PIONEERS
OF
ARMOUR
IN THE
GREAT WAR

PIONEERS
OF
ARMOUR
IN THE
GREAT WAR

DAVID A FINLAYSON & MICHAEL K CECIL

Pen & Sword
MILITARY

First published in Australia as *Pioneers of Australian Armour in the Great War*,
in 2015 by Big Sky Publishing Pty Ltd
PO Box 303, Newport, NSW 2106, Australia

Reprinted in hardback format in 2017 in Great Britain by
Pen & Sword MILITARY
An imprint of
Pen & Sword Books Ltd
47 Church Street, Barnsley
South Yorkshire
S70 2AS

Copyright © Big Sky Publishing, 2016, 2017

ISBN 978 1 52671 505 0

The right of David A Finlayson and Michael K Cecil to be identified
as Authors of this work has been asserted by them in accordance
with the Copyright, Designs and Patents Act 1988.

A CIP catalogue record for this book is
available from the British Library

Printed and bound in England
by TJ International Ltd, Padstow, Cornwall

Pen & Sword Books Ltd incorporates the Imprints of Pen & Sword Aviation,
Pen & Sword Family History, Pen & Sword Maritime, Pen & Sword Military,
Pen & Sword Discovery, Pen & Sword Politics, Pen & Sword Atlas,
Pen & Sword Archaeology, Wharncliffe Local History, Leo Cooper,
Wharncliffe True Crime, Wharncliffe Transport, Pen & Sword Select,
Pen & Sword Military Classics, The Praetorian Press, Claymore Press,
Remember When, Seaforth Publishing and Frontline Publishing

For a complete list of Pen & Sword titles please contact
PEN & SWORD BOOKS LIMITED
47 Church Street, Barnsley, South Yorkshire, S70 2AS, England
E-mail: enquiries@pen-and-sword.co.uk
Website: www.pen-and-sword.co.uk

For the pioneers of Australian armour during the Great War:
the members of the 1st Australian Armoured Section,
1st Australian Light Car Patrol and the Special Tank Crew.

CONTENTS

List of illustrations and maps

Part 1

A.   The December 1915 receipt for the purchase of armour plate by Captain James. The construction of the armoured cars was a considerable challenge in 1915 Melbourne.

1.   The 1st Armoured Car Battery in Egypt.

2.   Lieutenant Ernest Homewood James, 5th Australian Infantry Regiment, 1908.

3.   Military Order 213 of 1916.

4.   The vehicles of the 1st Australian Armoured Car Section at Royal Park, Melbourne, in mid-1916.

5.   The crews of the 1st Australian Armoured Car Section at Royal Park, Melbourne.

6.   The Daimler-based armoured car the crew named 'Silent Sue'.

7.   Armoured motorcar machine-gun and crew.

8. The Mercedes-based armoured car and crew at Victoria Barracks in May 1916.

9. The presentation of the 1st Armoured Car Section to the Minister for Defence, Senator G.F. Pearce, at Victoria Barracks, Melbourne, in May 1916.

10. First day out! June 1916.

11. Damage caused by storms in the Indian Ocean.

12. HMAT *Katuna* on arrival in the Suez Canal, August 1916.

13. The 1st Australian Armoured Car Battery awaiting departure for southern Egypt.

14. The Mercedes armoured car and crew on a railway flatcar preparing for the train journey from Moascar to Minia.

15. Minia Camp was the home of the British 11th and 12th Light Armoured Motor Batteries.

16. The Daimler armoured car in difficulties on the western frontier of Egypt.

17. The arrival of a shipment of new Model T Fords in southern Egypt.

18. Model T Fords were modified to suit local conditions.

19. Number 4 Block House.

20. The New Hudson motorcycle with its demountable sidecar.

21. Model T Ford LC427 of a British light car patrol with a badly bent front axle.

22. Sergeant Jack Langley and two other members of the 1st Australian Light Car Patrol aboard a heavily modified Model T Ford in early 1917.

23. The graves of two Royal Flying Corps airmen who were lost in the desert 40 miles west of Khara.

24. An Australian soldier stands in a line of defensive pits.

25. Sergeant Ivan Young, Corporal Bert Creek, Drivers George Jones and George McKay in their quarters with their Christmas gifts, 1916.

26. Members of the Armoured Car Battery with Christmas gifts provided by the Lady Mayoress' Fund.

27. Senussi prisoners on open railway trucks at Kharga.

28. Captured Senussi rifles stacked at Block House 6.

29. A member of the Light Car Patrol stands in front of a dug-in shelter in the Sinai.

30. Lieutenant James watches Sergeant Ivan Young operate the Colt machine-gun.

31. An overnight campsite.

32. Light Car Patrol members wear gas masks while completing anti-gas training.

33. Looking for enemy machines: the pedestal mount at the rear of one of the 1st Light Car Patrol's Model T Fords is used to engage an enemy aircraft.

34. Repairing a box-bodied Rolls Royce car in the desert.

35. Four of the Light Car Patrol's first issue of Model T Fords.

18. Grit takes its place in the Victory March through Melbourne on 19 May 1919.

19. Grit's final fundraising appearance near Luna Park, St Kilda.

20. Grit was transferred to the collection of the Australian War Museum in 1921, and was initially displayed in a semi-open area at the Exhibition Buildings in Melbourne.

21. The government transport service employees who moved Grit from the Canberra Railway Station to the Australian War Memorial pose on and around Grit in the area that later became the Western Courtyard.

22. Grit is delivered to the Australian War Memorial.

23. A newly repainted and conserved Grit in 2009.

24. Sappers William Kermack Marnie (left) and Arthur James Crampton, both of 2nd Field Company Engineers, outside their dugout at Anzac Cove.

List of diagrams

1. The first Australian armoured vehicle was Daimler-based 'Gentle Annie', designed and built by its enthusiastic crew.

2. The second armoured car, based on a Mercedes chassis, was christened 'Silent Sue' by its crew who considered it the quietest of the unit's vehicles.

3. The Model T Ford was one of the most widely recognised vehicles of its time.

4. The Mk. IV (Female) tank sent to Australia was a standard early 1918 vehicle produced by the Coventry Ordnance Works in Scotland.

List of Maps

1. Area of operations, Western Desert, southern Egypt and Libya, 1916–17

2. Area of operations, Sinai and Palestine, 1917–18

3. Area of operations, Palestine–Syria, 1918

AUTHORS' PREFACE

The Australian understanding of the Great War reflects the experiences of the infantry and light horse at Anzac and in the Middle East, France and Flanders, with the endeavours of small units sometimes lost within the big picture. Furthermore, our knowledge of armoured cars and tanks in this time period is based on the way British units operated them with our forces. As such it is understandable that the genuinely Australian experience of armour has been largely overlooked.

This uniquely Australian experience of armour can be found, however, in the stories of two little-known units: the Australian Armoured Car Section, later the 1st Australian Light Car Patrol, which operated from 1915 to 1919, and the Special Tank Section, AIF, formed in 1918. Both units embraced the power of the internal combustion engine, the firepower of machine-guns, and the protection of armour to demonstrate a new form of mechanised warfare on both wheels and tracks.

Lieutenant Ernest James and a small group of Edwardian motor enthusiasts designed, funded and constructed two armoured cars in Melbourne during 1915–16. Despite the potential challenges, particularly that of the hostile desert terrain, the Australian Armoured Car Section took these vehicles to the Middle East in 1916. Later re-equipped with Model T Fords and a change of title to the 1st Australian Light Car Patrol, the unit would demonstrate the value of speed, firepower and manoeuvre on wheels during the 1917–18 campaigns and the period immediately following the armistice with Turkey.

The story of 'Grit', Australia's first tank, began in 1917 when the Australian government requested its British counterpart to provide a tank for fundraising and recruiting purposes. Australian Army Service Corps drivers and artificers were trained at Bovington in the United Kingdom and then formed into the Special Tank Section, AIF, before travelling to Australia to await their vehicle. 'Grit', a Mk. IV (Female) tank, arrived in Port Melbourne in 1918. Over the next few years Grit and her successive crews demonstrated the capability of tanks to an awestruck public as they toured eastern Australia. Grit would eventually find a place of honour in the National Collection at the Australian War Memorial.

Pioneers of Australian Armour seeks to recognise the work of the members of these two small Australian units operating armoured fighting vehicles during the Great War. Their pioneering efforts laid the foundations for mechanised warfare and armour within the Australian Army.

In 2005, when this project was first considered, it seemed relatively straightforward. Captain James' unpublished manuscript 'The Motor Patrol', a little-known but complete text, was held at the Australian War Memorial and there was a small quantity of images available to support the text. Mike Cecil had documented Grit's history and that of the Special Tank Section over many years. The task was limited and appeared simple. However, by 2012, the situation had changed markedly: the internet and the current process of digitisation had produced a harvest of primary documents that could not have been accessed just a few years previously. The National Archives of Australia and the National Library website 'Trove' also uncovered a quantity of material that has provided vivid images of the period and the individuals concerned. In addition, the burgeoning interest in family history has produced on-line resources that document a person's life and allow contact between researchers. These contacts have enabled the descendants of members of the two units to participate in the documentation process. Their generous responses have expanded the project dramatically.

The authors intended to use primary documents wherever possible and this is reflected in the composition of *Pioneers*. While minimal editorial changes have removed spelling and typographical errors, minor inconsistencies in presentation and style and improved the readability of the text, the integrity of the original narrative has been respected and maintained. In preserving this text, views and language typically used during the Great War have been retained, some of which are no longer deemed acceptable. Likewise, many of the views expressed are certainly not those of the Australian Army nor the authors. However, these views and language have been left 'as found' as they are part of the historical record and their removal would diminish the value of the text as a means of understanding the past.

Pioneers of Australian Armour consists of two main parts. The first part comprises James' 'The Motor Patrol' in its entirety along with newspaper clippings from the time which provide a broader framework to the story. The second part tells the story of Grit, Australia's first tank, and the men who travelled eastern Australia providing demonstrations of the power of this extraordinary new weapon. Each part is followed by a section entitled '*Dramatis Personae*' which describes the lives of those pioneers of armour who served in each unit. The narrative is supplemented by a series of appendices which provide nominal rolls, technical information and summaries.

ACKNOWLEDGEMENTS

The authors are grateful for the considerable encouragement and support they have received throughout the life of this project. In 2012 this book was accepted as a project by the Army Tank Museum; in 2014 it was embraced by the Head of Corps and the Corps Council of the Royal Australian Armoured Corps as a worthwhile means to celebrate both the centenary of Lieutenant James' first tentative steps towards forming Australia's first armoured unit and the landing at Gallipoli. In 2014 the Army History Unit agreed to publish *Pioneers of Australian Armour* in the centenary year, 2015.

The concept of this project has extended over many years and *Pioneers of Australian Armour* could not have eventuated without significant help and encouragement from many. The authors wish to acknowledge those who have both assisted us and who have made this project a pleasure: Martin Pegler; Brad Manera, Manager, ANZAC Memorial, Sydney; Colonel Fred Dangar; Dianne Rutherford, Senior Curator, Military Heraldry and Technology, Australian War Memorial; Dr Roger Lee and Dr Andrew Richardson, Army History Unit; Lieutenant Colonels Stuart Cree and Andrew Abbot, Commanding Officers of the School of Armour; Major John Baines, Corps Historian, Royal Australian Armoured Corps; Major Peter Branagan, Office of Royal Australian Armoured Corps Head of Corps; Major Brian Gough, Manager, Army Tank Museum; Joe Linford, Curator, Army Tank Museum; Jane Carolan, Trinity Grammar; Jenny Pearce, The King's School; Carl Fitchett and John Italia, Defence Archives; Owen Gibbons, Jason Gibbons and Kate Lloyd of the Defence Publishing Service, Corporate Graphics; John Deckert, Nhill Aviation Heritage Centre; Michael Roberts, Collingwood Football Club; Greg Williams, Principal, Diamond Valley College; Shelley Cohn; Caroline Knaggs; Noel Troy and Krystii Melaine. Finally the editing skills of Catherine McCullagh and the high quality work of Denny Neave and his team at Big Sky Publishing brought this endeavour to a fitting conclusion producing the beautiful volume that is *Pioneers of Australian Armour*.

The families of James' original Armoured Car Section have also proven both welcoming and generous well beyond expectation. Many years ago Percy Cornwell's grandson arrived at the Army Tank Museum and handed over Percy's photo albums. In 2006 Henry Harkin's nephew donated family treasures to the Army Tank Museum. Along with Captain James' legacy, these artefacts enabled this project to come to fruition. Since 2013 the families of Ernest James, Ivan

Young, Bert Creek, Henry Morgan and Leo Cohn have produced material that will make the Armoured Car Section/Light Car Patrol one of the best documented units of the AIF. We wish to acknowledge the care of these families in the custody of such heritage and we thank them for sharing that heritage without hesitation.

And finally, a special thanks to our families who have encouraged, supported and, above all, tolerated our interests. You all played a vital part in the realisation of this project.

David A. Finlayson and Michael K. Cecil
2015

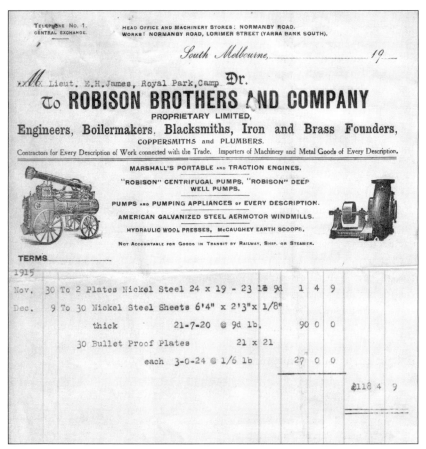

A. The December 1915 receipt for the purchase of armour plate by Captain James. The construction of the armoured cars was a considerable challenge in 1915 Melbourne.

FOREWORD

Pioneers of Australian Armour fills a significant gap in our understanding of the history of Australian armour. This important book describes the pioneering stages in the development of modern cavalry and tank capabilities. While the history of Australia's contribution to the Middle East Campaign of the Great War has been dominated by stories of the magnificent Light Horse for almost 100 years, there are other aspects of the campaign that deserve to be documented. *Pioneers* offers a unique account of a small force, the 1st Australian Light Car Patrol, mounted in armed cars, which performed an essential role as a scouting, security and intelligence-gathering asset for the Light Horse.

But *Pioneers* also tells another story that has long been neglected, providing a detailed account of 'Grit', Australia's first tank, and the men of the Special Tank Section. Grit arrived in Australia in mid-1918, its purpose to raise much-needed funds for the war effort. However the true contribution of Grit and the Special Tank Section was to educate the Australian public — the vast majority of whom had never seen a tank. Grit's tour of the eastern states demonstrated the capability of this modern war machine and showed Australians why the tank was fundamental to land combat. Indeed Grit played a key role in the genesis of armour in the Australian Army.

Pioneers is a truly fascinating account of a little-known facet of the Western Desert Campaign. What is perhaps most striking, however, are the qualities of resourcefulness, ingenuity, innovation and determination that emerge in descriptions of the men of both the 1st Australian Light Car Patrol and the Special Tank Section. These were essential qualities at a time when such technology was in its infancy and Australia was in the grip of wartime austerity. Yet these qualities remain just as essential in the modern Australian Army, reflected in the values of both the broader Army and the Royal Australian Armoured Corps — determination, courage, initiative and teamwork. The men of the 1st Australian Light Car Patrol and the Special Tank Section were trailblazers in the true sense of the word and left a legacy that characterises their modern counterparts despite the elapse of almost a century.

M.A. Brewer, CSC and Bar
Brigadier
Head of Corps
Royal Australian Armoured Corps.
Sydney, NSW
April 2015

PART 1

The Motor Patrol

The History of the 1st Australian Armoured Car Section

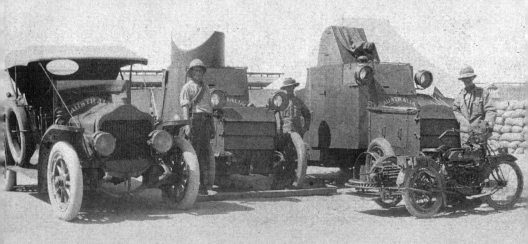

1. The 1st Armoured Car Battery in Egypt. The vehicles are, from left to right: the Minerva tender, the Mercedes armoured car, the Daimler armoured car, and in front of the Daimler, the New Hudson motorcycle and sidecar (AWM P02664.001).

TIMELINE

1st Australian Armoured Car Section/Battery and 1st Australian Light Car Patrol

1915–1919

1915

12 July	Lieutenant James (Reserve of Officers, 3rd Military District) writes to Minister for Defence and offers to raise and equip an armoured car section for the AIF.
14 July	Experimentation with various types of steel for armoured cars.
17 August	Designs and drawing submitted to the Department of Defence.
	Cars donated by I.S. Young and P. Cornwell. Both donors offer their services to the unit.
24 October	Work commences on the chassis at the Vulcan Engineering Works.

1916

7 February	Daimler car completed.
8 February	Mercedes car commenced.
27 February	Road trials and range practice of the Daimler car at Port Melbourne.
6 March	Lieutenants James and Cornwell mobilised at Swan Island Depot, 38th Fortress Company, Royal Australian Engineers.
16 March	Lieutenants James and Cornwell gazetted as officers in the Armoured Motor Section.
26 March	NCOs and men concentrated at the Royal Park Camp's 24th Depot Battalion.
28 March	Lieutenants James and Cornwell proceed to Machine Gun School at Randwick, New South Wales.
4 April	NCOs and men proceed to Machine Gun School at Port Melbourne.
28 April	Armoured cars presented to Senator Pearce at Victoria Barracks, Melbourne.

10 May	Officers, NCOs and men return to Royal Park from the Port Melbourne Machine Gun School.
16 June	Armoured cars and heavy baggage sent to Port Melbourne pending embarkation.
20 June	1st Australian Armoured Car Section embarks on HMAT A.13 *Katuna* at Port Melbourne for overseas service.
23 June	*Katuna* calls at Adelaide, South Australia.
2 July	*Katuna* calls at Fremantle, Western Australia.
18 July	*Katuna* arrives at Colombo, Ceylon.
20–29 July	*Katuna* experiences Indian Ocean gales.
9 August	*Katuna* arrives at Port Tewfik, Egypt.
10 August	1st Australian Armoured Car Section attached to the 2nd Light Horse Brigade at Moascar Camp.
August	1st Australian Armoured Car Section retitled the 1st Australian Armoured Car Battery to conform to British practice.
16 August	1st Australian Armoured Car Battery entrains for Minia, southern Egypt.
17 August	1st Australian Armoured Car Battery joins 11th and 12th Light Motor Batteries.
21 August	First patrol into the Libyan Desert.
22 August	Outbreak of Nile Fever: Lieutenant Cornwell and three men hospitalised.
4 December	Armoured cars and machine-guns despatched by train to Cairo where they are returned to the stores depot.
6 December	1st Australian Armoured Car Battery proceeds to the Southern Oasis.
8 December	1st Australian Armoured Car Battery is issued Ford Light Cars and machine-guns and is retitled the 1st Australian Light Car Patrol.
9 December	Crews are trained in the operation of Lewis machine-guns.
25 December	Christmas Day is celebrated at Water Dump A (WDA) near Kharga.

1917

January	Numerous patrols into the Western Desert.
11 May	2nd Light Car Patrol arrives at WDA and relieves 1st Australian Light Car Patrol.

15 May	Lieutenant Cornwell is detached to Topographical Survey Section, Sinai, at Khan Yunus.
18 May	1st Australian Light Car Patrol entrains for Khan Yunus and taken under command of the Desert Column.
25 May	1st Australian Light Car Patrol is inspected by Lieutenant General Chauvel.
26 May	First patrols in Palestine.
30 May	1st Australian Light Car Patrol receives reinforcements (Troopers Gray, Riley, Christensen).
6 June	Attached to the Imperial Mounted Division.
11 Jun	Lieutenant Gibbs, 7th Light Horse, attached for duty.
14 June	While escorting the Divisional Commander, a patrol engages enemy aircraft with Lewis gun fire.
4 September	Drivers Harkin and Riley's car attacked by a German aircraft.
18 September	Lieutenant Cornwell returns from detachment.
10–11 December	Exchange of vehicles for new equipment.

1918

25 April	1st Australian Light Car Patrol arrives at the Dead Sea and assists in the salvage of Turkish motor boats.
June–August	At the Dead Sea Post, the 1st Australian Light Car Patrol launches patrols on the Dead Sea using captured Turkish boats. Motor patrols also sent out from this post.
2 September	Capture of a German touring car retained for transport services.

1919

2 January	Sergeant Langley, DCM, dies of malaria.
3 March	Return of vehicles to the Stores Depot at Aleppo, Syria.
5 March	Members proceed by train to Egypt.
13 March	Captain Cornwell and remaining NCOs and men report to AIF Details Camp pending return to Australia.
	1st Australian Light Car Patrol is disbanded at Moascar.
16 May	Captain James and ten members of the 1st Australian Light Car Patrol embark on the HT *Kaiser-i-Hind* for return to Australia.

"THE MOTOR PATROL"

The History of the 1st Australian Armoured Car Section
In Egypt, Sinai, Palestine, Syria and Asia Minor

By

Captain Ernest Homewood James, MVO MC & VD

1st Australian Armoured Car Section.

Engineer of Hawthorn, Vic; born Melbourne, 22nd November 1879;
appointed a Lieutenant in the A.I.F. on 16/3/16; promoted Captain, 1/1/17;
appointment terminated 29/10/20.

The text is presented here as originally written by Captain James with
only minor editing for consistency and presentation. Place names are as
written by Captain James.

2. Lieutenant Ernest Homewood James, 5th Australian Infantry Regiment, 1908
(Martin collection Martin 001).

INTRODUCTION

The Great War saw the introduction of many new things. Not the least of these was the petrol driven machine, which took a prominent part both as a vehicle and as a weapon.

The experience gained has led to a very complete study being made of the part that mechanisation is likely to take in future armed conflicts.

The late war saw gradual development from petrol driven carriers of troops and weapons and eventually the complete weapon–vehicle: the tank. The light motors used in the Palestine Campaign armed with Lewis and Vickers guns were the forerunners of the modern armoured cars.

The wide expanse of territory embraced by the Commonwealth, the sparse population and the difficulties of inter-communication all tend to enhance the value of mechanized engines of war in the land defence of Australia.

Our Army authorities have naturally fully recognised this and the initial steps in mechanisation have been taken.

The following brief history of the first Australian mechanized unit, which operated in the Great War, should prove of interest and will undoubtedly provide ample food for thought for those interested in the subject of mechanized engines of war.

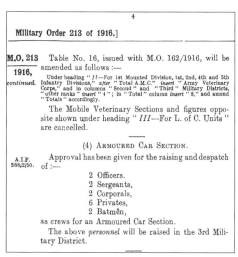

3. Military Order 213 of 1916 granted authority to both raise and despatch the Armoured Car Section for overseas service. This document formally establishes the first armoured unit in the Australian Army (ATM.LCP.Doc.002).

THE FIRST AUSTRALIAN ARMOURED CAR SECTION

In August 1914 when the dogs of war were let loose a number of motoring enthusiasts met together in Melbourne to talk over a scheme for building Armoured Cars for use with the Allied Armies and to form a unit to volunteer for service abroad. Cold water was thrown on the scheme from almost every quarter, as there was practically no information available as to what the proper design for an armoured car should be; how the guns should be mounted; what the equipment should consist of, and what the personnel should be.

Still fools rush in where angels fear to tread and being enthusiasts they persisted. After many months of searching and enquiries from various quarters, enough information was available to enable designs to be got out. Then other obstacles cropped up. Armoured Cars were very expensive luxuries and required commodious high-powered chassis to carry them. Armour plating and other expensive equipment was required. Three powerful chassis were donated for the purpose of Mr John Young of Horsham, Mr P. Cornwell of Coburg and Mr Sol Green of Melbourne. Designs and specifications that were drawn up were approved and ultimately through the untiring efforts of Colonel Osborne, authority was given for the unit to be formed and got ready as soon as possible for service at the front, the Imperial Government having accepted the offer of the unit complete. The necessary personnel were soon enrolled as members of the 1st Australian Armoured Car Section and they began to get busy.

The use of the plant at the Vulcan Engineering Works, South Melbourne, was obtained and as quite a number of the section were skilled engineers they decided to make the necessary alterations to the chassis and build the armour and gun mountings themselves.

Several Melbourne firms also very kindly gave considerable assistance by supplying valuable equipment. Conspicuous amongst these donors were the Victoria Rolling Mills, Messrs J. A. Linacre, W. Trill and W. P. Thompson & Co.

It was found that many difficulties had to be overcome, the greatest of these being the obtaining of suitable bullet resisting plate for the protection of the inmates and the vulnerable part of the chassis. Ordinary steel plating of the required thickness would be far too heavy to be of any use at all. Many suggestions were made by individuals who were prepared to sell us all kinds of wonderful metal and processes for toughening and hardening ordinary steel plate. We insisted that there was only one test, as far as we were concerned and that was the service bullet. Many tests were made at the rifle ranges and all these bullet proof metals were found useless. We also discovered that although these merchants were positive of the qualities of the plating none of them had enough faith in it to stand behind while rifles were fired at it.

One inventor in particular was quite amusing. He had an alloy, which appeared to contain a large percentage of aluminium, and which he claimed was extremely light and quite bullet proof at point blank range. He even went to the trouble of making a special helmet with which he wished the authorities to supply the troops at the front. During our tests we got one of our marksmen to try a shot at this helmet at a range of a couple of hundred yards. The bullet drilled a neat hole through the front but knocked a piece out of the back several inches square. The inventor's face was a picture when we gave him back his helmet. He apparently had no knowledge of the power of the modern 303 bullet.

Ultimately we got over our armour plate trouble as we discovered that there was a small supply in Melbourne of the special 3/32" steel plate imported from England some time previously for plating ammunition wagons. This plate is absolutely bullet proof at 500 yards and by doubling it, is proof at a much shorter range. We were fortunate in being able to purchase a supply of this and we used it in double thicknesses and in some places treble thicknesses on the vehicles. Louvers were fitted in front of the radiators. Colt Automatic guns were mounted in turrets (one on the top of each car). The turrets were revolving giving a complete arc of fire of 360 and a spare gun was carried inside each vehicle. On tests we found our cars were capable of a speed of between 50 and 60 miles per hour with their full load.

The crews went through intensive courses of machine-gun instruction and as the majority were very experienced motor car drivers, the personnel were in the ideal position of being able at a moment's notice to take the place of any vacancy through casualty or otherwise. Towards the end of 1915 the authorities were satisfied that the unit was well enough advanced for embarkation although it was well into 1916 before they got away on the old Transport A 13, HMAT *Katuna*, en route for an unknown port.

The account of this boat's peregrinations and how she took eight weeks from Melbourne to Suez sometimes drifting about in the Indian Ocean with engines broken down during the monsoons which were particularly severe, would fill a book; but ultimately men and cars were disembarked at Port Tewfik and sent by rail to join the Australian forces in Egypt.

4. The vehicles of the 1st Australian Armoured Car Section at Royal Park, Melbourne, in mid-1916. The armoured cars were the product of over two years' work by Lieutenant James and his motoring enthusiasts (Harkin collection ATM.LCP.HH.001).

5. The crews of the 1st Australian Armoured Car Section parade in front of their vehicles at Royal Park, Melbourne (Harkin collection ATM.LCP.HH.002).

Motors and Motoring

Although no official statement has been made, it is known by those associated with military work that the Defence department has all the motor ambulances it requires.

Armored motorcars will be acceptable, because the value of these machines has been demonstrated more and more as the war progresses. In Gallipoli they have been used with marked success to destroy the enemy's barbed wire entanglements. The writer has been told that the crew of an armored car runs little or no risk from rifle fire, because rifle and machine gun ammunition cannot penetrate the armor. Only big gun shells can damage them, and when they are driven up quickly they reach the enemy's trenches before the artillery gets its range, and when close up they cannot be attacked by field guns or mortars without the risk of blowing up their own men. Two cars are being fitted up from local designs, and various metal workers in Melbourne are submitting sheets of steel which will be tested against rifle fire at different ranges. The builders of these Australian armored cars believe they will be able to turn out vehicles equal in efficiency to those made in England and France.

(The *Leader*, 7 August 1915, p. 22)

6. The Daimler-based armoured car the crew named 'Gentle Annie'. The salient features are the bustle at the rear of the body and the gun shield instead of a turret (Young collection ATM LCP.IY.002).

Armoured Motor Cars.
Australian Officer's Enterprise.
A Year of Quiet Preparation.
Sergeant Ivan Young's Daimler Car.

After a year of battling against criticism of a new and strange enterprise, Lieutenant E. H. James has managed to have completed the first of two and probably three, armored motor cars, on which are to be mounted guns, for the Australian Expeditionary Forces.

It will be recalled in the communiqués from France, Flanders and even from Cape Helles that this class of car has at times played a large part in attacks and repulses of the enemy. At Cape Helles the cars, owing to the limited space, were not much used, but they fought their way to the very heart of the firing line along the Krithia road, and even to the Turkish trenches (then deserted), and grappling barb wire entanglements drew them back, and left a way clear for the infantry attacks.

The Australian armored car that has been completed is of different design from those motors at Cape Helles which were attached to the Royal Naval Air Service, and which were turret shaped armored bodies, mounted on Rolls-Royce chassis; it is different, too, from the French and Belgian of a similar type, which have little or no shield for the rapid firing gun.

An enthusiastic group of men, of whom Lieutenant James, besides being a practical engineer, was also an expert gun officer, commenced soon after the outbreak of the war to design armored cars and having obtained the sanction of the Minister of Defence during the early part of last year, commenced to collect the materials necessary for their construction.

Two power cars, each of 60 horsepower, were donated; one, a Daimler by Sergeant Ivan Young, (son of Mr. and Mrs John Young of "Yelholm", Nhill), and the other a Mercedes chassis, by Mr. P. Cornwell. Both of these men are expert mechanics, and will form part of the crew of the cars.

One of the greatest initial difficulties was the procuring of the required quantity of steel. It had to be light for the purpose, and yet with great resistance to be valuable. After travelling the Commonwealth sufficient was obtained (some of it still bears the German stamp), and by doubling and trebling the thickness of the vulnerable parts the proper protection was gained. Lieutenant James describes this steel as being as hard as diamonds. To cut it blunts all the tools, and special means have had to be adopted to cut it. Once this was obtained (and it was the work of months) it took little time to place it in the hands of a competent builder, who worked on the designs drawn up by Lieutenant James.

As the work proceeded various difficulties had to be overcome and modifications made to the original plans, but the result was Tuesday the nearly completed armored car, nick named by its crew, Gentle Annie. She weighs a ton and a half. Now the Daimler car (Sergeant Ivan Young's) has been the first completed, and a formidable looking object it is too, with its glistening and unpolished edges of steel plating and its strong bolts. Every vital part of the engines is protected by one, two, or three layers of grey steel plating.

At first thought to armor a car seems a simple object, but it had to be remembered that the whole of the car, not only the driver and engines has to be enclosed in an impregnable case of steel. There is just room for the driver to sit on the petrol tank, with a few inches between the crown of his head and the top of the armored top. Just behind him will stand the gun crew with the gun specially mounted behind a shield on the roof. The gun swings freely. It takes very little time to dismount the gun altogether, and then the crew can disappear below into the steel case, and the driver puts (if the car be too hotly attacked) as much space as he can between his deadly offensive weapon and the enemy. Any part of the engine can be reached from the interior of the car, radiators, crankshafts and gearbox. In a few days the car will be available for its trials.

The Mercedes, a German car, is called by its crew "Silent Sue", probably for the very reason that the powerful engine makes a throbbing like that of an aeroplane. Now that the first car has been completed (and many alterations had to be made as first one design and then another for certain sections were found wanting and altered), it will be very few weeks before the second car is completed.

Lieutenant James has insisted that every member of the crew belonging to each car and gun will be able to carry out each other's work. Every man will therefore be a mechanic and a gunner as well. Extra guns as well as spare wheels will be carried. It is probable that a third car will be constructed. The cost of construction is being borne by the donators of the cars and the designer, and will amount to several thousand pounds. The weight of the armor and the gun will be about one ton.

(*Nhill Free Press*, 11 February 1916, p. 3)

Armored Motor Car.
Australia's First Product.
A Grim-Looking Machine.
Goes Forward Firing.
A Satisfactory Trial.

Bearing down at over 30 miles an hour, an amored motor, with projecting weapon and just the top edge of a khaki cap showing above the rim of the gun shield. Looks a fearsome object. Watched steadily going forward, with the same gun spitting and barking fiercely, a faint smoke issuing from the muzzle, while the engine races, suggests a landscape swept bare of any enemy.

On the Port Melbourne rifle range on Friday, about noon, the trial was held of the first of such cars built in Melbourne, to the design of Lieutenant E. H. James.

The design of the car has already been described in the columns of "The Age", when it was shown that this was one of two powerful motor cars that had been donated, to be transformed into a bullet-proof turret on wheels, with a capacity of being hurled into action at the rate of 60 miles an hour. Space did not permit yesterday of the speed capacity of the machine being tried.

It was more with an idea of testing the working of the gun mounted on the top of the steel encasement that the little corps of mechanics and expert machine gunners that Lieutenant E. H. James has gathered round him scrambled inside their steel shell, and set off down to the rifle range, with a few belts of ammunition. Except, as has been stated, for the occasional glimpse of a head and shoulder of a soldier, this greenish-grey car, shaped like an old fashioned Cobb and Co. coach, with the stubborn-looking gun behind the protecting shield, no one was visible as guiding the movements of the car. But when it stopped there emerged from behind the steel door that swung back the crew, who had been crouched inside. Had they been going through a zone of shrapnel established by the enemy they would have been unscathed.

Sand, mounds and gutters formed no obstacles to the powerful motor, and once on the range a target was soon registered. Port Melbourne butts have seen many matches and tests, but none more interesting than the men behind the gun on the top of the turret of this armored motor sending round after round on to the target. It was in fact, considering that the machine gunners had never fired the gun before under such conditions, extremely creditable that they soon got on to the target, 600 yards away. A strong six point wind considerably influenced the flight of the bullets, but once picked up the gunners could make sure of their targets every time.

The test of firing as the motor was driven forward was more difficult, especially as the range is not exactly like the roads where the cars may be expected to be driven into fiction. Swinging round from various angles, the gunner picked up their target, und showed the mobility of the gun. In a few seconds it could have been dismantled and stored safely inside the shield, and the driver, crowding on all power, might have escaped from any enemy which threatened to destroy the unit.

For the most part, the armored motor may be regarded as a means of scouting and obtaining information. The gun mounted on it is a defensive weapon, as are the guns in an armored train rather than a means of commencing offensive tactics against the foe. For, with the terrible accuracy of artillery fire and the curtain of shellfire that is dropped before an advancing army, even with the high speed that such cars often obtain it would be a miracle if they escaped un-hit, though they might not be altogether put out of action.

In fact, looking at the car, there are no vulnerable points exposed, as far as one can see, and all that is required for success is nerve. One does not for a moment doubt that the men who are to form the little corps for the first armored cars to leave Australia will show their mettle as their engineer comrades in the trenches and in the air have proved themselves. But whatever work the men who guide these grim machines are to be engaged on, if perseverance, ingeniousness and courage can bring them through, they possess it. All that remains to be done is for each gun's crew to become thoroughly conversant with the work before it. They must be scouts, mechanics and gunners at the same time.

No doubt the designer will find many points to improve after his first trial, small but rather telling factors for complete and smooth working.

(The *Age*, 28 February 1916)

7. Armoured motorcar machine-gun and crew (Young Collection ATM. LCP.IY.003).

Armored Motor Car Machine Gun and Crew

Monday's Melbourne Herald contained two pictures of an armored motor machine gun, in which district residents have a special interest. The armored motor machine gun was constructed by the members of the crew, at their own expense, and is the first of these vehicles to be built for the Australian Armored Motor Machine Gun Corps, which is in course of formation. The main portion of the expense was borne by Sergeant Ivan Young, of the Australian Imperial Forces, who comes from Nhill, and is the son of Mr. John Young, J.P. He also gave the chassis, while Mr. H.W. Beckett, of the Vulcan Engineering works, South Melbourne, gave the free time of his plant, tools and shop. The plans and designs were drawn by Lieut. E. H. James, A.E., who supervised the work and organised the unit. The car, which is built of special bulletproof steel, is valued at about £1000. It is 60 h.p. and is capable of doing 60 miles an hour with a full load. Other cars are to be constructed, and another chassis has been given by Lieut. P. Cornwell, of the Engineers. Colonel Harley Tarrant, V.D., and Major W. H. Osborne, V.D., of the Motor Transport Board, gave valuable assistance in connection with the construction of the car. Behind the gun are Sergeant J. Langley; in front: Lieut. E. H. James, Sergeant Ivan Young (Nhill), Lieut P. Cornwell, Mr. H. W. Beckett, Sergeant Creek Horsham.

(The *Horsham Times*, 3 March 1916, p. 1)

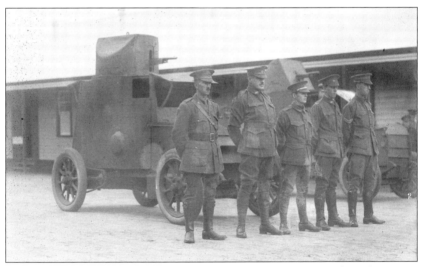

8. The Mercedes-based armoured car and crew at Victoria Barracks in May 1916. Left to right: Lieutenant Percy Cornwell, Lance Corporal Walter Thompson, Driver Robert McGibbon, unknown, and Corporal Leslie Millar (AWM DAOD2305).

9. The presentation of the 1st Armoured Car Section to the Minister for Defence, Senator G.F. Pearce, at Victoria Barracks, Melbourne, in May 1916 was attended by several dignitaries and a crowd of well-wishers. The two armoured cars were hand-built and each was unique. One of the more obvious differences was in the weapon mounting: the Mercedes 'Silent Sue' to the left of frame had a completely enclosed turret with sloped sides reminiscent of the British Army's Rolls Royce armoured cars of the period. The Daimler 'Gentle Anne' on the right had a gun shield with side wings but no protection at the rear (AWM DAOD2303).

Two Armored Motor Cars Presented to the Minister.

At the Victoria Barracks last week Senator G. F. Pearce, Minister for Defence, was presented with two armored motorcars carrying machineguns.

Lieutenants E. H. James and P. Cornwell, of the Armored Car Section of the Australian Imperial Force, gave a 60 h.p. Mercedes car, and Sergeant J. Young a 40 h.p. Daimler car fully armored and equipped for service abroad.

The crews for these cars have been selected, and the men are all in camp. They all assisted in the construction of the cars either in work or money.

Senator Pearce, in acknowledging the gifts, said that the manufacture of these cars showed that Australia had moved another step forward in the ability to equip her own armies. He heartily thanked the donors. Most of the work had been done at the Vulcan Engineering Works.

There was also on view a motorcycle with sidecar to carry a machine gun.

Among those present were Brigadier General R. E. Williams, State Commandant; Colonel R. Foster, Chief of the General Staff; Colonel T. H. Dodds, Adjutant-General; and Mr T. Trumble, Secretary of Defence.

(The *Weekly Times*, 6 May 1916, p. 23)

Across a Stormy Ocean.

Sergeant Ivan S. Young, only son of Mr. and Mrs. John Young of "Yelholm", Nelson Street, Nhill, writes:

"Indian Ocean more monsoons; left Colombo on Wednesday night about 10 o'clock, and had a fair run yesterday but about midnight struck a howling monsoon gale and rain, and at breakfast time things were only middling. Everybody and everybody's blankets soaking wet and water pours down hatchways in tons. About 7.30 I was in the washhouse when a wave came over and filled it to my waist; when I came out like a drowned rat. I saw two fellows pick themselves out from amongst the winches. Both wash houses and lavatories in a very precarious state. It will only want a few more waves like that and they'll go over.

10. First day out! June 1916 (Young collection ATM LCP.IY.050).

It just as well most Australians on board have a keen of a keen sense of humour We enjoy ourselves on a day like this seeing fellows getting drenched and knocked over every few minutes. My clothes were wet before 10 o'clock. I've been in wet cloth like everyone else, ever since. Luckily it's not cold, although the weather is remarkable. Had two blankets last night; hope this weather goes down soon. The day we reached Colombo there was a gale raging, and going on we passed dozens of catamarans fishing, or rather had been with sails blown to pieces others with masts gone. Before we were over 100 niggers missing they sent out a tug to try rescuing some. Just outside the breakwater the hull of the P. and O. liner Umbria, which ran ashore 20 months ago.

I just stopped writing, as I thought we were gone a terrific wave hit the hatchway way stripped it clean off a solid stream of water came down and flooded us out. As I write this, all hands are on deck baling out our quarters and engines have stopped. As I was going to say about the Umbria by the time we left she wasn't to be seen but was broken to pieces.

Had to stop last night, as our part of the deck was sealed down, and we slept on deck at the rear end of the boat. We were hove to and turned back east while they closed it down. It is a bit better today, but no one is allowed down. Talking about catamaran just before the pilot came aboard at Colombo, a catamaran with three niggers, one on the log went passed the ship in the same direction like streak before the gale. We were going 8 knots, so they must have been easily doing 15 knots - I wonder if they ever got home. We were marched ashore with our officers to stretch our legs to the barracks. After a while we were told the sentries were withdrawn. That did us; I and some others went to the "Gale Face". It was a wonderful sight along that promenade with the southwest gale blowing I never saw such breakers; the whole of the road was covered with white spume. When we got back to the barracks: where we had to fall in, you would have laughed to have seen us (our deep marching back to the boat with bunches of bananas over our shoulders, others with bunches of coconuts, some with pineapples, others with native bags full of limes, passion fruit, etc., and others again with parcels You never saw such a funny thing in your life, especially as some of them were pretty "shicker".

We got off again on the next morning, got a car and went out to Mt Lavinia and the Cinnamon Gardens etc., and got back to the boat about 2. We were to sail then, but they had part of the engine ashore getting repaired, and the dashed things didn't turn up until 9 at night, so we wasted our afternoon.

While waiting in the harbour a mail boat from Calcutta arrived the "City of New York" anchored along side of us and we had waving match and some "cooees" with a couple of girls on the saloon deck. Then the Mooltan bound for Fremantle arrived, in fact six boats came in while we were there and there are 20 in the harbour altogether.

Got your cable late the day we got there I was a bit disappointed when the letter bag came off with the pilot, and here was no telegram for me. The letters we sent all went to barracks, Colombo and expect to be censored. I wish you could see that hatch cover last night; it is fastened down with steel clamps and weights. I suppose a quarter of a ton. It was grappled clean off and left on top near by the winch if any one happened to be coming down just then they would have stood a good chance of being killed. Will ring off for a few days.

Wednesday 26th Still plodding along although only a little more than half way to Aden; should reach there about next Monday, sea, weather still moderate; it's that cool and clouded you can go all day without a hat and still sleep with blankets although pretty regularly every night we get a proper wind and rain storm for about an hour. I've discovered amongst the crew a chap from South Australia a cousin of Gordon's of Broughton. Have got a few decent snaps at Colombo, some good some bad. Hope you get them. So far as we know we are landing at Suez on Friday the 28th. Had a glorious day and enjoying it immensely. Since the morning the wind has increased to half a gale and the seas have risen tremendously. By dinner we all got our usual quota of drenching and falls. About 2 o'clock Bert Creek, George Morgan and myself got up the bit of a boat deck (there are only 2 life boats and 2 cutters) between the lifeboats and funnel, to see the tremendous seas better without getting washed about. We have been there 10 minutes before an enormous wave got her and broke over the side of the ship before she could rise. We didn't have time to sing out. I grabbed a wire rope and George a chain in the funnel and in an instant we were swept off our feet, talk about being drowned, anyway we thought after that we would be safer on the deck where there was a rail to stop us. About 4 o'clock another wave got her and flattened a row of 20 horse stalls like a pancake. You ought to see the wreckage. The cook and the bake house, all wood and bolted down to the deck near the rear of the ship were left a bit exposed when the horseboxes went. While the mess orderlies were getting tea the best wave of the lot came over, hit and knocked in one end of cook houses washed three men in it clean out and the mess orderlies with dixies full of tea overboard. Meat and men were all over the deck, and some of dixies overboard. All the bread was washed out of the bake house into the engine room and the skylight and the water filled the floor of the engine room 6 inches deep burst in the bulkhead of the engineers cabin and lifted the roof off the hospital, and knocked the chocks away from the port lifeboat. Every cabin on deck was flooded out and filled up over the bottom bunks. I suppose you understand there are no cabins or quarters below the deck, which is all cargo. All living quarters are on top, including ship officers, our own officers, stewards, etc. The only quarters below deck are ours right down forward, and the niggers right aft, and as it's too hot below, we live, smoke and eat in the open. We've had the time of our lives today and thoroughly enjoyed it, but were extremely lucky none have been killed. There were several hammocks slung in the horseboxes that were flattened, but luckily the occupants were out. Our little lot are mostly up in the forward horse stalls on the weather side, and have a canvas covering, but even they got pretty wet with the spray. We get a lot of fun for our money. However, we ought to reach shelter off Socolra tomorrow about midday when the weather may possibly moderate. Had machine gun examination yesterday to keep us occupied. I did pretty well, I think.

Tuesday, August 1st Six weeks since we left Melbourne and only in the Gulf of Aden. Beautifully cool weather, although getting hotter and quite a change not to have a gale blowing. We've only seen two ships pass us either way since leaving Australia, and they were about 7 miles off. I wish you could have seen the mess the decks were in the other day with the wreckage. The photo doesn't give you any idea of it. We have a guard every night now on the sheep pens near the niggers, as two or three have been missing over night. Expect to pass Perim about 7 o'clock to-morrow afternoon and reach Suez to-day week.

11. Damage caused by storms in the Indian Ocean (Young collection ATM LCP.IY.041).

8th August, Thursday—First day in Red Sea; pretty hot, although it is not too bad, as there is a nice breeze blowing. Passed six ships yesterday and today about six, including a hospital ship and a mail boat. We are averaging about 185 miles a day. Have just passed the "Twelve Apostles" (islands in the Red Sea). Sighted another ship. Friday—Terrible hot last night and today. This morning we started throwing buckets of water at one another, and it finished up in getting some big tubs and ducking' everybody, clothes and all. We also ducked all the officers (not ship's officers) and they took it like sports.

It was all right being wet all day; just had a pair of pants on, some not even that. It was 135 degrees in the engine room all yesterday and today. The electrician is a very nice chap, and if you happen to be in Melbourne when he gets back you ought to meet him. They expect to get back some time in October. All the engineers are good fellows, and three or four of us go round to their cabins of an evening and have a smoke, song, and a bit of supper.

Sunday: We are due to arrive about midnight Tuesday. Have passed numerous large boats outward bound today, all empty and very high out of the water. It does seem funny that they should be going out empty when it is such a hard job to get freight out from England. Have just had our last church service on board.

It is great weather, have had a lovely breeze all day; of course it's hot, but not so hot as some summer days at home. Haven't had a day's sickness, bar an occasional headache. Some of us are having a farewell banquet in the "banqueting hall" (horseboxes) the night before we reach Suez."
(*Nhill Free Press*, **29 Sept 1916, p. 3**)

12. HMAT *Katuna* on arrival in the Suez Canal after an eventful voyage, August 1916 (Young collection ATM LCP.IY.017).

On the Sands of the Desert.

Sergeant Ivan S. Young, only son of Mr. and Mrs. John Young, of "Yelholm", Nhill, writes as follows:

"… Have arrived at last. Hope you got my letter. Anchored off Port Zewfig midnight the 8th of August. Were just a day late for air raid on Suez. The morning before a couple of Taubes dropped bombs on the wharfs and town but did no damage. As you will see by papers the Australian Light Horse have been giving the Turks what for, and are doing still. Turks evidently had a big crowd because they have lost 5,000 men killed, wounded and prisoners. Trainload of prisoners went through here yesterday.

To step back to the steamer, some of us or rather 20 of the decent chaps on boat, including the doctor, two officers, all the engineer and the second mate, had a sort of a secret society on the boat and held lodge meeting about once or twice having something to drink besides hot lemonade, of course. It started with two or three; they would approach a chap and tell him a great tale about how useful it would be to belong to this society which consists of military and naval men that they had marvellous club rooms in London with cheap boarding and all sorts of inducements. The Duke of Westminster was President, anyway the chap would of course rush it and he would be blindfolded and in to the initiation ceremony. Of course it was all a lot of tales and made a fool of a chap, but as they only choose sports, the chap only laughed and waited to initiate the next chap. However, we had a final spree the night we got into Suez and demolished much ginger ale wine, etc.

Had about two hours sleep and were up again. After messing about all day we loaded cars on trains (goods) and we came on passenger train which arrived here about 8 o'clock with the Light Horse reinforcements dumped on the sands of the desert with no one knowing anything about us. However, we met a very obliging lot of chaps who did everything they could to make us comfortable gave us a feed and blankets. This is a very good camp. We get a swim every day and were up there at 6 this morning. Are right against the railway station. It was very pretty coming up along the fresh water canal seeing all the little irrigation plots, a clump of date trees leaded with nearly ripe dates.

Cars arrived this morning and we unloaded them, but heaven only knows what we'll do with them. There is only the main road through to Suez and if you get off the road you are settled.

Met a chap here from Horsham who knew all our people. The hours here are from 6 in the morning till 11 o'clock, then rest till 4 and work till 6. We've just had dinner and I'm sitting in the sand writing with the wind blowing sand and dirt in my cars. The climate will do me although I know we've passed the worst of the summer. We did look a dilapidated boat when we got in, all paint rusted off, broken and twisted wood and ironwork all over the place, and barnacles below the water line. I see in "Egyptian Mail" that South Australia is still having a good season. Hope you are. Although they are such horrible liars in this rag that not many troops trouble to buy it.

This is a good camp although on pure sand. All the Light Horse are ready at two hours notice to shift. There is a camp further along, but consists of "Tommies". All the horses are in fine nick and are good sorts. Corporal Millar is going to Cairo today to see about pay and also letters. We have an aerodrome here also aeroplanes; we were out in the morning. We are temporarily attached to a Squadron. All the original regiments are fighting the Turks, others are in reserve waiting. All these chaps that have been either here or on the Peninsula for last couple of years are totally different to a crowd of men say in camp in Australia. The whole lot, almost without exception, seem bigger, quieter, more reserved and nicer; perhaps I'm wrong, but that's the first impression. They are going to build 30 yards of road for us to run cars off the main road.

We are very comfortable here and have a good water supply. Sandland and Melville and the rest of the Light Horse who came over on the boat with us were suddenly bundled off with horses to the front to replace casualties out from Kantara. They left at 3 o'clock this morning. I'd grown very fond of them and feel it very much having to say good-bye to them so soon. If I'd had a chance I'd have gone with them. I'm sick of armoured cars in the desert, anyway. It's rather hard on Sandy and the others. They were only back in Australia for three months with enteric, and then to get sent off with only three days off the boat they'll be as soft as anything. Wish they'd sent us too. Wish you could see the long lines of horses and stables here, must a good two miles long double row of stables. We are looking forward to tomorrow as the last air raid dropped messages to beware of the 13th August, but I suppose it will come to nothing. Lots of railway traffic here, and miles of trucks laden with stores, etc., and a lot of passenger trains go through to Suez and Cairo; they are fine trains, the engines are first-class and quite equal to anything of ours, and to Cairo. Anyway, and a good deal faster. There is a big camp of British infantry. We can see from here the cruisers and auxiliaries anchored on the lake waiting for aeroplane attacks or any other kind. We've been shovelling sand all day off a patch of ground to run cars out to, and, it wasn't hot; Oh, no! It's remarkable how cold it gets at night here; we all sleep with two blankets over us. It starts to get cold about 9 at night, and is at its worst about 4 in the morning. They issue one packet of cigarettes or two oz. of tobacco per week per man here.

By the way, if you want to send any thing in the way of eatables, send a few tins of condensed coffee and milk (Nestles) it's great; Sandy gets it. It looks just like gear box grease, but get a cup of hot water and put a teaspoon of it in to dissolve and you have a lovely cup of coffee with milk already. Must leave this now as there is a train with reinforcements just come in from somewhere in open trucks with full equipment on they are "Tommies".

Sunday, 13th—The horses are to leave today, trains are waiting now. A hospital train went through last night with numerous wounded "Tommies", Australians, and a few Turks on board.

This is by far away the biggest attack yet made in Egypt, but they are doomed; it would take a million men to take the Canal. It is supposed to be practically impregnable. Went down for a swim before breakfast and are now waiting for the Taubes. We have got two machine guns mounted on cars in case they come down low enough to have a shot at them, although I believe there are plenty of special anti-aircraft guns in hidden positions in the sand hills. We have orders to leave here today. Am writing this in case I can't get a letter away within the next few days."

(*Nhill Free Press*, **10 Oct 1916, p. 3**)

13. The 1st Australian Armoured Car Battery awaiting departure for southern Egypt
    (Young collection ATM LCP.IY.046).

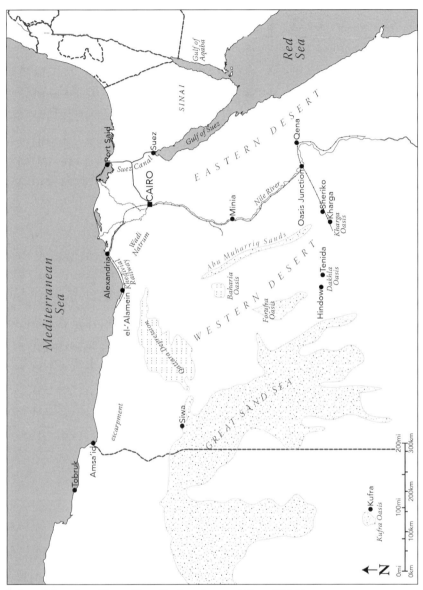

1. Area of Operations, Western Desert Southern Egypt and Libya, 1916-17.

THE LIBYAN DESERT

On August 15th, 1916, the Australian Armoured Car Battery received orders to entrain at Ismailia for the South of Egypt with their Armoured Cars. The battery was detained at Minia on the 17th and immediately took part in the operations between this point and the Baharia Oasis along a line of blockhouses through the Libyan Desert over one hundred miles in length. The unit worked in conjunction with the 11th and 12th Light Armoured Car Batteries, which were Imperial units, and were equipped with Rolls Royce Armoured Cars and the new Light Vickers Machine-guns. These vehicles were the envy of the Australians who were equipped with a mixed fleet of cars, which while satisfactory on hard ground, gave the drivers and gunners plenty of exertion in the soft sand of the desert. The Colt guns with which the Australian were equipped, worked well and the unit did good practice with these. While the unit was stationed at Minia the members suffered severely from Nile fever and welcomed the expeditions into the desert especially when they were detailed to relieve the garrisons occasionally in the desert blockhouses, where the conditions were much healthier although of course the heat was intense.

14. The Mercedes armoured car and crew on a railway flatcar preparing for the train journey from Moascar to Minia (Young collection ATM I.CP.IY.043).

The work operating the heavy cars in the desert was extremely strenuous on account of the many very soft patches in the sand, which called for skilled driving. All our drivers were accustomed to bush driving in Australia but nevertheless it was wonderful how the driving improved as they became more accustomed to the desert conditions. Efforts were made to lighten the cars by sacrificing some of the armour plating and other more or less unnecessary parts; and twin tyres were also devised for the rear wheels, which improved the going somewhat. The cars always worked in pairs, chiefly so that there would be plenty of manpower available when help was required in bad country. The chief work of the motor units was to patrol the desert west of the Nile and it was known that the Senussi were established in some of the oases and were in the habit of making small raids into Egypt across the Libyan Desert. These people could only travel by camels and would perhaps average about 20 miles a day, (while of course the motors could do this distance in an hour). This meant that if the motors patrolled on a line about 100 miles out, information of a raid could always be obtained about four days ahead.

15. Minia Camp was the home of the British 11th and 12th Light Armoured Motor Batteries. On arrival the Australian Armoured Car Section was retitled the 1st Australian Armoured Motor Battery to comply with British Army practice (Young collection).

16. An armoured car of the Australian Light Car Patrol, which was operating against the Senussi on the western frontier of Egypt, in difficulties. The wheels sank in a patch of soft sand and the car had to be dragged out over layers of board. Left to right: Sergeant A. Lloyd, Corporal N. Bisset, Lieutenant Holloway (British Army), Lieutenant E.H. James, Driver Oscar Hyman, Sergeant Ivan Young (inside car), Corporal G.F. Morgan, Sergeant H. Creek, Corporal W.P. Thompson (AWM B01769).

When patrolling, the crews of the cars would keep a keen watch on the sand for footmarks, which showed up very clearly, and any fresh tracks on the desert would always be followed until the people who made them were overhauled and interviewed. On September 6th, a couple of Imperial officers who were out with a car were surprised in the sand dunes near the Baharia Oasis by a party of tribesmen and were overpowered and shot. Next day a patrol car crew discovered the bodies in the sand with the emptied revolvers alongside them. Some days later a party of tribesmen were overhauled and captured by one of the Light Car Patrols.

On the 3rd December, orders were received by the unit for all cars, guns and vehicles, to be returned to G.H.Q. Cairo and the unit to proceed south and take over the Ford Light Cars and Lewis guns of a Light Car Patrol and the Australian unit was to take the name of No. 1 Light Car Patrol. The unit proceeded south by rail to Oasis Junction on 6th December. Next day they travelled by a narrow gauge Military Railway which had been built across the desert to Kharga Oasis and the unit detrained at a railhead which was known as Water Dump A. A camp was made near a railhead in the sand, and work was commenced on the

Ford Cars which had been taken over in a very dilapidated condition and which had apparently been allowed to run almost to destruction. All ranks worked night and day for the next couple of weeks overhauling and reconditioning the vehicles also in practising on the new Lewis guns. The strength of the unit was increased by the addition of some extra drivers also some dispatch riders with motor cycles who soon became very expert with their machines on the desert.

17. The arrival of a shipment of new Model T Fords in southern Egypt. These vehicles were still in factory condition but would soon be modified to suit local conditions. The second vehicle, LC0545, would be issued to the 1st Australian Motor Machine Gun Battery when its vehicles were returned to stores in December 1916 (Young collection ATM LCP.IY.183).

On 18th December the Divisional Commander and staff were escorted out to the Dakhla Oasis (about 80 miles) by a fleet of 8 cars and on the following day the British flag was officially hoisted at Tenida (the capital of the oasis) by Major General Watson. Two days afterwards the party returned to railhead.

On the 30th December, we took three cars and two motor cyclists with 6 days' rations, petrol, etc on a reconnaissance to discover alternative routes to the south of the Dakhla Oasis. The present route known as the "Gubari Road" is a very ancient caravan route across the desert with defined tracks made by the camels' pads, which have been crossing the same track for centuries. The surface is very rough and flinty and the sharp stones caused a lot of damage to the tyres of the motors.

18. On arrival, the Model T Fords were modified to suit local conditions. Driver Oscar Hyman at the wheel of a heavily laden patrol car (AWM P11419.006).

We spent a couple of days exploring the desert south of Mut (the most southern village of the Dakhla Oasis) and proceeded along another ancient route which runs for 220 miles due south to the wells of El Sheb.

19. Number 4 Block House. The defence of southern Egypt from the Senussi consisted of a number of 'block houses' that acted as both patrol bases and defensive positions (Young collection ATM LCP.IY.070).

We travelled mostly by the aid of the compass, but discovered that the instrument was very much affected by the magnetos of the motors and consequently had continually to be checked by stopping the cars and taken some distance away from the engine for bearings to be taken. Cairns of stones were erected in prominent positions and empty petrol tins placed on top of these to mark routes. These cairns would be seen for many miles, as the sun would be reflected off the shiny tin. In some cases we could see these tins as far as 20 miles away.

To the east of the El Sheb route runs a range of rocky hills which appeared to be impassable to cross with vehicles of any description. We climbed these hills on foot and discovered that the country was comparatively level to the east (the direction in which we desired to travel). After two days' searching, a practicable pass was discovered through the hills about 40 miles from Mut and from this point the cars were able to travel almost due east over splendid hard sand similar to the firm sand along the sea shore. High speeds could be obtained and we returned to Kharga Oasis by compass bearing after 4 days and nights in the desert.

Some weeks later we did this route again thoroughly, spending several days surveying and mapping. We afterwards prepared a comprehensive map of the various routes and landmarks between the two oases of Kharga and Dakhla. This was subsequently forwarded to the General Officer in charge of Southern Egypt and he later wrote and congratulated the unit on the result of the work.

Early in January 1917, we received instructions to move our camp from Water Dump A and endeavour to effect communication between the Dakhla Oasis and the oases to the east (Kufra and Farafra).

The first-named oasis was about 400 miles east of Dakhla while Farafra was about 100 miles north-east in a direct line (but very much farther the way motors would traverse, as several ranges of very rocky mountains would have to be avoided).

We decided to try the Kufra Oasis first. It was reported that no Europeans had ever reached this oasis. There was certainly no caravan route to the west in the direction of the Dahkla Oasis, the native caravans having always proceeded in a northerly direction towards the Mediterranean via Aujila.

The well-known explorer Harding King had made an expedition in 1911 to the south-east of Dakhla for 200 miles partly in the direction of Kufra but had to return on account of the very heavy country and complete absence of water.

We determined to make our route further north than King's. We spent a week making a dump in the desert about 80 miles out from our last camp. We buried stocks of petrol and water in Fantasses, also supplies of bully beef and biscuit here, as this was to be our jumping-off point and we naturally wished to start off with a full stock. Water and petrol would be the governing factors of the journey and in order not to waste any of the precious liquid in the radiators of the cars, we fitted condensers to the radiator caps and closed up the overflow pipes. The condensed water being caught in a 2-gallon petrol can and returned at intervals to the radiator again. By this means we saved fully 75% of the water generally lost through boiling.

Having completed our dump and got everything ready, we made a start with three Ford cars and a crew of two men on each. Two Motor Cyclist Despatch Riders accompanied the Patrol in order to keep up communications.

20. The New Hudson motorcycle with its demountable sidecar. The New Hudson was built by the New Hudson Cycle Company using a V-twin JAP engine. Mounted on the sidecar is a tripod with a Colt Model 1895 machine-gun. The version chambered for the .303 inch (7.7 x 56R mm) round had a much heavier barrel of uniform profile compared to the slimmer profile used for other calibres. The heavy barrel was an attempt to reduce the tendency of the standard design to overheat the chamber and uncontrollably 'cook off' rounds. As a result, the weapon was very heavy, at over 18 kilograms (Young collection ATM LCP.IY.182).

Every ounce that was not necessary was taken off the vehicles. For instance the cars had no bodies at all. The seats consisted of ration and ammunition boxes; the cushions were the men's blankets. Two of the cars were stripped of the Lewis guns and mountings. This meant that only one car was really armed but each car was provided with a rifle, and the crews all had their revolvers.

All the cars at the start were grossly overloaded, as of course this load would be rapidly diminished every mile traversed.

It was intended to leave one of the cars as an advanced dump at a point about 200 miles from our objective and make the final dash with two cars and a cyclist.

21. Model T Ford LC427 of a British Light Car Patrol. Sergeant Ivan Young wrote: 'Ford trying to rush a sand dune. Wheels twisted half way up. Result broken axle. Heavy Armoured Cars rush these dunes at 40 miles an hour, getting over the top about 15 miles an hour. Three of these dunes between Block House 6 and Bahria.' As illustrated, the learning curve was sometimes destructive. Driving fast at a sand dune in order to clear the crest resulted in a badly bent front axle on LC427. Establishing the limits of their vehicles and themselves was all part of the evolution of the unit into an adaptable and effective mechanised fighting force (Young collection ATM LCP.IY.175).

After leaving the last well, known as "Bir Sheikh Muhammad", the character of the desert began to change for the worse. Hitherto the sand, although perhaps soft underneath, generally had a hard crust. This meant that once a car got a start it could usually keep going. The crew would run along and push until a speed of 6 or 8 miles per hour was reached and then jump up onto the step. The nature of the ground was now quite different and seemed to be composed of very fine drift sand on the surface to a depth of about six inches. This meant very heavy going in low gear which of course was the very thing we wished to avoid, as it meant increased petrol and water consumption and reduced speed. However, we found that if one car led the way in low gear the others could follow in the tracks made (running in top gear), as the going was much easier for the following cars. Each car now took its turn half hourly to make the road. The cyclists travelled out on either flank to ascertain if there was any improvement in the ground.

Unfortunately there was no sign of improvement and after about 80 miles of this gruelling work one of the cars smashed its differential. We transferred some of the stores to the other two cars and pushed on, abandoning the disabled vehicle. We travelled for another day under similar gruelling conditions when a second car caved in under the terrible strain. Things now began to look serious. The two cyclists were sent ahead on a high hill on the horizon to try out the country and they returned that night to state that there was no improvement, so it was reluctantly decided to abandon the present attempt as there was well over 200 miles to go, and try again at a later date. The second car was temporarily repaired and the patrol returned to the well at "Bir Sheikh Muhammad" just as the last water can was emptied. The cars returned along the old tracks in less than half the time taken in the outgoing journey, as the road improved each time a vehicle used it, consequently, a second effort should be much easier than the first. We towed in the remaining broken car about a week later and began to make preparations for a second attempt.

The experience gained in the first trip was very useful and given reasonable luck we anticipated success next time. However, the second attempt was never made as before arrangements were completed, orders were received for the patrol to pack up and move into a new and more exciting theatre of the war, and early in May 1917, we started off on the long 1000 mile journey into Palestine.

22. Sergeant Jack Langley and two other members of the 1st Australian Light Car Patrol aboard a heavily modified Model T Ford in early 1917. The vehicle has had all its unnecessary weight removed. A copper pipe that connects the radiator with a condenser can be seen clearly. This simple adaptation helped prevent engine overheating while saving precious water (Young collection ATM LCP.IY.245).

Airmen in the Desert.

About the middle of last year Second Lieutenant Stewart Ridley of the RFC went out alone in his machine as escort to another pilot who had with him another pilot named J.A. Garside. Engine trouble developed when Lieutenant Ridley had been flying for an hour and a half, and as they could not put the matter right immediately they decided to camp where they were for the night the next morning, as Ridley's engine still proved obdurate, the second pilot decided to return to base, and return on the next day to the assistance of the two men. The programme was duly carried out, but when they got back the pilot found that Ridley and Garside, with the machine, had disappeared.

23. The graves of two Royal Flying Corps airmen who were lost in the desert 40 miles west of Khara. This tragedy led to the deployment of the light car patrols to the Libyan Desert (Creek collection ATM LCP.HC.040.HR).

A search party was immediately organized to scour the desert, and on the Sunday tracks were discovered. It was not until the Tuesday, however, that the missing plane was discovered. Beside it lay the dead bodies of Lieutenant Ridlev and Garside. A diary was found on the mechanic, and the brief entries therein tell the tragic story of those last hours better than pages of description. The diary reads as follows: "Friday. Mr. Gardiner left for Meheriq, and said he would come and pick one of us up. After he went we tried to get the machine going, and succeeded in flying for about twenty-five minutes, Engine then gave out. We tinkered engine up again, succeeded in flying about five miles next day (Saturday), but engine ran short of petrol. Sunday After trying to get engine started, but could not manage it owing to weakness, water running short, only half a bottle Mr. Ridley suggested walking up to the hills. Six p.m. (Sunday) - Found it was farther than we thought; got there eventually; very done up. No luck. Walked back; hardly any water-about a spoonful. Mr. Ridley shot himself at ten-thirty on Sunday whilst my back was turned. No water all day; don't know how to go on; got one Verey light; dozed all day; very weak; wish someone would come; cannot last much longer. Monday thought of water in compass, got half bottle seems to be some kind of spirit. Can last another day. Fired Lewis gun, about four rounds; shall fire my Verey tonight last hope without machine comes. Could last days if had water."

The Captain of the Imperial Camel Corps, with which the aviators were co-operating, formed the opinion that Lieutenant Ridley shot himself in the hope of saving the mechanic, the water they had being insufficient to last the two of them till help arrived. The Commanding officer of the RFC stated: "There is no doubt in my mind that he performed this act of self sacrifice in the hope of saving another man." The history of the RFC is a short one, but it is already full of glorious deeds.

(The *Egyptian* newspaper, July 1916, p. 55)

On the Rim of the Great Sahara

Sergeant Ivan S. Young, son of Mr. and Mrs. John Young, of "Yelholm", Nelson Street, Nhill, writes from somewhere in Egypt:

"On the sands of the desert with a vengeance while writing this. My outlook is nothing but sand dunes, immense outcrops of limestone, and the only evidences of civilization are the Egyptian Labor Corps working on the railhead, which is here now. It is not perfectly flat and monotonous as I expected but undulating hills and rises with not one single tree, shrub, or annual in the whole 100 miles, with the exception of the other blockhouses at intervals of 12 to 14 miles. The track is more or less along what might be ancient water courses, or wind courses perhaps; anyway along the bottom of innumerable valleys, in and out and everywhere, mostly fair going for cars, but intersected with numerous bad drifts and loose patches. There are also flat patches and hard outcrops of limestone occasionally. There is about five miles through what is called the S bend of heavy going, very similar to the two miles near Dadswell's, only between deep sand hills with not a stick on them. In places the Rolls Royce we came up on, with eleven men and baggage, would get up to 45 miles an hour. I don't think it was down to first gear all the way one cannot go where one likes over the desert for you have to work your way in and out, although there are several well known tracks or camel-pads, probably used for thousands of years. This is one we are on now, but to here it is very gravelly with ironstone and limestone rubbles, but right against us now are immense sand dunes about 25 miles wide, running north and south for about 100 miles or more. These dunes are ... well the one I can see in front of me is about 60 to 100 feet across quite round and smooth with the wind.

Two motorcyclists go out over them twice a day on patrol about 12 miles. It's marvellous to see them go up and down those dunes. On the way up, of course, we passed numerous camel transports mostly in charge of Australians, but the funniest thing is the Fords. They bring stores and transport stuff between the last two blockhouses. It's dead funny to be going along and all of a sudden coming over a bare sand hill a mile or so away to have a Ford pop up, then another and another; there might be twenty or more altogether. Needless to say with the rough track and the rough handling they get they are always breaking down, at least some of them. Before cars came here the track was lined, or rather blazed, all along with the bones and skeletons of camels. Now the track has got modernized, for with the camel bones every now and then you'll see the remains of a Ford. The name for them is "desert lice" and is very descriptive. The other side of these dunes, 2-5 miles away, is the Baharia Oasis, which the Senussi have evacuated and the Australian Camel Corps went in and took possession last Wednesday. There only remains one more oasis for them either to fight or to give in.

This desert must have been under the sea at some time for you can find shells and sandstone with mussel and other shell imprints on it, and again you can find any amount of petrified wood. In fact we found a section of a tree trunk about 2 foot in diameter, and about 1 foot high, petrified. It is far better here than at Minia; the sand is beautifully clean after the black dust of the Nile Valley, and the air is so fresh and clear after the unwholesome stinks, etc, of the natives of the valley. There are numerous high plateaus with tabletops of about an acre or two in extent, rising out of the desert 100 feet, or more high, and on one or two of these near the block houses are posted look-outs.

You ought to see the elaborate barbed wire entanglements all around us. It's a great life here—stand to arms for an hour every morning at four, start the engines of the cars, and then run out about 10 miles on patrol. Breakfast at 8. Either porridge or bacon and tea; dinner—tea and boiled dates; tea—tea and stewed beef. Usually to sleep about 7 o'clock as there is nothing else to do. It is great to be away from the mosquitoes and flies, although the flies are coming now the camels have started to camp here at night. There are little birds on the desert, something like sparrows, the same colour and size but with a sharper, longer beak, and a longer tail. In fact, like as a sparrow that showed some breeding. They won't eat bread, but evidently live on flies and meat. They are as tame as anything; they hop in and out of the shelter, on to our arms and shoulders, catching flies all day long. I suppose they have never seen white men before.

24. An unidentified Australian soldier stands in a line of defensive pits dug as cavalry traps (AWM P11419.003).

About a fortnight ago we were having a practice cricket match at the Minia camp, when the Adjutant, Captain Stout, an English County cricketer of some note said, "Give me a hand." He took the bat and Oscar Hyman, one of our fellows, began to bowl and bowled him out with the first four balls. We all laughed more or less, and Oscar called out to him, "did you know any other games, Sir?" He didn't say much, but that night at dinner he was telling the other officers the incident and he turned to James, our CO said, 'Yes, some of your Australians coolly asked me if I knew any other bally game. The other English officers went into hysterics for about 10 minutes. We are allowed 1 gallon of water per man per day for cooking, washing, drinking, etc- it is just enough, but you can't waste any. We save up and have a bath in half a kerosene tin of water about once a week, it costs about 7s a gallon to get it out here, although it should be cheaper now the line is about running.

Monday, 23rd October, Very dirty, today, strong wind and air full of sand pebbles, etc. Early this morning some of the Australian Camel Corps came across from the Biharia oasis with 40 prisoners and about £1000 worth of ivory. There is one Turkish lieutenant amongst them, and you ought to see the collection of old rifles they had: old percussion caps, smooth bore rifle, flint locks ordinary double barrel shotguns; etc., which of course would all make nasty holes in a fellow if he got close enough. Of course the majority of these men and equipment are what were left behind and the sick and wounded and so forth. The main able-bodied army has cleared out. They even have a variety of rifles, including English, Turkish, Mauser and others of all dates and patterns, several gold pieces and machine guns. This blockhouse is being made rather important, as it is the nearest blockhouse to --- filled up with water, stores, etc. Saw a great sight this afternoon, a convoy of 200 camels leaving with stores etc, for the ---- It was great seeing them disappear over the crest of the sand dunes.

They are in charge of an Australian Sergeant Major and he is a trick. He talks Arabic like a native, and whenever any of his natives deserve it he puts them over and has a big black Sudanese with a whip who gives them a good beating while all the others look on and laugh, they'd do anything for him, too.

We have just got a pigeon house built inside, with a dozen carrier pigeons, also a portable wireless outfit carried by two Fords, with a radius of 30 miles so we are all right for communications.

Some time ago we wrote to the commissioners of gifts for Australian soldiers telling them we were here, and the other day we received a case of goods. Talk about a Xmas party! If the people out there only could see and know the pleasure they gave us they'd be more than repaid. Each man got a tin of Tasmania preserved peaches, a big tin of caramels, a tin of 50 cigarettes, 2oz. of tobacco (from the V.R.C.), 2 packets of 20 cigarettes, writing pad and envelopes, soap, pickles, and tin of Swallow and Ariel's biscuits."

[The ancient camel route referred to by Sergeant Young is mentioned in Sir A. Conan Doyle's book *The Tragedy of the Korosko*.]

(***Nhill Free Press***, 8 December 1916, p. 2)

25. Sergeant Ivan Young, Corporal Bert Creek, Drivers George Jones and George McKay in their quarters with their Christmas gifts, 1916 (Young collection ATM LCP.IY.225).

Xmas in the Desert.
Lieut. P. Cornwell writes.

The following letter has been received from Lieut. P. Cornwell (Australian Armored Car Section), of Cornwell's Pottery, Brunswick:

Egypt, 25th December, 1916.

Dear Old Tom,

Xmas Day, and I am just writing a few words to let them know that I and we generally, are thinking of all you people at home, who were good enough to think of us in time to help us to have a swell Xmas dinner.

Our cook (Sergt. Millar) made a supreme effort to give the boys a dinner worth remembering. We have thirteen English Tommies attached to us now, so the boys have a pretty big mess as well, 25 in all. We divided the gifts up amongst the whole crowd of them, and the Tommies were delighted especially, as well as our boys. The Tommies did not have anything, so you can understand how pleased they were to share with our chaps.

The gifts they had doled out to them were all similar. A tray each was made out of part of the packing cases on which were stacked the different things, so that I could have them passed out of my mess hut as they filed past.

Called a parade yesterday morning at 10 a.m., and told them to form up so that I could say a "very" few words to them, and have a snapshot taken. (It took Sergt. Langley, Bisset and myself two days to go through the cases of gifts, and arrange every thing, so that each of the 25 would have similar items). Don't think the grocer is at the back door when you read the following list: I tin biscuits. 1 tin shortbread, 1 fruitcake, I tin preserved fruit, 1 tin cheese, 1 tin coffee and milk, 1 tin sweets, 1 tin sardines, 1 tin salmon or tongues, 5 packets cigarettes, 1 pipe, 1 tooth brush and paste, 1 towel, 1 pair socks, 1 writing pad and pencil, 1 plum pudding, and lots of little oddments, such as chewing gum, boot laces, handkerchiefs, etc. So we didn't do too badly, did we?

Yesterday afternoon (Xmas Eve), I sent Langley and another chap in one of our cars into the mud village of Kharga, about 30 miles away, to see what poultry they could get (as the meat which we had for our Xmas ration was not good enough to eat), and they brought back four turkeys. They returned about midnight, and it was a jolly good performance to get them back safe that night at all. The turkeys were killed and hung up in readiness for next day. Millar, with four orderlies as assistants, has cooked jellies, custards and a huge trifle. The brandy for the trifle and pudding sauce I obtained from the doctor here for the special occasions, and during the week

26. Members of the Armoured Car Battery with Christmas gifts provided by the Lady Mayoress' Fund (Young collection ATM LCP.IY.225).

I got fifty bottles of beer, four bottles of whisky, and gave them with the turkeys to the boys. There are also 24 bottles of ginger beer for the teetotallers (one or two, self included). The boys have invited me to the dinner. Later on, will send some snaps of them taken with their gifts.

Well, Tom, the desert is all right in its place, but one gets tired of it, and I won't be sorry to say farewell when the time comes to leave it. They are sending us eighty miles farther in next Wednesday, and, by the time they have finished with Susi we will fall over the other side of Africa and into the

Atlantic. As mentioned in previous letters, we have been out against the Senussi tribes, and the armoured cars have put in some good work.

Wishing you all a Happy New Year, Yours sincerely,

Percy Cornwell.

(The *Brunswick and Coburg Leader*, 9 March 1917, p. 3)

Extinguishing the Senussi.
Australian soldiers do their Share.

Particulars of the final stages of the successful British effort in destroying the Senussi Arab forces in the vicinity of Egypt show that Australian soldiers played an important part. Amongst the Australians who took part were Driver Norman Bisset, son of Mr. G. S. Bisset, of Golden-square, and Sergeant John Langley, nephew of the Anglican, Bishop of Bendigo. Both young soldiers were members of the armored car section, the rapid movements of which out maneuvered and bewildered the Arabs. This action was fought in the early part of February.

27. Senussi prisoners on open railway trucks at Kharga (Young collection ATM LCP.IY.196).

A Remote Vastness.

Siwa had been the headquarters of the Senussi forces since their expulsion from the eastern oasis in October. It is separated from the coast by 200 miles of desert, and the step escarpment, where the Libyan plateau dips sharply down into a hollow below the level of the sea, forms a natural wall, which shuts it off from the outer world.

The enterprise was a fitting climax to the series of brilliant successes, which our armored cars achieved in the western desert. A more lonely and desolate country than that between the coast and Siwa could hardly be imagined. After the first 50 miles the country is an absolute featureless, barren waste till the oasis is reached. It was bitterly cold at night, and as the force carried no tents each man had simply to scrape a hole for himself and creep into it. The 200 miles of desert were covered without mishap, every car that set out arriving. The dash had been carried out with such secrecy and dispatch that the enemy knew nothing about it till it was an accomplished fact. It was as if the cars had dropped from the skies. According to the statements of prisoners the first indication anyone had of our presence was hearing the noise of the motors. They thought at first that the sound came from an aeroplane; then through glasses they made out the cars, which had actually got down into the oasis, without even having been observed.

The Action.

The enemy was located in a strongly entrenched position on the rocky escarpment overlooking the detached oasis of Girba, some 15 miles to the west of Siwa. His strength was 800 rifles with two mountain guns and two machine guns. Our force at once attacked, and the engagement began at ten minutes past 10 by the armored cars dashing up to within 800 yards of the enemy's position and opening fire with their machine guns. Owing to the difficult nature of the ground over which the cars were operating two of the armored cars, which took part in the initial rush, got stuck in the marshy ground surrounding the springs in the oasis. One remarkable result of this was that when at a later period other cars were detached to both flanks to try and find a way of climbing the escarpment a single armored car was engaging the whole enemy force for three-quarters of an hour. Two Ford cars were sent along the road towards Siwa, and after going about six miles captured a convoy, which had been bringing food supplies.

The action at Girba took the form of a prolonged duel between our machine gun and the mountain guns, machine guns and rifles of the enemy. Fighting went on all through the night by moonlight. When day broke the beaten Senussi could be seen against the skyline moving off by the west on their camels. Unfortunately, the cars could not climb the cliff to pursue them, and they passed out of range. As soon as it was sufficiently light our men went up to the abandoned position, and set fire to everything that had not been burnt by the enemy. A large number of rifles and a considerable quantity of ammunition were captured. So ended an action, which was in its own way one of the most remarkable ever fought in Egypt. For 20 hours our machine guns had successfully engaged an enemy strongly posted in a prepared position, and had inflicted very heavy casualties almost without loss to themselves.

(The *Bendigonian*, 21 June 1917, p. 3)

28. Captured Senussi rifles stacked at Block House 6 (Young collection ATM LCP.IY.205).

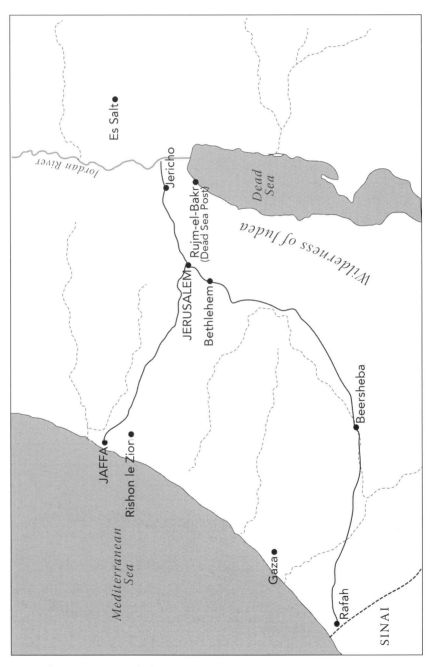

2. Area of Operations, Sinai and Palestine 1917-18.

SINAI

On the 18th May 1917, the Patrol loaded their cars and baggage on the trucks of the little narrow gauge Military Railway at Railhead Water Dump A.

Everything was securely roped up for the long journey to Egypt and at 6 p.m. the little engine whistled and puffed away on its long dusty trip across the Libyan Desert. The personnel spread themselves in their cars, as these were the only seats available on the train. We slept on board, as comfortably as could be expected under the circumstances and in the morning had our usual breakfast of bully beef and biscuit. The next day was a never-to-be-forgotten one. The temperature was between 119 and 120 degrees in the shade (which was difficult to find) and a genuine *Khamseen* (sand storm) was in full force. It seemed to us to be working itself up into an extra fury to give us a send off. The coarse grains of sand (from which it was impossible to get protection) would sting the face and hands like driving hailstones. The engine of our train was making heavy weather, as it had to rise nearly 1000 feet from the Kharga Oasis to the top of the scarp, which was the level of the ordinary desert. The difficulty was intensified by the drift sand, which covered the rails. The troops every few miles would walk ahead with shovels and clear the track to give the engine a chance to get going. Once on level ground the going was easier and the train made better progress.

29. A member of the Light Car Patrol stands in front of a dug-in shelter in the Sinai (Cornwell collection ATM LCP PC 011).

While on the subject of the oases it is just as well to mention that these are not exactly what they are popularly supposed to be. The oases in the deserts in the north of Africa are merely deep depressions in the ground. Some of them are very large and are generally from 20 to 100 miles in diameter. They owe their fertility to water, which comes from the mountains in the south, from underground sources. Most oases are populated by natives who sink wells and pump the water over the depression. They cultivate date palms principally. The dates are collected, dried and sent by camel to Egypt in exchange for other merchandise.

After spending the day in the train we ultimately arrived at the Nile Valley and transferred from the narrow gauge train to the broad gauge Egyptian State Railway's train at Oasis Junction and after another night and day in this train, we arrived at Cairo at 10 p.m. only to be immediately shunted off to the train to Kantara which we reached at 11.30 am on 21st May.

We unloaded here and packed our baggage once more on to our fleet of "Lizzies" and drove across the Canal at Kantara by the pontoon bridge to the terminus of the new Military Railways to Palestine.

Once more we loaded up and entrained for the new front, getting away after a hasty snack of lunch at 1 p.m. After a day and a night on board this train, we ultimately arrived at our new destination at the new front outside Gaza. We off loaded at a place known as Khan Yunis and were immediately welcomed at the new front by an enemy plane who promptly tried to bomb the train and was greeted by the "archies" whose spent shrapnel dropped all over us much to the annoyance of one of our drivers whose haversack and breakfast were ruined by a piece of shell case.

We moved off to our new camps which were in an old Arab orchard surrounded by prickly pears and we were told to dig dugouts for ourselves as the place was supposed to be popular with enemy aeroplanes especially on moonlight nights. Next morning we were introduced to General Sir Harry Chauvel, the Commander of the Desert Mounted Column, which was reputed to be the largest body of cavalry and mounted troops ever assembled. We were inspected and welcomed by the General and his staff and were informed that the motor units would co-operate with the mounted troops in forthcoming military operations. We were to get the hang of the country as quickly as possible and learn the various routes from one end of the front to the other.

On the 30th May, with two of our machine-gun cars accompanied by one car from No. 7 Patrol, two Rolls Armoured Cars and one wagon from the 11th Light Armoured Motor Battery, we took part in a reconnaissance from the

Wadi Ghuzzie in an easterly direction. About 20 miles out the country became very sandy and we decided to leave the heavy armoured cars in a commanding position and proceed further with two light patrol cars across the doubtful looking country. We ran across several of our light horse patrols who reported numerous small bodies of mounted Turks to the east in which direction we proceeded without encountering any of them, although they could be seen in the hills through the glasses. We reconnoitred the district for about an hour and returned to the armoured cars and then back to our camp in the evening.

During all movements such as these, we made it a fixed rule that all patrol cars must invariably work in pairs. This was necessary for several reasons.

First of all, in case of mechanical trouble one vehicle could always help the other out of difficulties or if necessary even tow it home. Secondly it was also a great advantage to have the extra manpower with two car crews in bad country when any manhandling of the vehicles had to be done. Thirdly, it was a great preventive of disaster. It rendered ambush almost impossible, provided the cars always kept their proper distances from each other on patrol; also in difficult crossings of creeks or depressions, etc. one vehicle could generally cover the other until it was across, when the first vehicle would in turn cover the crossing of the second and so on.

This patrol throughout its existence was remarkably free from bad accidents or disasters of any description and there is no doubt that our rule of working in pairs in this fashion was largely responsible for our good fortune in this respect.

30. Lieutenant James watches Sergeant Ivan Young operate the Colt machine-gun (Young collection ATM LCP.IY.165).

For the balance of the week we busied ourselves overhauling our engines and chassis and trying out our Lewis guns so that everything would be ready for any emergency and on the 5th June, we moved out to the outpost camp at Tel-el Fara and were attached to the Imperial Mounted Division. Next day we took part in an armed reconnaissance with the mounted troops for about 8 miles towards Beersheba. No serious opposition was offered by the enemy and our force, after obtaining the information required, returned to camp before 6 p.m.

On 8th June, instructions were received that the whole patrol would be required next day for an important reconnaissance at El Esani. We accordingly sent a couple of motorcyclists in company with one car to pick out the easiest crossings at Gorz Mabrook (a place where it was necessary to get the cars across deep wadis), as we did not wish to waste any time next day. Early next morning we picked up the Divisional Commander, Major General Hodgson and his General Staff officers and proceeded with four machine-gun cars reconnoitring the whole of the Esani district for four hours while the Light Horse Regiments were making a demonstration and engaging the Turks (towards the south-east) in order to distract their attention from our activities. We returned shortly after midday to camp without any untoward events except a misfiring engine, which was quickly rectified.

31. An overnight campsite. Tins of petrol have been used to tie down tarps to provide some comfort for the crews (AWM P11419).

On the 14th June we picked up the Corps Commander and staff again for another reconnaissance, which was carried out this time during the afternoon in the direction of Beersheba near a place called El Buggar. Everything proceeded satisfactorily except that an inquisitive enemy aeroplane became too interested in our movements and we were compelled to keep him busy by concentrating three of our Lewis guns on to him until he rose to a reasonable height again. We returned to camp before dark. All motor movements had to be made by daylight (except well behind the lines) as of course lights were not allowed to be used in any advanced positions. Although on moonlight nights very good work could often be done after sunset.

Next day one of our cars was out of action through being driven over a deep shell hole hidden in the long grass, with the result that a front axle was badly bent. However, we built a log fire in the evening and managed to get enough heat to straighten up the axle again, so the vehicle was ready for business as usual in the morning.

On the 20th June, we took the whole patrol on another inspection of the Turkish positions this time to the north-east to El Dammath and El Nagile. Much useful information was apparently obtained by the staff. We returned to camp before nightfall without our presence even being noticed by the enemy. About this time daily reconnaissances were made of all enemy positions until the 25th June when we took part in a new type of engagement. On this date it was decided to make a big drive on "no man's land" between the entrenched positions of both forces as it was suspected that small bodies of the enemy were secreted in various concealed places therein. Accordingly two bodies of mounted troops operating from each end of the position to be enveloped started out at daybreak and began to gradually converge.

The gun cars of No. 1 Light Car Patrol accompanied the Mounted Troops and we left a stores car with reserve ammunition and also a few important spares in a good concealed position known to our dispatch riders who could quickly find the spot if necessary. It was not to be expected that the enemy would ignore such a demonstration of force as this, and we were heavily shelled when passing the exposed positions between the Wadi Imleh to the Wadi Hannifish. However we suffered no casualties although a few mounted men were hit.

The chief duty of the Light Car Patrol was to cover the retirement of the mounted men when the movement was completed. We accordingly took up a position along a ridge and engaged the Turks with machine-gun fire until the mounted force was well back towards our own lines when we ceased fire and packed up our machine-guns and with our superior speed soon regained our own lines, picking up our stores car on the way, arriving back at our camp almost as soon as the rest of the force.

The operation was quite a success as a number of prisoners were roped in although not as many were expected. The day's work provided how usefully motor units could be utilised in covering a retirement.

Two days after this, Brigade Headquarters discovered a new use for a Light Car Patrol by sending us out to a position to draw fire.

Our instructions were to travel quickly over an exposed position making as much dust as possible as it was desired to know what sort of artillery the enemy had here. We were quite pleased to find out that our mission in this respect was not successful, as we did not draw the fire.

32. The Sinai presented new risks to the Light Car Patrol: members wear gas masks while completing anti-gas training (Creek collection, ATM LCP.HC.003).

About this time rumours had reached headquarters that gas attacks were being prepared for us by the Turks. Supplies of gas masks were issued to the various units. Gas instructors were detailed also to instruct all ranks how to use these. The men of the Armoured Car Sections and Light Car Patrols did gas drill along with others. No information was available as to how the motor vehicles would have behaved in a gas attack or what effect the gas would have on the running of the engines, so it was decided to try this out and one morning we had a full rehearsal. Gas masks were carefully fitted by the whole unit. The cars were lined up with full equipment and fully manned. A smoke and gas barrage was prepared in a suitable valley, and at the word "go" the whole unit drove quickly through the screen. On reaching the other side, the cars were turned round slowly driven back again along the same route to the starting point. All masks had been carefully adjusted and neither the smoke nor gas had any effect. It was thought that perhaps the running of the engines would be affected by the impure air mixture passing through the carburettors, but it made no apparent difference whatever as the motors seemed to run as steadily as usual without any misfiring being noticed. Possible they may not have developed their full power but as the cars were not fully extended we could not tell this. One thing was demonstrated however, and that was that the motor vehicles could operate in gas even if the animals could not.

During the month of July the patrol was engaged on many small stunts and reconnaissances along the whole front, but mainly towards the east. The chief object seemed to be to obtain more information about the country and roads for transport and the possibility of obtaining water for the horses and troops in the country ahead, in the event of an advance in this direction by our forces. Towards the end of the month there was a rumour that the Turks were evacuating Beersheba so we did a trip out in this direction but as we got well shelled for our inquisitiveness we did not persist; neither did we believe the rumours.

During August we were attached for duty to the Australian and New Zealand Mounted Division, Desert Mounted Corps, and later on to the Yeomanry Mounted Division. It was the custom for the various divisions to relieve each other periodically for the front line duty. The relieved division would move back a few miles and would have a bit of a spell from their more arduous duties. The Light Car Patrols however, generally stayed with the new duty division in order to put them "au-fait" with the country and roads.

Nothing really exciting happened in August until the 23rd and 24th, when the Patrol was operating with the Yeomanry Mounted Division which was bivouacked at Rashed Bek and reconnoitring the country around Ibin Said. During these operations the Divisional Commander Major General Barrow wished to view as closely as possible some enemy works being constructed near Gnaam. The patrol cars conveyed him and other staff officers to the spot required. By keeping well separated and under cover of the folds in the ground we managed to escape observation. However, when we left the observation point to return, our movements were evidently noticed as two shells immediately dropped beside us. The car drivers then took a track under cover of a slight rise in the ground and although this was out of sight of the enemy gunners they evidently had the range of it registered exactly for shells continued to drop along the track about every 25 yards. The road was too unhealthy a place to motor along consequently the cars had to take to the open ground. This meant travelling over very bad and bumpy country. It also meant that we were compelled to take a route which had to cross a deep wadi or creek. We travelled the side wadi looking for a suitable crossing for nearly half a mile till at last we discovered a possible track across and by dint of hard work with plenty of pushing and swearing all cars except one were safely across. When the last car was nearly over half way up the bank, some treacherous ground gave way with the result that the vehicle dropped to the bottom again (about a 15 foot fall). Fortunately, it dropped on its four wheels right side up. A quick examination showed a burst tyre, damaged wheel, some broken water joints and a cracked engine hanger. We hastily changed the wheel and tyre, patched up the water joints and braced up the broken hanger with some fencing wire. A rope was then fixed to the front axle and the other end to one of the cars that was across. Another ten minutes towing and pushing brought the damaged car to the top.

All the time the car was in the wadi, an attack was being very vigorously pushed by the Turks and a number of mounted men in our vicinity were being extremely hard pressed. At one time it looked as if the car would have to be burnt and abandoned but fortunately some reinforcements came up in time to push back the attack, giving us time to get everything clear away. During the whole operations of the war, No. 1 Light Car Patrol never lost a vehicle, but this occasion was the closest shave we had in this respect.

On the 4th of September, we carried out an interesting experiment in conjunction with the Signal Squadron Royal Engineers, during one of the armed reconnaissances, which were being conducted fairly frequently by us about this time. In these stunts, time was the essence of the contract and as much information as possible would be collected in the enemy's territory before he was able to bring up powerful reinforcements by which time we were generally back behind our own entrenchments again. In these affairs it was very important for the various Brigades and Divisional

Headquarters to be kept in constant touch with what was going on at the various points in their sectors. The most satisfactory way of doing this was by field telephones. These however, sometimes when done by hand took a considerable time to lay and pick up again after the stunt was over.

It was decided to do it by motorcar. Accordingly we took the machine-gun out of one of our Lizzies and in its place mounted a large cable drum, which had been prepared by the Royal Engineer men. This drum revolved on a spindle supported by a couple of bearings, a handle was fitted for paying out and winding up the cable as the motor was driven across country.

The trial provided very satisfactory and after the stunt was over the cable was being collected while the car travelled at about 12 or 15 miles an hour and was about half in when an enemy aeroplane became interested and began to take a hand in the proceedings.

Hal Harkin, the driver of the car who was also a very expert machine-gunner, was very upset at having left his machine-gun behind, when the pilot of the aeroplane began machine-gunning him from above. Two of the Royal Engineer men endeavoured to keep the plane up with their rifles but they were having a rough spin until another car came back to give them a hand when the plane rose and let them get back with their cable.

For the next few weeks, the patrol spent most of its time studying the ground and possible roads, tracks and water supply on the eastern flank of the force and, on the 18th of September, the Australian Mounted Division took over the outpost line from the Yeomanry Mounted Division who went back for a rest. We were now attached to the new division and things seemed to be getting busier. The raids began to go further into the enemy's lines and there was a feeling of a subdued excitement in the air as if something was going to happen at any moment. Orders are received to send all necessary equipment and baggage back to the dumps at Rafa. Evidently moves were contemplated so all weight was to be cut down to the minimum. On the 24th September a big reconnaissance took place to Asluj (a point on the Turkish Railway Line) and the whole district was reconnoitred very thoroughly and in the evening the force returned back to their old camp.

THE BATTLE OF BEERSHEBA

On the 30th of September, we were attached for duty to the Australian and New Zealand (Anzac) Mounted Division and on the 28th October the division moved forward to Asluj, which now became our headquarters. From now on things began to move fast and furiously. Most of the moves were done at night time. The air was generally thick with dust from the continual movement of horses, troops and transport, and the car drivers were generally smothered with white dust from head to foot. All our aeroplanes became intensely busy and were continuously in the air to prevent enemy planes from viewing what was going on in our lines.

On the 30th October, we sent a couple of cars some miles up the Beersheba Road to mark the track for a night march of the cavalry who moved off immediately after sundown in order to attack Beersheba from the rear. There was no sleep for anyone that night. Columns of troops with their transport were silently passing like shadows all night long on their way up the track marked by us the day before. Desert Mounted Corps Headquarters moved off from the Asluj Railway Station at midnight and at 4.30 next morning, before the first streaks of dawn, the Light Car Patrol moved out on its long task of overtaking all the troops that had been passing through the night. We processed for 14 miles in a north-easterly direction and then turned north-west behind Beersheba.

Shortly after daybreak the division was well in position behind the town and the New Zealanders attacked the hill of Tel-el-Saba, which they captured after a sharp fight. At 11 am we were attached for duty to the 2nd Light Horse Brigade under General Ryrie who were also hotly engaged in driving the Turks across the valley. The Turks were surprised at the flank attack, which was apparently unexpected. The Australian Mounted Division attacked the town from the other side and Colonel Scott's men made history by galloping across enemy trenches on horseback and charging with the sword. Meanwhile General Ryrie was using the Patrol Cars for making a hasty inspection of his front line.

As the general motored round his lines he probably attracted attention from snipers as plenty of odd bullets raised the dust but a quickly moving motorcar makes a very difficult target from any distance, and no hits were recorded in this instance. In the evening fires were burning in the town everywhere as the enemy retreated and it was not long after that the announcement was received that Beersheba had fallen.

33. Looking for enemy machines: the pedestal mount at the rear of one of the 1st Light Car Patrol's Model T Fords is used to engage an enemy aircraft. The Lewis is fitted with a wide bar-type foresight so the gunner can track the moving target with a degree of precision. Note the extent to which the patrol's early cars were stripped. They consisted of a flat wooden platform fixed to the chassis with large storage boxes as the seat bases for the front and gunner's seats (Creek collection, ATM LCP.HC.018HR).

The men of the patrol slept beside their motors that night while the outposts kept a constant vigil for counter attacks. Next morning at 4 am everybody was standing by as it was sure to be a busy day and everything was ready for moving at a moment's notice. The Patrol Cars were drawn up behind Brigade Headquarters, which was on a slight rise. At 7am two enemy aeroplanes appeared flying very low and began dropping bombs on any targets visible. One of these happened to be the field hospital, which suffered severely. The two planes then came straight for us apparently attracted by the groups around the Brigade Headquarters flag, and as they were flying so low that we could see the bombs ready for us we prepared to give them a hot reception. Our cars were equipped with Lewis guns and our machine-gunners had already had considerable experience in firing at moving planes. We knew that it was useless firing at any aeroplane unless it was moving either straight towards or away from the gun. We also had learnt that it was no use firing directly at the machine but the correct thing was to send a stream of bullets directly in front of the pilot through which he must pass. We accordingly reserved our fire waiting until he was coming in a straight line towards us and a few hundred yards away. We then let him have the concentrated fire of our four Lewis guns and every rifle we possessed. Our tactics were thoroughly successful. One plane turned sharply to the left and left us severely alone. The other one turned slightly and very nearly landed. Everyone cheered as we thought he was done. But suddenly he rose again and steered an erratic course to the left. We heard afterwards that he came down in our lines about a mile away. We found that the pilot had been shot and the observer had quickly seized the controls when the plane nearly came to earth the first time thus saving a smash. As he landed afterwards in the lines of one of the infantry regiments they probably received the credit of bringing him down. But there is no doubt that our fusillade had done it. We calculated that at the speed the plane was flying and the rate of fire of the Lewis guns the fuselage of the aeroplane should get about two bullets from each gun when passing through the stream of fire. This means that he would get about eight pretty effective hits as well as sundry rifle shots aimed at him. In any case, we think that everybody was pretty well relieved to see no bombs dropped.

The enemy put up a pretty stout resistance with machine-guns and light artillery during the rest of the day and very little advance was made. However, under cover of dark during the night he retired and entrenched in the hills. We bivouacked on the same position as on the previous night and the next day (the 2nd November) we advanced with the 2nd Light Horse Brigade for about 4 miles towards Dahariah, along the Hebron Road. We then met with some very steep hills where the Turks had their artillery and machine-guns posted with plenty of snipers scattered about. The Brigade Horse Artillery were having a duel with the camel guns in the hills and we dismounted our Lewis guns and leaving the cars hidden in a hollow, crept forward along the grass to a position where we thought we could get on to some machine-guns bothering us. But we found it very difficult to get a target as the enemy was well entrenched. A couple of the Rolls Armoured Cars endeavoured to proceed up the Hebron Road through a defile but the enemy had dug a deep trench across a narrow part of the road leaving no available route for wheeled traffic. The cars were plastered with bullets, which fell like hail on them, and one of them had its engine sump punctured by a bullet, which ricocheted off the road rising through the tray thus allowing the lubricating oil to run away. There was no room to turn on the narrow road and one car towed the other backwards after a couple of hours of very strenuous work. When they got back to cover every tyre had been punctured by bullets but the only casualty was one man injured by a piece of a door handle which had been struck from the outside by a bullet which forced through the door one of the broken pieces and this struck the machine-gunner in the leg. The crews of these two cars had a very difficult task in getting their vehicles out of an awkward position and the rear car was drawn up alongside the disabled one to afford cover to one of the men who fixed the tow rope while the machine-gunners did their best to keep the fire down.

34. Repairing a box-bodied Rolls Royce car in the desert. The 1st Armoured Car Battery appears to have been supplemented with British-owned Rolls Royce vehicles during its time in Egypt. There are several images showing the crews working with both open box-bodied cars and armoured cars in the desert (ATM ALC069).

For the rest of the day we endeavoured to keep the enemy busy with machine-gun and rifle fire while some of the men of the 2nd Light Horse Brigade tried to work round the enemy's right flank in the hills which are very steep and rough at this point. Our situation on the bend of the Hebron Road was known as Igery Corner and the sniping was particularly severe there. Everything showing round the bend of the hill was sure to attract attention from the Turkish sharpshooters and machine-guns. In the afternoon an ambulance wagon was so severely sniped that it was abandoned until nightfall when things quietened down considerably.

Early next morning (3rd November) we received a visit from an enemy aeroplane and kept him up with Lewis gun fire but he must have given our position away to the Turkish gunners as we were well shelled by them about midday and we were compelled to send the cars away to better cover behind a hill further back in order to prevent them being smashed up by shell fire and we spent the rest of the day getting a little of our own back by sniping the snipers and we bivouacked under the cars for the night. The next day was Sunday, 4th November, but it was not a day of rest. All had to stand to at 4 am. This hour was always the Turks' favourite time for a counter attack. It was very seldom that the enemy would attack at nighttime. He did not seem to like night operations and most of his attacks were made in the early hours of the morning.

35. Three of the four fighting cars of the Light Car Patrol's first issue of Model T Fords, which were stripped much further than the replacement vehicles received in December 1917. The Lewis light machine-gun's storage and transit case is fixed across the chassis at the rear of each vehicle, and a pedestal mount is bolted directly to the rear cross-member. (Creek Collection ATM LCP.HC.017)

As the advance on our sector was at a temporary standstill until the men on the hills had completed their outflanking there was not much use for the Armoured and Patrol Cars on their legitimate jobs, so we found other uses for them. Two cars were detached to bring up drinking water from some wells in the rear to the fighting men, one car was sent with six miles of signal wire to established telephone communication between Brigade Headquarters and the 6th Australian Light Horse Regiment up in the hills to the right flank and this was successfully accomplished by Corporal Hyman after a very rough trip over boulders and country that had certainly never had a motor car over it before.

Next day instructions were received to join Divisional Headquarters. We obtained supplies of rations, petrol, water etc. from a dump established at Beersheba and proceeded with the division in a northerly direction after the retreating Turks, for several days and nights. The Turks were fighting rear guard actions all the way and on the 7th we pressed hard on the enemy capturing large quantities of stores and railway. One of the patrol cars sighted a body of 20 mounted Turks and gave chase.

We opened fire with the Lewis guns giving them a couple of magazines. The Turks then scattered in various directions. As the cars could only follow one at a time and we had other important duties to attend to, we let them scatter. One car under Sergeant Langley was lent to the Camel Brigade to help their staff keep in touch with the various parts of their front, which was pretty extended. Next day we made a further advance of four miles, the enemy putting up a stout resistance all along the line, but still retreating. The cars got well shelled this day with shrapnel and some of the occupants almost wished they had their tin hats with them. (The drivers and gunners always preferred to wear their felt hats as the bumping of the motor cars over the rough roads knocked the helmets over their eyes, consequently they left their helmets behind). However, fortunately none of the occupants of the cars were struck although numerous shrapnel pellets were dug out of the woodwork of the motorcars that evening as souvenirs. That night we camped at Tel el Negile, a hill where the enemy made a strong stand and during the evening we were bombed twice by our own aeroplanes who evidently mistook us for the enemy. Some of our gunners were quite annoyed because they were not allowed to return the fire with their machine-guns. We complained during the night to the Air Force headquarters at being made a target for their bombs and the only satisfaction we received was to be told that we should not be so far ahead. Next day we continued the advance, which began to get more rapid as the enemy became more disorganised and large quantities of transport; ammunition and guns, which had been abandoned, were passed from time to time. Shortly after passing through Huj we were fortunate enough to capture one of the enemy's aerodromes so we were able to refill all our tanks with petrol, which had been abandoned by the Germans, and we took a few drums along with us in case we should lose touch with our own supplies. That night we bivouacked with the 2nd Light Horse Brigade behind the village of Suarfie-esh-Sherikye and had a fairly quiet night.

36. Two of the 1st Light Car Patrol's Model T Fords returning from a patrol. Each gun car was armed with a Lewis light machine-gun and had a crew of three — commander, gunner and driver. Each vehicle also carried a standardised load of fuel, food and spare parts. Two vehicles of the patrol were equipped as support vehicles — one carried the workshop stores and spare ammunition, while the other carried the bulk of the rations, mess stores, extra petrol and water (AWM B00054).

Next morning, 10th November, we sent some of the cars back to bring up fresh supplies of small arms ammunition, as owing to the rapidity of the advance it was difficult for the supplies to keep up with the mounted men. Our cars were gradually getting into a very decrepit state for want of adjustment etc, as owing to the continual movements by day and night it was impossible to give the attention to the machines that under normal circumstances they should have had. Practically all the travelling was done across country and any roads that existed were merely tracks of hard clay. Movements at night were particularly severe on the chassis as owing to the absence of lights the drivers had to be guided by instinct more than anything else. Some of the escapes from disaster during the night movements were almost miraculous and next morning we would often see where our tracks had been within a few inches of precipices and places that would make one's hair stand on end to drive over during daylight, let alone in darkness. On particularly dark nights in bad places the men would take it in turns to walk ahead and guide the drivers by the sound of their voices but generally this method of movement was too slow and we had to trust to luck. Needless to say, those on the cars would have a very rough passage as boulders or holes could not be seen until too late and it was quite a common occurrence for the occupants to be thrown out altogether. However, in the course of time, they became like flies and managed to hang on somehow no matter what the angle. This sort of work naturally was very hard on the vehicles, which were tied up with fencing wire and temporarily repaired with various makeshifts. As they were gradually getting to a state that would soon be beyond repair, we received instructions to proceed to Hamama for a day and do our best to get them to a reasonable state of security. So after darkness we set off via Mejdel to do our repairs. We waited until it was dark enough to hide our movements because enemy marksmen had been particularly active that afternoon and our course for a mile or two was very exposed as it led over a ridge where there was no cover whatever. About 7 p.m. we got clear away from the village, over the ridge without incident and drove steadily on for a couple of hours at a slow pace. The night was exceptionally black. There was no moon or glimmer of light whatever and we were only averaging about 8 to 10 miles an hour.

Progress was getting so slow and difficult that we were contemplating a few hours sleep leaving further travelling till some signs of dawn appeared, when suddenly, noises of angry men and a commotion sounded ahead. We stopped and walked ahead to ascertain the cause of the row and found a couple of Light Horsemen escorting about 200 Turkish prisoners back to a camp. The prisoners were beginning to get out of hand as they were very tired and thirsty and there was no water available. We arrived at the right time for the two troopers were at their wits end to keep the prisoners subdued. The escort had not had any sleep for a couple of nights so we decided to camp there and give them a hand. Fortunately we had a few gallons of drinking water on one of the cars, which assuaged the thirst of the prisoners who soon became subdued at the appearance of the armed patrol. We told the escort to have a sleep while our men took turns at guarding the prisoners until daylight. Then we packed up and went on our way after handing over the prisoners to their escort once more.

After a short run we arrived at our destination, Hamama via the village of Mejdel. We commenced at once to overhaul our vehicles and get them into reasonable order. Fortunately, we had a few necessary spares with which we replaced some of the most faulty units and everyone worked merrily away for about 18 hours by which time we had overcome the worst defects The only interruption we had was a visit from a couple of enemy aeroplanes, but a few rounds from Lewis guns made them move on again and they left us severely alone.

Next day we received orders to join the Yeomanry Mounted Division who we found at the village of Esdud, which they had just captured. The division was moving on to take possession of the village of Yebna during the afternoon where they stayed for the night moving eastward next day towards Akir.

Next morning, 15th November, an extended battle opened up first thing and the enemy retired eastward abandoning guns and ammunition all along the line. The division pressed on and we drove into Ramleh, the late German Headquarters and site of their aerodrome. We managed to get some more petrol here. That night we slept in the building that was the German Officers Mess. For the next day and night we rested in an olive orchard at Ramleh where we discovered some broken German motor cars. We managed to strip some parts such as springs etc. off our own vehicles, and install the good parts from the German cars. Next day we received fresh instructions to rejoin the Anzac Mounted Division and proceed with the New Zealand Brigade to the ancient town of Jaffa, which fell during the morning at 11 am. General Chaytor hoisted the British flag on the Town Hall in the presence of the local officials and inhabitants to the sound of cheering while the machine-guns and artillery at the back of the town made a suitable accompaniment for the occasion.

With the fall of Jaffa on the 18th November, another stage in the campaign was completed. The troops were now able to rest a little and consolidate their position. One of the difficulties of the Light Car units during the advance had been the problem of petrol supplies. We had been fortunate in being able to frequently replenish our tanks from supplies abandoned by the enemy during the retreat. The first thing we always did on overtaking an enemy motor lorry or car was to siphon out the petrol from the tanks into our own vehicles but sometimes we were forced to detach one of our own cars and send it back to the nearest supply depot. This would sometimes mean a long trip and by the time the vehicle returned, the unit may have moved many miles in some other direction, and perhaps would take a lot of finding. However, petrol along with other supplies was now being landed by boat at Jaffa.

The Division was now making its Headquarters at the town where we discovered a very well equipped German engineering shop with machine tools and first class equipment for repairs. Needless to say we did not waste any time in getting busy on our sadly neglected and overworked vehicles, we very shortly had them quite like respectable motor cars again.

At Jaffa the rainy season struck us, which was a new experience after many months of dry weather further south where the troops were never worried by moisture except the dew at night time. Needless to say the place was very soon a sea of mud with the constant movements of horse and motor transport, so in order to prevent the occupants looking like mud figures we had to extemporise mudguards on our cars which we did with the aid of a few boards taken from packing cases and fastened on with nails and the ubiquitous fencing wire. While we were at Jaffa, the cars were sent to the various surrounding villages with proclamations which were printed in the native languages ordering the inhabitants to hand in to the authorities all the arms and ammunition etc. in their possession and explaining a few regulations that must be observed. This work was carried out under the personal supervision of Major J. Urquhart, General Staff Officer of Desert Mounted Corps, and his suspicions were aroused in one of the villages at the actions of one of the inhabitants who was dressed as a native.

Major Urquhart, who is an excellent linguist in quite a number of languages, questioned this individual very closely and as his answers were unsatisfactory, we made him accompany us on one of the cars back to headquarters where we handed him over to the Military Police. We subsequently learnt that this supposed native was a Turkish officer disguised in native costume and he stayed behind in the village when his army retreated in order to transmit information of our movements back to his own people.

Needless to say he was sent away to a place where he would not cause any mischief until the end of the war.

On Sunday, 25th November, the enemy made a strong counter attack at the rear of the town and brought artillery up to shell the outskirts but the attack was driven back. Next day a squadron of hostile aeroplanes heavily bombed the town and our Lewis gunners had a little more machine-gun practise. The following evening one of the aeroplanes got even on one of our cars driven by Sergeant H. Creek, who was out on reconnaissance work. The aeroplane came down low and following the car machine-gunning all the time. Unfortunately, this particular car was not fitted with a Lewis Gun and no reply could be made, but it is understood that Sergeant Creek broke all existing motor records for that particular section of road. However, the pilot's shooting must have been bad, as he did no damage beyond stirring up the dust and perhaps taking a few more chips off the bodywork of the car.

On December 8th, the news was received of the fall of Jerusalem, which was now the other end of our line, which stretched from the coast at Jaffa to Jerusalem, which was about 3000ft. above sea level. The wet season had now set in earnest and it was apparent that things would probably settle down for a lull.

The unit moved into the village of Richon-Le-Zion on the Jaffa-Jerusalem road and were allotted billets. The first bit of comfort since the campaign began.

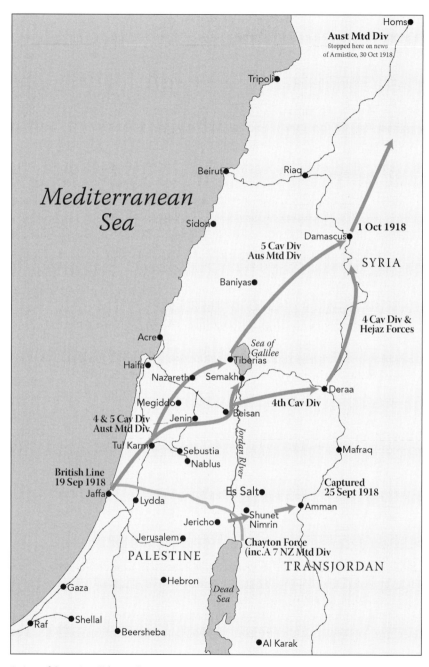

3. Area of Operations Palestine-Syria 1918.

PALESTINE

We were now in Palestine proper and settled down in billets in Richon where the Jewish villagers were doing their utmost to make us comfortable. In return we were able to give them our rations of sugar and tea, two luxuries they had been compelled to go without since the war began.

The 11th December was a red-letter day for the patrol. Instructions were received to hand in the old derelicts of cars that had served us so well over thousands of miles of all sorts of country and under all sorts of conditions.

We accordingly took them (with the mud of three continents and scars from many battles) to the headquarters of 956th Motor Transport Company who handed us out six new Fords in their place. The old buses had done their work nobly and it gave the drivers quite a pang to part with them when it came to the point. The drivers carefully removed the name plates before handing the machines in. Each car had been carefully named by its original crews and they were always known by their names in movements.

There was ANZAC (so named because it was supposed to have been used on the peninsula at Gallipoli) and was the oldest car in the patrol. Then came BILLZAC, which was generally the companion to ANZAC. OTASEL received its name from its tendency to warm the feet of its occupants and SILENT SUE because it was the quietest car in the fleet. IMSHI was so named on account of its speed capabilities. (IMSHI being the Egyptian word for clear out.) No 6 car was generally known as BUNG. This car carried the spare ammunition and some said that this was the reason for its name, but some held that there were other reasons.

Anyhow the old ones were gone and we now had to transfer our love to the new. For a couple of days we spent our time oiling, greasing and testing the mechanical parts, turning up engines, fitting up the machine-gun mountings, also our ration and ammunition containers to the best advantage. We were now able to dispense with the condensers, as owing to the cooler climate and harder ground these were not necessary for the radiators. The first job of the new vehicles was to distribute voting papers for the conscription referendum, which was done on the 13th December.

During the remainder of the month the Patrol was engaged in various small movements along the front. The weather had settled down to continuous rain and was extremely uncomfortable to all those moving outside their billets. Owing to the condition of the ground and the state of the roads neither side was able to make any very big movement. The patrol did quite a bit of escort work to and from Jerusalem along the road from Jaffa. This road, which was originally built a couple of thousand years back by the Romans, required extreme care in driving. The grades were very severe and the hairpin bends were too sharp for a vehicle with a long wheelbase to negotiate. Brakes on the motor cars and lorries were severely tested in coming down the 3000-foot drop from the Jerusalem hills to the plains below. Quite a number of motor vehicles were lost and unfortunately a number of men also through brake failures. At some of the bad corners the wrecks could be seen hundreds of feet below, generally with their four wheels upper-most and the contents scattered beneath. They were there forever and can probably still be seen by tourists where they act as a warning to fast drivers. The Jaffa-Jerusalem road in spite of its dangerous character was very important, and practically the only route from the coast to the hills of Judea. A large volume of motor transport was continually on the road carrying munitions, stores and food for the starving population and it soon became apparent that the road would not stand the heavy traffic.

Large numbers of native labourers were engaged in repairing and rebuilding the bad patches and several steamrollers were brought up. Fortunately, there was no shortage of road metal as the country on either side of the road was practically solid rock and was strewn with boulders and spalls, which only had to be broken and carried a few yards.

The women and girls from surrounding villages did a great deal of this work gathering the stones in baskets, which they carried, on their heads to the required places. These people were practically starving and they welcomed this work as they were fed and paid by the army authorities.

As our cars were continually journeying to and from Jerusalem along this road, we began to give serious consideration to the condition of the brakes. Although most of the British vehicles had ample braking surfaces this could not always be said for some of the cheaper type of cars used in the army and it was no exaggeration to say that sometimes a set of brake shoes would be worn out in one day's work descending these hills. Most of the accidents that took place were caused by some failure in the transmission such as broken tail shaft or universal joint, faulty crown wheels and pinions.

It is unlikely that any of the members of the Light Car Patrol will forget their first trip to Jerusalem. Several of the bridges had been blown up by the retreating Turks and crossings had to be made through streams that were fortunately not too deep to negotiate with our cars. The approaches to the streams however, were extremely rough and steep and many huge boulders had to be levered aside. There was plenty of manhandling in order to get the vehicles up the steep banks of "one in one" and back to the track again. On one bridge the crown of the arch only was blown out and here we were able to place a couple of stout planks across the gap over which we drove in comfort. In spite of all the hard work the trip was well worth it all. The views from the heights around Jerusalem were wonderful.

37. Typical semi-desert terrain encountered by the 1st Light Car Patrol in Palestine. Despite their narrow tyres, the cars performed extremely well in this type of country (ATM ALC.022).

The British Headquarters had been established in a large German building on the Mount of Olives from the tower of which could be seen the blue Mediterranean to the west and twenty five miles away to the east could be clearly seen the Dead Sea which appeared to be only about five miles off. This sea and the Jordan Valley with Jericho, was over twelve hundred feet below the level of the Mediterranean on the other side. The enemy still held all this country below and our batteries in a valley alongside were busy plastering him with shrapnel and High Explosive while an occasional burst of one of the enemy shells in the village alongside seemed somehow to be quite out of place with the surroundings. The weather was clear and the visibility was wonderful. The roads could be clearly distinguished through the glasses, winding up the hills, thirty or forty miles away. We were later to know quite a lot about this country from very close acquaintance when we found out that some of it at least looked much better from a distance.

The heights of Jerusalem were very cold after our long sojourn in the desert. It was now nearing the middle of winter and our drivers felt the hail and sleet very severely as there was no protection on the cars while driving and most of them were quite glad to return to the comparatively warm climate of Jaffa and Richon after their visits to the hills.

Christmas Day was celebrated at the Richon-El-Zion. There was comparative quiet at the front, although two days previously an engagement had taken place at Mulebbis (a village several miles out). The inhabitants turned out in force to celebrate the occasion and the famous wine cellars of the town were drawn upon for the troops who were supplied with a liberal ration of the beautiful Tokay for which the district is famous. We had a church parade in the morning and in the afternoon the inhabitants provided a free banquet. Unfortunately, it rained most of the time, but nevertheless the troops enjoyed the occasion.

38. A game of football somewhere in Palestine (Creek collection ATM LCP.HC.006).

Two days later we moved away through seas of mud and water to the village of Esdud. During the month of January 1918, the unit was kept continually busy reconnoitring the various roads and tracks along the whole front from Jerusalem to the coast, but on the 17th February, we moved with the Australian and New Zealand Division to Jerusalem as a big operation was brewing on that flank. Next day we proceeded with Engineer officers to Solomon's Pools on the Hebron Road to establish watering places for the horses and troops. On the 20th February the division proceeded along the back road to force the way to Jericho. Our orders were to take our cars and escort the motor transport along the Roman Road to Neby Musa, which overlooks Jericho. We proceeded satisfactorily for eight miles and after making a reconnaissance we found that the main road, which is very precipitous and steep, would be impassable for wheeled vehicles for many hours. We then went back to a rough track known as the "Pilgrims" road, which we worked along laboriously for about 4 miles until we came to the hill Gebel Ektief. Here we were compelled to stop as the hill was held in force by the enemy.

We placed the vehicles under cover of a neighbouring slope and climbed a hill opposite in time to view a wonderful charge by our infantry up the slopes of Gebel Ektief.

The hill had entrenchments near the summit and we noticed that the enemy troops in the trenches at the right flank at the approach of our infantry jumped out of the rear of their trenches and ran along the top of the trenches towards the other flank.

Later on we discovered that there was a sheer precipice behind them and they ran towards the other end to get away before it was too late. We were getting a wonderful dress circle view of the fight and in the excitement some of our men must have made themselves too conspicuous as a few minutes later we were plastered with shrapnel by the disgruntled enemy gunners.

Needless to say we soon left our front view seats and as the road was now comparatively clear of the enemy, we proceeded to our job of getting the transport along. We worked our way along for another very rough two miles when we came to a very steep decline of about 400 feet. This looked almost impossible, but we decided to try it out. So stripped every ounce possible off one of the vehicles and lowered it down the track with the men holding it back with ropes. We managed this successfully but decided to go on with the one car to reconnoitre the rest of the track before bringing more vehicles down the same way. We discovered however, that a little further on the track petered out altogether and any further progress was right out of the question, so we had over an hour's hard work hauling the car back again with ropes up the steep slope. By this time it was dark, so we decided to spend the night where we were and after posting sentries, we took turns to sleep under the tarpaulins of the cars. Everybody was moving at the first streaks of dawn and we soon packed up and moved back over the track we had taken back again to the old Roman Jericho Road, and we found that the engineers had been busy during the night to such an extent that the parts of the road which had been blown up were now almost negotiable for light traffic, so by dint of a little more of our customary pushing and manhandling, we got our "Lizzies" over the worst places. The previous evening one of the "Rolls" Armoured Cars of the Light Armoured Car Battery in endeavouring to get across the Pilgrim Road got out of control owing to the severe and rough nature of the ground and got rather badly smashed over one of the cliffs. However, we heard that it was hauled up again and repaired next day. We soon reached the rocky hill by Talat-El-Dum where an old stone building (supposed to be the Good Samaritan's Inn mentioned in the scriptures) gave us cover while we boiled the billy for breakfast. This building belied its name as throughout the night the machine-guns inside had kept up a continuous din, while the enemy gunners had made it their chief target for their artillery. We now had a large column of motor transport vehicles under our control and care and as we were very anxious to get these to the head of the column, we only spent a few minutes over breakfast. We pushed on with about a dozen motor vehicles following us and reached Headquarters at Neby Musa by midday. The Division now pushed on and took up positions at Jericho at 2 p.m. where Headquarters was established.

Apparently the enemy was aware of this fact as at 3.30 p.m. they began to drop shells there from a long range across the Jordan River.

The first shell that dropped caused considerable amusement. It could be heard whining for quite a time before it dropped. One of the natives of the village heard it coming and dropped flat on the ground. Strange to say the shell dropped in the mud almost beside him and smothered him with earth but did no further damage. The native then jumped up and ran until out of sight to the screams of laughter of the troops. One of the next shells went clean through the radiator of the Divisional Commander's car and as this was one of the vehicles under our charge, we had to get busy. Things were getting too warm at this spot, so we moved camp to a new position about 400 yards away. We towed the General's car away and dismantled the broken parts. After dark we sent a car back along the road towards Jerusalem for about 10 miles where some advanced motor transport stores were kept and he managed to obtain a new radiator, which he brought to us before midnight. Before daybreak the car was repaired and ready to move off with the rest of the fleet at reveille.

39. The tough conditions of the Palestine Campaign forced the 1st Light Car Patrol to become self-sufficient. Members of the unit undertake major repairs and servicing of their vehicles in makeshift circumstances (ATMLCP.002).

In the morning one half of the unit was ordered to patrol the road from Jericho to Jordan and the other half to reconnoitre a road marked on the map from Umm-Elha-Dumm to Neby Musa and the Jericho Road. We found this road to be merely a packhorse track, unfit for wheeled vehicles. We reconnoitred on foot for a few miles and made our report and received orders to proceed to Jerusalem where we arrived at 6 p.m. setting up camp in the cold and wet: very different to the warm valley at Jericho only twenty five miles away.

This was the middle of February, which was probably the coldest time of the year. For the next few weeks the patrol had very little excitement beyond a few reconnaissances around Jerusalem, Nailin and other parts of the front now extending from the River Jordan to the coast north of Jaffa. However, on the 13th March, we received orders to make the Jordan Valley our headquarters and this was apparently the flank where any future movements were to take place. Ten days afterwards we crossed the Jordan River by a pontoon bridge and received orders to reconnoitre the roads from the river to the base of the hills on the east now occupied by the Turkish Army. We found that most of the roads petered out into mule tracks once the hills were reached and only one road (that leading from Ghoranyeh where we had established a bridgehead) was suitable for wheeled transport. Next night, the Australian and New Zealand Mounted Division pushed on up the mule tracks and left their transport behind them. The men led their horses all night long up the steep hills in the rain and in the morning the division was on top of the hills pushing on towards Amman with the surprised enemy running before them.

40. A forward outpost manned by the 1st Light Car Patrol on the Jordan River. The patrol would increasingly assume traditional cavalry roles of flank protection and lines of communication duties during the Palestine Campaign (Cornwell collection ATM.LCP.PC.014).

The Light Car Patrol received orders to proceed up the Ghoranyeh road with the infantry via Es Salt, which we did. We however, found considerable difficulty in getting through the heavy columns of the transport accompanying the infantry who had about six hours' start of us and they had also added to the difficulties by churning the mud up along the road to the consistency of butter. By dusk we were within three miles of the town of Es Salt which had not yet been captured and as it was too dark to see where we were going there was nothing to do but camp for the night which we did alongside the road. Beyond an occasional shot from a few snipers in the hills, we had a fairly peaceful night. At daybreak next morning we were packed up and on the move again, shortly afterwards we drove into the town of Es Salt. The villagers welcomed us by firing fusillades from their rifles into the air. The villagers were very friendly to us and during the night they had prevented the Turks taking a battery of artillery away with them, the result that it fell into our hands next morning. We could not afford to waste much time in the town, as our instructions were to push on along the road taken by the retreating enemy in a north-easterly direction and soon left the infantry behind. We were now acting on our own in the open land between the two divisions without the slightest knowledge of where our own division was.

The so-called road was a veritable quagmire as during the night the whole of the Turkish and German transport had ploughed it until the mud was knee deep and the continuous rain during the night had not improved it. About 2 p.m. we captured a Turkish prisoner who had been wounded and as he could speak Arabic we learnt from him that his army was about two hours ahead in full retreat. We directed him to the rear and proceeded on our way. Two miles further on we overtook two German motor lorries hopelessly bogged. The first thing we did was to siphon the petrol tanks into our own as the heavy going was using our supplies of "juice" up too rapidly for our liking. We also put the engines out of action and pushed on. After another hour's hard pushing and driving we came in sight of a large body of transport surrounded by men. On examining them through field glasses we saw that the transport consisted of 23 German army motor lorries and a number of cars. These had been abandoned and the men around them were hoards of Bedouins busy looting. A couple of rounds from the Lewis guns soon cleared this mob away and we shortly came up to inspect our new find. We discovered however, that the lorries and cars were all axle deep in mud and that it was almost impossible for us to proceed ourselves. We got a little more petrol and oil and after rendering the enemy vehicles hors-de-combat, we decided as it was rapidly getting dark we had better make ourselves secure for the night. We moved back along the road to a small hill about half a mile back which was comparatively dry and which commanded a fair view of the surrounding country and here we parked our cars in a square with a Lewis gun at each corner and after posting sentries we endeavoured to take turns at sleeping. This however, was not an easy matter as every now and then loud bursts of rifle fire kept occurring from various quarters. This turned out afterwards to be fights between various Circassian and Bedouin villages who were having a little war on their own and apparently were quite disinterested in our doings. We unfortunately did not know which of these were friendly or otherwise so had to keep all villagers at a distance. We sent a small patrol on foot under Sergeant Langley towards the east in order to get in touch with headquarters of the Mounted Division as we estimated that owing to the distance we had come we could not be more than a few miles away from them. Our estimate was not very far out as our patrol ran across their outposts about three miles away.

The patrol informed headquarters of our position and brought back the information that the mounted men were having a very rough time. Numbers of the wounded were dying from exposure, as no ambulances were able to traverse the country. When our patrol returned in the morning they brought back instructions for us to stay in the present position for the day and before dark to return to Es Salt. Fortunately, the day was dry and we spent the time drying our blankets and salvaging the magnetos and other useful parts from the German vehicles (these we handed in later on to the officer in charge of the motor workshops). During the day we got in touch with some men from the Anzac Division Signals who required petrol for the motor on their wireless outfit and we were able to spare them some of our loot for this purpose. Before dark according to instructions we retired to Es Salt, which we reached in time to make a comfortable camp for the night. However, before leaving our position of the night before, the advance party of the infantry division had reached us and was well on its way to junction with the mounted division.

We stayed next day at Es Salt and sent messages through to Divisional Headquarters asking for orders. Next day was Good Friday which we spent (also the three following days) in driving along the Es Salt to Amman Road and bringing in loads of wounded who were compelled to walk, as it was not possible for the ambulances to reach them. We were able, however, to give a pretty rough ride to quite a number of these poor chaps who were nearly dead with wounds, cold and exposure. Later on some of the light ambulances managed to get up into the hills and we received instructions to protect them from interference, which we did by continually patrolling the road.

The troops were having a pretty rough spin altogether. The weather was bitterly cold and wet and most of them were soaked to the skin, day and night. Some of the natives were also giving some trouble and there were rumours of retirement. All day and night the population of Es Salt and the surrounding district were slowly evacuating their homes and with their valuables packed began to march down the long road through the hills to the Jordan Valley over twenty miles below. Word had evidently reached the villagers that we intended to retire to the valley again shortly and they were fearful of the vengeance that the Turks, on their return, would turn upon them for helping the British during the advance. The road was becoming filled with refugees and it was pitiful to see tiny children and old people quite unfit for such a journey endeavouring to do the long walk with their bundles. On the 1st of April we received orders to evacuate Es Salt and return to Shunet Nimrin and the foot of the hills.

The trouble apparently was not that we could not hold our own in the hills but the difficulties of transport for supplies and ammunition were too great to keep up for an extended period. We now saw the worst side of war as we had to force our way through the panic stricken population and we could imagine what a retreat meant. Numbers of footsore and crying villagers asked for seats in our patrol cars and many of the men were quite willing to walk and let these poor people have their seats but this could not be allowed as military considerations had to come first and we had to be hard hearted and keep to our schedules. We left Shunet Nimrin at 6.30 am next day and proceeded to cross the Jordan at the Ghoranyeh Bridge about an hour later while the enemy aeroplanes were making things very lively by bombing the road and bridge-head. However, we managed to run the gauntlet without suffering in any respect and joined our old comrades the Anzac Mounted Division at Jericho about 11 o'clock and learnt of the rough times they had experienced in their retirement and how the Circassians and Bedouins who had feted them on their advance had sniped them from every rock on their return journey. So this was the end of the first Amman Stunt.

Next morning the enemy reminded us that the war was still on by bombing our camp at daybreak from their planes. However, our chaps were so tired or else were getting used to bombs to such an extent that the majority of them would not stir from their blankets.

The enemy was beginning to get a bit cheeky and they evidently thought that as we had retired from the hills we were beaten and on the 11th April they came down from the hills and after a lot of shelling they began to attack our bridgeheads on the Jordan. The Light Car Patrol received orders to take the Lewis guns out of the cars and to reinforce the 1st Light Horse Brigade who were holding the foothills across the river. We placed our guns in the trenches under orders from the Brigade and very soon had plenty of machine-gun practice opening up at 1200 yards, which was reduced later down to 500 yards range.

41. Detail of the Lewis light machine-gun and mounting on one of the Light Car Patrol's Model T Fords. Part of the 'Australia' insignia can also be seen (ATM ALC019).

Next morning a large number of dead Turks were buried in front of our position so apparently the couple of thousand rounds of ammunition used by us was not all wasted. Our chaps relished the change of sitting down behind cover to do the shooting as generally the position was reversed and they were the targets. During the night the enemy retired to the hills again, sadder but wiser and it was quite a time before he picked up courage to make another attack.

After their attack on the 11th of April, the enemy became very quiet and un-enterprising. So a demonstration was made into his territory on the 18th and 19th to keep him busy and on the 24th the Armoured Cars and Light Car Patrols made a dash across the river and proceeded north for about 7 or 8 miles into enemy territory to have a look at his territory and dispositions. We toured around for a couple of hours and beyond provoking some of the batteries of artillery, which shelled us, we were not interfered with. The shelling did not affect us as the enemy discovered that quick moving motor cars make a very difficult target especially when they do not adhere to a fixed road. We returned back again to camp shortly after midday by our old pontoon bridge. Next day we crossed the river again and this time we proceeded in a southerly direction through scrub and new country along the east coast of the Dead Sea. Our duty this time was to cover a working party who were endeavouring to salvage a damaged enemy motor boat, which had been beached along the coast some miles south-east of the mouth of the Jordan. We encountered about half a squadron of enemy cavalry about four miles along the coast. These men scattered to the hills on seeing our cars and as our job was to cover the working party we did not give chase and left them alone after firing a few shots to hurry them along. The working party managed to get the boat afloat and they towed it with a motor boat to Rujm-el-Bahr, a rendezvous on the north of the Dead Sea. We arrived back at Headquarters about 4 o'clock in the afternoon with several broken springs owing to the extremely rough ground covered along the coast. We found on examination that there was scarcely a sound spring on any car in the patrol so in the evening we sent off a car post-haste to Richon and Ludd via Jerusalem, a trip of about 60 miles each way to fetch back a fresh supply of spring plates. We received these next evening and after a busy night we had all springs repaired and replaced, the cars ready for anything but the men rather weary.

42. Light cars in various states of repair at a desert encampment in Palestine with three drivers working on mechanical problems (ATM. LCP. 001).

On Tuesday 30th April and Wednesday 1st May, another big attack was made on Shunet Nimrin by the infantry and further north by the Light Horse Regiments. This attack was not altogether a success from all points of view and at times things were very mixed. We were ordered to stand by with cars ready for a dash at any moment to places that might need assistance. About noon on the Wednesday, word was received that the 4th Light Horse Regiment had been cut off by the enemy, and that General Chaytor the Divisional Commander was motoring with his escort directly into the enemy's lines. One of our cars was sent off to chase him at full speed and warn the party of its danger but fortunately we discovered that they had already been warned of the enemy's new position. Our base of operations for this two days' fighting was a place known as Um-esh-skirt and we slept in the scrub for the night. Next morning an enemy bombing squadron dropped a large number of bombs amongst our forces but did very little damage considering the large numbers of troops moving about.

We had a little more machine-gun practise at the aeroplane but with no apparent result. At 6 o'clock that evening we were all back again at Jericho as the attack was over and everything was quiet once more except for occasional shots from outposts.

Throughout the month of May the Patrol was stationed alternately around Jericho and at different points along the river front. The heat by day was very severe and almost unbearable and the dust was choking. The flies were a black mass over everything and at night the sand flies and mosquitoes took over their duties to make our lives as miserable as possible. The flies were so thick that it was absolutely impossible to get food to one's mouth without some flies going with it. In fact, many of us cut our meals down to two a day (one in the early morning before the flies were up and the other in the evening after they went to bed). One genius discovered a method of beating the flies for the midday meal. He built a small frame with sticks large enough to sit in. This he surrounded it with a mosquito net into which he took his tin of jam, biscuits and mug of tea. He then proceeded to kill off the flies inside the curtain and then calmly ate his meal to the maddened buzz of the insects outside the curtain who could not reach him. After he had finished his meal others would take their turn. The men on outpost work near the river at night time had a miserable time as the swarms of sand flies and mosquitoes would leave their faces and hands like raw beef. After three months of this misery in the Jordan Valley we were given a fortnight's leave to overhaul our cars and recuperate up in the hills at Bethlehem. The cooler climate was a great relief after the uncomfortable valley but we were all very sorry when the two weeks was up and we had to return to the heat, filth and flies again.

43. Brew up: crews enjoy a meal somewhere in Palestine in 1917 (Creek collection ATMLCP.HC.081).

This time our camp was made at the base of Mount Kurun-tel, which was nearly ten miles from the enemy's front line. A few days afterwards we were very surprised to find high velocity shells exploding around us, as under ordinary circumstances this would have been out of range. We heard afterwards that the Turks had taken some of the long range naval guns from the old "Goebern" and had manoeuvred them overland to the hills opposite where they were enjoying themselves at our expense. However, the range was too long for them to see what they were doing and most of their shooting was harmless.

THE DEAD SEA

Towards the end of June the Light Car Patrol received instructions to patrol the River Jordan from Hajla and Henu to the mouth, where the River enters the Dead Sea. The orders were to patrol twice daily (at dawn and in the evening before dark) and to report the result to Divisional Headquarters. On either bank of the river there were clay foothills over which we soon made motor tracks. These hills commanded a good view of the surrounding country for about 10 miles and by the aid of field glasses any movement could quickly be seen. The river was nominally the dividing line between the two forces but actually the British held both banks for most of the distance. This patrolling of the river banks meant that the unit spent considerable amount of time travelling backwards and forwards from the camp north of Jericho to the Dead Sea, which was the starting point of the line to be patrolled and in order to reduce this dead mileage we applied to have our camp moved down towards our starting point. This request was granted by Headquarters and accordingly on 12th July we were transferred to Rujm-el-Bahr on the coast and generally known as the Dead Sea Post. This new move was a very welcome one to all members of the unit. It meant that we got away from the choking and blinding dust encountered wherever bodies of horsemen were moving (and this was practically all the time near Light Horse camp) but what was far more welcome was the fact that we were near the water and bathing could be indulged in. We built our bivvies right alongside the water and in the morning rolled out of the blankets into the sea for our swim. The Dead Sea would be a good place for non-swimmers, as it would be practically impossible to drown. The buoyancy of the water is such that a person may stand in deep water and hold his arms up out of the water and the water will not rise over his neck. A swimmer used to fresher water however, will notice that it is very difficult to get speed up. This is probably because of the density of the water and of the difficulty of keeping the feet down as they have a tendency to rise to the surface all the time. One of the chief amusements of the place was to encourage visitors to dive into the water head first. The water was intensely bitter and if any of it went up the nose or got into the mouth the victims would probably cough and splutter for half an hour or until he managed to wash out his throat with fresh water again. If the water got into the eyes it would sting very severely for quite a while. A peculiar effect of a dive into the water was the speed with which the diver shot up out of the water again and sometimes if a person dived straight down he shot out feet first again.

44. At the Dead Sea post the mechanical skills of the members of the Light Car Patrol were put to good use running captured Turkish patrol boats (Creek collection ATM LCP.PC.006 HR).

The Dead Sea Post was an ideal spot from many points of view for our camp. There was a workshop there and a forge, which were extremely useful to us. One of the first things we did after being stationed there, was to remove the wheels from our cars and leave them overnight or as long as possible soaking in the Sea. Our wheels were only wooden ones (as the pressed steel wheels were not available at that time) and we had experienced considerable difficulty in keeping wheels tight owing to the extreme heat and in some cases we had narrow escapes from wheels practically collapsing altogether. The result of the soaking was to swell the wood making the spokes and felloes tight. This was not merely a temporary remedy because the brine soaked right into the wood and although the wood appeared perfectly dry in the day time, in the night air the salt would always get damp again causing the joints to swell.

There was stationed quite a fleet of motor boats at our post. These included a couple of fast six cylinder "Wolseley" speed launches each fitted with a Vickers gun. There were also some ships' boats with outbound motors and later on two large Thornycroft twin screw gun boats each fitted with a three pounder were transported overland by tractors and launched near our camp. These boats greatly appealed to the men of our units who were nearly all good mechanics and expert machine-gunners and on many expeditions across the water the Dead Sea fleet was manned by the members of the Light Car Patrol who became known as the "Amphibians". Quite a lot of work was done by these boats after dark as we would then run our "agents" across the sea, land them in enemy territory and pick them up at prearranged spots after they had completed their mission. On certain nights the boats would cruise along the enemy coast keeping watch for lights as if one of our men wished to be picked up he would light a fire under a cliff or overhanging ground so that the light would not show inland. The boat would then move quickly in towards the light and pick him up. Great caution of course had to be exercised as there was always the risk of treachery but this was never experienced. One of the agents, an old native, who appeared to be well trusted by Headquarters, had made many trips backwards and forwards and seemed to bring back a lot of information. This old chap was generally very regular in keeping his appointments with the boat, but one night he did not turn up and after the third night of cruising he was given up for lost by the crew. But about a week later the lookout reported a light some miles south of the usual position. A boat was sent down and after carefully cruising towards the light they discovered the old chap nearly dead, laying on the beach alongside a fire, which he had lighted. He was carried on board and given some food and water after which he seemed to revive. He had been badly wounded in the foot and he was taken across as soon as possible to be attended to. There was a large hole in his foot where a bullet had gone through it and it was expected that the leg would probably have to be amputated. It appeared that the old fellow had been seen by some of the Turkish sentries as he was passing through their lines and they had fired at him, one shot getting him in the foot. In spite of his wound however, he managed to get away to hide in the scrub during the day and crawled down to the beach at night time, where he slept and rested for about twenty-four hours. He put his foot into the water and left it there. The next evening he managed to crawl to a spot where he could light a fire and there he was found by the boat's crew. The doctor told us afterwards that they managed to save the foot after all. They were afraid that the gangrene had set in but it appeared that the wound was filled with almost solid salt from the Dead Sea, the healing properties of which had saved the foot.

The Dead Sea Post was quite an interesting place from many points of view and we had numbers of episodes of various types to keep us from becoming dreary.

One morning the enemy dragged an old camel gun down the hills opposite to us and began to bombard the post at extreme range for an hour or two until pursuit was arranged and he was chased back over the hills again. The shelling did not do any harm as all the missiles exploded either in the water or in the mud behind. Another morning several of us who were standing in the water's edge were surprised to see a large column of water shoot up into the air about half a mile out to sea. Some of the members of the unit (who had at one time been members of the Submarine Miners Corps) immediately came to the conclusion that a mine had gone off under the water and were marvelling where it could have come from, when a few minutes afterwards another explosion was heard from behind and a column of mud from the land side shot up into the air about a quarter of a mile behind us. We then discovered that an enemy aeroplane was dropping bombs from a great height. He was flying so high that he could not be heard and barely seen even with the glasses. As his nearest shot was over a quarter of a mile from its target, he did not cause much anxiety to anybody.

Amongst the stuff left behind at the Dead Sea Post when captured, were all the parts of a large steam tug, which had been taken to pieces at Haifa and transported overland in sections by the Germans and Turks. It must have taken a large amount of labour and time to do this as every piece had to be brought by road over the steep hills for something like 100 miles. All the parts were there except the engines and these could not be found. These had either not been brought or had been sunk in the water. Divers were sent down to search but no trace could be discovered. The British authorities decided to assemble the boat as all the parts were so conveniently left for them, and internal combustion engines from some of the Tractors were to be installed. Some shipwrights were brought down and the frames and plates of the boat were all riveted up. When we left the Jordan Valley some months afterwards the hull seemed to be all ready for launching but we never heard whether this had ever been done.

On the 14th July (a few days after our move to the Dead Sea Post) our two cars on morning patrol work at about 5 a.m. noticed movements of enemy troops some miles east of the Jordan. This information was immediately sent back to Headquarters and in the meantime parties of the enemy could be heard being engaged by our outposts. Apparently there was to be another attack on the riverfront. Sergeant J. Langley (a Bendigo boy) was in charge of the morning patrol that day and after sending back full particulars of enemy movements, he reported to the officer in charge of the lower bridgehead asking permission to cross and engage the enemy in front. This was granted to him and he immediately took his two cars across the bridge proceeding to some hills about a mile to the east where he dismounted his Lewis guns and carried them to a spot commanding the approaches in his direction. He left his two cars below headed for the bridge ready to move off in a hurry if necessary.

Meanwhile he entrenched and waited. Shortly afterwards a column of packhorses came along and a Machine Gun Section. These were allowed to get well into range when both Lewis guns opened on to them with deadly effect. The horses were stampeded and some of them killed.

Meantime one of the enemy machine-guns managed to get into action and a duel began in which the Turkish machine-gunners came off worst. Some time afterwards the rest of the patrol came up to relieve the morning men but when they arrived the ground in front was strewn with enemy debris. The remaining men of the Turkish section in front of us fled, abandoning their machine-guns and equipment which were captured. In that engagement we fired 5000 rounds out of our Lewis guns and two of the barrels were so damaged in the rifling owing to the continuous fire that they had to be renewed. Beyond this the only damage suffered by the patrol was some slight injury to the casing on one of the Lewis guns by an enemy bullet. The Turks retired from this attack along the line leaving large numbers of dead and prisoners.

Sergeant J. Langley was awarded the DCM for his conduct during this attack and that was the end of the second big attack on the Jordan Valley. The enemy now seemed to lose all interest in us for a couple of weeks and we arranged a big cricket match between the Australian Light Cars and the garrison of the post who consisted of English units. This was looked on as a test match and created a lot of interest for miles around. The weather of course was intensely hot as usual, but the fielders were able to have a swim in between each batman's hand. I'm pleased to say that Australia won this test by 110 to 36 runs.

45. Boys playing cricket in the Jordan Valley. Sport played a significant part in the pre-war lives of many members of the Light Car Patrol (Cornwell collection ATM.LCP.PC.005).

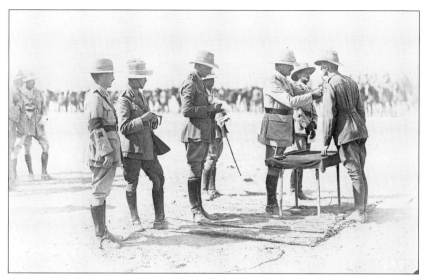

46. General Allenby decorating Sergeant Langley of No. 1 Light Car Patrol with the Distinguished
Conduct Medal (AWM B00249).

Bendigonians Gain Distinction
Distinguished Conduct Medal

The news reached Bendigo yesterday that Sergeant Jack Langley grandson of the Most Rev. Dr. Langley, Bishop of Bendigo and Sergeant Norman Bisset son of Mr. G.S. Bisset of Golden Square, had been awarded the Distinguished Conduct Medal.[2]

These soldiers are in Palestine, and are attached to the Australian Light Armored Car Patrol. Sergeant Bisset is an Anzac, and returned to Bendigo about two year ago, and after a brief stay again left for the front. He took part in the Senussi Campaign in Egypt. Sergeant Langley prior to enlisting was residing with Bishop Langley. He left for abroad in June 1916 and is 23 years of age."

In connection with the announcement of the awards the following extract from a Letter from Gunner Leo Cohn by his parents will be interestedly read:"The Jackos (Turks) made a big attack last week, and got all they wanted. Six of our little unit, including Jack Langley and Norman Bisset and myself, were on our usual early morning patrol with two cars when we first got word of their advance right up to our lines during the night. We had to leave the cars about half a mile back and go on as infantry machine gun section. Our position overlooked that of the enemy's flank, we had a perfect enfilade fire. They left their horses in gullies, and, although 1400 yards away, the observation was so good that we got right on them and stampeded the lot. About 7 o'clock they got four machine guns to try to quieten us, but we got right into them and repulsed them. Later a regiment of Indians came along on our right and put the enemy to flight.

"It was just like shooting rabbits"
Trooper Leo Cohn

The original text of Cohn's letter provides a clearer understanding of the courage of the small patrol:

"*The Jackos made a very lively attack on the 14th. Two of our cars got into it and we had a splendid day's shooting. Jack Langley was in charge and Norman Bissett of our car. Norman is the gunner and I am the driver but as our boss is always cooling off we have to get another hand, as we had to this day. We had to leave the cars and carried on as a dismounted machine gun section. We got right up and got on to one of the Jackos' flanks, which by the way were practically all Huns. We got on to one big crowd of horses and scattered them, leaving dead and kicking horses all the way up the gully. About two in the afternoon a Regiment of Indians had worked well up on the right and made a beautiful charge with the lances. The Huns had to run right again across our front to try and find their horses. It was just like shooting rabbits.*

A few evenings later a big concert was held up in Jerusalem by Lena Ashwell's party and permission was granted for a carload to go to Jerusalem for the night. Needless to say the car was well filled. On the morning of the 25th July during our morning patrol, we discovered a homemade boat and some oars hidden in the reeds skirting a lagoon close to the mouth of the river. We had not noticed this boat previously so concluded it must have been brought across the river during the night probably by an enemy agent. We were anxious to see how the boat was brought into the lagoon, so a couple of us embarked and pushed off when the boat promptly sank with us both, and we just had time to throw our watches and revolvers ashore as we disappeared below the surface to the amusement of the rest of the patrol. The boat had only sufficient buoyancy for one person, so evidently only one had to come across in it. We discovered that there was a narrow but deep entrance through the reeds into the sea through which the boat had been brought. We replaced the boat where we had found it after making it leaky enough to prevent it crossing the river again and reported particulars to the nearest intelligence officer who arranged for a watch to be kept beside the boat for the return of the navigator, but he must have received news of the boat's discovery for he never turned up again. When we returned from the morning patrol, the water had dried on our clothes after the immersion and the white salt had dried and left us white like a couple of ghosts to the great enjoyment of the troops in the vicinity who thought it was some new game for their amusement.

Things seemed to be settling down about this time and no events of importance took place much in the valley. The enemy made a small demonstration on the 6th September and the whole patrol received orders to cross the river at Hajla Bridge, which we did first thing in the morning. We travelled at full speed to the north-east where we joined the Central India Horse with whom we crossed the Wady Rame. The enemy however changed their minds and retreated at full speed to the hills again. We received orders to return and were back at our post again in plenty of time for lunch. Nothing more of importance happened until 13th September when orders were received to leave the valley. We packed up after having been there for six months to a day. They were the six hottest months of the year and we were not sorry to leave. We were not to see the Jordan Valley any more. Events were shortly going to happen on the other flank of the Mediterranean Coast and we were to be there for the kick off. Orders were received for the cars to proceed singly at half hour intervals so as not to excite any particular interest and we were to take two days over the move. We arrived at Ramleh on the evening of the 15th September and proceeded to Sarona a couple of days later. All movements were now done at nighttime, so as not to arouse the enemy's suspicions of the concentration on this flank. We now joined the 4th Cavalry Division and on the 18th September the officers were called to a conference where the Commander in Chief (General Allenby) explained that the big smash through the enemy's lines was to be attempted at dawn the next morning. He explained that speed was to be the essence of the whole operation. The artillery and infantry were to make a break on the enemy's western flank when the mounted troops and motor units were to pour through at full speed and take the enemy in the rear." [3]

(The *Bendigonian*, 12 September 1918, p. 9)

THE BATTLE OF MEGIDDO

It was the morning of the 19th September 1918. Our orders were to stand to at 3.30 a.m. and have everything ready to move off at a moment's notice. We were attached to the 4th Cavalry Division for these operations and we were to protect the convoy of the whole of the divisional motor cars and transport. Our starting point was to be one mile east of El Jeliel. The bombardment on the enemy's front line began at 4.30 a.m. and it was the best thing in the way of bombardment that any of us had ever seen. Every gun, howitzer and mortar in existence seemed to be going off at once and all the batteries from the 13 pounders up to the big sixty's seemed to be working overtime. For about an hour or so the air appeared to be filled with fire and shrieking shells, after that there was a lull and in a little while the sound of cheering could be heard in the distance as the infantry did their part of the job and cleared a gap through the trenches. At 8 o'clock the road was clear and we got the word to go. Every horse in the division went forward at the trot with the motors alongside them. The barbed wire entanglements were trampled down by hundreds of hoofs and wheels, the trenches filled in and crossed; and away went the whole division complete into the north via Tabsor never slowing down once until after midday when a brief stop for half an hour for lunch and a spell for the horses was made. Then on again till 6 p.m. when Kakon was reached where another brief stop for tea was made. The division then pushed on with all speed throughout the night as it was very important to get through the Mus Mus pass before the enemy had time to collect reinforcements and hold us up there. This we were able to do and the dawn breaking found us through the hills with the plains of Esdraelon at our feet. At 7 a.m., 20th September we entered Leggun where the division rested for a couple of hours. The night travelling had been more trying for the motor drivers than for the horsemen. The only light we had was what we got from the moon and it was impossible to see the ground owing to the clouds of dust from the horses' hoofs. The motor drivers had to just drive blindly on and trust to luck, which generally was with us. Both our motor cyclists came to grief early the first evening and smashed their machines on rough ground and they had to drop out of the chase. Shortly afterwards one of our gun cars crashed on to a huge boulder in the dark, which went through the sump of the engine making a complete stop. We hastily transferred the guns and ammunition off this car on to one of our transport vehicles and left our corporal mechanic with the driver and his assistant to make the best repair possible while we pushed on with the division. The cyclist and this car overtook us a day or two later, so they must have made good use of their time in repairing their machines which were all working again.

47. Broken down on the desert 10 miles from home two of the chaps had to walk back for another car. This is a typical photo here you see a car that has been over rocks and has not seen a road for 12 months. We strip all the body off and tie our blankets, duffle and machine gun whilst on patrol. Lt Cornwell and I have just had lunch [and] he snapped me. (Morgan collection ATM LCP. GM.001).

After a couple of hours at Leggun we pushed on towards El Afule, an important railway town and junction, also signal station and German aerodrome. Here we met our first serious opposition. The enemy had hastily rushed some troops forward with machine-guns but they had not received enough notice of our coming to entrench properly. The division halted momentarily while the 11th Light Armoured Motor Battery was rushed forward. This battery was equipped with Rolls Royce armour-plated cars and light Vickers machine-guns. The battery drove down the main road and simply mowed down all machine-gun sections sent up to oppose the advance. A detachment of Indian Lancers then went forward at the gallop to mop up what was left. That ended the opposition and the enemy machine-guns were all abandoned in the fields. Shortly afterwards we drove into Afule where everything was in a state of chaos. Much material was captured including a number of German motor lorries, which we put out of action by dismantling the magnetos etc. We promptly pushed forward to the aerodrome, as petrol was a very important item for us. Our tanks were getting low and we did not wish to wait for the supply train, which was following. Fortunately we managed to get enough to fill all the tanks of the Patrol and Armoured Cars. While we were engaged on this a German aeroplane unsuspectingly landed in the aerodrome and the pilot was promptly made a prisoner to his surprise and anger. Shortly afterwards another plane was seen to be landing but just as he reached the ground something aroused his suspicions and he rose again. One of our Armoured Cars promptly opened fire on him then and the pilot was killed. The observer was wounded in the head and taken prisoner. He told us afterwards that it was the felt hats of the Australians in the aerodrome that made them suspicious that something was wrong.

As soon as we got enough petrol, oil and water for our cars, we had a hurried lunch at the German Officers Mess where the late occupants had very obligingly set the table for us before they left for other parts. After lunch a couple of us wandered down the road for a few hundred yards to stretch our legs when we noticed a number of motor lorries coming along and we remarked that our supply column must have made wonderfully good time in following up so soon. Just then the vehicles drew up alongside us when we found that they were filled with armed Germans who immediately jumped out of their vehicles and held up their hands as a token of surrender. We did not know what to do with such a large number of prisoners so we jumped up into the leading vehicle and directed the driver to drive into the town where we had plenty of men to disarm them. We signalled the remaining vehicles to follow which they did. On arriving in the town we handed over the convoy to the Area Provost Marshal who was responsible for collecting the prisoners of war. I don't suppose any haul of prisoners was so easily made before. The prisoners seemed to be quite content with their lot and were apparently not looking for any fight.

The divisions next pushed on to Beisan about 16 miles east of El Afule where we were promised some sleep. This was sorely needed by the drivers who had been at the wheel for 40 hours without any rest whatever. We discovered that the horseman has a decided advantage over a motor driver in the matter of sleep. The former can nod off and still keep in the saddle as the old horse jogs along and follows the track, but if the motor driver closes his eyes for an instant, he will probably crash into a rock or over a cliff. On the way to Beisan we noticed a motor car about half a mile off the road in difficulties. On examining this through the glasses we noticed some men making frantic efforts to get a touring car (that was bogged) out of the mud. We sent a car across and the occupants promptly bolted into the scrub. The car had the German coat of arms painted on the door and it was apparently one of their staff cars. So we hitched a rope on to it and hauled it out with one of our own cars. We found that car very useful and kept it for nearly six months. We used it for carrying extra petrol and baggage about with us on our peregrinations. The late occupants who took to the hills would probably have had their throats cut by the Arabs who are always ready to murder and rob the underdog. On arriving at Beisan, we discovered that there was not to be too much sleep after all. The road from Beisan to Shutta had to be patrolled through the night with cars to take prisoners who were expected to be coming back from the fight that was still going on at part of the enemy's front lines. Our division now had a line about 40 miles long and it was about 30 miles behind the enemy's front lines. The Turks were now in a thorough trap and could not escape any way. Although the road had to be patrolled, we found that a couple of cars could manage it all right and the drivers took one-hour shifts so the majority managed to get a reasonable amount of sleep after all. We bivouacked for the night at Beisan but next morning all the cars were required to patrol the roads and collect numerous enemy fugitives who were more or less demoralised and pouring in from all quarters.

48. A light car in fighting order. Trooper Leo Cohn described the cars as nothing more than 'a flying bedstead' (Creek collection ATM LCP.HC.052).

The divisional commander asked us to send a car up to Jesi Majame, a railway crossing where there is a bridge across the river a few miles south of Lake Tiberias or the Sea of Galilee. A party of engineers was there to mine the railway bridge and one of the officers had his hand injured with explosives. A car was required to bring him back to Beisan, the nearest field ambulance.

It was explained that an armed car was not necessary, as the road had been cleared. All our patrol cars were busy on the road in the other direction gathering up prisoners, but we dug up a ration car and one of the drivers who had been having a well-earned sleep. A couple of us pushed off as quickly as possible. We found that the road was littered with abandoned transport and broken down vehicles of all descriptions and we frequently were compelled to drive off the road altogether in order to get past these obstructions. We had proceeded several miles on our journey when a loud report seemed to come from under the car. Thinking that one of the tyres had blown out we were slowing down when another report occurred from behind us. We discovered that the tyres were all right but the reports were gunshots and as we were the target we decided the best thing was to get a move on. There were growing crops alongside the road and in there were concealed the marksmen. It was impossible to see them so it was no use trying to shoot back at them. Fortunately, they were atrocious shots and they did no damage beyond making us break the speed record. We ran the gauntlet for about five miles like this (it seemed like ten) when we came to a spot on the road that was completely blocked by a train of German motor lorries that had been abandoned. Hundreds of natives from an adjoining village were busy looting these vehicles and at first there were too busy to take any notice of us. We got busy clearing a track for our car and had nearly got it through when the natives who were all armed with rifles and knives began to congregate around us. Several of them began to snatch things out of our car such as our haversacks, field glasses etc. By this time we were practically clear and we covered them with our revolvers. The natives began to get their rifles ready and to flourish their knives and the prospects looked ugly. Meantime, the driver got his engine going and we grabbed a native boy who was hanging around the car, pulled him in and held him between us and the tribesmen while we did the next mile in record time and not a shot was fired at us. When we were out of range we kicked the boy out. After another two or three miles, we arrived at our destination and we were not sorry to see a detachment of Indian Lancers.

We explained to the officer in charge that we had a fairly eventful drive up and that we did not relish the idea of the trip back again, it was bad enough with two of us coming up with our hands free but to go back encumbered with a wounded man who would be in pain and not able to stand the jolting and bumping of the car was driven at speed was certainly looking for trouble.

We got away as quickly as possible with our charge and the mounted escort who must have been seen coming for when we arrived back at the scene of trouble there was not a man to be seen anywhere and the village was absolutely deserted. We said goodbye to our Indian friends then and did the twelve miles back to Beisan without a shot being fired at us. We arrived just as it was getting dark and handed our charge over to the doctor. We then explained to Headquarters how 'clear' the road was on our outward journey. The divisional commander sent messages next morning to all villages along the road that if any more sniping occurred along the route that he would burn all the crops on both sides. This had the desired effect as no more shooting took place by the tribesmen along that route.

Next day the unit received instructions to join the 11th Light Armoured Car Battery and proceed back to Lejjun where the Desert Mounted Corps Headquarters was stationed. We arrived there in the dark and bivouacked for the night. Next day we were to join the 5th Cavalry Division who were making a dash on the town of Haifa, which was still in the hands of the enemy. The town was attacked during the afternoon and fell about 4 o'clock. Shortly afterwards we drove in and took possession. We slept in an olive grove that night and next morning our orders were to proceed south (around Mount Carmel) along the coast and search the villages for enemy and rifles etc. We went through the villages of Athlit and Tantura and although we found none of the enemy left we got large supplies of rifles, 30 cases of ammunition and a bag of bombs, which we handed in. We returned to Haifa and slept in our old quarters again.

On the 27th September the Corps pushed on through Nazareth to Tiberias where we stayed for the night. We had considerable difficulty in getting through the mountains near Nazareth. Our aeroplanes the day before had severely bombed an enemy mechanical transport column as it was in the pass and had played havoc with them. The result was that in places the road was blocked by disabled vehicles, which we had to push over the side into the valley below in order to get past.

We arrived at Tiberias on the shores of the lake in time for tea and stayed there for the night. The blue waters of the Sea of Galilee looked very refreshing after the dry and dusty journey and most of the men indulged in a bath at the first opportunity. We also had fresh meat that day which was a welcome change after weeks of 'bully'. One of our machine-gunners found a sheep on the journey up and soon had it skinned and cut up in professional style. Nobody asked any questions as to how the sheep was found, but it certainly tasted all right. Next day our orders were to push on to El-Kunneitra but to leave two gun cars with their crews at Tiberias to guard the town which was a rather important point in our line of communication. The road to El-

Kunneitra was in very bad condition and the transport of the retreating Turks had not improved it, but we arrived there at dusk and camped for the night. Next morning, at daybreak, again we were off to Kaukab where we stayed the following night, but not to sleep as we were getting very close to our destination, the City of Damascus — the oldest city of the world, and a great Turkish stronghold. We placed our guns in position for the night but were undisturbed. The next day was a great day for our army. As soon as it was light enough to see we started on a road reconnaissance. We found a good track and proceeded with all vehicles to Kiswe, a few miles south of Damascus. Coming over the hills we got a magnificent view of the great city about ten miles away in the hollow. The morning mists were just rising and the view was beautiful. We could see the minarets and towers peeping through the green foliage. Numbers of streams of fresh water winding through the orchards and vineyards, and in every direction could be seen thin columns of dust rising through the green trees as bodies of troops, armoured cars, transport and cavalry were all converging along every possible road and track towards the one centre. Every now and then a puff of white smoke could be seen, as a shell would burst in the distance. The sight was a never-to-be-forgotten one. Away on the horizon (always well out of range) were hordes of Lawrence's Arab 'allies' hanging around for their share of loot when the city fell. Within an hour the leading regiments were in the city. The 3rd Light Horse Brigade secured positions above the Abana Gorge the night before where they inflicted terrible losses on the retreating enemy. This completed the enemy's discomfiture and at 11a.m. we formed a grand procession through the city. The whole of the native population turned out to see us come in and expressed their feelings by firing their guns into the air and, as every member of the city seemed to have a rifle or a gun of some description, the row can be imagined. We drove through the street that is called Straight. By this time our other cars from Tiberias had joined us and we made a good show with the cars of the other armoured car batteries as we did the conquering hero stunt up to the Town Hall where we stopped for a while for the chiefs to take over the keys of the Town etc. While waiting we did not forget to try the fruit and the other dainties on sale in the bazaars. Damascus is certainly best from the distance — just far enough away not to notice the filth and smells. Most of us thought we knew enough of the east but Damascus certainly beat all the other cities that we had been in for smells. We did not think it possible to get such a variety of stink in one town.

The streets were certainly not made for motor traffic and our drivers had to keep their eyes open when moving about in the town. Holes full of filthy water abounded everywhere. Some of the streets were pitched, but the pitchers were laid anyway, some on top of each other. One of our drivers just missed a manhole in the street with the cover missing. The hole was a well about 10ft deep. An electric tram ran through the city but it puzzled everyone how it kept on the rails as these in some cases bulged nearly a foot above the level of the road and in other places were lost in a sea of mud. Our drivers had to give these rails a wide berth, as they would drag the tyres off the wheels if caught in them. We received orders to proceed to the north end of the city to camp for the night. We tried to get through the gorge where Colonel Scott's Light Horsemen had their picnic the night before, but found it impossible to get along until we had spent an hour or so clearing the track of dead men and horses which were heaped across the road everywhere. We had to lever smashed up vehicles of all descriptions into the river while there were machine-guns lying about in hundreds. The gutters literally ran with blood. Through the narrow gorge ran a railway line, a river and a road and there was no room for anything else. The railway was blocked with a smashed train of trucks. The river was a racing torrent full of debris and the road was a conglomeration of vehicles and bodies. Eventually we cleared a track through the mess and arrived at our camping position on a hill overlooking the town. Next day we had to patrol the road from Damascus back to El-Kunneitra as the Commander in Chief was motoring up to enter the city officially. We stayed at Damascus for a couple of weeks and took the opportunity to do a number of necessary repairs to our motor vehicles and equipment in between a lot of necessary road patrolling along the various routes, but chiefly between Beirut on the coast and Damascus. In the meantime, the 5th Cavalry Division under General MacAndrew had pushed on from Damascus and had reached Baalbek en route for a dash at Aleppo, the headquarters of one of the Turkish armies and the junction of the Mespot and Syrian Railway system on the main line from Constantinople. One of our cars had already been attached to this division for some days and on the 19th October orders were received for the whole unit to join the 5th Cavalry Division. We accordingly pushed right away and arrived at Zahli (the junction of the Beirut and Aleppo roads) about midnight. We stayed here until daylight and rushed on with all speed to the north joining the division that afternoon. And now began what was (from the motor unit's point of view) the most eventful part of the campaign, and it was probably the first time in history that a complete series of operations was carried out on motor vehicles against an opposing army.

49. The Battle of Megiddo saw the collapse of the Turkish forces in Syria. Trophies of the victor included the guns of an Austrian artillery battery (Creek collection ATM LCP.HC.001).

The Battle of Megiddo from the Driver's Seat

By Trooper Leo Cohn.

Syria October 8, 1918

Dear Mother,

This is the first chance I have had to write since the stunt started and now Lord knows when I shall get a chance to post it.

Looks as if we have wiped Jacko properly off the slate this time. We are all anxiously waiting to see if the fight is finished. It looks very much like it. At present we are in Damascus and are just sitting tight waiting for the squadron, which, of course, means rations. We went on that fast and captured so many prisoners that rations have been a thing of the past. Anyhow, it has not affected us much as we have had plenty chances to buy food in the towns. Where we are camped at present there are vegetable gardens stretching for miles around. About every second day we buy a sheep from the natives.

It is no good starting at the end of the stunt, so I shall tell you what happened right from the hop-off. September 19th: Camped at Sarsouin and moved up at 3 a.m. and waited just behind the line. At 5 a.m. the Artillery started and at 5.30AM the Infantry hopped over on about a two mile front and took the first line of trenches. The three mounted divisions, Australian Division and the two Indian Divisions went straight through and made one rush and did sixty one miles in twenty four hours, right round to the back of Nablas and cut the whole main army off. Anyway my wish was pretty right as I had only gone about eight miles over the trenches when I broke the handlebars of my bike and as one of the cars was having a good deal of trouble I dumped the bike with them. When we got about thirty miles on we struck one of our cars and the other cyclist, both broken down. So on the afternoon of the 20th I got a lift way out to within about seven miles of the bike that night. Had a fruit tin. Tea, sugar and biscuits with me so had a feed and rolled into my blanket for a few hours. Got up at daybreak and started out and found my bike about eight o'clock. Luckily nobody had seen it and everything was complete. Rode back with one handlebar to a motor depot about ten miles away and put in new handles. Rode back to Sarona and had lunch with a Canteen fellow that I know. After an afternoon riding I arrived back at the broken down car at sundown. Next morning (23rd) I started and reached Desert Corps HQ at about 9 a.m. Enquired where the unit was and was told they were with the 4th Indian Division at Biesan about thirty miles on the right very nearly on the Jordon. Passed through El Arcale which had been a big Turkish railway centre and aerodrome and arrived at Bresan at midday. There I was informed that they had been sent over to the 5th Indian Division and were advancing on Hafar. Went back through Arfile and passed through Magaherta at dusk and pushed on, arrived at Haifa at about 7 a.m in the pitch dark. The town was taken about 4 p.m. after a pretty stiff little fight. Went to the boss hotel of the town and saw some of the staff who absolutely swore there was no such thing as an Australian Light Car Patrol. Eventually one fellow told me that they had been sent on to Aine. I told them that I was homeless and mighty hungry so they ordered a room for me and dinner. Went up and had a look at the room. Shook the dust out of my clothes and had a bath. Had a dinner and retired to the sheets after drinking with a couple of fellows that had been captured and recaptured the same afternoon. Got up in the morning and went down to the pier for a dip and after breakfast went up to HQ and met the patrol going out on a job along the beach. A convoy reported that they had been fired on near a German Colony. Captured a good few eggs and a couple of rifles and returned back to Haifa. Camped down and had a spell all the next day. Next day (26th) we went back to Desert Corps, about six miles the far side of Arfule. Next day we shifted up again through Mugareta and reached Tiberius that night. The view of the Sea of Galillee and Tiberius with its old ruined walls on its shore looked something wonderful from the hill above.

Next day we shifted on to a village on the Jordon just below Lab Hulleh. Next day on the Kanetra a Sarcassian village. Next day we shifted to Damascus. That night the Turks fired the railway station and huge ammunition dumps and all night the whole sky was lit up and the place practically shook with the rumble of explosions. Next day Oct 1st Australian Division took the town. The Sheriff's men were supposed to have got there the night before but if they did you can be sure there was nobody there left to stop them. We stopped in the outskirts that night and moved in the next morning and have been here ever since. At present Jack's and Norman's cars are out on the Beirut road somewhere but otherwise we have had a good six days rest. A French Division has landed at Beirut but the Jackos had had to clear out days before. I am afraid we are not going to get along too well with the Hedjaz crowd. The genuine army are alright but it is the thousands of looting Bedouins that follow them about that cause the trouble.

The town itself is one of the filthiest I have ever been in but from a distance it looks beautiful. It is built in the centre of a huge plain surrounded by hills. For miles around it is one sea of green with the grey houses in the middle and every here and there Mosques with their minarets standing out. Anyhow we can buy a 'bit of feed' here so it is not so bad. Well that is not so bad for a plain old raspberry like me and it is nearly teatime. Needless to say we are living in a house and are making ourselves pretty comfortable. Anyhow our War is over and they seem to be doing wonders in France and collapse ought to bring things to a close, very soon and I can tell you all about this part of the world and that will be easier than writing.

Love to all.

Your loving son,

Leo.

57588

Each issue of Orders will be issued consecutively throughout the year. A fresh series to be commenced with the first issue in each year.

Army Form O. 1810
All Arms.

Unit No1 Australian Light Car Patrol

DAILY ORDERS. PART II. No. 5

N.B.—The Sub. No. of Order and Subject are to be shown in cols. 1 and 2, thus :—1.—Cour's Martial.

Station Cairo EGYPT

Date 22-2-19.

Regimental No., Rank and Name.	Sqdn. Batty. or Co.	Particulars of Casualties, etc., and Date.
10 APPOINTMENT		
10 M.T.Dvr Hyman O.H.		Appointed A/Lance Corpl. 9-3-18.
1 INVALIDING		
12 M Cpl.Morgan C.F.		Embarked HT"MARGHA"at Suez29-1-19.for Australia. Malaria.
2 EMBARKATION		
LIEUT.F.V.N.CORNWELL		Embarked HT"ASCANIUS"at Suez 21-2-19. for Australia.Compassionate leave. (Auth:Def:Cable WR879 dated21-11-18)
3 BURIAL		
3 Sgt Langley J.H."DCM"BAR		Buried 4-1-19.by Capt E.N.D.Bourney. Gravesite:-Grave No4 Aleppo Military Cemetery.
4 EVACUATION MT.DVR.		
4 10 A/L/Cpl.Hyman	O.H.	To hospital sick 3-1-19
5 1351 Tpr Pines	M.C.	do do
6 3013 " Riley	J.C.	do 27-1-19
7 REJOINED UNIT		
3013 Tpr Riley	J.C.	Rejoined fromsick 18-2-19
8 3138a " Jarvis	B.C.	do 3-1-19
9 10A/L/Cpl.M.T.Dvr Hyman	O.H.	do 25-1-19
20 3021 Tpr Bosanquet	L.C.V.	do 5-1-19
1 1039 " Colm	L.R.	do 19-1-19
2 34a " Rhodes	J.P	do 14-2-19
3 HONOURS & REWARDS		
CAPT.E.H.JAMES		Awarded The Military Cross.6-12-18 G.H.Q.E.E.F.List No 499 dated5-1-19

Australian Headquarters(EGYPT)
E. E. F.

(sgd.) J. Val. Boyle
..............................LIEUT
For o.i/c Records

D. D. & L., London E.C.
(P11036) Wt. W2739/P939 3,512,000 9/13 W45
Forms/O1810/78

Officer Commanding or Adjutant.

49a. Daily Orders Part II dated 22-2-1919.

THE MOTOR DASH ON ALEPPO

When Major General MacAndrew left Damascus with the 5th Cavalry Division with Aleppo as his objective it was known that he had a pretty tough proposition in hand. Aleppo was a Turkish Military depot where several divisions were stationed with large supply and ammunition reserves. It was also a railway depot and junction of the two railway systems to Bagdad and Damascus and was in direct communication with Constantinople.

50. The vehicle park of the 1st Australian Light Car Patrol and the British Armoured Car Batteries in Syria, 1918 (ATM LCP 006).

On the other hand the 5th Division was only about half strength on account of the losses through disease and battle etc. The horses were more or less done on account of the strenuous operations preceding the taking of Damascus and there was over 200 miles to go before reaching the objective with perhaps the prospect of strong enemy resistance anywhere on the route. Nevertheless, the division made excellent progress considering the conditions for over a third of the distance when it was realised that progress was getting considerably slower and the horses were becoming more or less done.

General MacAndrew or "Fighting Mac" as he was known, realised that something else would have to be done if the operations were to be successful as speed was one of the main factors necessary for success. The General then decided when the division reached Homs to collect all the available motors together and make a rush for the enemy's base leaving the division to follow on as soon as possible. Three Armoured Car Batteries (Nos. 2, 11 and 12 Light Armoured Motor Batteries) and three Light Car Patrols (Nos. 1, 2 and 7 Light Car Patrol) hastily collected together their necessary transport vehicles. Each armoured car battery consisted of four 50 hp Rolls Royce armoured cars, each mounted with a Vickers machine-gun and each Light Car Patrol consisted of four light cars each mounted with a Lewis gun. Both units of course had necessary tenders accompanying them with extra petrol, oil, water, rations and ammunition. Thus the fleet mounted between them twenty-four machine-guns with their crews and transport. The armoured cars were the battleships of the fleet, but owing to their weight they were more or less compelled to stick to the hard ground. The cars of the Light Car Patrols, while they did not have the protection of the larger vehicles, could venture on to places where the others could not go and were like the light cruisers of the fleet.

This little mobile army with General MacAndrew in command himself left Hama at daybreak on the morning of the 22nd of October 1918 and said good-bye to the rest of the division.

After driving due north for an hour or two a fleet of enemy motor vehicles hove into view; these vehicles consisted of a German armoured car and a number of German motor lorries fitted with steel tyres and each mounting a machine-gun and then began one of the prettiest little fights that has probably ever been witnessed. This was probably the first occasion on record of a battle between two fleets of motor vehicles. The German vehicles saw that they were outnumbered and were making all haste to get away north firing frantically with their machine-guns from the rear of the lorries as they bounced and jolted over the rough ground. The big German armoured car endeavoured to cover the retreat of the other vehicles. Our armoured cars rushed up alongside the enemy vehicles and a running fight ensued at a speed of about thirty miles per hour with the Light Car Patrols hovering round to get a shot in now and then, while some of them rushed ahead in order to cut off the enemy vehicles. The shooting from the German lorries was very erratic, as owing to the roughness of the ground, the speed at which they were travelling, the gunners one minute would be firing into the ground and the next into the clouds. After a few minutes of this running fight the German armoured car suddenly stopped, a door opened at the side and the crew rushed out towards some barley crops growing alongside the track only to be shot down as they ran. The other lorries were then gradually surrounded and captured and some caught fire and were burnt. On examining the enemy armoured car we found that the engine was still running and we soon discovered why the crew left it so hurriedly. The fact being that it was a very unhealthy place to be as the bullets from our vehicles were penetrating the supposed armour plating and going clean through both sides at close range. The bullets from the German cars only fell harmlessly from the plating of our armoured cars, so the fight was more or less a one sided one. After this little delay the column pushed on once more and by evening we had reached the village of Seraikin where it was decided to stay for the night. Outposts and machine-guns were placed around the camp and everyone took their turns at watching through the night. The village of Seraikin contained an aeroplane depot and we surprised the occupants in time to prevent any planes from rising.

51. A smiling Captain James in typical officer's working dress, complete with necktie and a Light Horse emu plume in his slouch hat. The car, LC-1216, was one of the new cars taken on strength in December 1917. Note the two u-shaped mounts for the Lewis light machine-gun, and the pedestal-type mount in the rear of the vehicle to provide elevation for firing at aircraft. The insignia 'Australia' has been stencilled above the registration number (Cornwell collection ATM LCP.PC.013).

When we arrived at Seraikin we were fortunate in being quick enough to prevent the aeroplanes there from taking off and flying to Aleppo with the information of our proximity. We were especially anxious that the enemy should not know what a comparatively insignificant force was advancing against them. The General wished to use the element of surprise to gain as much advantage as possible. Near the village we discovered a small gun with a calibre of about 1.5 inches. It was mounted on a small folding carriage something like the German Maxim gun tripod. There was also a case of shells. These were something after the style of the Pom Poms and would be under one pound in weight. We put the lot into the back of one of the cars and they came in very useful later on. Next morning we made an early start as usual and proceeded north until we came to Khan Tuman. Here the cars suddenly and unexpectedly ran into a small detachment of Turkish Cavalry. There was a sudden burst of fire from the Lewis Guns and a couple of the Cavalrymen fell wounded. Some of the Light Cars then made a rush to head off the horsemen from the direction of Aleppo, which they succeeded in doing. The officer in charge and a party of his men were surrounded and they surrendered. A few of the remainder galloped off to the west where they got into some rough timbered country where the motors could not penetrate without a lot of trouble. As they were cut off from Aleppo it did not matter very much what happened to them. After this little episode the force pushed on again and was almost in sight of Aleppo before any serious opposition was encountered.

The flying motor force had been particularly fortunate. First of all the enemy motor vehicles had been encountered and exterminated. Next the aeroplanes had been caught before they had time to rise and then the cavalry patrol had been cut off. So the enemy headquarters had practically received no news whatever of what was happening and the surprise was complete. They were evidently very anxious thinking that something was wrong and were nervous. However, on reaching a position within view of town it could be seen that the place was alive with troops. Trenches had been dug all round the city and the troops could be seen in these through the field glasses. A couple of armoured cars drove down the road towards the city and encountered a storm of rifle and machine-gun fire. Some batteries of artillery also opened up with shrapnel High Explosive. The General then called a halt and collected his small force under shelter of a friendly hill for a council of war. He then decided to make as much display of force as possible. The armoured cars manoeuvred on the skyline making as much display and dust as possible. Some of the Lewis guns were taken off the light cars, which were also driven about in view. The guns were carried along under cover of some stonewalls and rocks so as to get within range of the trenches and make as much noise as possible. In the meantime, our "brave" allies the Arabs apparently began to think something was doing and could smell loot for they began to collect in thousands on the horizon in every direction. In the distance it looked like an army collecting on the doomed city.

Several hundred of these Arabs mounted on horseback collected in the rear of our cars and one of them who was apparently a man of importance after talking with our interpreter began to harangue his followers with the result that they all sprang into the saddle and rode forward up to the motor car column. Apparently this was not enough for their leader for he began to talk and yell at them seriously for about ten minutes or a quarter of an hour which presumably had the effect desired as they all rode forward onto the skyline. Immediately about ten machine-guns and a couple of batteries of artillery opened fire. That was enough. The horsemen all turned tail and galloped until they were out of sight to the yells and jeers of the British and Australian onlookers. It was now our turn to make some show and several parties of machine-gunners crept forward with their Lewis guns. We also carried along our captured Pom Pom and sent across all the little shells from various positions at extreme range. Although they did no damage they made plenty of smoke and noise, which is what we wanted, for it looked to the Turks that we were bringing artillery up. After this the General decided on a bold stroke and resolved to send a demand to the Turkish Commander in Chief to surrender. Accordingly in the afternoon Lieutenant McIntyre of No.7 Light Car Patrol drove into the enemy's lines in a car under a white flag with documents for the Turkish Commander. No shots were fired at the car, but when the Turkish trenches were reached the car was stopped. McIntyre was blindfolded and taken through on foot to an officer who took him to the Turkish Commander who was very courteous. General MacAndrew's ultimatum requested the immediate surrender of all troops, arms and materiel in the town. In return the General promised safe custody and the best treatment given to prisoners of war.

There was no sign of the car with the white flag returning and it was decided that McIntyre must have been taken prisoner but after about four hours' absence, he returned with a reply.

This was to the effect that the Turkish Commandant of the town could not reply to the demand, as he would have to communicate with Constantinople for instructions. However, the reply showed weakness. We found out afterwards that the Turks' chief fear was of the hordes of Arabs hovering around, as these gentry were always ready to fall on the defeated side and cut the throats of as many as possible. The Turks were very nervous about these fellows and although we found them useless as fighters they were indirectly of use on account of their reputation. That evening as we stood on the hills watching the city fires began to break out everywhere, explosions occurred in the city and railway stations and yards. Then we knew that the bluff had worked and the Turks were preparing to evacuate. We could see railway trains leaving the other side of the town. The sky was lit up over the town all night. Next morning we drove into the city without opposition and as the last train drove out of the town with Turkish troops on one side the Armoured Cars and Light Car Patrol drove in along the road on the other side to the accompaniment of cheers and the usual banging of rifles of the inhabitants. As we drove into the town an enterprising moving picture operator took views of the column entering and a few days afterwards we saw views of the entry of the town in the local cinema theatre.

A peculiar feature about the operations of the day before during the manoeuvring of the cars outside the town was the fact that although the enemy batteries shelled us heavily and although nearly everyone in the Light Car Patrols received a pellet of some description, nobody was hurt. Some of the bullets seemed to have no penetrating power and did not even penetrate the uniforms. Lieutenant Cornwell picked a pellet out of his Sam Brown belt that would have gone through the region of the heart if it had only had enough power. Numbers of splinters and pellets next day were dug out of the woodwork on the cars while one driver got one on the knuckles of his hand when driving, making him momentarily release the steering wheel with a yell but beyond a slight cut his hand was uninjured. We came to the conclusion afterwards that the shrapnel must have been stuff that been kept for many years and had lost its power, fortunately for us.

However, Aleppo was the Grand Finale of the best stunt we had had. By this time the advance men of the Mounted Division were well on our heels and we soon had a strong force in the town, although nothing like the number of troops that had just left it. For the first couple of days we had to quieten the Arab and Bedouin looters who started to rob all the inhabitants of the town as soon as the Turks withdrew but we soon had these fellows under control.

The capture of Aleppo took place on the 26th October. The Turks withdrew to the north-west and established a line of trenches about 15 miles out. The division followed and took up positions outside the town across the road to Alexandretta, the Armoured Car Batteries and Light Car Patrols taking up their share of this work.

The armoured cars attempted a reconnaissance a few days afterwards to test the Turkish defences. They found that the enemy had blown up all the culverts and bridges along the road and had dug trenches and pits at narrow crossings to make it difficult for vehicles to traverse. They got well shelled all along the road and found that the enemy was in strength and after about an hour of this they returned to camp intending to try other routes later on but on the 31st October at noon an Armistice was declared with Turkey and all fighting was off.

AFTER THE ARMISTICE

Because an Armistice was on it did not mean that work ceased for members of the motor units. As a matter of fact, the numbers of duties to be attended to seemed to increase rather than otherwise.

Car crews had to be out on outpost duties the same as usual and relieved one another for day and night shifts as the front lines were kept intact and no armed bodies were allowed to approach. Numerous trips were undertaken to quell disturbances caused chiefly by bodies of unfriendly Arabs and tribesmen in the various villages and towns in the vicinity.

In fact, we came to the conclusion that the whole population of Asia Minor and Syria were more or less cutthroats and robbers. The tribe that was strongest generally murdered and robbed the weaker ones.

52. No. 1 Australian Light Car Patrol at Aleppo Railway Station in November 1918. From left to right: two Model T Ford 'fighting' cars armed with Lewis machine-guns, a Ford tender, German Loreley, another Ford Tender, two 'fighting' cars and two motorcycles. Clearly some effort has been made to reassemble the cars at the end of the war (AWM B00707).

The Light Car Patrols owing to their mobility were gradually taking over the job of policing the occupied territory and had to take numberless excursions by night and day in all directions on both real and false alarms. One of the first undertakings of the British at Aleppo was to get the railway intact and trains running through to Damascus again. Several of the bridges had been blown up and most of the locomotives had been damaged before the Turks left the town.

A small shunting engine had been overlooked and this came in very useful for moving construction material. Several German motor lorries with flanged wheels to use as rail motors were also discovered and, in a very few days, Major Alexander, the Commander Royal Engineers, had the line clear for the first train from Damascus and a daily service was soon in vogue.

Several miles north of Aleppo was Muslemeye which was a very important point on the railway line as the junction of the two lines from Constantinople and Bagdad took place there. At this junction was stationed a large German Mechanical Transport Depot with stores and workshops. In the yards we were surprised to see quite a number of the German army lorries, which we had put out of action several months previously on the Amman and Es Salt Road. They were in for reconstruction, but practically nothing had been done to them and they were in the same state as we had left them on the road, some with their water jackets smashed and others with gear boxes blown in. We could imagine the tremendous amount of work the enemy had put in in getting these vehicles back over the road and then on to the rail again, only to be abandoned once more several miles north.

53. Sergeant Bert Creek and Driver Hal Harkin with Turkish prisoners, 150 miles from Alexandretta (Cohn collection ATM LCP.HC 016).

On the 24th November, we had an interesting trip into the enemy country under arrangements made between the British, French and Turkish authorities.

Our instructions were to make a road reconnaissance up to the town of Erzin which is west of the Taurus Mountains in Asia Minor as it was proposed to send ambulances to this point to pick up sick and wounded prisoners in Turkish hands and bring them back to our own hospitals before the weather became too wet for travelling. We accordingly took a couple of our own cars and borrowed one of the Rolls' tenders from the 11th Light Armoured Motor Battery Squadron and drove westward over the Hills of Bailin to the Mediterranean at Alexandretta (about 100 miles) where we stayed for the night in a liquorice factory on the sea coast.

In the morning we picked up the English Base Commandant and the French Military Governor (as Alexandretta was in the French sphere).

We made an early start and drove north under a white flag until we came to the Turkish line of trenches where we were halted. The Turkish Authorities had been advised and had raised no obstacles to the expedition. After a short delay we crossed the trenches, picked up a Turkish Officer as a guide and drove along the coast for a while then proceeded inland passing numbers of Turkish and Armenian villages (most of the latter being deserted and looted). There were very few travellers on the roads and the few that we passed ignored us probably thinking we were German. We arrived in time to have a late lunch at Erzin and after interviews between the British and Turkish local authorities who all seemed to talk in French we drove back to Alexandretta arriving at the French lines before dark. We found the tracks rough but quite negotiable for motor ambulances provided the weather was dry but quite hopeless after any heavy rain and we made our report accordingly. Next morning we left Alexandretta and got back to Aleppo in the afternoon.

On the 4th December, we had another interesting trip and under orders from the General Officer Commanding we proceeded to Katna, a railway town, to take over from the Turks a train load of guns and machine-guns from the Turkish southern line. These were to be handed over to us under the terms of the Armistice. We arrived at Katna in the morning expecting the train to be in about midday and waited all day in the teeming rain without any sign of it. Late in the afternoon a message was received that the train was delayed owing to the lack of fuel, and the firewood gathered along the route was wet and unsuitable. We camped on the railway platform for the night and next morning the train slowly steamed in.

G.269
Headquarters 5th Cavalry Division.
3rd December 1918

PRESSING.

TO   No. 11 L.A.M. Battery.
       No. 1 L.C. Patrol.
       13th Cavalry Brigade.
       15th Cavalry Brigade.
       Divl. Train.
       'Q.'

1. The 11th L.A.M. Battery and the No.1 L.C. Patrol under an Officer not below the rank of Major to be detailed by the 13th Cavalry Brigade, will proceed to MASHALE station to-morrow December 4th to receive the surrender of the guns Light and Heavy, machine guns and ammunition of Turkish Forces, South of the line KILLIS-ISLAHIE.

2. The guns will be handed over at MASHALE station at 1200. The number to be surrendered is not known, but the officer in charge will give a detailed receipt for all guns, machine guns and ammunition taken over.

3. The machine guns and ammunition will be brought back to ALEPPO by the lorries detailed in QX/916 of 2nd, which will move to MASHALE station for this purpose after depositing their loads at KATNA.

4. The surrendered guns will be towed to ALEPPO by these lorries, and rope and tackle for this purpose will be taken out by the lorries.

5. In the event of the lorries being unable to bring in all the surrendered guns and ammunition, they will be dumped at MASHALE under guard of No. 1 L.C. Patrol and the fact reported by wireless from KATNA to Divisional H.Qrs.

6. Rations for 3 days are to be taken by No.1 L.C. Patrol.

7. Name of the Officer detailed by 13th Cavalry Brigade to be wired to Divl. H.Quarters.

8. The 13th Cavalry Brigade will detail an Officer to proceed with this party to reconnoitre and report on suitable site for a camp at or near KATNA for one cavalry regiment.

9. Acknowledge.

Lieut-Colonel
General Staff
5th Cavalry Division.

H.Qtrs 5th Cav. Div.
3rd December 1918[4]

We went through the inventory of the guns and stores on board and found these correct. The Turkish Officer in Charge seemed to be quite pleased to hand over his charge. He said he was finished with military duties and was going back to his farm. He had had quite enough of war and handed to the writer his dagger as a souvenir. We placed a guard in the train which was the first one through from the Turkish direction since the Armistice and after about an hour's wait to get up a sufficient head of steam the train slowly proceeded on to Aleppo.

We drove there by road and arrived a couple of hours ahead of the train. Two days later we received orders at midnight to turn out and kill or capture a party of bandits who were attacking our telegraph linesmen along the road about 60 miles west. The night was black, cold, wet and miserable but after about five minutes grumbling the unit was going full speed, splashing through sheets of water and mud and all soaked through to the skin, only to arrive at our destination (with the first streaks of dawn) to find that the bandits had bolted to the mountains hours before, probably long before we started. However, this was only what we expected, so we picked up the linesmen and returned to our camp near Aleppo.

54. General Allenby, mounted, taking a salute from paraded drivers and crew of armoured cars from the 2nd, 11th and 12th Light Armoured Motor Batteries, Machine Gun Corps, the 1st Australian Armoured Car Section and the Scottish 7th Light Car Patrol (AWM P11419.007).

On the 11th we had a different sort of turnout. All cars and guns were cleaned up and polished and everyone had his best uniform on for the occasion as this was the day of the Grand Procession through the city on the official entry of General Allenby (the Commander in Chief). The inhabitants had to be impressed properly and the mounted forces with the various motor units in full strength made a good display as they paraded through the principal streets.

Two days later, we had another excursion after bandits in the direction of El Hamman. This time we managed to capture one of them. We brought him in and handed him over to the authorities to deal with.

The weather at this time of the year being the wet season was very cold and miserable and the members of the patrol were feeling it very severely after their long sojourn in the extreme heat of the Jordan Valley. Many of them who managed to survive the malaria while in the hot and unhealthy parts were now succumbing to it although in a district where malaria was not prevalent, and one after another the men were being drafted off to hospital. Fortunately, we were able to get sufficient reinforcements to carry on with.

On the 28th December, the unit drew petrol and supplies for ten days and received orders to move north about 100 miles to the Turkish town of Ain Tab which was to be the centre of our operations until further orders. Ain Tab is at the foot of the mountains and is a very cold place in the winter and as it happened to be nearly midwinter we arrived there at the coldest time of the year. We drove into the town at 4 p.m. and were met by Major Mills, the British representative there. We were allotted quarters in an American school which was empty and were glad to get under a roof once more. We soon had some firewood brought up and a cheerful fire burning. Next morning when we woke up a snowstorm was in full progress and the ground was under a mantle of white. Motoring was more or less out of the question and we hoped that no orders for any more moves would be received for some time. New Year's Day broke out fine and we took the opportunity of sending back to Aleppo to bring up further supplies of petrol. The following night the car returned to Ain Tab with supplies after a very rough trip; the driver reported that the rains had washed innumerable stones on to the roads and he had had no fewer than fourteen punctures on the trip back. We found out afterwards that the stones were not wholly responsible for our tyre trouble as the tyres themselves were somewhat to blame. The Motor Transport stores had received a consignment of tyres of American manufacture which had been sent from Egypt and these we discovered were far from being up to the standard of the quality of the usual tyres of British manufacture which we had received previously.

This day the 2nd January, was a day of gloom with the unit. Sergeant J. Langley, the gallant Non-Commissioned Officer who had led his car into numerous fights and who was the admiration of the whole unit, died at Aleppo hospital from malaria. He was a man of splendid physique, young, healthy and full of vigour, yet he died the second day after going to hospital. He received a bar to his DCM the week previously. He was buried with full military honours at Aleppo Cemetery.

55. Sergeant John Langley's grave marker in the military cemetery at Aleppo, Syria. He was later reinterred in the Commonwealth section of the Beirut War Cemetery in Beirut, Lebanon (Creek collection ATM LCP.LC.005).

"Absolutely in Peace"
Trooper Leo Cohn

Aleppo.
January 12, 1919

Dear Mother,
Isn't it sad about poor Jack. Mrs. Mackay's death, Pies, Bert Henderson, Hugh McColl, what terrible lists for the past month or so. It quite takes the glow off this wonderful Peace that we have prayed for so long.

I have been out of hospital for a few days now and am all right once more. The unit is still up in the mountain but I am putting in a week or so with a Scottish Horse Patrol until I am properly fit.

I do not know whether Jack was in hospital last time I wrote. He had intended to go back to Puchc [sic] to see about our kit left there before the stunt and from there to Cairo. He had had slight jaundice but reckoned on the mild climate back further to fix him up. He grew that bad that he was persuaded to go into hospital for a week or so first and then down the line. The day after he was admitted I was able to get him to the next bed to me. He had grown a bit worse, but jaundice is such common complaint just now that the Doctor just put him on milk diet and said he would be right in few days. The next day he was semi-conscious and had passed a very bad night, so first thing in the morning I got the Doctor to come and have another good look at him. He suspected Malaria straight away, took a blood test but it proved negative but he was certain and gave him an injection of quinine.

Later in the day he gave him two more injections. All the next day and night he lay unconscious. The next afternoon he was just the same and although in the morning the Doctor said that most likely he would come too before night he had grown worse and the Doctor told us there was very little chance. At this time there were two more of the Patrol in hospital also. He was a little better after tea and two of us decided to sit up all night. I had been sitting with him for an hour or so when suddenly his breathing stopped or rather just faded away and he passed out absolutely in peace.

I wired to the ALCP and next day he arrived down with Norman and another fellow. Next we buried him in a small military cemetery just outside the town.

This has been a great blow to us all. He was a fine fellow and most of us idealized him. I don't think you could have found a cleaner living fellow and that does more good amongst a crowd of men than Bible banging.

It was only our limited little unit that kept him from making a name for himself for he had a great personality.

Norman has gone off on the Hickson on a Cairo trip. He expects to be away six weeks or more. A fortnight would be the very shortest time I should say that he would work his way back to Palestine ….
Your loving son,
Leo.

Particulars Required for the Roll of Honour of Australia in the Memorial War Museum.

1. Name (in full) of Fallen Soldier *John Hudson Langley*
2. Unit and Number (if known) *No.3 1st Australian Light Car Patrol.*
3. With what Town or District in Australia was he chiefly connected (under which his name ought to come on the Memorial)—
   Town (if any) *Bendigo* District *Bendigo* State *Victoria*
4. What was his Birthplace *Melbourne*
5. Date of Death *Jan 2nd 1919.*
6. Place where Killed or Wounded *Died Malignant Malaria Aleppo —*

Particulars Required for the Nation's Histories.

1. What was his Calling *Engineer*
2. Age at time of Death *25 years —*
3. What was his School *Trinity Grammar School Kew —*
4. What was his other Training *Thompson's Engineering Works Castlemaine*
5. If born in Britain or Abroad, at what age did he come to Australia.
6. Had he ever served in any Military or Naval Force before Enlisting in the A.I.F. (Please state particulars)
   Citizens Forces — Lieutenant —
7. Any other biographical details likely to be of interest to the Historian of the A.I.F., or of his Regiment:—
   Both in School, in Citizen Forces + Army Life shewed remarkable powers for Leadership + he always stood for Justice + Fair Play —

8. Was he connected with any other Member of the A.I.F. who died or who distinguished himself. (Please state Relationship)—

9. Name and Address of the Parent or other person giving this information—
   Name *J H Langley*
   Relationship to Soldier *Father*
   Address *aranuka. Gilbert Islands.*

10. Names and Addresses of any other persons to whom reference could be made by the Historian for further information—
    Name *General Chauvel —* *Sergeant Norman Bisset*
    Address *Melbourne —* *Middle Park Hotel Middle Park*

NOTE.—This Folder is Addressed to the Secretary, Department of Defence, Melbourne. Please fold in four, and stick down gummed flap so that the addressed portion is outside. The information is required urgently.

P.1685/10.11.—C.16706.

Young, Young Bros Whill — Leo Colin Barkly Place Bendigo —

NOTED ON H. R. CARD

56. Jack Langley's Roll of Honour circular for the Australian War Memorial.

Jack Langley.
An appreciation, by
Captain Alexander Barrett Keage
Master in Charge,
Trinity Grammar Cadets.

All those who were contemporaries of Jack Langley eight or nine years ago must have felt a sincere pang of regret when they learned that he had died of malaria at Aleppo at the beginning of the year. Jack had fought with distinction all through the Palestine Campaign, and had taken part in the adventurous dash, under the Duke of Westminster into the Sahara where they rescued the crew of an English ship from the Senussi.[5]

It is a painful reflection that while his audacious campaigns against the Turks were nearing a victorious end he was obstinately fighting a malignant foe in the form of Malaria, contracted some weeks previous in the Jordan Valley and to this insidious enemy he surrendered his life on 2nd January. Those who were intimately acquainted with Jack in 1910-11 need not be told that he was a brave as a lion. We guessed that, and we were not surprised to learn that he had been awarded the Distinguished Conduct Medal. He also has been personally recommended by his General for a Bar to the DCM a few weeks before he died.

It seems to be a characteristic of brave and chivalrous men to be also gentle and good-natured. It was this trait, no doubt, which endeared him to his comrades both at School and the Front. His O.C. Captain James speaks of him as: "Dear Sergeant Langley, my right hand man, and the finest fellow that ever lived." He also refers to him as "Dear Old Jack my old comrade he has been with us from the very beginning, and has really been the backbone of the Battery since the day of its formation. The whole unit was broken up at the sad news, as he was undoubtedly the most popular man in our part of the force."

Jack will always be remembered by his old friends and comrades for his cheerfulness and good temper, nothing, except injustice or wrong, could disturb his imperturbable good temper and equanimity and he was always straight and dependable: altogether, one of those for whom we have to thank god for making tradition of Trinity.

John Hudson Langley
Born 10th April 1894
Entered the School 9th February 1909.
No 310 on School Roll.
Left December 1911.
Died of Malaria at Aleppo, 2nd January 1919.

For noble deeds as simple duty done,
In their Christlikeness known to god alone;
For high, heroic bearing under stress;
Fore hearts that no ill fortune could depress;
For every helpful word and kindly deed;
That formed occasion in brother's need
We thank Thee Lord.
(The *Mitre*, May 1919, p. 40)

57. John H. Langley as a student at Trinity Grammar, Melbourne, 1911 (Trinity Grammar School Trinity 001).

Ain Tab
26/1/19 &
31/1/19,

Dear Mother,
Have been very busy this last week so excuse change of date. Have been out of hospital or, rather out of Aleppo for over a week now and am with the Unit at Ain Tab, a filthy little Turkish and Armenian town. We are pretty short-handed and since being back I have had two trips to Aleppo, eighty miles of rotten roads and as cold as charity. They have been arresting some of the Young Turk (Party) and we have had to run them to Aleppo. It is Turkish territory and we were not too sure how they would take it, but there hasn't been any fuss so far.

My fellow was the most evil looking man I have ever seen. He must weigh about twenty-one stone, huge face, pock-marked and with a Hindenburg moustache. I must send you a snap of him sitting beside me in the car and a fellow behind him with a rifle ready to pop him off if any of his crowd tried to hold us up on the road. He was supposed to have killed three or four hundred women and kids and while down in Mespot he was in charge of two labour battalions and instead of taking the trouble and transport to bring them back, he murdered the lot. Of course they were all Armenians. He confided in me going down and from what I could make out, Allah was responsible. I gave him plenty of spiritual advice, mostly because of a bag of gold-boys that he had …

… As soon as I hear any definite word of being sent home I shall cable. There are rumours that the French are coming to take over all country north of Jerusalem.

Best love to all.

Your loving son
Leo …

58. Troopers Cohn and Richardson escort a Turkish officer wanted for crimes in Mesopotamia (Cohn collection ATM LCP.LC.006).

THE BATTLE WITH THE KURDISH BANDITS

The 12th January 1919 was our last scrap. We claimed that we fired the last shot in connection with the Great War. This is how it happened. The Town of Ain Tab where we were stationed was an inland town in the mountains. Although well inside the Turkish line at the signing of the Armistice, the town now had both British and Turkish Commandant residing there. Any person who had a grievance or a complaint to make went to both and if he was up to the usual standard of eastern artfulness he would try and work one against the other. Well to get on with the story, a party of Armenians looking very sorrowful and woebegone on the day in question, arrived at the house of the Turkish Commandant and explained to him with tears in their eyes that they had been waylaid and stripped of their clothes and robbed of all their possessions by brigands on the main road between Killis and Ain Tab. The Turkish official said that he was very sorry to hear the sad news, but explained that the matter had nothing to do with him and they had better run across and tell the British Commandant. Perhaps he might be able to get their clothes and possessions back again for them.

They took his advice and went across to Major Mills, the British official, who questioned them and managed to get the story out of them and the position of their caravan when robbed. He then sent across for the Officer in Charge of the Light Car Patrol who immediately got a couple of his cars ready with instructions to chase the brigands. We were told these gentlemen were about four miles down the main road so we took one of the Armenians who could speak some English, as a guide to the position and although expecting the usual wild goose chase, we set off at full speed in the direction of the trouble, everyone being very sarcastic on the subject of bandits in general, but sure enough, when we had gone about four miles down the road we saw a long camel caravan halted in the middle of the road and a squad of armed horsemen holding them up with rifles in the true highway fashion. Joy beat in the hearts of the motor patrol. At last, they were going to get even with somebody for all the miserable expeditions at midnight in the cold and wet that they had endured for the last few weeks.

No questions were asked by either side. The bandits knew they had been caught red-handed and could expect no quarter. They all started firing wildly with their rifles and revolvers from horseback as they galloped down the road, which had stonewalls along each side at this particular spot. The horses apparently were not much in the steeple chasing line so their riders rode straight on hoping to get gaps in the walls. The two cars tore on (on either side of the caravan) holding their fire until up to the horses then they let go at the riders who fired from the hips as they ran along side by side. However, owing to the speed and the bumping of the cars and the elusiveness of the target the shooting on both sides was very bad. The writer, who at one time rather fancied himself as a bit if a revolver shot, still remembers his disgust at emptying every shot in his Webley at point blank range at a Kurdish horseman without the slightest effect. We then concentrated on the horses which were much more difficult to miss with the result that the animals were soon all on the ground except one which galloped away without the rider who was wounded. The rider however, jumped over the wall and began shooting from behind cover at us so we divided, (each car's crew going to opposite ends of the wall) and we opened up on them from both flanks with rifles and Lewis guns. This soon fetched them up and they tried to bolt away through some ploughed ground. However, our shooting was better now and we picked them off as they ran up the hill. We accounted for the whole band who were all either killed or wounded. We found that some of them had three or four bullets through before they dropped. While this little running fight was taking place, the men on the caravan who had been held up were yelling with glee and excitement and when they saw their late aggressors lying on the ground they rushed up to our chaps and began patting them on the back while the Armenian who came with us was apparently a hero for all time among his compatriots. By the time the shooting was over and we had collected the spoils to return to the people who had lost it, and had picked up one of the brigands who was only half dead to take back to town, it was getting dark. So we thought it was time to get back to make our report. We turned for home again and the caravan followed along after us.

Before we reached Ain Tab however, we were met by a large crowd of the townspeople coming down the road to meet us. They had heard all the shooting down the road and this noise had been increased by the echoes in the mountains as each shot was repeated backwards and forwards from hill to hill until it must have sounded like a general engagement to the people in the town. We felt quite elated on reaching the town to be told that the tribe we had exterminated had been preying on travellers for years and they had been a thorn in the side of the Turks right through the war even interfering with their army transport.

Hitherto, all attempts to trace or run them down had been ineffective with the result that they had got bold enough to attack quite large convoys. We handed over the wounded man to the Turkish Authorities and we heard afterwards that they had their own methods of dealing with him. They put their 'third degree' across him and got information as to the village he came from and where they kept their loot etc. Anyhow, we believe the man died a day or so afterwards.

After this little episode the Australians were looked upon as quite a lot of little tin gods by the Turks and local inhabitants. The Turkish Commandant wished to have the members of the Patrol decorated with a Turkish medal of some description, but of course it was not allowed for British to accept decorations from an enemy country. However, he insisted on the writer accepting as a souvenir a decoration of his own, which he had received from his own Government.

After tea that evening, the sentry in from of No. 1 Light Car Patrol's quarters was surprised to see a large deputation arrive headed by the interpreter or the 'Interrupter' as he was known by the troops. He explained to the sentry that the deputation consisted of the principal Armenians of the town and the head man or patriarch who had come down to express their thanks to the men who has delivered their countrymen from the brigands. He also explained that it was the custom there to express their gratitude by their head man kissing the victim on the forehead. At this there was much amusement among the rest of the troops who were lining up to see what the excitement was all about.

The Commandant was appealed to, but he only grinned and said that the ordeal must be gone through otherwise the town would be offended for evermore. One man suggested that he would go through with it if they sent their daughters up instead, but apparently that was not allowed. Finally the five victims were lined up by their mates, while the patriarch solemnly carried out his duty to the accompaniment of yells of laughter from the onlookers. After it was over it was discovered that one of the men had bribed a substitute to take his place by offering him his week's issue of rum. The Ain Tab scrap was the last shooting the Patrol did although shortly afterwards a detachment was sent up into the mountains to augment No. 7 Patrol (The Scottie) who were at Marash as it was rumoured that the inhabitants in that district were talking of rising up and driving the small British garrisons back into the sea. However, the threat was never put into execution. About this time also, we sent another detachment across to the Euphrates to join up with a party from Mespot, who had come across from Bagdad thus joining up the British forces in Palestine and Mesopotamia.

On the 1st March we received orders to return to Aleppo and we were relieved by No. 3 Patrol. We did not take long to do the 100 miles back although it had been snowing a couple of days previously. Two days afterwards great was the joy throughout the unit when orders were received to hand in all guns and cars as the unit was to proceed to Egypt ready for return to Australia. We handed in all our war-worn and battered, but still serviceable outfits and received clean receipts. The German car, which we captured at Afule, was handed over to the Commandant at Aleppo. We had managed to keep this car on the road ever since we grabbed it and had done many thousands of miles with it. Although spares were unobtainable, we had always managed to devise substitutes and we had a sneaking idea that we might smuggle the outfit down to Egypt somehow and finally get it to Australia, but it was not to be.

However, there was only one subject in everybody's mind and that was home. On the evening of the 5th March, we embarked on the train at Aleppo for Damascus where we arrived at 11 p.m. the following night. It was quite interesting viewing the country that we had travelled and fought over previously from the train. We changed trains at Damascus and next morning left by the narrow gauge train for Haifa via Dersa and Semak. We stayed the next night at Haifa and after another day and night in the broad gauge military railway we arrived at the Canal at Kantara. We crossed over the pontoon bridge (this time on foot) and that evening were in Cairo.

Next day the native revolution broke out. All the other Light Car Patrols and Armoured Car Batteries were immediately sent to the various towns where disturbances were taking place to make the niggers learn sense. However, we were useless as we had no guns or cars (our teeth had been drawn) and we were sent to camp at Ismailia to await news for embarkation. On the 16th May we embarked on the *Kaiser-i-Hind* with the Air Force for Australia and four weeks later we arrived at Melbourne where we had embarked three years previously almost to the day.

It was with mixed feelings that we arrived at our home ports. There was no doubt about everyone being glad to get home to their dear ones again. Nevertheless, there was a distinct air of sadness at each port as old comrades parted. No. 1 Light Car Patrol was certainly an interstate unit, as its personnel consisted of Victorians, New South Welshmen, South Australians, Queenslanders and Westerners.

These men had been comrades in arms on three continents; some of them had been together for four years or more. They had fought together and had shared the good and bad times and had always played the game towards each other. There must have been many occasions with all when the prospects of ever returning home again looked hopeless.

No wonder then, that eyes looked a little dim as each man shook hands all round and wished his mates "Good Luck" before disembarking. Friendships such as these will last through all time.

"OLD SOLDIERS NEVER DIE – THEY SIMPLY FADE AWAY"

58a. Crews standing with their vehicles at Minia Camp in late 1916. The New Hudson Motorcycle with sidecar, Silent Sue the Mercedes armoured car, the Minerva tender and "Gentle Annie" the Daimler armoured car. In the hanger are new Model T Fords that will soon replace the Australian designed and made vehicles. This small group of motor enthusiast were the pioneers of Australian armour, who combined speed, firepower, and manoeuvre into start of a tactical doctrine that continues in the modern world. (Morgan collection ATM.LC.HM.100).

DRAMATIS PERSONAE
OF THE MOTOR PATROL

59. The 'originals' of the 1st Australian Armoured Car Section as they appeared prior to embarkation. Members had funded, designed and constructed Australia's first armoured fighting vehicles (Harkin collection ATM.LCP.HH.004).

The 'originals' of 1916–20:
Captain E.H. James, RVO, MC & Bar, VD
Lieutenant P.V.R. Cornwell
Sergeant I.S. Young
Sergeant H. Creek, DCM, RVM
Motor Transport Driver R.W. McGibbon
Lance Corporal O.H. Hyman
Lance Corporal W.P. Thompson
Motor Transport Driver H.L.F. Harkin, RMV
Lance Sergeant L.G. Millar
Motor Transport Driver G.A. McKay
Lance Corporal N.S. Bisset
Motor Transport Driver S.G. Jones
Sergeant J.H. Langley, DCM & Bar
Corporal G.F. Morgan

THE MEN OF THE ORIGINAL ARMOURED CAR SECTION[6]

The Armoured Car Section (later the 1st Australian Light Car Patrol) was unique in the Australian Imperial Force (AIF), as it was a self-contained unit with just 33 men serving between its formation in 1915 and disbandment in 1919. As such, it has been possible to trace the lives of all these men and identify trends such as factors in their enlistment and those that influenced their lives.

60: Ernest James behind the wheel of an early motorcar. James passionately embraced motorcars in the years prior to the Great War (James collection ATM LCP.EJ.001).

The unit consisted of two distinct groups. The first group comprised the 'originals' —James' motoring enthusiasts of 1915–16 who committed time, effort and finances to make his vision a reality. As the war progressed, the circumstances of military service saw a call for reinforcements as members of the original group were transferred to other units. The second group consisted of reinforcements who were already serving in the Middle East when the Armoured Car Section arrived in August 1916. It is evident that, while these two groups were different in many ways, they also had a great deal in common.

The demographics of the 1916 Armoured Car Section originals reveal some interesting trends. The youngest member at the time of enlistment was Driver Harkin who was just 18, the oldest Lance Corporal Thompson, who was 41 years of age. The average age was 28. All were native-born Australians and only Driver Hyman had ancestors who hailed from outside the Anglo-Irish tradition.

Religious affiliations show an overwhelmingly protestant influence as six were members of the Church of England, seven were Presbyterians and one Methodist. The originals were all Victorian apart from Hyman, who was South Australian and the lone enlistee from outside Victoria. Five men were married, the rest single.

In terms of the rural-urban divide, eight came from either Melbourne or Adelaide while six hailed from regional centres or smaller country towns. Thus 57% could be described as being of urban origin. However, the occupational status of the section reveals that none came from a traditional rural occupation. Nine members or 64% claimed engineering and technical backgrounds, and the remaining five came from the commercial world. Some men listed their occupations variously. Sergeant Young, for example, described himself as a clerk on some documents but not on others. It is evident, however, that all members were employed at the time of their enlistment.

There are several indicators of wealth or social class. At least five original members were educated at elite private school such as Coburg and Geelong Colleges, Melbourne and Trinity Grammars. Four held qualifications such as engineering or accountancy that required recognised qualifications. At least four members made significant financial donations to James' project: Cornwell and Young donated expensive private motorcars, Thompson and Hyman made significant financial contributions. In Hyman's case the figure of £100 was quoted. A comparison of this donation to his pay rate of 8/- per day as a motor transport driver suggests that he had donated 250 days' pay just to join the unit!

The originals and their families were also active citizens within their communities. Among their parents and grandparents were a member of the Victorian Legislative Assembly, the Secretary of Education, a magistrate, one doctor, two Justices of the Peace, two Shire Presidents and an Anglican bishop. Both Cornwell and Young are recorded as benefactors to local charities and good causes.

Sporting achievements are also evident in the pre-war lives of the originals and during their military service. Local newspapers of the period recorded the cricketing and football achievements of Young, Hyman and Creek. Hyman was a gifted athlete, raced at the top professional levels in his native South Australia, Western Australia and Victoria, and played in both the South Australian and Victorian Football Leagues. Young and Hyman both owned racehorses. Millar managed the Richmond Racetrack where both horse and motor racing took place. Cornwell embraced speed racing of both cars and motorboats. In 1914 he and his brother won the Australian Motorboat Championship in Sydney.

61. Cadet Corporal Henry Harkin of the Melbourne Grammar School Cadet Unit. Many members of the AIF had their first military experience in the cadets or Militia (Harkin collection ATM LCP.HH.002).

Membership of the Militia and rifle clubs was also popular in Federation Australia. Of the originals, Captain James was the first to enter military service with the Victorian Defence Force prior to Federation, later serving with the 5th Australian Infantry Regiment, Commonwealth Military Forces, although by 1914 he had transferred to the Reserve of Officers. Millar had served in the Senior Cadets and with the Victorian Bushmen and Imperial Forces in the South African War. Sergeant Langley and Driver Morgan served with the 66th Infantry and Driver McGibbon with the Fortress Engineers. Others had also served in the cadet system. It is apparent that there were at least five members of the originals who had some military experience prior to 1915. A late arrival to the unit was Driver Bisset who had returned from service at Gallipoli in 1915.

A typical member of the 1915–16 originals would be protestant, 28 years of age, well educated by the standards of the day, employed in a technical or professional role, single, Victorian, and have Anglo-Irish ancestry.

On departure in 1916, the 1st Australian Armoured Car Section would boast significant engineering, technical and driving experience in its ranks. There was also a range of prior military experience, with several having served in the Citizen Military Force (CMF) and two seeing active service either in South Africa or the 1915 Gallipoli campaign.[7]

Unlike most other units of the AIF, the 1st Australian Armoured Car Section, and later the 1st Australian Light Car Patrol, did not receive dedicated reinforcement drafts from Australia. New members to fill vacancies and bring the unit up to strength came from the resources of the Australian Mounted Division. In all, 19 officers and men joined the 1st Australian Light Car Patrol between May 1917 and January 1918. The reinforcements present a very different profile to the men of 1915–16.

Ernest Homewood James
MVO, MC & Bar, VD

Ernest Homewood James was born in Richmond, Victoria, on 22 November 1879, the son of Charles and Mary James. Charles James was a prominent public servant who at one stage served as the Victorian Secretary for Education. Their son Ernest married Kate Melville, the daughter of the Honourable Donald Melville, MLC, and Catherine Melville at Brunswick in March 1909. In 1910 Ernest and Kate's only child, Alice James, was born in Hawthorn.

62. The wedding party of Lieutenant Ernest James and Kate Melville in Brunswick in 1908. Next to James is Lieutenant Colonel Elliot, DCM. The Militia had been part of James' life since the late 1890s (James collection ATM LCP.EJ.001).

Ernest James demonstrated a passion for engineering and motor transport from an early age. An article in the Melbourne *Argus* in 1938 reported: 'One of his earliest recollections is being found in the pool of oil beneath an engine at the Centennial International Exhibition of 1888 by an anxious mother who had searched several hours for her mechanically minded son.' His experience in automotive design and construction dated back to the 1890s when he witnessed the construction of the first successful steam-driven car built in Australia by Herbert Thompson of Armadale. At the age of 18, he and his brother Cyril built one of the first steam-driven launches on the Yarra River. James also developed a lifelong interest in scale models.

63 Pre-embarkation studio portrait of Lieutenant Ernest Homewood James, taken at Broadmeadows Camp in May 1916. The portrait is part of the Darge Photographic Company collection. The Darge company had a concession to photograph personnel at both Broadmeadows and Seymour camps. The portraits of several members of the 1st Armoured Car Section were consecutively numbered by the Darge staff, indicating the unit's personnel were all in attendance at Broadmeadows Camp at the same time, probably to make final preparations for overseas service (AWM DACS0120).

James' military career began when he enlisted in the Victorian Military Forces circa 1897 and served with the Senior Cadets and 1st Victorian Infantry Regiment. With the formation of the Commonwealth, he transferred to the Australian Military Forces (AMF) on 1 July 1903 and served with the 5th Australian Infantry Regiment. On 28 August 1911 he transferred to the Reserve of Officers (3rd Military District).

In 1914 he appears on the electoral roll as a merchant residing in Riversdale Road, Hawthorn, Victoria. On other documentation his occupation is shown as an engineer. In the Edwardian years James promoted various technical innovations such as the use of suction gas technology for the lighting and heating of the greater Melbourne area. The interest in motor vehicles seems a logical extension of his childhood passion.

On the outbreak of the Great War in August 1914 James was one of a small group of motoring enthusiasts who pressured the Commonwealth government over the potential value of armoured cars as a weapon of war. At first James' efforts made little headway with the Commonwealth, but later, with the support of Colonel Osborne of the Motor Transport Board, approval was granted for the design and construction of two armoured cars, a tender and a motorcycle with sidecar. The Vulcan Engineering Works in South Melbourne provided workshop space and support for this grand design.

Lieutenant James was transferred from the Reserve of Officers to the CMF on 1 April 1915 and posted to the 38th Fortress Company, Australian Engineers. From this posting, Lieutenant James oversaw the construction of the vehicles and recruitment for the Armoured Car Section. On 3 March 1916 Lieutenant James was appointed Officer Commanding the 1st Australian Armoured Car Section, Australian Motor Machine Gun Corps, AIF. He transferred to the AIF on the same day.

Lieutenant James and his section embarked for overseas service on HMAT A13 *Katuna* in Port Melbourne on 20 June 1916. Disembarking at Port Tewfik, Egypt, the 1st Australian Armoured Car Section joined the Egyptian Expeditionary Force on 9 August 1916. The section soon entrained for southern Egypt to serve with the British 11th and 12th Light Armoured Car Batteries in operations against the Senussi tribesmen. On 3 December 1916 Lieutenant James received orders that the section was to be redesignated the 1st Australian Light Car Patrol. They were to hand in their vehicles and would be re-equipped with Model T Fords. On 1 January 1917 James was promoted captain. Between January 1917 and the Light Car Patrol's disbandment in 1919, Captain James remained as officer commanding.

Captain James was recognised for his leadership in January 1919 with the award of the Military Cross 'for continuous good work in command of his unit when he showed marked zeal and ability especially when acting with cavalry reconnaissances.' In March 1919, a second Military Cross was awarded for actions 'at Aleppo, on 24 and 25 October 1918, [where] he displayed great dash and perseverance in the way he attacked and drove enemy cavalry off the hills south of the town. He so disposed his cars that he held a strong force of enemy in check and denied them the crest and observation. All through the operations he displayed courage and resourcefulness.'

Captain James embarked on the *Kaiser-i-Hind* at Port Said, Egypt, on 15 May 1919 and disembarked at Port Melbourne on 23 June 1919. On return to Melbourne he did not seek an early discharge but was retained for duties with the entourage of His Royal Highness the Prince of Wales. James was to control six motorcars and their drivers as the Prince of Wales toured south-eastern Australia. For his services during this royal visit, Captain James was awarded the Royal Victorian Order (5th Class) in October 1920. In the same year he was also awarded the Volunteers Decoration.[8]

Captain James' appointment to the AIF was terminated in Melbourne on 29 October 1920. For his services he had been awarded the Royal Victorian Order, the Military Cross and Bar, the British War and Victory Medals, the Volunteers Decoration and the Returned Soldier's Badge.

Captain James resumed his service in the CMF with the 38th Fortress Engineers Company in South Melbourne on 1 January 1920. He transferred to the Reserve of Officers on 1 April 1924. His period of military service finally ended when he was placed on the retired list with the rank of honorary major on 31 March 1942.

James always remained a passionate advocate for Australia's automotive future. In 1923, while Assistant Controller of the Australasian Equipment Company Ltd, he wrote a detailed letter to Melbourne's *Argus* newspaper promoting the use of buses to ease congestion on Melbourne roads. Several other letters would appear in Melbourne newspapers promoting motoring interests. In 1924 James was the secretary of the Australian Omnibus Company of Victoria Street, Melbourne. Around 1930 James and a friend established the Model Dockyard in Swanston Street, a business that would become a Melbourne institution. While running this store James, a renowned maker of scale models, fostered several modelling clubs.

Like many old soldiers James retained his interest in the Australian Army. During the Second World War he wrote an extended letter to the Army outlining the tactical use of light cars and advocating their employment with the Volunteer Defence Corps (VDC). Later he donated his papers to the Royal Australian Armoured Corps Directorate. These were 'lost' for a time but have since found their way to the Army Tank Museum in Puckapunyal. The Army newspaper and RAAC Bulletin reported James' death and described him as one of the Army's most colourful characters. Both publications also included a reflection James had made on his service: 'My worst job in the Army was acting lance corporal. I had everybody on my back at the same time!' James died in Heidelberg, Victoria, in 1960.

Percy Reginald Vernon Cornwell

Percy Reginald Vernon Cornwell was born in Brunswick, Victoria, on 23 August 1882, the son of Alfred and Eleanor Cornwell. Alfred was an immigrant from Cambridge, England, and Eleanor a native of Wicklow in Ireland. Alfred established the colony of Victoria's first industrial pottery kiln in Phoenix Street, Brunswick, in 1859.[9] By 1900 Cornwell's Pottery was a successful business, providing stoneware pipes to various municipalities throughout Victoria as well as exporting to the Americas.

Percy Cornwell was educated at Brunswick College where he attained excellent academic results.[10] In 1905 he joined Cornwell's Pottery as an apprentice, learning the manufacturing aspects of the family enterprise from the 'bottom up'. Between 1910 and 1912 he graduated to travelling for the firm. He and his brother Fredrick were well schooled in all aspects of the business when they assumed management of the kilns and associated business in 1912.

Cornwell's inclusion in Ernest James' group of motoring enthusiasts in August 1914 would have come as little surprise to those who knew him. Cornwell, like many well-to-do businessmen of the Edwardian era, lived a life in which public service and the adoption of new ideas and challenges were considered a civic duty. Cornwell embraced both charitable works and the internal combustion engine with equal zest.

In October 1904 the *Brunswick Leader* reported a singing competition held in the Brunswick Town Hall for the benefit of the La Trobe Street Ragged Boys Mission and Home. As secretary, Cornwell was described as having worked 'indefatigably to make the competition a success.'[11] In 1909 Cornwell's Pottery celebrated its Golden Jubilee and Percy Cornwell assumed a major role in organising the festivities. These included a works picnic at Mordialloc where he expended much effort in organising sports and entertainment for his workers.

The day concluded with speeches that provide a genuine insight into the firm's success: the engineering skills and innovation of Cr Allard, the works manager, the sense of community and common purpose, and the manufacture of a product that was 'second to none'. The final presentation on behalf of the staff was to 'Mr. Percy Cornwell on the occasion of the jubilee of his father's works' and expressed the hope that 'as he was only a young man, he would live long and be a credit to the works.'[12] In 1914 Cornwell demonstrated his patriotic spirit by presenting revolvers to staff members who were leaving the firm to enlist in the AIF.[13]

64 Portrait of Second Lieutenant Percy Cornwell, taken at Broadmeadows Camp in May 1916. Cornwell was a well-known motor racing identity who donated his private vehicle for conversion as an armoured car (AWM DACS0119).

Percy and his brother Fredrick shared a love of speed and Percy raced both cars and powerboats. In early 1913 he toured New Zealand with his motorcar, demonstrating racing techniques, the *New Zealand* newspaper even reporting a crash at Alexandra Park. After returning to Australia Percy became involved in the Richmond races. In November he lent his 90hp Mercedes racing car to the American Douglas Campbell who raced at the Richmond Race Track before a crowd of 10,000 which reportedly attended with the 'half pleasurable anticipation of an accident.'[14] Cornwell also raced that day in the ten-mile event, although the race was forced to an early stop by rain. In February 1914 the Cornwell brothers travelled to Sydney Harbour with their boat the *Nautilus II* to compete in the Motorboat Championship of Australia. Percy sped overland from Melbourne to Sydney in his 75hp Mercedes, while Frederick embarked on the more traditional means of transport between capitals, the steamer *Yarra*.[15] The championship boat race was conducted between Rose Bay and Manly. The *Leader* reported, 'The Victorian boat beat her rival easily. Fred and Percy Cornwell had their engines in perfect order and maintained an average speed of 85 miles per hour.'[16] Percy also had interests in less frenetic sports as a member of the Melbourne Cricket Club.

By the outbreak of the Great War in August 1914, Cornwell had established himself as a successful community leader, businessman and sportsman. He appears on the electoral roll as a manger residing at 'The Grove', 35 Moreland Road, Brunswick. His attestation papers in 1915 noted that he was a mechanical engineer.

It is unclear when or how Cornwell became involved in James' group of car enthusiasts. The first clear evidence can be found in late August 1915 when the Melbourne *Leader* newspaper reported in its motoring column 'Motors and Motoring': 'The Armour of the experimental armoured cars has been tested and the work of constructing them is now in hand. Mr. Percy Cornwell has donated a powerful car, to be transformed into one of these war machines. He has volunteered to take an armoured car to Gallipoli.'[17]

In Australia prior to the Great War, the supply of a motorcar to the Department of Defence also gained the donor an honorary commission. However, Cornwell's engineering, manufacturing and motoring experience would have made him a natural candidate for a leadership role in the new Armoured Car Section. Cornwell's donation of a Mercedes is consistent with his previous history of public service and interest in motorcars.

65 Lieutenant Percy Cornwell leaning over the engine of a Rolls Royce. Cornwell's engineering abilities proved an asset to both the Australian Light Car Patrol and the British units (Young collection ATM LCP.IY.240).

Cornwell's military service began when he was appointed provisional lieutenant in the CMF on 10 October 1915 and posted to the 38th Fortress Company, Australian Engineers. From this posting, Lieutenant Cornwell assisted with the construction of the armoured vehicles and the training of the Armoured Car Section. On 16 March 1916 Lieutenant Cornwell was appointed second lieutenant in the 1st Australian Armoured Car Section, Australian Motor Machine Gun Corps, AIF. He was administratively transferred to the AIF on the same day. In March 1916 Second Lieutenant Cornwell attended a Special Machine Gun Course in Randwick, New South Wales (NSW).

Prior to his departure on active service, Cornwell was given a send-off by the members of the Victorian Stoneware Pipe, Tile and Potter Manufacturers Association at Café Francis where his generosity and patriotism were recognised with the presentation of a portable typewriter suitable for use on active service.[18]

Second Lieutenant Cornwell and the other members of the Armoured Car Section and their vehicles embarked for overseas service on HMAT A13 *Katuna* in Port Melbourne on 20 June 1916. Disembarking at Port Tewfik, Egypt, the 1st Australian Armoured Car Section joined the Egyptian Expeditionary Force on 9 August 1916. The section soon entrained for southern Egypt to serve with the British Army's 11th and 12th Light Armoured Car Batteries in operations against the Senussi tribesmen. The section was later redesignated the

1st Australian Light Car Patrol and re-equipped with Model T Fords. On 1 January 1917 Cornwell was promoted lieutenant. He remained with the 1st Australian Light Car Patrol for the majority of the Palestine Campaign other than for some brief periods of hospitalisation, training and a detachment to the Topographical Survey Section, Sinai, at Khan Yunus between 15 May and 18 September 1917. On 1 February 1919 he left the 1st Australian Light Car Patrol to return to Australia on compassionate grounds. He embarked on the HMAT A11 *Ascanius* at Suez on 21 February 1919 and disembarked in Port Melbourne on 3 April 1919.

Lieutenant Cornwell's appointment to the AIF was terminated in Melbourne on 11 May 1919. For his services he was awarded the British War and Victory Medals and the Returned Soldier's Badge. Lieutenant Cornwell was appointed to the Reserve of Officers, Australian Engineers, on 1 November 1920. He continued in that capacity until placed on the retired list on 30 June 1942.

On return to Australia in 1919 Cornwell returned to his role at Cornwell's Pottery works. On 21 January 1920 he married Adele Sleeman. In the early 1920s Cornwell renovated 'Annandale' in Waterdale Road, Ivanhoe, his home showcasing the terracotta products of Cornwell's Pottery works.[19] In the late 1940s the Cornwells relocated to Glenferry Road in Malvern. Percy Cornwell died in Armadale on 26 April 1962 and was cremated at the Springvale Cemetery where his ashes were interred in the memorial garden.

Ivan Sinclair Young, J. P.

Ivan Sinclair Young was born in Nhill, Victoria, on 7 July 1889, the son of John and Louisa Young. John Young was a prominent Wimmera businessman and citizen with interests in agriculture and stock and station supplies. He was also the president, at various times, of the Nhill Agricultural Society and Shire Council, member of the Nhill Water Trust, and a Justice of the Peace.[20] By the outbreak of the Great War, Young Brothers Auctioneers, Stock and Station Agents, was a well-established trading company in the Wimmera region.

Ivan was educated at the Nhill School and Geelong College, where he distinguished himself in academics and sport.[21] He pursued higher education at Roseworthy Agricultural College in Adelaide, South Australia, in 1911 where he graduated with first class honours in dairying and surveying. He was also an active sportsman, batting for the Nhill cricket team, playing golf, and as a member of the Nhill Football Club. In 1914 Young showed an interest in politics, becoming secretary of the Nhill branch of the People's Party.[22]

Ivan Young enlisted in the AIF in Melbourne on 9 July 1915 and was allocated to C Company, 31st Infantry Battalion. In Broadmeadows Camp, Young was reunited with Private Herbert Creek, who was formerly employed by Young Brothers as a mechanic, and friend Sergeant John Langley of Bendigo. All three men would soon be recruited into the new Armoured Car Section.

Young's enlistment was not as straightforward as his service record indicates. Young had donated his private car, a Daimler, to provide a chassis for Captain James' project. This action gained him a position in the Armoured Car Section and promotion to sergeant on 19 January 1916. As part of James' team he assisted in the conversion of the vehicles to armoured cars.

66 Sergeant Ivan Young, who donated his Daimler car for conversion to the armoured car 'Gentle Annie', photographed in the Darge Photographic Company's temporary studio at Broadmeadows Camp, Victoria, in May 1916 (AWM DACS0131).

67. Lieutenant Ivan Young, Australian Flying Corps, wearing his flying suit at Bishop's Court, Bendigo, in 1918 (Young collection ATM LCP.IY.249).

The *Horsham Times* records the emotion and patriotic feelings of the time that characterised Private Young's farewell at Nhill's Royal Hotel, which it reported in detail:

A social to Private Ivan Young was tendered at the Royal Hotel, when the occasion was also availed to say good-bye to Sergeant J. Langley and Corporal W. Nunan. Private Young was handed a gold-mounted fountain pen and wished well by his friends. In acknowledging the toast of the parents, Mr. John Young said that right from the beginning he knew well that Ivan wanted to enlist. Had he been in his son's place he would also have enlisted for active service. He knew how Ivan felt, and told him if he desired to go to the front he would not stand in his way. The titanic struggle was not a question of "my country, right or wrong" but right against being completely crushed, before a lasting and honourable peace, could be attained. Realizing that Great Britain had entered into this great conflict on the side of liberty, justice and freedom, Mrs. Young and himself offered not the least objection to Ivan's decision to volunteer for active service.[23]

Sergeant Young embarked for overseas service on HMAT A13 *Katuna* in Port Melbourne on 20 June, disembarking at Port Tewfik, Egypt, where the 1st Australian Armoured Car Section joined the Egyptian Expeditionary Force on 9 August 1916. Young remained with the 1st Australian Armoured Car Section and later the 1st Australian Light Car Patrol during the Egyptian Campaign until March 1917 when a new opportunity presented itself.

On 10 March Young was detached from the Light Car Patrol to attend a school of instruction at Abbassia. Having completed the course, he proceeded to the School of Aeronautics on 24 March and was taken on strength by the 58th Reserve Squadron, Royal Flying Corps (RFC), on 12 April. Between 6 and 15 May he attended a wireless course at the School of Aero Gunnery at 20th Wing, RFC. On graduation he was promoted second lieutenant and, on 26 May, posted to the 67th Squadron, Australian Flying Corps (AFC), at Moascar as an air observer.

The *Nhill Free Press* published a letter from Lieutenant Young in September 1917 in which he describes his experiences in the AFC:

Things are pretty quiet here for the present. We were at Jaffa for a while but have now shifted to a place called Din el Bulah right in amongst thick orchards of big fig trees and vines which at present are laden with fruit which should be ripe in about a month. It's as hot as anything, but luckily we have a sea bath fairly often. As you know we are still in front of Sampson's city, Gaza, which the Turks strongly hold and with whom we had two scraps, called the first and second battles of Gaza. Some people at home think it's a holiday out here. Old Gallipoli men say that April 19 was worse than any day they had on the Peninsula. We have just about got on even terms with the Hun in the air. So far I've been lucky enough to dodge any stray Huns and their "Archies". The latter is the thing to shake you up. When you are sailing round at 7000 or 8000 feet viewing proceedings below, High Explosive or shrapnel bursts fairly close and you hear the pieces whistle, you are wondering all the time if they've chipped any part of the machine or whether it will collapse with you and it's a dammed long way down to mother earth. The armored cars are near here on our right flank with the Light Horse at a place called To el Para; it's very interesting seeing these old biblical places even if it's from a fair height. Have seen Jerusalem and the Dead Sea from a distance and have sailed over Beersheba, Hebron, Giza, Irgey, Hareira, Sharia, and other places, and you get a few "Archies" put up at you from most of them, so, needless to say, one doesn't dwell for a week over them. We have lost two men in the last couple of weeks, so we have just about got the Hun bluffed; for the previous couple of months our air casualties were very heavy. You ought to see the caterpillar tractors here pulling enormous loads over sand dunes. They are built on the same principle as the tanks and no sand dunes ever made will stop them. Remember me to all the boys.[24]

In July 1917 John Young Senior died suddenly in Nhill, leaving the management of Young Brothers in serious difficulties.[25] Soon after, Lieutenant Young was granted compassionate leave to return to Australia to settle his father's estate.[26] He embarked on the HMAT A42 *Boorara* at Suez on 23 August and disembarked in Port Melbourne on 27 September.

Lieutenant Young's appointment to the AIF was terminated in Melbourne on 22 October 1917. For his services he was awarded the British War and Victory Medals and the Returned Soldier's Badge.[27] Lieutenant Young was appointed to the Reserve of Officers in 1920 and remained on the reserve list until the 1930s when he returned to the Militia as Officer Commanding B Squadron of the newly raised 19th Light Horse (Armoured Car) Regiment. He relinquished this position when he left the district and returned to the Reserve of Officers.[28] He was placed on the retired list on 19 December 1944 with the rank of honorary captain in the Australian Armoured Corps.[29]

Young's return to Nhill appears to have been not altogether a pleasant experience. His late father had been a strong advocate for the introduction of conscription in 1916; furthermore, many local families had suffered hardship caused by the absence of fathers, sons and husbands on active service. Nhill also had many entries on the local honour roll by the end of 1917. Lieutenant Young's return on compassionate and business grounds caused significant disquiet in some sections of the community. By December the local Member of the House of Representatives, Mr A.S. Rodgers, had entered the debate when he spoke at a Reinforcements Referendum Campaign at Nhill's Theatre Royal:

Before he commenced his address Mr. Rodgers said he wanted to refer to another matter, a matter which caused him considerable pain, viz the fact that certain people had seen fit to defame Lieutenant Ivan S. Young of the Royal Australian Flying Corps. Now he wanted the true facts in regard to Lieutenant Young's case to be known to the people of Nhill and District. On July 3rd last. Mr. John Young died. Lieutenant

Young was on active service, and a cable was dispatched asking for leave of absence for Lieutenant Young, which was granted. Mr. Thomas Young, of Horsham, one of the principals of Messrs. Young Brothers interviewed the speaker and said he believed the altered circumstances with regard to the family life and business in Nhill, which represented the life's work of the late Mr. Young, were such that Lieutenant Young should take up his father's and the family's responsibilities, he being the only male member of the family — the mother being in delicate health and there being only two single daughters and the latter could not be expected to supervise family and business matters.

He (Mr. Rodgers) was asked to put full particulars of the request before the military authorities which he did; therefore, the proposal was made that Lieutenant Young be relieved from further military duty. He took the full responsibility and submitted to the family request in making the application, and the case rested solely on its merits. His relationship with the Defence Department was purely official. He had no private interview over the matter with the authorities; it was done by official letter, a copy of which Mr. Rodgers read to the audience. However, a somewhat similar case had previously come before the military authorities when the request was granted. Lieutenant Young was still a soldier of the king, he is not yet discharged although, Mr. Rodgers believed that, in the altered circumstances of the family, his request would be granted.

The slanderers of Lieutenant Young doubtless were not aware of the fact that he was on active service for 14 months and 7 months he served against the enemy in the Libyan Desert, and afterwards joined the Royal Australian Flying Corps. For three months now was flying over enemy territory in Palestine where, it is stated, on an average 600 shells per day are fired at each airman who participates in reconnoitring work. It ill becomes anyone in this district to slander a local soldier who has daily risked his life in the defence of his country and for those who remained at home.[30]

On return to Australia, Ivan Young married Nancy Chisholm in Sydney on 20 March 1918. The Reverend Doctor Langley, Bishop of Bendigo, celebrated the wedding. Young became a member of the Nhill Racing Club and a racehorse owner. His love of technological progress also extended to the world of aviation. In 1920 the *Nhill Free Press* reported that he had received a wire from Sir Ross Smith that he would fly his Vickers Vimy over Nhill during his flight from Adelaide to Melbourne.[31] Young Brothers also provided the land for the first aircraft landing ground at Nhill. In November 1933 Young and his wife were part of the official party that greeted Sir Charles Kingsford Smith at Nhill during his visit to the Nhill Aerodrome.[32] Young also showed a keen interest in photography and early home movies.[33]

In the twenties and thirties he was prominent in many community activities in the Nhill district. He retired from an active role in the management of Young Brothers in January 1936, later relocating to central Victoria where he took up the pastoral property Zintara at Trawool. In 1943 he was appointed a Justice of the Peace.[34] Prior to 1949, Young relocated to the Melbourne area where he died in Kew on 12 July 1966.

Ivan Young's son John served as a sergeant in the 2nd Cavalry Division Signals during the Second World War.

Herbert Creek, DCM, RVM

Herbert Creek was born in Hamilton, Victoria, on 2 March 1888, the son of Joseph and Ellen Creek. At the time of his enlistment he was a motor mechanic employed at Young Brothers' Motor Department in Horsham. In 1911 he acted as chauffeur for the Governor of Victoria, Sir Thomas Gibson-Carmichael, when he toured the Western District. Advertisements for new cars sold by Young Brothers in 1914 promised that Bert Creek would act as an instructor to all who purchased cars. Creek was also a talented footballer, playing in the centre for Horsham prior to the Great War.

68. Herbert Creek standing outside McDonald's Motor Garage, Hamilton, circa 1912. Creek would be one of the first men in Victoria to make his living from this new technology (Creek collection ATM LCP.HC.021).

Creek enlisted in the AIF in Melbourne on 2 July 1915. He was taken on strength by A Company, Depot Battalion, at Flemington. On 12 July he was posted to C Company, 31st Infantry Battalion, at Broadmeadows. His former employer, Ivan Young, was also serving in the 31st Battalion and it is likely that Creek accompanied Young to the Royal Park Depot where his mechanical and driving skills were used in the construction of the armoured cars. On 17 January 1916 he was promoted corporal and was taken on strength by the Armoured Car Section. The *Horsham Times* of 15 February reported that Ivan Young and Bert Creek were part of the new Armoured Car Section and that Creek would be a driver.[35]

69. Studio portrait of Corporal Herbert Creek taken at Broadmeadows Camp in May 1916. Creek was later promoted sergeant and commanded one of the 1st Light Car Patrol's gun cars equipped with a Lewis light machine-gun (AWM DACS0132).

Creek embarked for overseas service on HMAT A13 *Katuna* in Port Melbourne on 20 June 1916. After disembarking at Port Tewfik, Egypt, the 1st Australian Armoured Car Section joined the Egyptian Expeditionary Force on 9 August 1916. The section soon entrained for southern Egypt to serve with the British 11th and 12th Light Armoured Car Batteries in operations against the Senussi tribesmen.

On 1 August 1917 Creek was promoted sergeant. Other than a period of hospitalisation for malaria in early 1918, Creek remained with the Light Car Patrol in the Palestine Campaign until the end of hostilities. On 20 September 1918 Creek's driving skills and courage were tested close to Ajule where his patrol encountered three enemy motor lorries containing men and equipment. He boldly cut the lorries' avenue of escape, forcing them to surrender. For this action he was awarded the Distinguished Conduct Medal.

In December 1918 an extended letter from Bert Creek appeared in the *Hamilton Spectator*:

Private Bert Creek, who up to the time of his enlistment was employed in Messrs. Young Brothers motor department Horsham, writing to his mother from Damascus, states "that the Allied advance from the Dead Sea to Damascus was an eventful one". At the time of writing (October 11) he was quartered on the outskirts of the city. "The place," he added, "was rather out of order when we got there, but our people are getting it cleaned up, and put in order. The trams were not running, but were getting ready." On the advance, sometimes travelling all night, the Allies captured in one instance an aerodrome, four aeroplanes, motorcars, motor lorries, and a quantity of material. At Bieran they had practically surrounded the Turkish army, so they stayed there patrolling the roads and collecting prisoners who were wandering about in all directions, and did not know what to do or where to go. At Iliafia, Private Creek's patrol, the only Australians among the British and Indian troops, watched the coast for 20 miles. Subsequently they proceeded through Nazareth and on to Tiberius (where they had a swim in the lake), crossing the Jordan at Lake Hula, and then the advance proceeded to Damascus. The Turks burnt their petrol and ammunition dumps, and "it was", Private Creek adds, "the biggest and best fire I have ever seen." Next morning, the town was theirs, and Private Creek, who escorted the general through the town, states that the population came out into the streets and cheered and clapped. Nearly all the prisoners taken were in a state of starvation, and although the army of occupation was put on half rations in order that the prisoners might be fed, the latter died in hundreds. As there were a lot of grapes, vegetables, and sheep about, he could not understand why the Turks starved. The 150 miles' advance had been somewhat difficult, and supplies had to be kept up to the troops by means of motor lorries but when the railways were running again things would improve.[36]

On 15 March 1919 Creek was posted to the AIF Details Camp pending his return to Australia. He embarked on the HT *Kaiser-i-Hind* at Suez on 16 May and disembarked in Port Melbourne 16 June. Sergeant Creek was discharged on 31 July. For his service he was entitled to the Distinguished Conduct, British War and Victory Medals and the Returned Soldier's Badge.[37]

On arrival in Australia, he joined the 1919 Royal Tour of His Royal Highness the Prince of Wales as a driver, along with Motor Transport Driver Harkin, another former Light Car Patrol driver. The *Horsham Times* newspaper reported that Sergeant Herbert Creek of Horsham, son of

> Mr. and Mrs. Joseph Creek, of Hamilton, was employed as one of the drivers in connection with the visit of HRH The Prince of Wales, on his recent visit, had a unique compliment paid to him. At the Prince's request he was invited on board HMS *Renown*, and made the recipient of a valuable tie pin and decorated with the Victoria Medal in recognition of the faithful and conscientious manner in which he had discharged his duties. There are only six Victoria medallists in Australia, so that the honor conferred on Sergeant Creek is a valued one. The Prince also gave one of his photographs to Sergeant Creek.[38]

70. Herbert Creek at the wheel of HRH the Prince of Wales' limousine during the Prince's Australian tour (Creek collection ATM LCP.HC.032).

In 1954 Bert Creek recalled his time with the Prince of Wales to a South Australian journalist who wrote that Creek was:

No. 1 of four chauffeurs engaged to drive the Prince of Wales on HRH's Australian tour. "I drove the Prince round when he had an extra seven days off the record," Bert told us. "He went along very quietly. I took him to Caulfield where he tried a horse over the fences and to Elsternwick for golf, to Morphettville racecourse for another private ride." Lord Mountbatten was the Prince's companion on these unofficial trips. The Prince was a likeable man. "When he said goodbye on the Man-o-War steps in Sydney Harbour, he gave us an autographed photograph of himself, and a medal. He also gave me a platinum tie pin with his crest on it." Bert Creek won the DCM in Palestine with the Armoured Car Section (Capt. E. H. James, MC).[39]

For this service Creek was awarded the Royal Victorian Medal on 1 January 1920.

After the Royal Tour, Creek returned to Horsham where he resumed his trade as a mechanic and hire car operator. He married Mary McClounan at the Presbyterian Church in Horsham on 18 September 1922. It is apparent that Creek lived a colourful life. In September 1930 the *Horsham Times* newspaper reported on a raid by Melbourne detectives at the Royal Hotel where off-course gambling was taking place. Creek, with fellow returned soldier Murphy, were charged with being 'SP bookies'.[40] Later,

… in the Magistrates Court the police prosecutor called for a minimum penalty of £20 be imposed. Murphy was a returned soldier and was incapacitated from work by war wounds and he was trying to eke out a living in these unfortunate circumstances. Mr. Bennett entered a plea for Creek, who was also a returned soldier, and added that the defendant had already been fined £20; he had been awarded high war honours and had served the Prince of Wales as a motor driver. If the defendant were fined it would inflict great hardship. The prosecuting sergeant suggested to the Magistrate that the further hearing of the defendant's case be adjourned. Mr. Bennett: "It would be a better corrective than penalizing him." The Magistrate asked defendant Creek, "if he was prepared to give up the practice." The defendant said he was prepared to do so as a licensed bookmaker because he could not follow his trade of a motor mechanic. The Magistrate said: "You see betting is not a very profitable game." Defendant Creek replied: "Not after today!"[41]

In his later years, Creek was interviewed several times by journalists about his experiences in the Great War and the 1919 Royal Tour. Herbert Creek retired to an aged care home in Bendigo where he died on 8 April 1980.

Robert Wilson McGibbon

Robert Wilson McGibbon was born in Albert Park, Victoria, on 11 June 1896, the son of John and Mary Margret McGibbon. At the time of his enlistment he was a mechanic residing in Mowbray Street, Albert Park.

71. Portrait of Driver Robert McGibbon, one of the 1st Armoured Car Section 'originals', who transferred to the Australian Flying Corps as an air mechanic in August 1917. At war's end he remained in Palestine working with the American Red Cross where he met his future wife, Ruby, an American nurse. The McGibbons eventually settled in Maryland, USA (AWM DACS0126).

McGibbon enlisted in the 34th Electrical Company, Australian Engineers, CMF, in Melbourne in June 1915. He transferred to the AIF in Melbourne on 25 March 1916. On 3 April he was posted to C Company, 22nd Depot Battalion, at Royal Park, followed by a posting to the 24th Depot Battalion at Royal Park on 12 May.

On 20 June McGibbon was taken on strength by the Armoured Car Section as a motor transport driver and embarked for overseas service on HMAT A13 *Katuna* in Port Melbourne. After disembarking at Port Tewfik, Egypt, the 1st Australian Armoured Car Section joined the Egyptian Expeditionary Force on 9 August. The section soon entrained for southern Egypt to serve with the British 11th and 12th Light Armoured Car Batteries in operations against the Senussi tribesmen. On 8 December the section was redesignated the 1st Australian Light Car Patrol and re-equipped with Model T Fords.

On 6 August 1917 McGibbon was posted to the 67th Squadron, RFC (later 1st Squadron, AFC), and was mustered as a second class air mechanic (fitter and turner). He was promoted to first class air mechanic on 1 March 1918. On 19 July he was re-mustered as a motor transport driver.

In January 1919 McGibbon was approached by the American Red Cross in Palestine and the Near East with an offer to take charge of the repair workshops in Jerusalem. He accepted this offer and was discharged in Cairo on 11 February. McGibbon's further service in Palestine with the Red Cross is undocumented. For his service in the AIF he was entitled to the British War and Victory Medals and the Returned Soldier's Badge.[42]

McGibbon returned to Australia in 1920 with an American war bride, Ruby, who had served as a nurse with American forces during the war.[43] They settled in Abbotsford, Victoria, where he resumed his civilian engineering trade, However his return to Australia was short-lived as the McGibbons emigrated to the United States (US) in 1925. Robert travelled to the UK and resided briefly at Jeaturgh Road in London prior to embarking on the SS *Minnekahda* for New York on 11 July. The McGibbons settled in Midland, Maryland, where he worked as a machinist and, in November 1925, became a US citizen. The family finally settled in Allegany, Maryland, where McGibbon worked for the Celanese Corporation of America. During the Second World War there are numerous reports in the Cumberland newspapers of the McGibbons' undertaking Red Cross and hospital work. In 1942 McGibbon registered for Selective Service but was not called up. Robert McGibbon died in Washington, District of Columbia.

During World War II, McGibbon's father, John McGibbon, served in the CMF as a corporal with the 115th Australian Military Hospital at Heidelberg between 1941 and 1947. McGibbon's son, David Allan McGibbon, served in Headquarters 2nd Battalion, 115th Infantry Regiment of the Maryland National Guard.[44]

Oscar Henric Hyman

Oscar Henric Hyman was born in Mitcham, South Australia, on 25 November 1877, the son of Robert and Sarah Hyman. He married Harriette Brennan on 16 November 1898. Hyman held the licenses for several hotels in the Adelaide area including the General Havelock, the Caledonian, Earl of Zetland, and the United Service Club. At the time of enlistment in 1916 he was a licensed victualler and resided in Dover Street, Malvern, South Australia.

Prior to the Great War, Hyman demonstrated considerable sporting talent, playing Australian Rules Football for South Adelaide in the South Australian Football League and for Collingwood in the Victoria Football League. He concluded his playing career in 1910 having represented South Australia on nine occasions and played 41 games with Collingwood.[45]

In August 1905 Hyman played for Collingwood in a match in Broken Hill. The *Barrier Miner* reported a post-match incident in dramatic terms:

Sunday Night's Outrage. The young man Oscar Hyman, a member of the Collingwood team of footballers, who had his skull fractured by a blow from a stone thrown in Blende Street on Sunday night, is still in the Hospital. He is no worse than he was yesterday. He will require rest and quietness for a time, and will probably be compelled to remain in the institution for a couple of weeks to come. "J.F. Dunn" writes to express his indignation at the fact that a visitor to the city should have been treated as Oscar Hyman, the Collingwood footballer, was on Sunday evening. He hastens to insist that the assault was not the work of any worker. Our correspondent's sentiments will be universally shared, but the fact that a man is under arrest on a charge of having assaulted Hyman it is obviously improper to at present discuss the most regrettable happening.[46]

This story appeared in newspapers across Australia. The case's conclusion at the Magistrate's Court in November was reported in some detail:

Stone throwing Outrage. The defence was that the quarrel was caused by the aggressiveness of Hyman and the Collingwood footballers who were in his company on the night of the alleged wounding. William A.

Hutchinson and John Dorman both swore that McCourt acted in self-defence. He, in the first place, courteously bid the Collingwood men 'Good-night,' but received an unseemly reply and was knocked down. Accused went into the witness box and swore that he was set upon by the Collingwood men and knocked down. He got up and tried to get away, but was rushed a second time, and in defence picked up a stone and threw it. He had been very roughly handled by the Collingwood men. After hearing the evidence of these witnesses the jury informed his Honor that they were satisfied accused had acted in self defence, and on his Honor's direction returned a formal verdict of not guilty.[47]

Hyman was also a gifted runner, competing in Western Australia, South Australia and Victoria. In 1896 he won the Sheffield Handicap, South Australia's premier professional athletic event.[48] In 1904 he came third in the Stawell Gift, returning in 1905 and 1906. Hyman's sporting interests also included the owning of racehorses such as Major Booth, which ran in the 1910 South Australian Derby.[49] On Hyman's enlistment in 1916 he was described by the *Barrier Miner* as: 'a good patron of the turf, owning several fair horses, but none of them did much stake collecting.'[50]

At the time of the outbreak of the Great War in 1914, Oscar Hyman was a well-known racing identity and sportsman in South Australia with both family and business responsibilities. Although still fit, he was by then in his late thirties and was under no obligation to enlist. Like several other members of the Armoured Car Section, Hyman's enlistment proved unusual. The 'Sporting Gossip' section of the *Port Pirie Recorder* reported: 'The old Adelaide and Melbourne footballer, Mr. Oscar Hyman, paid £100 to become an Australian soldier. A little while ago two armoured motorcars were presented to the Victorian Military Authorities by a few young men, who, in addition to contributing the cost of the motors, also armed themselves. For his seat, as one of the detachment, Mr. Hyman paid £100. The cars have been taken over by the Military Authorities, and attached to the 22nd Infantry.'[51]

Hyman travelled from South Australia and enlisted in the AIF in Melbourne on 28 March 1916. He was briefly posted to the 22nd Depot Battalion on 3 April but joined the other members of the Armoured Car Section at the 24th Depot Battalion at Royal Park where he would have participated in the final construction work on the armoured cars. On June 20 he was appointed a motor transport driver and taken on strength by the Armoured Car Section, embarking for overseas service on HMAT A13 *Katuna* at Port Melbourne on the same day. Disembarking at Port Tewfik, Egypt, the 1st Australian Armoured Car

Section joined the Egyptian Expeditionary Force on 9 August. The section soon entrained for southern Egypt to serve with the British 11th and 12th Light Armour Car Batteries in operations against the Senussi tribesmen. Hyman was a member of the section when it was re-equipped and designated the 1st Australian Light Car Patrol on 8 December.

72. Driver Oscar Hyman's studio portrait taken at Broadmeadows Camp in May 1916. Hyman was an accomplished athlete and a wealthy hotelier by the time of his enlistment in March 1916 (AWM DACS0127).

Hyman recorded his first Christmas overseas in a letter published in the *Adelaide Register*:

Oscar Hyman, of the Australian Armoured Car Section in Egypt, writing to a friend in Adelaide, says: "I am penning these few lines in the hope that they will be published in the *Register*, just to give the public of South Australia an idea of how our little camp (consisting of small units necessary to keep the advanced base camp going) spent their Christmas Day in the desert.

We are located out in the wilderness, 500 miles from Cairo and 150 miles from the Nile, and, thanks to the generosity of Lieut. Cornwell and the ladies of Australia, we spent a most enjoyable and never-to-be-forgotten day. We were favoured with very fine weather, and a programme of sports arranged by a committee was successfully carried out. Prizes or the most part were donated by Mr. McDiarmid of the Y.M.C.A. A feature of the sports was the donkey race, and it caused endless amusement. The donkeys were specially brought from Kharga, 20 miles away, for the occasion. There was also a tug-of-war between different units (eight men a side), and our unit, the Australian Armoured Car section (now increased to 20 men, in order to take over light car patrol work and responsibility), after beating two other teams, were unlucky enough to run up against a better team in the final. We had one win to our credit, your humble servant succeeding in winning the 100 yards scratch race.

After a very interesting afternoon we left for our respective camps, ready to do justice to the good things in store. Our marquee was decorated with a few flags, and the table set for our Christmas dinner, with 27 of us stated at 6 p.m., Lieut. Cornwell in the chair. A start was made on the good things provided, the menu consisting of pea soup, roast turkey, baked potatoes, plum pudding, trifle, jelly, blancmange, and fruit, walnuts, almonds, raisins, and bonbons.

The liquid refreshments were bottled beer, whisky, and lemonade, so you can see we had a real Christmas dinner. A musical evening followed naturally and several toasts were honoured. The toast of the evening was 'The Ladies' Leagues of Australia', the splendid work done by them in sending 'billies' and Christmas cheer of all description being freely commented on.

They can rest assured that their untiring efforts, accompanied by good wishes, are very much appreciated by the boys so for from home. The work of the women of Australia was an eye opener to those of the Tommy regiments attached to us (who participated), and the toast was followed by prolonged cheering. It was atop a great send off to our unit, who are getting ready to move off to patrol and explore a way to another oasis some 400 miles further into the desert. It will probably mean months and months of work shifting the Senussi tribes."[52]

Hyman served with the 1st Australian Light Car Patrol in Egypt, Palestine and Syria until the end of the Great War, remaining with the unit for the entire campaign other than during brief periods of hospitalisation. He was promoted lance corporal on 8 March 1918. On 15 March 1919 Hyman was posted to the AIF Details Camp pending his return to Australia. He embarked on the HT *Kaiser-i-Hind* at Suez on 16 May and disembarked at Port Adelaide 14 June. Lance Corporal Hyman was discharged on 29 July and was entitled to the British War and Victory Medals and the Returned Soldier's Badge for his service.[53]

Hyman returned to his business commitments and, in April 1922, opened a billiard saloon in Unley.[54] In January 1926 he was appointed the handicapper for the Tattersalls Club.[55] In this new position Hyman became both successful and well respected in racing circles. In 1930 he visited the UK as a representative for Tattersalls. He was later the senior handicapper for the South Australian Jockey Club and the Australian Racing Club. After a long and successful career he retired in June 1948. His retirement was reported in the *Adelaide Chronicle*:

> Mr. Oscar Hyman announced at the weekend that he had resigned as handicapper to the SAJC and ARC. He was appointed in 1941. Mr. Hyman stated in his resignation to the two committees that ill health prevents him from continuing with his duties after the end of the racing season. … Mr. Hyman, who is 70, is widely known in sporting circles and until he was appointed to his present position he was handicapper for Tattersalls Club for 16 years. He was a star footballer in his youth and played league standard in three States. He played with North, South, West Torrens and Sturt. He captained Sturt for two years and led the State team in the 1908 carnival. His last season was 1910. A returned soldier from the First World War, Mr. Hyman saw three years' active service with a fighting unit in Egypt, Palestine and Asia Minor. At a meeting of the committee of the SAJC on Monday it was decided to place on record appreciation of Mr. Hyman's services.[56]

Hyman died in Mitcham on 11 January 1955.

Walter Perrin Thompson

Walter Perrin Thompson was born in Kew, Victoria, in 1874, the son of Henry and Elizabeth Thompson. He married Fanny May White in 1904. The Thompsons had two daughters: Gwyneth, born in 1904 and Elizabeth, who arrived in 1911. The electoral rolls prior to the Great War recorded Thompson as an accountant or merchant residing in the Hawthorn-Kew area. His address on the outbreak of war was Berkely Street, Hawthorn. Thompson was part-owner of W.P. Thompson and Co Pty Ltd of Lonsdale Street, Melbourne. By the standards of the day it appeared to be a successful company; in November 1920 a business report in the Melbourne *Argus* stated that the firm was General Merchant, Saddlers and Ironmonger with capital of £75,000 issued in £1 shares.[57]

It is likely that Thompson was one of the motoring enthusiasts described by James. His age, wealth and social position would have made him a likely candidate for motorcar ownership in Edwardian Melbourne. One could also imagine his angst as he made the difficult decision between family and business management responsibilities, and his strong patriotic feelings.

Thompson chose the latter, joining the AIF on 25 March 1916 when Lieutenant James, the Officer Commanding the Motor Machine Gun Corps, gave him a letter stating that he was willing to accept Thompson into the Armoured Car Section. He was allotted to C Company, 22nd Deport Battalion, on 3 April and, while at Royal Park, assisted with the construction of the armoured cars. On 17 May he was promoted lance corporal. Once the armoured cars were accepted by the Defence Department and training had been completed, Thompson embarked for overseas service on HMAT A13 *Katuna* in Port Melbourne on 20 June. After disembarking at Port Tewfik, Egypt, the 1st Australian Armoured Car Section joined the Egyptian Expeditionary Force on 9 August.

The section soon entrained for southern Egypt to serve in operations against the Senussi tribesmen. During this period Lance Corporal Thompson was thrown from a patrol motorcar and injured his left knee. He was treated at a field ambulance and later evacuated to Cairo where he developed rheumatism. On 17 August 1917 he was transferred to the Australian Army Pay Corps at AIF Headquarters Middle East. However 1918 saw further admissions to the 14th Australian General Hospital where he was medically boarded as B1 on 13 January. On 1 March Thompson was promoted to extra regimental corporal, later reverting to lance corporal on embarkation for Australia. He boarded HMAT A15 *Port Sydney* at Suez on 19 May and disembarked in Port Melbourne on 4 July.

73. Studio portrait of Lance Corporal Walter Thompson taken at Broadmeadows Camp in May 1916, just prior to his embarkation with the 1st Armoured Car Section (AWM DACS0125).

Lance Corporal Thompson was discharged as medically unfit for service on 14 August 1918. For his service he was entitled to the British War and Victory Medals, the Silver War and Returned Soldier's Badges.[58]

Following discharge Walter Thompson returned to Berkely Street, Hawthorn, and resumed his business activities. During the 1920s and 1930s he wrote several extended letters to the *Argus* newspaper on Melbourne's history. He died on 9 August 1934 and was buried in Kew Cemetery. When probate was granted on 30 May 1935 his estate was valued at £78,387-4, a considerable fortune in that era.[59]

Henry Lloyd Fitzmaurice Harkin, RVM

Henry Lloyd Fitzmaurice Harkin was born in Chiltern, Victoria, in 1897, the son of Dr Charles Harkin J.P. and Emily Harkin.

The Harkin family were early pioneers of Victoria's north-east. Henry Harkin Junior was named after his paternal grandfather, Henry Charles Harkin, who was an early member of the Victorian Police at Wodonga and later rose to the rank of police sergeant. After leaving the police force he became a successful businessman and later a magistrate. In 1917 his death was widely reported in the newspapers of the area and he was described as Wodonga's oldest citizen.

Charles Harkin attended Dublin University and qualified as a doctor. On his return he practised in Albury, NSW, and Chiltern in Victoria. Dr Harkin was an active citizen with an extensive list of achievements that included President of the Chiltern Rifle Club, Justice of the Peace, Shire Councillor, Shire President, director of several local gold mines and President of the Overseas Wine Marketing Board. In 1911, when gold mining declined in the district, Dr Harkin led a group of local businessmen in founding the Chiltern Vineyard Company in an attempt to establish new industries in the area. He was also the first owner of a motor vehicle in Chiltern — a Stanley Steamer.[60]

Henry Harkin Junior was educated at Melbourne Grammar School between 1912 and 1915 where he reached the rank of cadet sergeant in the Grammar cadets. By 1916 Harkin had served in the junior cadets for two years and the senior cadets for four. In March 1916 he was still a member of the 29th Battalion of the Senior Cadets. His nephew, Henry Harkin, in an interview in 2006, recalled that Henry lived for cars and that he was passionate about every aspect of motors and motoring. On enlistment in 1916 he stated that he was a motor mechanic by trade.[61] In March 1916 he was given a letter by Lieutenant James which stated that he was 'willing to enrol H. Harkin as a member of the armoured motor crew when enlisted.'[62]

Harkin enlisted in the AIF in Melbourne on 30 March 1916. At 18 years and seven months, he was to become the youngest member of the Armoured Car Section. Interestingly, his attestation paper was marked with the comment that he had defective vision and that he was only suitable for mechanical (motor) services and should wear spectacles. He was taken on strength by C Company, 22nd Depot Battalion, on 3 April but was posted to the 24th Depot Battalion on 12 April where he participated in the final stages of Lieutenant James' project. On 20 June Harkin was posted to the 1st Armoured Car Section and, on the same day, embarked for overseas service on HMAT A13 *Katuna* in

Port Melbourne. Harkin remained with the Armoured Car Section and the 1st Australian Light Car Patrol until the end of hostilities. During that time his dossier remarkably records no illness or hospitalisations until he is diagnosed with malaria just prior to his return to Australia in March 1919.

74. Studio portrait of Driver Henry Harkin, the youngest recruit to the 1st Armoured Car Section, taken at Broadmeadows Camp in May 1916. He became Lieutenant Percy Cornwell's driver in the Light Car Patrol (AWM DACS0130).

On 15 March 1919 he was posted to the AIF Details Camp pending his return to Australia. He embarked on the HT *Dorset* at Suez on 29 April, and disembarked in Fremantle, Western Australia, on 29 May due to influenza. Sufficiently recovered from his illness, he re-embarked on the HT *Dorset*, finally arriving in Port Melbourne on 11 June. Motor Transport Driver Harkin was discharged as medically unfit on 13 August. He was entitled to the British War and Victory Medals and the Silver War and Returned Soldier's Badges for his service.

On arrival in Australia, Harkin and Sergeant Creek joined the 1919 Royal Tour of His Royal Highness the Prince of Wales as drivers. For this service Harkin was awarded the Royal Victorian Medal on 1 January 1920. Harkin returned to Chiltern following the Royal Tour, his family recalling that he returned to the vineyard in very poor health and seemed unable to gain weight. A short while later he did not have the energy to walk from the vineyard back to the house. He was diagnosed with Juvenile Diabetes and died from this illness at 'Kilara' in Mentone on 18 January 1922.

In 2006, Henry Harkin donated his uncle's effects to the Army Tank Museum. These included personal items Henry carried with him during his Army service, his Royal Victorian Medal and the personal keepsakes presented to him by His Royal Highness the Prince of Wales for the 1919 tour. There were also photos of the Armoured Car Section in Melbourne in 1916.

Leslie John Millar

Leslie John Millar was born in Melbourne on 12 September 1877, the son of Thomas and Helen Millar. At the time of his enlistment in 1916 his next of kin was his wife, Isabella Millar, of William Street, Melbourne. He listed his occupation as accountant and motorcar expert.

Millar's military service began in 1900 when he enlisted in the 3rd Victorian Bushmen. On enlistment he stated that he was a boundary rider and resided at the Doutta Galla Hotel, Flemington, Victoria. Millar embarked on the SS *Euryalus* at Port Melbourne on 10 March 1900 and disembarked at Beira in Portuguese East Africa on 3 April. He served with the Rhodesian Field Force and was present at the siege of Elands River between 10 and 16 August 1900. He returned to Victoria aboard the SS *Morayshire*, disembarking in Port Melbourne on 5 June 1901. He was discharged on 8 August. Millar subsequently returned to South Africa where he served in the Imperial Military Railways.[63]

Following his return from South Africa, Millar settled in William Street, Melbourne, and became a commercial traveller, marrying Isabella Monteith in 1906. On the 1914 electoral roll his occupation was listed as eye specialist and he was residing at Dundas Place, Albert Park.

Millar was an early user of motorcars and, in November 1911, he learnt of the dangers of road use first hand:

Knocked Down by a motorcar. A motor accident occurred in Beaconsfield Parade yesterday afternoon, the victim being Ray Phelan, 7 years of age ... he was playing with several other lads in one of the rockeries, and, rushing on to the parade, was struck by a motor driven by Leslie Millar, of Dundas Place, Albert Park. The Car was travelling at not more than five miles an hour, and the boy appeared to run under the wheels. When picked up the boy was badly bruised on the face and the body. In company with Constable Hall, Mr. Millar drove the lad to the Homeopathic Hospital where he received attention from Dr. Gould. No bones were broken, and the case is not regarded as serious.[64]

Millar's interest in motorcars also extended to the infant sport of motor racing. In 1913 he was manager of the Richmond Racecourse where Percy Cornwell raced his Mercedes.[65]

75. Corporal Leslie Millar, prior to embarking for overseas service with the 1st Armoured Car Section. Note the ribbons of the Queen's and King's South Africa medals on his uniform tunic that indicate his prior service (AWM DACS0123).

Millar enlisted in the CMF (Home Service) sometime after the outbreak of the Great War and served with the Australian Army Pay Corps. He transferred to the AIF on 3 April 1916 in Melbourne and was taken on strength by C Company, 22nd Depot Battalion, and promoted corporal. He was posted to the 24th Depot Battalion at Royal Park on 13 April. On 20 June he was appointed lance sergeant and quartermaster sergeant of the Armoured Car Section. Millar embarked for overseas service on HMAT A13 *Katuna* in Port Melbourne on 20 June 1916. In April 1917 his health declined and a series of hospitalisations followed. On 19 September he was posted to the AIF Details Camp at Moascar. In the year that followed, Millar was repeatedly admitted to hospital for a wasting condition that affected his left leg and right knee. Eventually he was medically boarded and classified as unfit for further service. He embarked on the HMAT A18 *Wiltshire* at Suez on 30 August 1918 and disembarked in Port Melbourne on 4 October.

Lance Sergeant Millar was discharged as medically unfit on 29 May 1919. For his service in the South African and Great War he was entitled to the Queen's South Africa Medal (Bars: Cape Colony, Transvaal, Rhodesia and South Africa 1901), the King's South Africa Medal (Bar 1902), British War and Victory Medals and the Returned Soldier's and Silver War Badges.[66]

Following his discharge Millar resided at Alexandra Mansions in South Melbourne. The 1919 electoral roll lists his occupation as manager. Sometime in the late 1920s he relocated to Whitehorse Road, Balwyn, and returned to commercial travelling. Millar died at the Mont Park Hospital in Macleod on 21 November 1956 and was cremated at Springvale.

Gordon Alexander McKay

Gordon Alexander McKay was born in Brunswick, Victoria, on 7 January 1887, the son of Andrew and Christina McKay, and joined Havelock Tobacco Company in 1902 as an office lad. He married Annie Forbes in March 1913. At the time of his enlistment he was a clerk residing in Bruce Street, Preston.

McKay enlisted in the AIF in Melbourne on 1 July 1915. He was promoted corporal and taken on strength by Headquarters Company at Ascot Vale Camp on 12 July. On 27 November he was transferred to the invalid list due to chronic arthritis. His file contains a note that he could only be employed in Australia as a clerk, while other documents recommended discharge on medical grounds. After time spent at the Melbourne Hospital, McKay returned to the Ascot Vale Camp on 14 February 1916 and was promoted acting sergeant. On 25 April he was posted to D Company, 23rd Depot Battalion, at Royal Park only to be posted again on 18 May, this time to the 24th Depot Battalion, also at Royal Park. On this occasion he reverted to private at his own request.

On 20 June he was taken on strength by the Armoured Car Section as a motor transport driver and embarked for overseas service on HMAT A13 *Katuna* in Port Melbourne. McKay served with the Armoured Car Section and the 1st Australian Light Car Patrol until July 1917, with only a short period of detachment between 19 and 27 May 1917 to act as Lieutenant Cornwell's batman with the survey party in the Sinai area.

76. Driver Gordon Alexander McKay, Armoured Car Section (DACS0238).

On 20 July 1917 McKay was posted to the AIF Canteens Service. He was promoted acting sergeant on 31 May 1918, extra regimental staff sergeant on 10 November and warrant officer Class I the following day. On 27 November McKay boarded the HT *Harden Castle* bound for Gallipoli where he was part of the occupation forces. He later returned to Egypt pending his return to Australia. He embarked on the HT *Ulimaroa* at Suez on 13 March 1919 and disembarked in Port Melbourne on 22 April. Warrant Officer Class I McKay was discharged as medically unfit on 13 June. He was entitled to the British War and Victory Medals and the Returned Soldier's and Silver War Badges for his service.[67]

Following discharge McKay returned briefly to Preston but soon relocated to Cowra, NSW, where he took up farming. He died on 25 April 1922 as a consequence of an accident. The *Canowindra Star* and *Eugowra News* reported:

> Death at Cowra. The death occurred last week of Mr. Gordon Alexander McKay, one of the Victorian farmers who came to Cowra some years ago and took up lucerne land at Mr. C. N. Grieves' property. Several months ago the late Mr. McKay had one of his knees seriously injured (through being run over by a wagon at Billimari) and blood poisoning set in and he died as stated at the early age of 35 years, at Nurse Matheson's Private Hospital, despite the best medical attention and the most skilled nursing. He leaves a sorrowing widow and a young family.[68]

He was buried at Cowra the following day.

McKay's two sons both served in the Second World War. Keith Ronald McKay enlisted in the AIF on 6 June 1940 and served as a lance corporal with the 2/8th Field Company. In May 1941 he was captured in Greece and remained a prisoner of war in Europe until 1945.[69] Alan Murray McKay enlisted in the CMF on 15 August 1940 and served as a gunner with the 2nd Medium Regiment. He left the Army and enlisted in the Royal Australian Air Force (RAAF) in September 1941, training as a wireless and radar mechanic. McKay served with the 79th Squadron in the Pacific before returning to Australia where he was posted to the 1st Operational Training Unit based at East Sale, Victoria. He was engaged in radar tests when he was killed in an air accident on 23 February 1945. The Lockheed Ventura twin-engine bomber in which he was flying crashed 12 miles east of Sale, the aircraft disintegrating on impact and killing all those on board.[70]

Norman Sinclair Bisset

Norman Sinclair Bisset was born in Sandhurst, Victoria, in 1887, the son of

George and Malvena Bisset. Norman was educated at Golden Square and Sandhurst High School. He played lawn tennis for the Bendigo Lawn Tennis Club[71] and was a member of St Andrew's Presbyterian Church.[72] At the time of his enlistment in 1914 he was an accountant employed by the Bendigo Permanent Land and Building Society and resided in Wade Street, Golden Square.[73]

Bisset enlisted in the AIF in Bendigo on 15 November 1914. He was soon allocated to the 1st Reinforcements, 16th Battalion, with whom he embarked on HMAT A35 *Berrima* on 22 December in Port Melbourne.

After a period of training in Egypt he was detached to the Administrative Headquarters Staff, although this was not recorded in his military records. However he describes his experiences in Egypt in a letter published in the *Bendigonian* in March 1915:

Headquarters Base Details, Camp Abbassia, 15th February, 1915. As I have a few moments to spare, I will spend them with you. You will see by the heading I am now stationed on the headquarters staff and don't I know it. It's a case of getting a move on as early in the morning as possible, take as little time as is safe to your meals, and burn as much midnight oil as you can. We have no time we can really call our own. Our hours are "get through it", and we have to go for it. I am the correspondence clerk, and have to register and file all letters that come in and go out. It is interesting in so much that I know what is going on in our sphere, but would rather be at some of the other work, getting experience in something that I am not used to. I have also other duties, for which I am responsible, and between the lot I get plenty of "hurry up". I will now give you the details since my last letter. I was doing some clerical work a week ago with our company clerk, when I was told to report at the Orderly Room. I did so and was picked with nine others to go into the Headquarters in Cairo, and was told to report at 12.30. In the meantime I learned that we would likely be stuck in Cairo for good, and I didn't fancy the experience, so I went to the Adjutant and asked if the change meant that I would not see any service, and he said, "practically, no." I then asked if I could strike my name off the list. He asked me what I had been used to, when I told him he asked me to join his staff, which meant that we would always move with the troops. I agreed, so here I am. The offices are in a part of the barracks, which practically surround the camp, and I eat and sleep here. Compared with the rest of the troops we are fed like prize turkeys, so it works both ways. What do you think of this for a day's menu? Yesterday we had four eggs each, bacon, coffee, bread and jam for breakfast; mutton, three vegetables, plumb duff and tea for dinner; bread and jam and pancakes for tea. How is that for active service living? We have two cooks between twelve of us. "Bowie" and V. Ryan came in from Mena yesterday, and looked me up, and we went into Cairo together. They are camped near the Pyramids. When going through the camp we ran into W. Dawe. He has been camping about six tents from me and I did not know he was here. I keep running up against fellows from Bendigo all the time. One day our telephone orderly said to me, "You will be missing the dances this year." I looked at him and said. "What do you know about my dancing?" He said, "Oh, I often saw you at the Town Hall; my father is caretaker there." He is a son of Mr. Green. I haven't seen much of the sights yet, and goodness knows when I will. The best place about here is Heliopolis, half a mile from the camp, and I believe it is a magnificent town. It was originally built to be a rival to Monte Carlo, and money wasn't considered; but it did not come off. The main building is now used as a military hospital. There is a Luna Park, lit up just like the St. Kilda one, scenic railway and all. The inhabitants are mostly English and French, and there are no slums or poor parts. Every residence, they say, is a model. Another place I must get to is the Dead City, near Cairo, and the Pyramids go without saying. Some of our chaps went there yesterday, and I saw a native make a bet of 5/- to run down the biggest from top to bottom in two minutes. He surprised them by doing it in a minute and a half. I have just heard that the rest of the Australians are on the water. All the reinforcements are being taken from Abbassia to make room for those who are coming, and soon it will be a new crowd altogether.[74]

While it was not recorded precisely when Bisset rejoined his battalion or arrived at Gallipoli, the *Bendigonian* reported his probable departure as mid-November 1914 and thus it is likely he reached Gallipoli sometime after August. At Gallipoli he developed a septic hand and was evacuated on 10 November to the 1st Australian General Hospital at Heliopolis. After a period of hospitalisation and convalescence Bisset returned to his unit on 5 February 1916.

On 19 March 1916 he embarked on HMAT A64 *Demosthenes* at Suez to be returned to Australia as an escort, disembarking at Port Melbourne on 19 April.

His return home was reported in the *Bendigo Advertiser* on April 29:

Corporal Norman Bisset, who was recently invalided to Australia, and who returned to his home in Bendigo last Saturday, tells of the appreciation of Bendigo and what Bendigonians are doing for the troops, as expressed by a soldier whom he met in Egypt. Whilst riding in a tramcar Corporal Bisset was reading a 'Bendigonian' which had been sent to him when a strange soldier, who was seated next to him, asked to be allowed to peruse the journal. The stranger, on learning that Corporal Bisset came from Bendigo, read the 'Bendigonian' and then went on to express his appreciation of Bendigonians. He said that before leaving for the front, he was attached to the Bendigo camp, which he considered to be the best he had ever been in. In the course of his conversation he referred to three young Bendigo ladies whom he had met, and spoke highly of the work which was being done for soldiers by the ladies of the Bendigo Y.M.C.A.[75]

After a brief period of home leave, he returned to duty.

It is likely that fellow Bendigonian Sergeant John Langley recruited him into the Armoured Car Section. On 7 June Bisset reverted to the rank of private at his own request and joined the 24th Depot Battalion at Royal Park. On 20 June he was posted to the Armoured Car Section as a motor transport driver and embarked for the second occasion for overseas service on HMAT A13 *Katuna* at Port Melbourne on 20 June 1916. Bisset would serve almost continuously with the Armoured Car Section and the 1st Australian Light Car Patrol throughout the Egyptian and Palestine campaigns. On 7 August 1917 he was promoted corporal. On 15 March 1919 he was posted to the AIF Details Camp pending his return to Australia. He embarked on the HT *Kaiser-i-Hind* at Suez on 16 May and disembarked in Port Melbourne on 16 June. He was finally discharged from the AIF on 15 August.

In 1919 General Allenby recognised Bisset for his conspicuous service with the award of a Mentioned in Despatches. For his service in the Great War, Bisset was entitled to the 1914–15 Star, British War and Victory Medals, Mention in Despatches, and the Returned Soldier's Badge.[76]

Bisset married Rita Jackson in 1922 and relocated to the St Kilda-Elsternwick area at around the same time. In the mid-1920s he joined the Country Roads Board where he rose to the position of assistant accountant. He died suddenly at St Kilda on 23 December 1941 and was buried in Bendigo.[77]

77. Driver Norman Bisset joined the Armoured Car Section after being invalided to Australia following the Gallipoli Campaign (Young collection ATM.LCP.IY.127).

Stanley George Jones

Stanley George Jones was born in Bendigo, Victoria, on 12 August 1890, the son of William and Margaret Jones. At the time of his enlistment in 1916, his next of kin was his father, William Jones, of 61 Page Street, Albert Park. He listed his occupation as clerk and motor mechanic.

Jones' military service began in 1915 when he enlisted in the CMF (Home Service), serving with the Australian Army Pay Corps. He transferred to the AIF at Royal Park on 23 May 1916 and was taken on strength by the 24th Depot Battalion, also at Royal Park, before transferring to the newly formed 1st Australian Armoured Car Section. On 20 June he embarked on HMAT A13 *Katuna* at Port Melbourne for overseas service.

On 23 September 1917 Jones was admitted to the 3rd Light Horse Field Ambulance with septic sores and evacuated to the 14th Australian General Hospital on 29 September. His health declined and a series of hospitalisations followed. He returned to the 1st Australian Light Car Patrol on 26 October; however his return was to be short-lived and he was readmitted to the 44th Stationary Hospital on 21 November with enteritis and septic stores. He was medically boarded on 17 December and classified as unfit for service due to general debility. He embarked on the New Zealand Transport *Tofua* at Suez on 28 December and disembarked in Port Melbourne on 30 January 1918. He was discharged as medically unfit on 4 March.[78]

Following his discharge, Jones returned to the South Melbourne-Albert Park area where he lived for most of the rest of his life. His occupations as listed in the electoral rolls of this time were either clerk or traveller.

On 22 January 1940, in the early days of the Second World War, Jones enlisted in the CMF at Broadmeadows, Victoria. At this time he stated he was a traveller by occupation and was residing in Dank Street, Albert Park, his next of kin Alice Jones, his elder sister. He was posted to the 12th Garrison Battalion. He was promoted staff sergeant on 3 April 1940 and graded as a Clerk Group III. He had several postings over the next few years, mostly to infantry training units.

Jones' health declined in July 1944 and he had several hospitalisations at the 115th Australian General Hospital at Heidelberg. On 28 October he was medically classified Class D and discharged as medically unfit on 30 October at Royal Park.[79]

For his service in two world wars he was entitled to the British War, Victory, War (1939–45) and Australian Service Medals and the Silver War, Returned Soldier's and Australian Service Badges. Jones died at Heidelberg, Victoria, in 1976.

John Hudson Langley, DCM and Bar

John Hudson Langley was born in Kew, Victoria, on 10 April 1894, the son of John and Eda Langley. Langley's parents separated and divorced and his aunt Louisa Langley raised him. The Langleys were a prominent Victorian family in religious and educational circles. At times members of the Langley clan served as the Anglican Archdeacons of Gippsland, Melbourne and Geelong, and Bishop of Bendigo. Members of the Langley family also founded several independent schools.[80] Langley was educated at Sandhurst Corporate High School, Trinity Grammar School, where he was a prefect and a member of the Senior Cadets, and Castlemaine Technical School. He later completed an electrical apprenticeship at Thomson and Company Engineering Works at Castlemaine and was still employed with this firm in 1915.

78. Sergeant John Langley served with the 1st Armoured Car Section and the 1st Light Car Patrol and was awarded a DCM and Bar in late 1918. His death in January 1919 due to illness was a bitter blow to the unit (AWM DACS0128).

Langley's military service began when he enlisted in the 66th (Mount Alexander) Infantry Regiment sometime in 1911 and, by 1915, he had attained the rank of sergeant. At the time of his enlistment in the AIF on 12 July 1915, he was an electrician residing at Whitehills, Bendigo, and his next of kin was his father, John Langley, who was employed by the Pacific Phosphate Company in the Gilbert Islands in the South Pacific. His mother Eda had remarried and was residing in North Sydney.

On arrival in camp Langley was taken on strength by A Company, Flemington Depot Battalion, as a sergeant. On 12 August he was posted again, this time to C Company, 31st Infantry Battalion, at Broadmeadows. In the 31st Battalion, Langley encountered Ivan Young from Nhill. The Langley and Young families were closely connected and the social columns of both the Nhill and Bendigo papers make several mentions of the families exchanging visits during this period. Ivan Young would later marry Langley's cousin, Nancy Chisolm, the marriage officiated by Langley's uncle. The *Nhill Free Press* reported that both Langley and Young took leave in Nhill in November 1915: 'Sergeant John Langley, and Private Ivan S Young, only son of Mr. and Mrs. John Young, of "Yothom" Nelson Street Nhill, is now on a visit to the town. Sergeant Langley and Private Young are members of one of the motor machine gun sections of the Australian Imperial Expeditionary Force and will leave Australia shortly for Egypt. Both young soldiers received a hearty welcome from their Nhill friends.'[81] With his previous military, electrical and engineering experience, Langley would have been a prime recruit for Lieutenant James' armoured car venture. Langley was posted to the 24th Depot Battalion and took a leading role in the construction of the armoured cars. He was formally taken on strength by the Armoured Car Section on 20 June 1916. He would also recruit George Morgan, a close friend from Thomson's engineering works and the CMF, into the Armoured Car Section.

Sergeant Langley embarked for overseas service on HMAT A13 *Katuna* at Port Melbourne on 20 June 1916. During the voyage he held the position of Ship's Sergeant Major. Langley would serve almost continuously with the Armoured Car Section and the 1st Australian Light Car Patrol throughout the Egyptian and Palestine campaigns.

Langley was an outstanding non-commissioned officer (NCO) and leader. In August 1917 Captain James recommended Langley for a commission in the absence of Lieutenant Cornwell and, although this promotion was approved, it did not eventuate as Cornwell returned from his detachment. In November 1918 Langley was awarded the Distinguished Conduct Medal 'for conspicuous gallantry and devotion to duty. When in charge of a Lewis Gun section he twice stampeded an enemy machine gun section, enfiladed a trench causing many casualties and dispersed several digging parties. He captured a machine gun killing some of the gunners and putting the rest to flight. He showed marked skill throughout.' The award of a Bar to the Distinguished Conduct Medal followed: 'On the 23rd October, 1918, at Khan Tuman, he pursued in an armoured car, over very rough ground, an enemy patrol which had approached the armoured car position. His quickness and dash enabled him to kill one of the enemy and capture four. He set a brilliant example of determination and initiative.'

Sergeant Langley was admitted to the 14th Mounted Brigade Field Ambulance at Aleppo on 1 January 1919 with malignant malaria and died on 2 January. It was a bitter blow to the unit. Captain James wrote after Sergeant Langley's death that Langley was 'my right hand man and the finest fellow that ever lived.'[82] Langley was buried by Captain E. Bourney on 4 January at Aleppo Military Cemetery. His grave was later relocated to the Beirut War Cemetery. For his service in the Great War, Langley was entitled to the Distinguished Conduct Medal and Bar, British War and Victory Medals.[83]

George Foy Morgan

George Foy Morgan was born in Castlemaine, Victoria, on 20 January 1894, the son of David and Annie Morgan. At the time of enlistment his next of kin was his stepmother, Mary Moore Morgan. He married Mary Lipplegoes on 10 March 1916. Morgan had completed an apprenticeship as a motor mechanic and was employed at Thomson and Company Engineering Works at Castlemaine. He also enlisted in the 66th (Mount Alexander Infantry) sometime in 1912 and was still an active member in 1916.

Morgan's first attempt to enlist in the AIF occurred in Melbourne, Victoria, on 23 July 1915, when he joined the Munition Workers Company. The *Mount Alexander Mail* reported that Morgan was one of 116 men from the district who enlisted in the first two weeks of July.[84] Morgan's service proved short-lived as he was discharged on 16 October 1915 to return to industry to make munitions.

Morgan's second — and successful — attempt to enlist occurred in Melbourne on 31 March 1916. It is highly likely that Sergeant Langley recruited Morgan into the Armoured Car Section prior to his enlistment. They had both been apprenticed and worked at Thomson's Engineering Works, were members of the same Militia Regiment, and were close friends. Morgan was taken on strength by C Company, 22nd Depot Battalion, on 3 April and then posted to the 24th Depot Battalion at Royal Park where his mechanical skills were put to use in the construction of Captain James' armoured cars. On 19 June he was appointed as a motor transport driver and was taken on strength by the Armoured Car Section.

79. Studio portrait of Driver George Morgan taken at Broadmeadows Camp in May 1916. Morgan had completed an apprenticeship as a motor mechanic prior to enlistment — a prized skill in a mechanised unit that had to rely largely on its own resources for maintenance and repairs. After his promotion to corporal, Morgan commanded the 1st Light Car Patrol's workshop and spare ammunition tender (AWM DACS0129).

Morgan embarked for overseas service on HMAT A13 *Katuna* in Port
Melbourne on 20 June 1916. On 1 August 1917 he was promoted corporal,
remaining with the Light Car Patrol until the end of hostilities. In late December
1918 he contracted cerebral malaria and was evacuated on the hospital ship
Assaye at Alexandretta in Turkey, arriving in Alexandria, Egypt, where he was
admitted to the 14th Australian General Hospital. He embarked on HT *Marghs*
at Suez on 29 January 1919 and disembarked in Port Melbourne on 4 March
1919.[85]

Corporal Morgan was discharged as medically unfit on 12 April. He was
entitled to the British War and Victory Medals and the Returned Soldier's
and Silver War Badges for his service. After discharge Morgan returned to
Castlemaine where he resumed his trade as a fitter. He died on 27 June 1965 at
Castlemaine, Victoria, and was buried at the Chewton Cemetery.

80. A light car and crew at Aleppo in November 1918.

THE REINFORCEMENTS

The demographics of the reinforcements were quite different to those of the originals. The youngest member of the reinforcements at the time of his enlistment was 18, the oldest 39. The average age was 23, five years younger than the originals. The ethnic origin of the group was once again predominantly British, although two had Scandinavian heritage. The reinforcements proved overwhelmingly protestant with only one Roman Catholic. Two were born in the United Kingdom (UK), while the rest were native-born Australians. Unlike the Victorian flavour of the originals, the reinforcements were an all-Australian mix: four Victorians, two Queenslanders, nine New South Welshmen and two South Australians. Only three of the reinforcements were married.

Of the reinforcements, nine came from rural areas while ten came from major cities. This equates to 53% from urban backgrounds; thus the rural-city divide of both the originals and the reinforcements appears very similar. Of the nine rural members, eight came from traditional agricultural occupations including farmers, overseers, station hands and a grazier. The ten city dwellers held a variety of employments: a motor expert, a baker, cabinetmaker, driver, clerk, accountant, commercial traveller and chemist. None identified himself as unemployed. In this area a distinct difference emerges between the skilled engineering backgrounds of the 1916 originals of the Armoured Car Section and those who followed.

The reinforcements were drawn from the units of the Australian Mounted Division in both Egypt and Palestine. The 4th, 8th, 9th and 10th Light Horse Regiments each provided individual troopers, seven members of the 6th and two troopers from the 7th Light Horse Regiments, five from training regiments and units, and a lone signaller from the 1st Australian Pack Wireless Troop. The majority of these men had been serving in the AIF since 1915; two were 1914 enlistments, the remaining six had served since 1916. On average they had 26 months of military service at the time they were taken on strength by the 1st Light Car Patrol. The reinforcements added considerable active service experience to their new unit. Several of these men also had prior experience in the colonial, CMF and naval forces.

Thus a typical reinforcement was native born, single, protestant, 24 years of age, employed in a traditional rural or urban occupation, and had ancestry with origins in the UK.

The reinforcements 1917–19
Private L.A. Gray
Private G. Christensen
Private J.C. Riley
Private J.A. Driscoll
Lieutenant A.C. Gibbs
Private F. Rhoades
Private K.C. Riley
Private B.C. Jarvis
Private L.R. Cohn
Private S.C.K. Forsyth
Private A. Eddie
Private G.V. Somny
Private J.B. McKay
Private M.C. Pines
Private C.L Richardson
Private R.J. Simpson
Driver A.G. Holley
Private L.G.V. Bosanquet
Private F. Arnott, MM

Laurence Alfred Gray

Laurence Alfred Gray was born in Victor Harbour, South Australia, on 22 October 1896, the son of Henry and Alice Gray. At the time of his enlistment in 1916 he was a farmer.

Gray enlisted in the CMF in late 1914 and served with the 22nd Light Horse Regiment. Prior to this he had been a member of the Senior Cadets, Area 74B. On 8 March 1916 he enlisted in the AIF in Adelaide. While in training in South Australia he served with the 2nd Depot Battalion, Base Light Horse Depot, the Musketry and NCO Schools, 23rd Reinforcements 9th Light Horse, and the 23rd Reinforcements 3rd Light Horse. During this period Gray held provisional ranks of both sergeant and corporal. He reverted to trooper on 1 December.[86]

On 15 January 1917 he embarked for overseas service on HMAT A45 *Bulla* in Adelaide, disembarking at Port Said on 16 March. He was taken on strength by the Details Camp at Moascar and posted to the 1st Light Horse Training Regiment on 4 April. During this period he attended a course of instruction on the Hotchkiss machine-gun. On 30 May he was posted to the 1st Australian Light Car Patrol.

Trooper Gray marched into the Details Camp on 15 March 1918, later embarking on the HT *Kaiser-i-Hind* at Port Said on 16 May and disembarking in Adelaide on 14 June. He was discharged on 22 July. For his military service he was entitled to the British War and Victory Medals and Returned Soldier's Badge.

Gray returned to the CMF after the Great War. He was commissioned as a provisional lieutenant with the 18th Light Horse Regiment on 16 September 1921 and in July 1922 transferred to the 3rd Light Horse Regiment. During this period Gray attended several machine-gun courses. On 18 November 1925 he resigned his commission and left the CMF. On the outbreak of the Second World War Gray returned to the Reserve of Officers (Cavalry) in the 3rd Military District and retired from this position on 19 December 1944 without returning to full-time service.

On return to Australia following the Great War, Gray married Mabel Lord. He died in Adelaide on 25 October 1967 and was buried in Mitcham Cemetery.

George Christensen
(George Christian Christensen)

George Christian Christensen was born in Port Melbourne, Victoria, on 26 August 1887, the son of Christian and Emma Christensen. He married Catherine Williams on 16 October 1916 at St John's in Footscray. He served in the CMF with the 5th Battalion, the Victorian Scottish Regiment. At the time of his enlistment in 1915 he was a baker residing in Yarraville.

Christensen enlisted in the AIF in Melbourne on 12 July 1915. He served with the 14th Depot in Ballarat, but was discharged as medically unfit on 9 March 1916. He re-enlisted in the AIF in Melbourne on 2 January 1917, training at Royal Park and the Seymour Army Camp in Victoria before being posted to the 25th Reinforcements, 8th Light Horse.

George Christensen embarked for overseas service on 2 February 1917 aboard the HMAT A57 RMS *Malakuta*, disembarking at Port Said on 11 March and was taken on strength by the Details Camp at Moascar. He was posted to the 8th Light Horse Regiment on 1 April. Between April 12 and 29 Christensen was detached to the Cookery School. On 30 May he transferred to the 1st Australian Light Car Patrol. He remained with the Light Car Patrol until 16 October when he was evacuated sick to the 2nd Light Horse Field Ambulance. On 16 February

1918, following a period of hospitalisation and convalescence, he was posted to the AIF Kit Store. He returned to the 8th Light Horse on 15 June before contracting malaria on 18 August and being evacuated to hospital where he remained until November when he returned to his unit. Trooper Christensen marched into the Details Camp on 15 March 1919 and later embarked on the HT *City of Poona* at Port Said on 7 April, disembarking in Melbourne in 14 May. He was discharged as medically unfit on 17 August.

On his return to Australia, Christensen went first to Yarraville but soon relocated to Springvale. Sometime prior to the late 1930s the Christensen family returned once more to Yarraville. During this period he listed his occupation as either an oiler or linesman with the Post Master General's Department.

On 4 September 1939 Christensen applied to serve with the CMF. He enlisted at ANZAC House in Melbourne on 30 October. His address at this time was Adeleigh Street, Yarraville, and he gave his occupation as a cook. He served in Victoria with the General Depot from 16 October, then with the 12th Garrison Battalion and the 3rd Military District Workshops from 28 September 1941, the Area Signals from 20 October, the 15th Line Maintenance Section from 10 August 1943, and Signals Land Headquarters, Northern Section, from 11 February 1944.

Christensen was employed initially as a specialist cook until 16 June 1940 when he was graded as a Group II Linesman. He was promoted lance corporal on 26 January 1942, acting corporal on 12 January 1943 and corporal on 12 April 1944. In 1944 his health declined and he was medically boarded in late 1944 and subsequently discharged as medically unfit on 5 October.

For his military service in two wars he was entitled to the British War, Victory, the War (1939–45) and Australian Service Medals, Silver War, Returned Soldier's and General Service Badges.

On his discharge from the CMF Christensen returned to Yarraville. He died in Heidelberg on 14 October 1964.[87]

James Cory Riley

James Cory Riley was born in Warialda, NSW, in 1887, the son of Alick and Louisa Riley. At the time of his enlistment in 1916 he was an overseer at Emmet Downs Station, Queensland. His family was residing at Fairview, Yass, NSW.

Riley enlisted at Casula, NSW, on 7 February 1916 and was posted to E Company, Depot Battalion, and the Depot Regiment, Australian Light Horse.

After training he was allocated to the 22nd Reinforcements, 6th Australian Light Horse. He embarked for overseas service on HMAT A13 *Katuna* at Sydney on 23 November, disembarking at Port Said on 2 January 1917. Riley was taken on strength by the 2nd Light Horse Brigade Training Regiment at Tel el Kebir on 22 January. After attending a school of instruction he was briefly posted to the 5th Light Horse Details on 16 May. On 28 May he was posted to the 1st Australian Light Car Patrol. Other than for periods of sickness and hospitalisation caused by malaria, Riley remained with the unit for the rest of the war.

On 12 August Riley's younger brother, Trooper Kenrick Riley, also joined the Light Car Patrol. However this reunion was not to last long as Kenrick returned to the 6th Light Horse on 4 February 1918 and was killed in action on 27 March.

On 13 March 1919 James Riley marched into the AIF Details Camp pending his return to Australia. Trooper Riley embarked on the HT *Dorset* at Port Said, Egypt, on 29 April 1919 and disembarked in Sydney on 11 June. Riley was discharged as medically unfit on 22 July. For his service he was entitled to the British War and Victory Medals and the Silver War and Returned Soldier's Badges.[88]

Following discharge he returned to Queensland where he was employed as an overseer and station manager at Yaraka and Isis Downs stations, later returning to Yass before moving to the Winton district where he managed the Venture Downs Station, Corfield. Riley married Eileen Stanton in Penrith on 28 June 1928. He died on 20 July 1955 at Winton Hospital, Queensland. The *Nepean Times* reported his death:

> Fatal Fall from Horse. Grandson of Penrith's First Mayor. Mr. James Cory Riley, of 'Venture Downs', Corfield, Queensland, died on July 20 from injuries received as horse rider when mustering. He was a grandson of the late J.J. Riley, first Mayor of Penrith, and spent his early days in this district. 'Venture Downs' is out from Winton, in Central Queensland. There Mr. Jim Riley was mustering sheep at the time. His horse shied, Jim fell, and the horse fell on to him. He was taken to Winton Hospital and died two days later. Jim Riley was born at Warialda, the son of Mr. and Mrs. Alek C. Riley. Years ago he lived in Penrith, and was married at 'Ormonde', High Street, to Eileen, daughter of the late Mr. and Mrs. J. Stanton, and sister of Mrs. Honey and Mrs. Gimbert, of Penrith. He served with the 6th Light Horse in the 1st World War. Deceased is survived by his wife and by three

sons and two daughters. Kenrick (Teric Station, Blackall, Queensland), John (a veterinary surgeon, at Mackay, Queensland), Margaret, Jane and Jimmie (all of 'Venture Downs'). Sisters and brother of Mr. Riley are Eena (Mrs. C. C. Hope, Roseville), Jeanette (Yass), Kenrick (1st A.I.F., killed), Ula (Roseville), Nell (Mrs. Willott, Fiji). Jim Riley had been managing at Venture Downs for four or five years and previously had been at Forest Hill, out of Blackall, for many years …[89]

John Anthony Driscoll

John Anthony Driscoll was born in Delegate, NSW, on 25 May 1896, the son of John and Lucy Driscoll. At the time of his enlistment in 1915 he was a labourer residing in Surry Hills.

Driscoll enlisted in the AIF in Liverpool on 28 December 1915 and was allotted to the 19th Reinforcements, 7th Light Horse Regiment. He embarked for overseas service on 8 July 1916 aboard the HT *Mongolia* in Sydney, disembarking at Port Said on 11 August. On arrival he was taken on strength by the 2nd Light Horse Brigade Training Regiment at Moascar. On 25 August he was posted to the 7th Light Horse Regiment.

On the night of 15 November he was found asleep and drunk while on guard duty and court-martialled on 20 November at Hassaniya. He was found guilty on both charges and sentenced to nine months' hard labour. The court recommended a commutation of sentence due to his very good character and the fact that, as he was virtually a teetotaller, he was unused to alcohol and had fallen asleep as a consequence. He served his sentence at the Cairo Detention Barracks from 30 November 1916.

On 20 March 1917 Driscoll's sentence was suspended and he was released from the Detention Barracks and returned to his regiment. He was immediately detached for duty with the Divisional Army Service Corps (ASC) Train and then, on 10 June, to the 1st Australian Light Car Patrol. He returned to the 7th Light Horse on 20 July. On 21 August he was detached to the AIF Railway Construction Section between 21 August 1917 and 31 July 1918 when he was posted to the 2nd Light Horse Brigade Training Regiment at Moascar. In September he was hospitalised with influenza at the 14th Australian General Hospital. He rejoined his regiment on 14 October. On 10 December he boarded the *Indarra* at Port Said for the Dardanelles where he served with the occupation force. On 26 January 1919 he embarked at Chanak, Turkey, aboard the HT *Kandy*, disembarking in Alexandria on 2 February.[90]

Driscoll boarded the HT *Madras* at Kantara, Egypt, on 26 June and disembarked in Sydney on 3 August. He was discharged on 18 September. For his military service he was entitled to the British War and Victory Medals and Returned Soldier's Badge.[91]

On his return to Australia Driscoll initially lived in Sydney where he worked as a labourer and rabbiter. He married Louisa Harmer at Paddington, Sydney, in 1920. Their first child died in infancy that same year. While there appear to be no records of a divorce or annulment of Driscoll's marriage, Louisa died in Tumut in 1959 under her maiden name. On 21 October 1926 he married Vera Kerr in Tasmania. As with many returned soldiers, the 1920s and the Great Depression that followed saw Driscoll and his family suffer considerable difficulties and hardships, and the electoral rolls show numerous residences in Surry Hills, Botany and Helensburg between 1927 and the outbreak of the Second World War.

At the height of the Great Depression it appears Driscoll's fortunes completely failed him. The *Sydney Morning Herald* reported that Driscoll and his brother William were committed to trial at the Central Police Court for counterfeiting coins. The men were found in possession of coins and moulds and silver nitrate batteries they intended to use to make coins. The police reported that, when Driscoll opened the door, he stated: 'You have me at last. There you are: there is all you want.'[92] Driscoll appeared at the quarter sessions the following February where he was 'charged with having in his possession, at Sydney, on November 18, 1934, 20 counterfeit coins resembling shillings, knowing them to be counterfeit. He was further charged with making 20 such counterfeit coins, and having in his possession certain metal with intent to use it in the manufacture of counterfeit coins. Accused, who was said to be a married man with three children, pleaded guilty to each of the three charges, and was sentenced to 18 months' hard labour on each, the sentences to be concurrent.'[93]

The Second World War offered Driscoll the opportunity to return to military service which, following the trials of the Depression, would have promised him and his family a sense of security. He enlisted in the CMF on 15 October 1939 at Wollongong. At this time he stated that he was a labourer by occupation and was residing in Postman's Track, Helensburg, his next of kin Vera Driscoll. He was posted to the 2nd Garrison Battalion at Port Kembla but was discharged as medically unfit on 29 February 1940. He re-enlisted in the CMF at Paddington on 1 August 1941 and served with the 7th Garrison Battalion but was again discharged as medically unfit on 6 January 1942. He enlisted in the VDC on 9 July 1942 in Sydney and was discharged on 15 May 1943, once again deemed medically unfit.[94]

Driscoll's final years also proved a tragic time for the old soldier. In July 1944 Driscoll was arrested in Newcastle for public drunkenness and found in possession of a number of counterfeit two-shilling coins.[95] In November he appeared before the Newcastle Sessions Court where in evidence it was mentioned that Driscoll had worked on a fruit barrow in the Sydney Market and was addicted to drink. He was found guilty and sentenced to 12 months' imprisonment.[96] Driscoll died at Coledale Hospital on 8 January 1946.

Archibald Cecil Gibbs

Archibald Cecil Gibbs was born in Kenthurst, NSW, on 3 July 1876, the son of Charles and Elizabeth Gibbs. He married Jessie Moore at Castle Hill on 25 December 1899 and the couple had two children. In the late 1890s Gibbs played cricket for Kenthurst and was Secretary of the Kenthurst School of the Arts.[97] In 1904 Gibbs was elected to the Leichardt Council and served until September 1907 when he was defeated in the council elections.[98] This electoral defeat came as a result of his questionable commercial dealings as an agent for the Cumberland Valley Fruit Producers. The *Cumberland Argus and Fruitgrowers Advocate* contains several articles that question his business practices.[99] At the time of his enlistment in 1915 Gibbs was residing in Coogee and employed as a commercial traveller for the Perdrian Rubber Company.

Gibbs enlisted in the AIF in Adelaide on 9 September 1915. On enlistment he stated that he had previously served with the Sydney Lancers (1st Light Horse Regiment) for three and half years. His postings in NSW included the Depot Training School and Light Horse Depot at Liverpool Camp. On 11 November Gibbs applied for a commission which was granted on 6 January 1916. Second Lieutenant Gibbs was posted to the 18th Reinforcements, 7th Light Horse Regiment, in October 1916.

Gibbs embarked for overseas service on HMAT A20 *Hororata* in Sydney on 2 May, disembarking at Port Said, Egypt, on 29 June. He reported to the 2nd Light Horse Training Regiment at Tel el Kebir on arrival. After further training he was assigned to C Squadron, 7th Light Horse, on 20 September; however he remained seconded to the Training Regiment until 24 December when he joined the 7th Light Horse at Hassaniya. He was promoted lieutenant on 22 October. Gibbs was detached for duty with other units on numerous occasions: the Camel Transport Corps between 18 February and 18 March 1917; the

Divisional ASC Train between 21 March and 22 April; the 1st Australian Light Car Patrol between 10 June and 27 July; and the AIF Railway Construction Party from 21 August to 17 November 1918. He rejoined the 7th Light Horse on 19 November.

During his service in the Middle East, Lieutenant Gibbs wrote several letters that were published in various Australian newspapers. In one account he expresses his gratitude for the gifts delivered to his men by the Australian Comforts Fund:

Overcoming Difficulties. Comforts Fund in Palestine. Lieutenant A. C. Gibbs (OC AIF railway construction in Palestine) writes as follows: "last December I was engaged in the construction of the line from Gaza to Ludd. The weather was atrocious. One rainstorm following another with persistent regularity. The line was being washed away constantly, the roads such as they were, were impassable, and this country resembled a quagmire. The camps were under water frequently, and the men were wet through night and day. Many times they worked all night to enable trains to get through, and owing to the small number of trains the men were on half rations.

In the midst of those conditions Mr. Coward (of the Australian Comforts Fund) rode into our camp, and asked whether he could assist us in any way. Did ever the A.C.F. arrive in a more opportune moment? One can realize how weary and depressed the men were and the prospect of relief from A.C.F. was welcomed by everyone. A couple of days later a consignment, of most acceptable goods reached us by train. How Mr. Coward managed to arrange the transit, despite the fact that every inch of space was required urgently by the military is known only to himself. It is beyond my comprehension. The distribution allowed us to have a really excellent Christmas repast, despite the dismal surroundings. Our chief regret was that Mr. Coward was not with us there to partake of it. That is no isolated instance of how the A.C.F. has come to the help of the A.I.F. in strenuous times, and has given just those extra comforts which have made the difference. I wish the public of Australia could be made to realize the real benefits accruing to the troops, through the good service of the A.C.F., which spares no efforts to rub off some of the hardships of campaigning and does cheerfully. Its agents do not ask for or expect thanks. They sell nothing, but give all and with each giving there are apologies for not being able to give more.[100]

On 10 December he boarded the *Indarra* at Port Said for the Dardanelles where he served as part of the occupation force. He embarked on the HT *Kandy* at Chanak on 21 January and disembarked in Alexandria on 31 January, returning to the 7th Light Horse. On 3 July 1919 he boarded the HT *Malta* at Port Said, reaching Sydney on 10 August. His AIF appointment was terminated in Sydney on 25 September. For his service in the Great War he was entitled to the British War and Victory Medals, the Mentioned in Despatches emblem and the Returned Soldier's Badge.[101]

Gibbs' service in the Great War raises some questions. He served only six weeks with the 7th Light Horse Regiment before being sent on a series of detachments that continued until after the war's end. In a confidential report in 1919, Lieutenant Colonel Richardson writes of Gibbs: 'This reinforcement officer has seen very little work with the Regiment and hardly any fighting. He has shown very little capacity for handling men in the field, has a bad manner with men, and is certainly unfitted for promotion to higher rank.' A contrasting view was expressed on 14 June 1918 when General Allenby mentioned Lieutenant Gibbs in his despatches 'for distinguished and gallant services and devotion to duty'. A notation in his file links this award to his service with the AIF Railway Construction Party. It is apparent that, while not suited to regimental duties, Gibbs was regarded as a capable officer in an unglamorous but important logistics role.

On his return to Australia, Gibbs made his way back to Sydney and resumed his business pursuits. His marriage ended in divorce in March 1928.[102] With the onset of the Depression and his loss of employment, other aspects of Gibbs' life also became fraught with difficulty. On 29 August 1931 he appeared before the Sydney Police Courts 'charged with having fraudulently converted to his own use £60, of which he was the bailee. Archibald Cecil Gibbs, 48, salesman, was committed for trial from the Central Police Court yesterday by Mr. Williams, S.M. Bail of £60 was allowed.'[103] The circumstances of this case involved one 'Catherine O'Byrne [who] said that she drew £97 from the Government Savings Bank. She asked defendant to mind £60 for her until she came out of hospital. After coming out of hospital she asked defendant if he had used her money. He said, "I have. I am expecting £200 in a week or two, and I am going to put it back." She has not received it.' In September the *Sydney Morning Herald* reported: 'Archibald Cecil Gibbs ... was charged with larceny as a bailee, the amount involved being £60, the property of Catherine O'Byrne. The jury returned a verdict of guilty, and Gibbs was remanded till Friday for sentence.'[104] Gibbs was sentenced to hard labour, the judge noting that, if restitution of £60 was made, he would recommend some remission of the sentence.[105] Gibbs appealed his conviction for larceny as a bailee and sentence of 12 months' imprisonment passed by Judge White at the Sydney Quarter Sessions on September 23, but was unsuccessful.[106]

Gibbs' death on 8 June 1932 completes the tragedy of his final years. The *Sydney Morning Herald's* headlines proclaimed:

Man shot dead outside Children's Court, Women Charged with Murder. Archibald Cecil Gibbs, aged 55 years, of Glebe Road, Glebe, was shot dead in Albion Street, Surry Hills, yesterday afternoon. One shot passed through his heart, but the police believe that four other shots were fired, as they found five empty shells in a revolver. Gibbs was shot after he had accompanied a woman, who was carrying her one-year-old daughter, from the precincts of the Children's Court. They had been involved in a case concerning the child, and were quarrelling bitterly. Several shots rang out. Gibbs made no sound. He clutched his side, and fell heavily on the footpath. A dense crowd soon gathered in the street, surrounding the dead man and the excited woman. Detectives were rushed to the scene within a few minutes. They seized a revolver and five empty cartridge shells. The detectives had difficulty in gathering information from the large crowd in the street, and received a number of conflicting stories. However, Detective-sergeants Quinn and Swasbrick, who handled the case for the police, soon secured the salient features of the tragedy. Detectives stated that Gibbs and the woman with the child had lived together. About 12 months ago they had frequent disputes, which ended in court proceedings. Gibbs was sentenced to 12 months' imprisonment for taking £60 of the woman's money. He had the benefit of a remission of sentence owing to good behaviour, and had been released only a few days ago from the Tuncurry Afforestation Camp ...[107]

The Coroner's Inquest was held two weeks later and fully reported in the *Sydney Morning Herald*:

WOMAN'S STORY. Shooting of Archibald Gibbs. ACCUSED DISCHARGED. The shooting of Archibald Cecil Gibbs, outside the Children's Court on June 8, was inquired into by the City Coroner yesterday morning. Catherine O'Byrne, who had been remanded on a charge of having murdered Gibbs, was discharged.

Detective Sergeant Hayes said that O'Byrne told him she had first met Gibbs in Queanbeyan in 1923; she was not married to him, but had taken the name of Gibbs. He was the father of her child, which was a year and

10 months old. She had summoned Gibbs before the Children's Court for maintenance. The case was put off for a while, and after leaving the court Gibbs sat on the steps of the court. She said to her little girl, "This is your daddy, dear," whereupon he replied, "I don't want her; I will kill her," and tore up two of her photos, and threw the pieces to the ground. She said, Gibbs then grabbed hold of the child, and said, "I will kill her." She struggled with him, and took the child, and walked down Albion Street. He walked down the street too, and on the way he again said he would kill the child, grabbed the child, and declared that he would never pay a penny for her support. He stooped down and commenced to open up a parcel he was carrying, and again said, "I will kill her." O'Byrne said she thought he was getting out a razor or a revolver to kill her child, and she took a revolver from her pocket, and said, "I came prepared today as I was told that you were going to crucify me and my child when you came out of gaol." He made a grab at the revolver, and said, "I will blow your brains out now and the kid's too."

Ernest Hudspeth gave evidence as to seeing the struggle, which preceded the shooting, and, in reply to Mr. Sproule, said the woman was holding the pistol apparently to frighten Gibbs but he became the aggressor, and rushed her. To the Coroner: "In my opinion, Gibbs was shot accidentally."

The Coroner returned a verdict of death from bullet wounds accidentally received, and said the unfortunate woman was in trying circumstances, afraid for her child, and one could quite understand that the gun might have gone off accidentally while the man grasped her hand. It would be a travesty of justice to send her for trial, and no jury could convict. He did not intend even to mention her name in his finding …'[108]

Gibbs was cremated at the Rookwood Crematorium on 10 June 1932.

Frank Rhoades
(Frank Hetherset Huntington Rhoades)

Frank Hetherset Huntington Rhoades was born in Brisbane, Queensland, on 22 June 1890, the son of Thomas and Eva Rhoades. He married Margaret Irvine on 8 June 1916 in Brisbane. Rhoades had completed an apprenticeship with Benjamin Winston of Brown Street, New Farm, prior to the Great War. At the time of his enlistment in 1914 he was a cabinetmaker residing at New Farm. He had also served six months in the Naval Institute Cadets.

Rhoades enlisted in Brisbane on 28 September 1914 and was posted to the 1st Australian General Hospital, Australian Army Medical Corps (AAMC).[109] He embarked for overseas service on HMAT A55 *Kyarra* in Brisbane on 21 November, disembarking in Port Said in December. In March 1915 he returned to Australia on the *Ulysses* as a medical orderly for invalids. He was granted leave from the Convalescent Home at Osborne House, Geelong, Victoria, on 28 April but failed to return and was later declared a deserter. There are no records describing his return to the Army, although it is clear that he travelled to Queensland where he married in 1916.

The military records do not contain any detail of Rhoades' activities until 9 May 1917 when he embarked on HMAT A15 *Port Sydney* with the 19th Reinforcements, 11th Light Horse Regiment, in Sydney. Rhoades disembarked at Suez on 20 June 1917 and, after further training with the 4th Light Horse Brigade Training Regiment, he was posted to the 1st Australian Light Car Patrol on 16 August. He remained with the Light Car Patrol until the end of the Great War apart from a period at the Cookery School and a short hospitalisation in August 1918. On 1 January 1919 he was posted to the AIF Details Camp pending his return to Australia.

Rhoades embarked on the HT *Kaiser-i-Hind* at Port Said on 16 May 1919 and disembarked in Sydney on 19 June. He was discharged on 20 July. For his services he was entitled to the 1914–15 Star, the British War and Victory Medals and Returned Soldier's Badge.[110]

Following discharge Rhoades returned to New Farm where he resumed his trade. He later relocated to Wilston, finally settling in Southport on the Queensland Gold Coast in the 1950s. Rhoades died in Southport on 11 July 1971 and was buried in the Southport Lawn Cemetery.

Kenrick Cory Riley

Kenrick Cory Riley was born in Mulgoa, Penrith, NSW, in 1892, the son of Alick and Louisa Riley. He was educated at Newington College, Sydney. At the time of his enlistment in 1916 he was a station hand at the Bulgroo Station, Windorah, Queensland. His family was residing at Fairview, Yass, NSW.

Riley enlisted in Liverpool, NSW, on 27 January 1916 and was allocated to the 16th Reinforcements, 6th Australian Light Horse. After training he embarked for overseas service on HMAT A1 *Hymettus* in Sydney on 3 May, disembarking at Port Said. During the voyage a group of soldiers including

Riley decided to send a letter in a bottle, as the *Sydney Morning Herald* reported in 1919:

A Bottle's Long Drift. A bottle containing letters written by Troopers B.J. Graham (2320), A.A. Hislop (2330), K.C. Riley (2120), and J.W. Chisholm (2111) was dropped overboard from the troopship Hymettus on May 4, 1916, when the vessel was off Green Cape. It was picked up in Souta Bay, Palm Island, Queensland, on 13 August 1919, having been drifting for three years and three months. The point at which the bottle was picked up was 1700 miles from the spot at which it had been thrown overboard though the total distance which the bottle drifted must have been much greater than this.[111]

81. Trooper Kenrick Cory Riley, 16th Reinforcements, 6th Light Horse Regiment, of Warialda, NSW. He was killed in action on 27 March 1918 in Amman, Palestine, aged 26 years, while carrying a fallen comrade, Sergeant Lionel William Loveland, who later died from his wounds (AWM P05032.001).

Trooper Riley was taken on strength by the 2nd Light Horse Brigade Training Regiment at Tel el Kebir. After further training he was posted to the 6th Light Horse on 12 October. He remained with the regiment until 12 August 1917 when he was transferred to the 1st Australian Light Car Patrol at Marakeb. His older brother, James, had been a driver with the Light Cars since May. While on the Hebron Road, Kenrick Riley became ill with malaria which resulted in his hospitalisation on 27 October. After treatment at the 44th Stationary and 14th Australian General Hospitals, he returned to his unit on 15 November. On 4 February 1918 he was transferred back to his original regiment, the 6th Light Horse.

Trooper Riley was killed in action on 27 March 1918 near Amman, Syria, and buried by Reverend Maley the following day. In July his family received news that Riley's effects had arrived in Australia via the *Port Darwin*. His father wrote a heartfelt letter to the authorities:

Dear Sir,

I am in receipt of your letter of 11 September 18 enclosing list of belongings of the late K.C. Riley, I have also received the parcel containing articles as listed. I have pleasure in enclosing the receipt as requested and I take this opportunity of thanking you and the Military Department for the several informations concerning our dear soldier boy.

Yours faithfully
A.C. Riley[112]

In December 1918 the Principal of Newington College, Sydney, unveiled a memorial tablet for Trooper Kenrick Riley.[113] His remains were later exhumed from his temporary grave and reburied in the Commonwealth War Graves Cemetery in Damascus. For his service, Trooper Riley was entitled to the British War and Victory Medals.

Basil Clarence Jarvis

Basil Clarence Jarvis was born in the Inman Valley, South Australia, on 9 August 1896, the son of Walter and Adelaide Jarvis. At the time of his enlistment in 1916 he was a farmer.

Jarvis enlisted in the CMF in June 1915 and served with B Squadron, 22nd Light Horse Regiment. On 8 March 1916 he enlisted in the AIF in Adelaide.

While in training in South Australia he served with the 2nd Depot Battalion, 3rd and 4th Reinforcements 48th Battalion, Base Light Horse Depot, 21st Reinforcements 9th Light Horse, the Musketry and NCO schools, 24th Reinforcements 9th Light Horse, and the 25th Reinforcements 3rd Light Horse.

On 1 January 1917 he was appointed provisional corporal and allocated to the 24th Reinforcements, 9th Australian Light Horse. On 5 February he embarked for overseas service on HMAT A6 *Clan MacGorquodale* in Adelaide, disembarking in Port Said on 12 March. He was taken on strength by the Details Camp at Moascar and promoted temporary corporal. However he reverted to trooper on 26 March when he was posted to the 3rd Light Horse Regiment. He transferred to the 9th Light Horse Regiment on 3 August. This posting proved brief as he was then posted to the 1st Australian Light Car Patrol on 31 August.

82. Troopers Basil Jarvis and Leo Cohn with Sergeant Creek in Syria in 1919 (Cohn collection ATM LCP.LC 001).

Jarvis remained with the Light Cars until 18 October 1918 when he was evacuated to the 31st General Hospital via HMHS *Dunluce Castle* with malaria. After hospitalisation and convalescence he returned to the Light Cars on 2 January 1919. Trooper Jarvis marched into the Details Camp on 15 March and later embarked on the HT *Kaiser-i-Hind* at Port Said on 16 May, disembarking in Adelaide on 14 June. He was discharged on 22 July. For his military service he was entitled to the British War and Victory Medals and Returned Soldier's Badge.[114]

On his return to Australia Jarvis married Elizabeth McCallun in 1921. By 1969 he was residing in Victor Harbour where he died on 16 June 1977.

Leo Reoch Cohn, OBE

Leo Reoch Cohn was born in Bendigo, Victoria, on 12 May 1897, the son of Julius and Sarah Helen Cohn. He was educated at St Andrew's College and the Continuation School, Bendigo.

83. Trooper Leo Cohn, 8th Light Horse Regiment, prior to embarkation in 1915 (Cohn collection ATM LCP.LC 009).

The Cohns were a prominent Bendigo and colonial Victorian family. Leo Cohn's grandfather, Moritz Cohn, had emigrated from Denmark and settled in Bendigo in 1853 with his brothers Julius Isaac and Jacob. The three brothers established a cordial factory that later expanded to brewing and foodstuffs. They held prominent local government roles, two becoming mayors of Bendigo. Among other organisations they helped establish the Bendigo Land and Building Society which later became the Bendigo Bank. Jacob Cohn was the Danish Consul for Victoria. After Moritz died, Leo Cohn's father, Julius, trained as a brewer in Worms, Germany, and joined the family business as Head Brewer on his return. He is reputed to have brewed the first lager beer in Australia.

At the time of his enlistment in 1915, Leo Cohn was a clerk residing at his family home, The Bungalow, 21 Barkley Place, Bendigo. He was also serving in the 68th Battalion, Senior Cadets. He enlisted in Bendigo on 6 May 1915 and was allocated to the 8th Reinforcements, 22nd Battalion. On 12 September he was transferred to the 7th Reinforcements, 8th Australian Light Horse, and embarked for overseas service on HMAT A57 *Malakuta* at Port Melbourne on 24 September, disembarking at Port Said in October. He was taken on strength by the 8th Light Horse Regiment Details at Heliopolis on 26 December.

Cohn served with the 8th Light Horse in the Sinai until 30 December 1916 when he was briefly detached to the Australian Base Post Office at Moascar. He returned to the 8th Light Horse on 16 January 1917. In July and August he suffered a period of ill health and hospitalisation. In a letter home in September 1917, Cohn wrote of his transfer from the Light Horse:

> While I was in hospital I had a letter from Jack (Langley) to say that there was a vacancy and if I could get out of the 8th, I would be able to get in at the other end. That is why I worked my way out of hospital so soon. I never dreamt that they would grant my application but by being down at Moascar I put it in there and got a Captain that I know very well to recommend it. I had just been with the Regiment a couple of days when it came through. I was very sorry to leave the boys and all the old horses but the dust was beginning to get me down and it would only have been a matter of a month or so before I was in hospital again …

He was transferred to the 1st Australian Light Car Patrol on 8 September where he remained until the end of the war other than for periods of hospitalisation. On 15 March 1919 he was posted to the AIF Details Camp pending his return to Australia. He embarked on the HT *Kaiser-i-Hind* in Suez on 16 May and disembarked at Port Melbourne on 16 June. He was discharged on 8 August.

Following his discharge Cohn's health declined rapidly and he was admitted to a rehabilitation hospital in Caulfield where he spent several months regaining his strength. He returned to Bendigo where the electoral rolls initially record his occupation as a farmer. He applied for a war service farm in the Mallee but was persuaded to return to the commercial world. He was accepted back into the family business on the proviso he complete a Diploma of Science in Organic Chemistry at the Bendigo School of Mines. He worked in the firm as a travelling salesman while undertaking his studies. In September 1924 he married Beatrice Pitman and relocated to Swan Hill where he established and managed the Cohn Brothers' Soft Drink Factory and Tomato Cannery and raised four children.

In 1944 he reported on the difficulties of producing canned goods in wartime Australia:

> Tomatoes take a high place in Swan Hill's production. The Cohn Bros Ltd.'s factory handled more than 1,000 tons last year for sauce making and pulping, drawing supplies from growers. Mr L. R. Cohn, manager, said the factory was to have canned a target of 2,500 tons, but the programme had to be greatly curtailed because of inability to get delivery of machinery and equipment. That machinery is now coming to hand and we expect to process more than 2,000 tons of tomatoes, and also carrots, beet, and peas, next season. We feel there will be no difficulty in getting the produce. We have erected a modern hygienic canning factory and a fruit-receiving shed. Labour was short during the processing season, but local women responded well to an appeal for part-time workers. Citrus formerly processed by the factory is now sent to the Bendigo factory.

Cohn would become a pillar of the community in Swan Hill and later Bendigo. He was an active member of Rotary, the Masonic Lodge, the Returned Service League and Legacy. He was also the local Commissioner of Scouts, the government nominee for the Mallee Regional Commission, the Portland Harbour Trust, and the Swan Hill Waterworks and Sewage Authority. He was a patron of the Bendigo Base Hospital and the Bendigo Art Gallery. His granddaughter, Shelley Cohn, recalled that there were also less public aspects to his welfare work. During the 1920s, the Depression, and after World War II, a number of unemployed and homeless ex-diggers were living rough along the banks of the Murray River. On his morning walks Leo would check on these men and do whatever possible to improve their welfare.

On 18 May 1942 Cohn returned to military service when he enlisted in the CMF at Swan Hill. He served with the 21st Battalion, VDC, where he was promoted lieutenant on 26 June. On enlistment he stated his civilian occupation as Foodstuff Factory Manager, adding that he was also a qualified chemist. He served on a part-time basis until 31 October 1945 when the VDC was disbanded. He joined the Reserve of Officers on 1 November 1945.

In 1957 Cohn returned to Bendigo as Managing Director of Cohn Bros. He had been a Company Director since 1937. He went on to become Chairman of Cohn Bros and the Company's nominee Director of Carlton and United Breweries in 1961. He was also a Director of Sandhurst Trustees Ltd.

Cohn also gave his time to other projects that assisted regional Victoria. In the 1960s he helped establish and became Chairman of Bendigo TV and was the Mallee Regional Committee representative for the Western League. On the Queen's Birthday List in June 1964 he was made an Officer in the Civil Division of the Most Excellent Order of the British Empire (OBE) for services to the community. On four Anzac days in the 1970s, Cohn was one of four Great War Light Horsemen who led the march on horseback. Leo Cohn died in Bendigo on 5 July 1984.

For his military service during two wars, he was entitled to the 1914–15 Star, the British War and Victory Medals and the Returned Soldier's Badge for the Great War, and the Australian Service Medal 1939–45 for the Second World War.

Cohn's son, John Magnus Cohn, served in the Second World War as an able seaman with the Royal Australian Navy Reserve between April 1945 and December 1946.

Sydney Colin Kenneth Forsyth

Sydney Colin Kenneth Forsyth was born in Collingwood, Victoria, on 10 June 1894, the son of Alexander and Elizabeth Forsyth.[115] At the time of his enlistment in 1916 he was a driver residing in East Perth. He was also a member of the CMF.

Forsyth enlisted in Brisbane on 10 April 1916 and was initially posted to the 62nd Depot Battalion. On 1 May he was taken on strength by the 21st Reinforcements, 11th Battalion. His training continued in Adelaide where he was transferred to the 22nd Reinforcements, 10th Light Horse Regiment, on 15 August. He embarked for overseas service on HMAT A55 *Bakara* in Adelaide on 4 November, disembarking at Port Said on 4 December. He was taken on strength by the 3rd Light Horse Training Regiment at Moascar on 14 December. After further training he was posted to the 10th Light Horse Regiment on 16 January 1917. He joined the 1st Australian Light Car Patrol on 29 September, this posting proving brief as Forsyth returned to the 10th Light Horse on 4 November. On return to his regiment he had several periods of hospitalisation.

Forsyth embarked on the HT *Oxfordshire* at Port Said on 19 July 1918 and disembarked in Perth on 4 August. He was discharged as medically unfit on 8 November. In 1919 Forsyth returned to Perth where he was initially employed as a wool merchant. He later settled in Osborne Park and became a carrier. He married Laura Scott in Perth on 31 October 1920.

Forsyth's military service continued in the Second World War when he enlisted in the CMF on 8 March 1941 in Western Australia and served on a part-time basis as a sapper with the 22nd Field Company. At the end of 1941 he was required to return to essential war industries and discharged from the Army. Forsyth died in Perth in 1969.

For his services in the Great War he was entitled to the British War and Victory Medals, the Silver War and Returned Soldier's Badges.[116]

Alexander Eddie

Alexander Eddie was born in Richmond, Victoria, on 8 September 1888, the son of Alexander and Annie Eddie. At the time of his enlistment in 1916 he was an accountant residing in Newmarket.

Eddie enlisted in the AIF in Melbourne on 8 November 1916. While in training in Victoria he served with the AIF Signal School and the 8th Reinforcements, 3rd Australian Camel Regiment. He embarked for overseas service on 2 February 1917 aboard the RMS *Karmala* in Port Melbourne, disembarking at Port Said on 11 March. On arrival he was taken on strength by the Details Camp at Moascar and on 2 April posted to the 4th Light Horse Regiment where he was promoted acting sergeant on 26 May. Eddie reverted to the rank of trooper and transferred to the 1st Australian Light Car Patrol on 11 September. He remained with the Light Cars until 15 March 1919 when he marched into the Details Camp pending his return to Australia. He embarked on the HT *Kaiser-i-Hind* at Port Said, Egypt, on 16 May and disembarked in Melbourne on 14 June. He was discharged on 24 July. For his military service he was entitled to the British War and Victory Medals and Returned Soldier's Badge.[117]

84. A moment to relax at the Dead Sea post in 1918. Included in this group are Harkin, Hyman, Cohn, Bosanquet, Langley, Morgan and Eddie (Cohn collection ATM LCP.LC 002).

On his return to Australia Eddie initially moved to Newmarket, resumed his accountancy work and married Clarice Bishop in 1920. He later became a builder and contractor and had moved to Balaclava by 1924, relocating to Healesville by 1931. The Eddies lived in Kew in the 1950s before settling in Pearcedale Road, Cranbourne, in the early 1960s. Alexander Eddie died in Frankston on 19 April 1971 and was buried at the Cranbourne Cemetery.

Gaston Victor Somny

Gaston Victor Somny was born in Hanwell, Middlesex, UK, on 9 March 1891, the son of Joseph and Cecelia Somny. In the 1911 English census Somny is recorded as living with his parents at Hanwell and employed as a ship's librarian. At the outbreak of the Great War he was residing in Perth, Western Australia. At the time of his enlistment in 1914 he described himself as a motor expert and had completed an apprenticeship with the Dagenham Car Company. His next of kin was his father, Joseph Somny, of Portman Square, London.[118]

Somny enlisted at Helena Vale on 17 August 1914 and was allocated to A Company, 11th Infantry Battalion, on the same day. After training at Blackboy Camp, he embarked for overseas service on HMAT A11 *Ascanius* in Fremantle on 2 November, disembarking at Port Said on 13 December. Following training in Egypt, the 11th Battalion boarded the *Suffolk* on 1 March 1915 to join the Mediterranean Expeditionary Force off the island of Lemnos. During March the battalion continued training and practised landings on Lemnos but remained aboard the *Suffolk*. On 25 April Private Somny landed on the Gallipoli Peninsula. He was later evacuated with dysentery to the HMHS *Grantully Castle* and admitted to the 15th Stationary Hospital on Mudros on 11 June. On 7 July he was a patient at the 2nd Australian Hospital at Ghezireh and was diagnosed with shell shock. He was posted to the Base Details at Zeitoun on 22 July. It is evident that his pre-war skills were recognised as he was posted as a machine artificer at an armoury. It is likely that Somny was promoted to acting sergeant in this position.

In March 1917 Acting Sergeant Somny was posted to the Inventions Board, General Headquarters, Egyptian Expeditionary Force. He remained with the headquarters until 22 July when he was posted to the armoury at the Australian and New Zealand Training Camp at Moascar. On 23 September he transferred to the 1st Australian Light Car Patrol, although it appears that his health may have been poor as he was marched out within the week. After periods of hospitalisation and convalescence, he returned to the Australian Camp at Suez. He remained on cinema projectionist duties for some time before transferring to the 58th Squadron, Royal Air Force (RAF), on 15 July 1918. However illness and hospitalisation prevented him from taking up this posting. His medical records clearly show that Somny's health had declined rapidly as a result of his war service.

Private Somny embarked on the HT *Somali* at Port Said on 26 December 1918 and disembarked in Fremantle on 21 January 1919. He was discharged as medically unfit on 6 April. For his services he was entitled to the 1914–15 Star, the British War and Victory Medals and the Silver War and Returned Soldier's Badges.[119]

Soon after his discharge, Somny returned to the UK where he married Doris Meacock on 12 November 1921. However he died in tragic circumstances on 10 December 1935 as the *West Australian* reported:

AIR DISASTER. BELGIAN PLANE CRASHES. ELEVEN KILLED. THREE BRITISH VICTIMS. LONDON, Dec. 10: Flying from Brussels to London, a Belgian airliner carrying seven passengers and a crew of four crashed into a hill near Tatsfield, Surrey today. So terrific was the crash that the noise was heard two miles away. The machine was smashed to pieces and the eleven occupants were killed. The bodies were terribly mutilated and a woman was decapitated. There has never been a worse disaster to a civil aeroplane to England. In addition to the pilot Mr. Schoon Brodt, the crew comprised of an engineer, a wireless operator and a steward. Of the seven passengers, three were British and four were

Germans travelling from Cologne to London. The British passengers included Sir John Carden, a noted engineer, and designer of aeroplane engines, and Mr. G. V. Somny, who served with the Australian army in the Great War.

The weather was bad for flying during the day and it was very cold, windy and raining when the crash occurred at dusk. The machine, an Italian three-engine Savoia monoplane owned by a Belgian Company, was in touch with the Croydon aerodrome control tower by wireless until a few minutes before the disaster. The operator of the control tower was awaiting the pilot's signal asking for permission to land when the news of the crash was telephoned by the local police.

Wing Touches Trees. — The plane was observed near Tatfield flying low, presumably owing to ice on the wings. People in the neighbourhood saw one wing hit the treetops on a small hill near Pitsie Hill. The machine staggered as the pilot apparently tried to gain height but the plane crashed into the summit of Pitsie Hill. Many persons rushed the scene, but the passengers and crew were seemingly killed instantly … Mr G V Somny who was 42 years of age was employed by the Ford Motor Company at its Dagenham factory. He went to Australia at the age of 17. He joined the AIF and served at Gallipoli: he returned to England after the Great War. Entered the motor trade, specializing in tractor and aero engines and agricultural machinery. Mr. Somny was of French descent; his wife and daughter (aged 12) were listening to the wireless news bulletin and heard a description of the crash, at first without realizing that Mr. Somny was travelling by air. Mrs. Somny telephoned to the Air Ministry and received tragic confirmation. Mr. Somny, who disliked flying, went to Belgium at the weekend and returned today with Sir John Carden with whom he was associated in business …[120]

John Beverley McKay

John Beverley McKay was born in Dubbo, NSW, on 6 December 1892, the son of John and Mary Ann McKay. At the time of his enlistment in 1915 he was a station overseer residing at the 'Over Flow' in Warren.

McKay enlisted in Liverpool, NSW, on 20 July 1915. At the Light Horse Depot in Liverpool Camp he was allocated to the 10th Reinforcements, 6th Australian Light Horse, and embarked for overseas service on HMAT A4 *Pera* in Sydney on 12 October, disembarking at Port Said in November. He was taken on strength by the 6th Light Horse Regiment Details at Maadi on 27 December. On 23 February 1916 he marched into the 6th Light Horse at Serapeum. After a period of hospitalisation, he was posted to the 2nd Light Horse Training Regiment at Moascar on 13 April. In May he attended a Lewis gun course and qualified as a first class machine-gunner. On 5 July McKay returned to the 6th Light Horse Regiment before attending a Hotchkiss machine-gun course in September. He joined the 1st Australian Light Car Patrol on 4 October 1917, remaining with the Light Cars until 13 March 1919 when he marched into the AIF Details Camp pending his repatriation. Trooper McKay embarked on the HT *Dorset* at Port Said on 29 April and disembarked in Sydney on 11 June. He was discharged on 3 August 1919.

For his service in the Great War he was entitled to the 1914–15 Star, the British War and Victory Medals and the Returned Soldier's Badge.[121]

McKay married Florence Edward on 15 June 1927 at Darlinghurst in Sydney. By 1930 he had returned to rural life and was recorded as a station overseer at Pigeonbah near Warren. By 1936 he had returned to the family property, the 'Over Flow' near Warren, where his occupation was recorded as a grazier. He died on 6 July 1956 and was buried in the Roman Catholic section of the Warren General Cemetery.

Martin Cleveland Pines

Martin Cleveland Pines was born in Balmain, NSW, on 6 November 1892, the son of Frederick and Eleanor Pines. At the time of his enlistment in 1915 he was a station overseer.

Pines enlisted in Liverpool, NSW, on 26 June 1915. At the Light Horse Depot in Liverpool Camp on 1 July he was allocated to the 10th Reinforcements, 6th Australian Light Horse, and embarked for overseas service on HMAT A4 *Pera* in Sydney on 12 October, disembarking at Port Said in November. He was taken on strength by the 6th Light Horse Regiment Details at Maadi on 27 December and marched into the 6th Light Horse at Serapeum on 23 February 1916. In August 1917 he attended a school of instruction to become an officer's batman. He joined the 1st Australian Light Car Patrol on 4 November and remained with the Light Cars until he was evacuated with malaria on 4 January 1919 and hospitalised at the 14th Australian General Hospital. Trooper Pines embarked on the HMAT A14 *Euripedes* at Kantara, Egypt, on 15 March 1919 and disembarked in Sydney on 25 April. He was discharged as medically unfit on 10 August 1919.

On his return to Australia, Pines married Helen Nossiter in Ryde in 1927. He returned to farming and, in 1930, he was a grazier residing at Kallamondah, Boggabri. By 1935 he had relocated to Neutral Bay. It appears that Pines had fallen on hard times as the following year he changed address again and was living in Lane Cove. The electoral roll records no occupation at this point in his life.

On 3 October 1939, following the outbreak of the Second World War, Pines enlisted in the CMF at North Sydney. His stated occupation at this time was farmer and his place of residence Mosman. He also stated that he had been unemployed since 1936. He was posted to the 2nd Garrison Battalion on 16 October 1939 and transferred to the 7th Garrison Battalion on 13 December 1940. This posting proved short-lived as he was taken on strength by Headquarters Eastern Command on December 17. On 4 April 1941 he was promoted corporal and, on 20 March 1942, posted to the 5th Supply Personnel Company. Promotion to sergeant occurred on 1 June 1942 and a final posting to the 12th Supply Personnel Company took effect on 27 July 1942. From this point Pines' health deteriorated and there were several hospital admissions. He was discharged as medically unfit on 24 May 1943. He died on 12 August 1970.

For his military service he was entitled to the 1914–15 Star, the British War and Victory Medals and the Silver War and Returned Soldier's Badges for the Great War. His service in the Second World War earned him the War and Australian Services Medals and Australian Service Badge.[122]

Charles Longden Richardson

Charles Longden Richardson was born in Queanbeyan, NSW, on 2 February 1893, the son of Dr Sidney and Mrs Minna Richardson. He was educated at the Queanbeyan Primary School and The King's School at Parramatta and was a member of the school's cadet unit. At the time of his enlistment in 1915 he was an analytical chemist at the Colonial Sugar Refining Company and his home address was 'The Elms', Queanbeyan.

Richardson enlisted in Liverpool on 18 April 1915. He was allocated to the 8th Reinforcements, 6th Australian Light Horse, and embarked for overseas service on HMAT A23 *Suffolk* in Sydney on 28 July, disembarking at Port Said in September. Richardson was taken on strength by the 6th Light Horse Regimental Details at Maadi on 27 December. He joined the 6th Light Horse Regiment on 23 February 1916 and remained with the regiment until 21

October 1917 when he was detached to the ANZAC Mounted Division Supply Dump for a brief period. From this location he joined the 1st Australian Light Car Patrol on 3 November. Apart from periods of illness, Richardson served with the unit for the remainder of the war.

Trooper Richardson embarked on the HMAT A15 *Port Sydney* at Port Said on 5 March 1919 and disembarked in Sydney on 11 April. He was discharged as medically unfit on 13 June. For his services he was entitled to the 1914–15 Star, the British War and Victory Medals and the Silver War and Returned Soldier's Badges.[123]

Following his discharge Richardson returned to NSW where he married Helen Mallam in 1933. In the 1930s he relocated to Childers in Queensland where he was employed as a field chemist with the Colonial Sugar Refinery. Later moves took him to the Hambledon Mill in Gordonvale and Fiji. During the 1930s and the war years Richardson was involved with the Pest Boards which sought to increase sugar production by removing pests from the cane fields. The *Cairns Post* in May 1941 reported a paper presented by:

> Mr. C. L. Richardson, of Hambledon, and Mr. B. W. Mungumery, of Meringa, on the control of the Frenchii grub pest showed that control could be effected by suitable fallowing and cultivation of infested fields. Mr. Richardson's investigations showed that the giant toad may be doing effective work in destroying a large number of Frenchii cane beetles. The increase in bird life following the large-scale surrender of firearms was referred to. It was decided to ask the Government to consider the licensing of firearms and their strict control in bird life sanctuaries. It was also decided to ask the Government for a greater measure of autonomy for pest boards in the conduct of their domestic pest control campaigns.[124]

Perhaps his advocacy of the cane toad was not Richardson's best professional moment. During the Second World War he moved to South Australia to establish a grain distillery at Wallaroo. Sometime after the end of the war he settled in Double Bay, NSW, where he died in 1979.[125]

Royden John Simpson

Royden John Simpson was born in Baerami, near Muswellbrook, NSW, on 17 October 1889, the son of George and Isobel Simpson. The Simpsons were pioneers of the Muswellbrook-Maitland region. At the time of his enlistment in 1915 he was a grazier residing in Emu Vale, Kurrabee. Simpson was a well-known sportsman in the Muswellbrook district, achieving particular prominence as a batsman for the Denman cricket team.

Simpson enlisted at Liverpool on 4 May 1915. After training at the Australian Light Horse Depot in Liverpool he was allocated to the 8th Reinforcements, 6th Australian Light Horse, on 1 July and embarked for overseas service on HMAT A23 *Suffolk* in Sydney on 28 July, disembarking at Port Said in September. Soon after, he was sent to Gallipoli where he was taken on strength by the 6th Light Horse Regiment. He was admitted to the 16th Stationary Hospital on Mudros on 12 January 1916 with a case of diphtheria and was evacuated to Malta aboard HMHS *Panama* on 21 January, arriving at St David's Hospital, Malta, on 26 January. Here his diagnosis was amended to severe enteric fever. After hospitalisation and convalescence he returned to Alexandria on 27 March. Following a further period of hospitalisation at the British Red Cross and No. 3 Auxiliary Hospitals, he returned to the 6th Light Horse at Tel el Kebir on 30 April. Simpson remained with the regiment until 21 October 1917 when he was detached to the ANZAC Mounted Division Supply Dump for a brief period. From this location he joined the 1st Australian Light Car Patrol on 3 November. Other than for periods of illness, Simpson served with the unit for the remainder of the war. He was posted to the AIF Details Camp on 15 March 1919 prior to his return to Australia.

85. Privates Bosanquet and Simpson with fish caught in the Jordan River, 1918 (Cornwell collection ATM LCP. PC. 012).

Trooper Simpson embarked on the HT *Kaiser-i-Hind* at Port Said on 18 May 1919 and disembarked in Sydney on 19 June where he was discharged on 18 August. For his services he was entitled to the 1914–15 Star, the British War and Victory Medals and the Returned Soldier's Badge.[126]

On return to civilian life after the Great War, Simpson married Kathleen Vindon at Morpeth on 18 January 1922. He acted as manager for the Widden Stud Farm until 1925, when the *Muswellbrook Chronicle* reported:

A visit to Widden Stud Farm, made last week, showed that everything was spic and span at that old-established property. The whole of the stock, which includes the patriarch Linacre, as well as Kenilworth, Claroi and others of lesser renown in the equestrian world, are looking exceedingly well; and the brood mares and their progeny are also in fine fettle. During a short chat with Mr. Roy Simpson, the genial and capable manager of the stud farm, the fact was elicited that the champion sire Valais would arrive at Widden in about a fortnight. It is a matter for regret that Mr. Simpson, after putting in over three years' yeoman service, has resigned his position as manager, and leaves Widden before the end of the month.[127]

Simpson returned to the family property at Emu Vale.

On the outbreak of the Second World War Simpson joined the Muswellbrook Recruiting Committee.[128] In 1941 the *Muswellbrook Chronicle* reported that he was relinquishing his interest in dairying at Emu Vale.[129] On 15 August 1942 he returned to military service when he enlisted in the CMF at Baerami, NSW. He served with the 6th Battalion, VDC, as a private and was discharged on 29 June 1944.

In the late 1940s Simpson moved to the Dunoon Estate where he assumed the position of caretaker. By the late 1950s he had moved to Mount Cole where he was employed as a groundskeeper. Simpson maintained an active life. The *Singleton Argus* of 1952 reported his admission to the Maitland Hospital with a broken collarbone after falling from a horse.[130] Simpson had also earlier returned to the Denman cricket team, batting on a regular basis until the late 1930s. He died at St Leonards on 12 April 1973 and was buried at the Mount Dangar Cemetery.

Albert Gordon Holley

Albert Gordon Holley was born in Fulham, London, on 20 February 1894, the son of Cornelius and Ellen Holley. He was educated at Grafton Road School,

Islington. In the 1911 census his occupation was recorded as builder's clerk. On 26 February 1914 he embarked on the HMAT A24 *Benella* for Melbourne, arriving on 10 April. At the time of his enlistment in 1915 he was a labourer residing in Mornington and his next of kin was his sister, Ada Holley, of Burnfoot Avenue, Fulham.

86. Driver Albert Gordon Holley, No. 1 Pack Wireless Signal Troop (AWM DA13770).

Holley enlisted in the AIF in Melbourne on 14 September 1915. He initially served with A Company, 24th Depot Battalion, at Royal Park and D Company, 20th Depot Battalion, at Castlemaine before being allocated to the 1st Australian Pack Wireless Signal Troop on 4 January 1916. He embarked for overseas service on HMAT A12 *Salandah* in Melbourne on 5 February, disembarking in Colombo, Ceylon, on 24 February. The following day Holley transferred to the HS *Varela* which was due to sail to Bombay, India, on 28 February. On 10 March he embarked for Mesopotamia, disembarking at Basra on 20 March. He was taken on strength by the 1st Australian and New Zealand Wireless Signal Squadron on arrival, although his service with the squadron would prove brief. He was invalided to India via the HS *Varela* on 5 August. On 20 October he boarded the HMHS *Alexa* at Bombay for Egypt via Aden, arriving on 7 November 1916. On 23 February 1917 he was attached to Headquarters ANZAC Training Centre and Details Camp in Egypt. On 9 June he was detached to the 3rd Light Horse Brigade Headquarters before returning to the Details Camp at Moascar on 15 October.

Holley joined the 1st Australian Light Car Patrol on 1 November. He remained with the Light Car Patrol until 7 September 1918 when he was admitted to the 36th Stationary Hospital and later transferred to the 14th Australian General Hospital. He did not return to his unit until 15 December. He remained with the Light Cars until 8 February 1919 when he marched into the AIF Details Camp pending his repatriation.

In March 1919 Holley was granted a month's leave in the UK and boarded the HT *Malwa* at Port Said, bound for Taranto, Italy, on 28 March, eventually arriving in the UK on 11 April where he was taken on strength by Headquarters AIF. Following his leave he was granted non-military employment as part of the AIF's repatriation program. He attended a commercial course at Clark's College, Chancellery Lane, London.

Holley embarked on the HT *Devon* at Southampton on 16 September and disembarked in Melbourne on 27 November. He was discharged as medically unfit on 26 March 1920. For his service in the Great War he was entitled to the British War and Victory Medals and the Silver War and Returned Soldier's Badges.[131]

Following his discharge he initially moved to Mornington, later settling in Brunswick where his occupation was recorded as a clerk. He died at Glenlyon Road, Brunswick, on 21 September 1925. His memorial notice described him as 'one of nature's gentlemen'.[132] In a joint memorial notice in the *Argus* a year after Holley's death, a friend wrote: 'two of the best gone but not forgotten'.[133]

Lancelot George Vivian Bosanquet

Lancelot George Vivian Bosanquet was born in McKay, Queensland, on 25 September 1879, the son of George and Mary Bosanquet. Commander Bosanquet RN was a prominent member of the NSW Colonial Defence Forces where he was in charge of Naval Artillery Volunteers and the torpedo defences of Sydney Harbour for a number of years.[134]

Lancelot Bosanquet enlisted in the 3rd NSW Imperial Bushmen in early 1900. The *Cumberland Argus and Fruitgrowers Advocate* reported in April 1900 that George Lancelot Bosanquet of Moorebank had been selected to go to South Africa with the Imperial Bushmen, describing him as 'a fine young fellow who won his bush experience in Queensland'.[135] He embarked on the *Armenian* in Sydney on 23 April and arrived in South Africa on 4 May. Bosanquet served with A Squadron in the Western Transvaal, Cape Colony, Orange Free State and Rhodesia before returning to NSW in 1901 where he was discharged after 16 months of service.

Following his return from South Africa, Bosanquet resumed farming and married Annie Kennedy at Port Macquarie, NSW, on 9 February 1905. At the time of his enlistment in the AIF in 1916, his next of kin was his wife, Annie Bosanquet of Forrest House, Comboyne.

Bosanquet enlisted in the AIF at Bathurst on 18 February 1916 and was taken on strength by the Bathurst Depot Battalion. His enlistment was reported in the *Richmond River Herald* in February 1916: 'Mr. Lancelot Bosanquet (married) has left the Comboyne to enlist. Mr. Bosanquet is an old South African soldier, and a descendant of a fine old English family. He is closely related to Admiral Bosanquet.'[136]

He was promoted corporal and posted to D Company, 53rd Battalion, on 24 May before being posted back to the Depot Battalion at Bathurst on 5 July. On 9 October Bosanquet was posted to the 22nd Reinforcements, 7th Light Horse Regiment, appointed sergeant (voyage only) and embarked for overseas service on HMAT A65 *Clan McEwan* at Port Melbourne. After disembarking in Egypt he reverted to trooper and was taken on strength by the 2nd Light Horse Training Regiment on 9 November. He joined the 7th Light Horse Regiment on 13 February 1917. On Christmas Day 1917 he wrote to Lieutenant James and requested a transfer to the Light Car Patrol as either a gunner or mechanic based on his civilian garage experience. His request was evidently successful as he was posted to the 1st Australian Light Car Patrol on 14 February 1918. Other than for periods of hospitalisation, he remained with the Light Cars until 15 March 1919 when he was posted to the AIF Details

Camp pending his return to Australia. He embarked on the HT *Kaiser-i-Hind* at Suez on 16 May and disembarked in Sydney on 19 June. Bosanquet was discharged on 27 July 1919 and returned to his farm at Comboyne.

Bosanquet returned to military service for the third time in 1940 when he enlisted in the CMF on 23 December at Port Macquarie. On enlistment he stated that he was a grazier who resided at Wauchope. He was posted to the 8th Garrison Battalion at Adamstown where he was promoted acting sergeant on 19 December 1941. He was discharged as medically unfit on 17 July 1942. In the late 1940s he relocated to Panania and, by 1959, he had settled in Pambula, where he died on 10 May 1962.

For his service in South Africa, the Great War and Second World War he was entitled to: the Queen's South Africa Medal (Bars: Cape Colony, Orange Free State, Transvaal, Rhodesia and South Africa 1901), British War, Victory, the War and Australian Service Medals and Returned Soldier's and General Service Badges.[137]

Bosanquet's sons served in the second AIF: George Stanley Bosanquet enlisted on 1 August 1940 and served as a major with the 32nd Works Company and was discharged on 17 May 1946. Angus Lancelot Bosanquet enlisted on 21 August 1942 and served as a lance corporal with the 2/2nd Australian Tank Transporter Company, Australian Army Service Corps (AASC). He was discharged on 13 December 1943. Robert Eric Bosanquet graduated as a doctor in Edinburgh, Scotland, in 1943 and served in the British Army.

Frank Arnott, MM

Frank Arnott was born in Wagga Wagga, NSW, in 1889, the son of George and Catherine Arnott. He was educated at The King's School in Parramatta where he was a boarder between 1905 and 1908. At King's he was a school monitor, cadet lieutenant, and a gifted rugby player, awarded an Honour Cap for the First Fifteen in both 1906 and 1907.[138] At the time of his enlistment in 1915 he was a clerk residing at 'St Claire', Bradley's Head, Mosman.

Arnott enlisted at Liverpool on 21 April 1915. At the Light Horse Depot in Liverpool Camp he was allocated to the 8th Reinforcements, 6th Australian Light Horse, and embarked for overseas service on HMAT A23 *Suffolk* in Sydney on 28 July, disembarking at Port Said in September. There he was taken on strength by the 6th Light Horse Regiment Details at Maadi.

Arnott was then transferred to A Squadron, 6th Light Horse, at Gallipoli on 14 November. In December he was evacuated from Gallipoli with his regiment, embarking on the HMAT A72 *Beltana* and arriving in Alexandria on Christmas Day 1915. On 2 August 1916 Arnott was wounded in action at Romani, suffering a gunshot wound to his left knee. He was evacuated to the 2nd Light Horse Field Ambulance and later the 3rd Australian General Hospital in Cairo. He returned to the 6th Light Horse on 9 September. In August 1917 he attended a Hotchkiss machine-gun course and was awarded a first class gunner's qualification. On 9 December he was awarded the Military Medal for bravery in the field and, on 6 January 1918, promoted lance corporal. On 10 March he reverted to the rank of trooper and was transferred to the 1st Australian Light Car Patrol where he remained until 31 July when he was evacuated to the 76th Casualty Clearing Station with an infection in his left leg. Following hospitalisation at the 36th and 44th Stationary Hospitals and the 14th Australian General Hospital and a period of convalescent leave, he returned to the Light Cars on 13 October.[139]

87. Captain Ernest James, MC, with Trooper Frank Arnott, MM, at Aleppo, Syria (AWM B01074).

On 14 March 1919 Arnott marched into the AIF Details Camp pending his repatriation. He embarked on the HMAT A15 *Port Sydney* at Kantara, Egypt, on 4 March 1919 and disembarked in Sydney on 21 April. He was discharged as medically unfit on 13 June.

For his service in the Great War he was entitled to the Military Medal, 1914–15 Star, the British War and Victory Medals and the Silver War and Returned Soldier's Badges.

Following his discharge he married Dorothy Pike at St Clement's Church in Mosman on 22 January 1921. Arnott settled in Mosman where he returned to his pre-war occupation as a clerk. He died on 5 August 1968.

Arnott's son, Edwin Chapman Arnott, served in the Second World War as a lieutenant with the anti-aircraft branch of the Royal Australian Artillery between September 1942 and June 1945.

OLD SOLDIERS FADING AWAY

88. Officers and other ranks of No. 1 Australian Light Car Patrol (AWM B00708).

Two images of the last days of the 1st Australian Light Car Patrol stand out. The first is a photo taken in Aleppo, Syria, where 19 of the patrol's 21 members pose for a group portrait. At the rear of the image a light car is visible on the left and two Lewis guns sit in the foreground. The war had either ended or was about to end and there is a sense of pride and unity projecting from the group. The second, a word image, comprises the final lines of James' 'The Motor Patrol'. It is a parody of the song *Kind thoughts can never die* which British soldiers turned to *Old soldiers never die — they simply fade away.* In these few words James encapsulates the emotion behind the disbandment of a very close and unique unit of the AIF and hints of a future life in peacetime Australia.

The 1st Australian Light Car Patrol in Aleppo in 1918

With the surrender of the Ottoman Empire in October 1918, the 1st Australian Light Car Patrol's establishment consisted of two officers and 19 NCOs and men who manned six Model T Fords and the captured German touring car. During its existence, 33 members of the AIF had been on the unit's posted strength as well as an unknown number of British Army soldiers who were attached at various stages, usually driver-mechanics from the ASC and despatch riders. Since August 1916 the Armoured Car Battery and, later, Light Car Patrol, had seen 27 months of active service in two distinct campaigns.

The leadership of the Light Cars was extraordinarily stable. Captain James was both the driving force behind the unit and the only officer commanding from its formation in March 1916 to its disbandment in March 1919. His involvement also included the period from April 1915 when he initiated the project. Lieutenant Cornwell also served with the patrol through its entire service, less one month while on detachment. Sergeants Langley and Creek were also foundation members whose service dated back to 1915 at Royal Park. The three corporals, Hyman, Bissett and Morgan, all dated their service to the days of the Deport Battalion in Melbourne. These men all served between 28 and 31 months with the Armoured Cars or Light Cars. This service would have been far longer had time at the depot battalion been included.

The composition of the unit in October 1919 is worth examining. Some 38% had embarked in June 1916 with the Armoured Car Section in Melbourne, while 62% were reinforcements. The average full-time service was 36 months with two members serving 47 months; the shortest full-time service was 23 months. The average service with the patrol was 19 months with the longest 31 and the shortest eight. The morale of the unit appears to have remained high throughout its existence. The two key indicators of this are the incidence of military offences and venereal disease — there are no recorded cases of either in the personnel files of men while serving with the unit.

The demographics of the patrol also illustrate some interesting trends. The average age was 29 years with the oldest member 41 and the youngest 22. The largest proportion enlisted from rural areas at 66%. Overwhelmingly protestant and native-born Australian, only one member was born overseas and one was Roman Catholic.

It is evident that, by October 1918, the Light Car Patrol was a very settled unit with a stable leadership at all levels. This was also an experienced group with all members having extended service in both the Light Cars and the broader AIF. The average age of 29 also suggests a degree of maturity among its members. Since August 1916 the Light Car Patrol had operated in both Egypt and Palestine without any casualties due to enemy action, while hospitalisations were limited to vehicle accidents and illness. Again this is a tribute to the leadership and skills of the members of the Light Cars.

Old soldiers never die — they simply fade away

Following the armistice in the Middle East in 1918, the thoughts of the men of the Light Cars must have turned to their futures and what peace would bring. In most cases unit histories end with the disbandment and return to Australia, and the future experiences of unit members are not part of the story. James' sentimental lines at the close of 'The Motor Patrol' end his story. However, the explosion of archival databases and family history sites in recent years enables the story to be continued into the post-war era. With various degrees of success it is now possible to see how the men of Light Car Patrol 'faded away'.

Of the 33 men who served in the Armoured and Light Cars, only three had returned to Australia by the end of December 1918, one due to family reasons, the others assessed as medically unfit. Trooper K.C. Riley was the only one not to survive the war. He had returned to the 6th Light Horse and was killed in action shortly after. The New Year of 1919 brought tragedy to the Light Cars when one of its foundation members and stalwarts, Sergeant Langley, was admitted to hospital with cerebral malaria. He died the following day, thus becoming the unit's only casualty in 30 months of active service.

Like most AIF units, the process of fading away began in 1919. Corporal Morgan and Private Pines were victims of the outbreak of illness in the winter of 1919 and were evacuated to the 14th Australian General Hospital and later returned to Australia for medical reasons.

It is evident that the period between January and March was not the happiest time for the members of the Light Car Patrol. They were surrounded by the chaos and suffering caused by the collapse of the Ottoman Empire and the outbreak of tribal warfare and hatred. Some of the events they witnessed were truly horrific in nature. Alongside these issues was a sense of isolation as AIF formations were withdrawn to Egypt and the Light Car Patrol remained under Imperial control. Above all, the members experienced the overwhelming desire to return home to Australia.

Trooper Leo Cohn's letters of early 1919 document both a yearning for home and a sense of frustration at the end of an extended period of overseas service:

> It is absolutely scandalous the way we are treated. We are the only Australians up here and are attached to a division of Indian Regulars and worst of all we have got an OC who sits back and takes what they give him. All the rest of the AIF are down at Suez ready to get on the boat as soon as they come along and we are stuck up here as "Army of Occupation". There is a rumour that we are shifting down on the

Euphrates in a few days. One thing it might be a bit warmer if we get out of the hills. It snowed this morning and has been blowing all day. Am afraid I have got the blues today. Anyway I don't suppose they can get us all home in five minutes, still it is hard to be among the last.[140]

89. Members of the Light Car Patrol enjoy a trip to the pyramids and the Sphinx in their final days in Egypt (Creek collection ATM LCP.HC.010 HR).

The members of the Light Cars were gradually posted to the AIF Details Camp pending their return to Australia. In early March the vehicles were returned to the stores depot. Leo Cohn recorded the last days of the Light Car Patrol: 'We were recalled from Ain Tab three weeks ago, gave in our cars and guns and landed down here expecting to get on a boat any day. The day we landed, of course, the Jacko must run amuck and upset everything. Anyway we are in the embarkation camp and are down amongst the first to leave, so as soon as things settle down we will get away…' His letter continues to describe both the chaos of Syria and the journey to Egypt:

I will try and tell you what we have done since leaving Ain Tab. We drove to Aleppo and handed the cars and guns over. The night before we arrived there had been a bit of an Armenian massacre. But we were quite surprised that was all … Then we had five days of sitting in trucks, changing trains, getting out and walking over damaged bridges and all troubles and trials that of course you must expect about eight hundred miles of indifferently constructed lines of communication. To us it was all terribly interesting to see the places we had chased Jacko over and which we were seeing for the last time. The trip from Dera to Samuk on the Sea of Galilee was simply wonderful. The line follows the Jarmuk River for about twenty miles. One minute straight above will be immense waterfalls, next you can look down in the ravine with water rushing everywhere. At one place there are two tunnels through the same hill. It was something worth seeing. At Kantara we decided that it would do us all the world of good to have a few days in Cairo. Although we were a bit frightened of missing a boat, a few days feeding us would be very tempting. We had only been there a few hours when the trouble began. At first it was all a good joke and we spent our time walking about with sticks. When we arrived at Moascar all was bustle and they were talking of giving us cars again but it blew over. The Light Horse was reissued with horses and are scattered all over Egypt.

On 13 March Captain James and the final ten members of the unit marched into the AIF Details Camp to await their return to Australia and their homes and loved ones. This was three years to the day from James' initial appointment to the Armoured Car Section.

The wait for the troopship at the Details Camp at Moascar proved a frustrating period, and again the letters home from Leo Cohn record increasing irritation and impatience:

Another boat goes tomorrow and we are going to be left behind again. We had been led to believe that we were certain to go and yesterday the boat-roll went up and our names were not on it. One of our fellows named Harkin is going and is going to post this when he arrives and has promised to ring you up.

Received two letters from you, two from O and one from Dad. So pleased to hear that the wee fellow is doing well, but wish Lorne was better. What an awful time you must have had with the 'flu scare. By the cable news it seems to be pretty well in hand now.

Slight interruption caused by an Indignation Meeting to find out why we are here and when we are going home. We got poor satisfaction but they promised to write to HQ and see that we get on the next boat. We lost faith in our OC so are doing a lot on our own. He doesn't want to lose his good job ... Nearly every day there is a boat going through from France, but they seem to have forgotten that we want to get back to civilisation. Anyway I don't suppose it will be more than a few weeks before we get away so I sincerely hope that before you receive this we will be well on our way back.[141]

90. Hurry up and wait! Members of the Light Car Patrol waiting for transport to the *Kaiser-i-Hind* in May 1919 (Cohn collection ATM LCP.LC 003).

91. Homeward Bound! *Kaiser-i-Hind* in May 1919 (Cohn collection ATM LCP.LC 007).

Typically, men would return to Australia as transport became available and when their turn came, given the quota system on which repatriation was based. Under this system, the AIF and its units simply 'faded away' as the men trickled home in small numbers. However, James and his ten men all returned to Australia together on the *Kaiser-i-Hind* on 16 May, arriving in June 1919. Two men chose different paths home. McGibbon, who had transferred to the AFC in August 1917, was discharged in Palestine to take up a commission with the American Red Cross where he became the workshop manager in Jerusalem. He would return to Australia sometime in 1920 with an American war bride. Driver Holley was posted to AIF Headquarters in London to complete a commercial course with the Non-Military Employment Program. He would be the last member of the Light Cars to return to Australia, finally reaching familiar shores in November 1919.

On arrival in Australia, medical examination and discharge awaited. The majority of men were discharged within weeks of their arrival, Captain James the last in October 1920. The average length of service was 42 months, the longest Captain James at 66 and the shortest Driver Jones at 22.

92. The return home was not smooth sailing for all. Leo Cohn pictured at Caulfield Rehabilitation Hospital with a group of returned soldiers. He took almost six months to regain his health following discharge (Cohn collection ATM LCP.LC 008).

The electoral rolls and correspondence found on individual files allows a glimpse into the lives of these men following their return to Australia. Some 65% resumed their pre-war lives and settled close to where they had previously resided. Of the remainder, 35% relocated shortly after the end of the war. Around 14% shifted from rural areas to metropolitan centres while 13% either relocated from metropolitan areas to rural areas or from one rural district to another. The remaining men left Australia in the 1920s. McGibbon returned to Australia briefly and then migrated with his young family to the US. Somny returned to his home in the UK in the 1920s. The electoral rolls also show that most men returned to their pre-war occupations.

93. Home! George Morgan with Mabel in Castlemaine, 1919 (Morgan collection ATM.LC.GM.020).

Return to Australia following the Great War also allowed lives to be resumed after the interruption of the war years. Fourteen members married between 1918 and 1922. All but one man would eventually marry. The economic circumstances of the 1920s and the Great Depression would also cause considerable hardship to many. Ivan Young's family business, Young Brothers, would be sold in the 1930s as a consequence of the financial pressures of the Great Depression. It appears that Martin Pines lost his farm in the early 1930s and relocated to several addresses in Sydney in the following years. In 1939, in his application to join the CMF, he stated that he had been unemployed since 1937. Two men who saw only very brief service in the Light Cars, Archibald Gibb and John Driscoll, were dogged by misfortune in the post-war world. Archibald Gibbs' pre-war life had been touched by scandal several times, and this pattern would resume on his return to Australia. His marriage was dissolved in 1928 and he became unemployed during the Great Depression. In 1931 he was jailed for converting funds for his own use; on his release in 1932 he was killed during a domestic dispute. John Driscoll appears never to have settled well to civilian life. He worked as a rabbiter and labourer, his first marriage dissolved and he moved addresses frequently. His later life was marked by two major criminal convictions and alcoholism. His service in the Second World War would provide a brief period of stability. He would die in 1946 at the early age of 50. There is little doubt that many of these men suffered considerable stress in post-war Australia.

Some men returned to the situation they left when they enlisted. Typical was George Morgan who returned to Castlemaine in 1919 to his wife and young daughter. Family legend has him returning to Thomson's Engineering with a request to see his former employer concerning re-employment. The manager refused to allow such a direct approach and blocked the door. George then picked the man up and removed the obstacle. He subsequently returned to work and remained with Thomson's until his retirement. He would raise a family, work and retire in his home at Castlemaine and live an ordinary life that revolved around his community and family. Like many other old diggers, he would not speak openly about his wartime experiences, but would sit with other old diggers every Anzac Day and quietly share a drink, remembering his lost brother and dear friend Jack Langley.

Further military service would have been a distant thought for many of the men of the Light Car Patrol as they returned to Australia in 1919. However a small number immediately returned to the militia. Lieutenants Cornwell and Young were appointed to the 3rd Military District Reserve of Officers and remained so until the 1940s when their appointments were terminated without recall for service. Captain James would be appointed to the 38th Fortress Company, Royal Australian Engineers (RAE), in 1920 and play a part in rebuilding the CMF after the Great War. He would retire as a major in 1924 and remain on the Reserve of Officers until 1942. Trooper Gray joined the 18th Light Horse Regiment in South Australia in 1921 where he was commissioned as a lieutenant. He resigned his commission in 1925. He was appointed to the Reserve of Officers, 3rd Military District, in 1939 and remained until 1944.

The outbreak of another world war in 1939 would see several members return to the colours. Between 1939 and 1941 Bosanquet, Driscoll, Forsyth, Jones, Pines and Christensen all enlisted in the CMF. For Driscoll and Pines, the return to uniform appears to have provided much-needed economic security and stability, as each was unemployed at the time. These men served in garrison battalions, lines of communications or training units. None would see active service outside Australia and all were discharged by 1944. Cohn, Simpson and, after his second discharge from the CMF, Driscoll, would join the part-time and unpaid VDC in 1942. In far-off America, McGibbon would have to register for selective service with the American Armed Forces.

One the great tragedies that befell the diggers of the Great War was that, a mere 20 years later, their children would also be required to serve in a world war. It has been possible to identify eight children who served in the Second World War period, although the number is probably far greater. Six served in the AMF: one in the Royal Australian Navy (RAN), four in the Army, and one in the RAAF. Two would serve in foreign forces: one as a doctor in the Royal Army Medical Corps and another in the US National Guard. The children of Gordon McKay, who died on Anzac Day 1922, deserve special mention. Lance Corporal Keith McKay would be taken prisoner in the campaign in Greece in May 1941 and would not return home until 1945. His brother Alan would serve in the CMF before transferring to the RAAF where he was killed in an air accident at East Sale in 1945.

The circumstances of the deaths of all the members of the Armoured and Light Cars have been documented except for one. Two died on service in the Middle East while the remaining deaths spanned the years from 1922 to 1984 when the last survivor, Leo Cohn, died aged 87. There was an initial spate of deaths soon after the Great War. In 1922 the unit's youngest member, Henry Harkin, died of juvenile diabetes, the same year as George McKay, who had relocated to a soldier settler farm in Cowra. McKay died from complications following a farm accident. Albert Holley passed away in 1925. Three died as a result of misadventure. Archibald Gibbs was shot dead outside the Surrey Hills Court in 1933 after a domestic dispute. Gaston Somny died in one of the UK's first commercial aviation accidents in 1935 and James Riley was thrown from a horse in 1955 while mustering sheep. The average age at death was 70 years of age, the oldest Bert Creek at 92 in 1980 and the youngest Henry Harkin at 25.

As with any group, the men of the Armoured and Light Cars enjoyed mixed success and achievement, and the last two survivors, Bert Creek and Leo Cohn, both lived in Bendigo in their final years. Bert became a local identity who was regularly interviewed around Anzac Day when he would recount his adventures in the Palestine campaign and driving for the Prince of Wales. If alive today he would be regarded as a 'living treasure'. Leo Cohn, a successful businessman, championed the interests of north-west Victoria and, unsurprisingly, the development of the regional television networks. He received an Order of the British Empire in 1964 for service to his community. Each man had embraced a technology that, in 1914, was regarded as cutting edge in that era. Both men served their nation in time of war and, in the post-war world, resumed their lives and continued to serve their families, communities and nation.

Thus it was that the men of Australia's first mechanised military unit finally faded away.

94. Ernest James sits inside one of his scale models (James collection ATM LCP.EJ 003).

Grown Up Toys
Hobby Becomes an Industry
By R. B. IRVING

THERE is a big difference between models and mere toys, as every youngster knows. Although there is not a toy in the building, a visit to the Model Dockyard, in Swanston Street, would gladden the heart of any boy. The shop is filled with models of trains, aero planes, steam engines, and ships, ranging from models in high glass cases to fully rigged sailing ships and power-driven liners. The Model Dockyard not only sells models, but encourages craftsmen of all ages to make their own. The manager of the Dockyard (Captain E. H. James) has helped the formation of five clubs, whose activities cover the modelling of ships, powerboats, trains, and aeroplanes.

Captain James has been interested in the making of models all his life. One of his earliest recollections is of being found lying in a pool of oil beneath an engine at the Centennial International Exhibition of 1888 by an anxious mother, who had searched several hours for her mechanically minded son. In the early nineties of last century he watched the construction of the first successful steam-driven car built in Australia, at the workshop of Mr. Herbert Thompson, of Armadale. Later this car was driven to Sydney at an average speed of 8 m.p.h. The journey occupied a fortnight. When aged l8 years, Captain James and his brother built one of the first steam driven launches in Melbourne. During the war Captain James was a member of the first Australian Armoured Car Section, which built the first armoured car in Australia at the works of the Vulcan Engineering Company in South Melbourne.

Men Like It

About six years ago Captain James and a friend, who had been making models together for years, found that they had enough models in their workshop to stock a shop, so they started a business in Flinders Street. The shop soon proved too small, so the dockyard was moved to larger premises in Elizabeth Street. The dockyard soon outgrew these premises too, and last year was moved to its present situation in Swanston Street. Captain James finds that his models interest not only boys but men. He exhibited some models at the International Motor Show this year. There was a large crowd round the exhibit all night. The front row was composed almost entirely of fathers. From small boys on the edge of the crowd was frequently heard the cry, "Let's have a look, Dad."

Captain James has high praise for the skill of many craftsmen who come to him for advice and materials. In his shop he has a model of the Bounty, which was built according to instructions published in "The Argus" in 1935. Model aeroplanes, made in Australia, are recognized as the best in the world, he says. They are exported in large quantities to England, America, Sweden, and South Africa. Shortly after the war two war pilots, Captain Hervey and Mr. Gordon, started a factory for model aeroplanes. These models became famous not only in Victoria but overseas, and probably were the first of their kind in the world. Thus Victoria had an early lead in the industry, of which its hundreds of model aeroplane clubs have taken advantage.

Rides for Children
A model train running on a quarter of a mile of track will be the chief feature of the exhibit at 'The Argus' 20th Century Exhibition. The engine is a replica of the AA locomotives which were used to draw the Sydney express until 1907. It has a scale speed of 45 M.P.H., and draws five vans and carriages. The largest of these carriages, which is 3ft. 6in. in height, will hold eight children. It is fitted with windows, doors, and electric lights. All the carriages are fitted with spring buffers and steam brakes. The train was built by Captain James in his backyard at Hawthorn. The engine took three years to build.

Other exhibits at the Model Dockyard stand will include models of trains, steam engines, ships, and petrol-driven aeroplanes, made by members of the Victorian Model Railways Society, the Victorian Model Engineers' Society, the Victorian Model Ship Builders' Society, and the Victorian Model Power Plane Society.

(The *Argus*, 29 July 1937)

Bert recalls desert war

From ROY WITHELL

HORSHAM. — A Horsham man who operated with the legendary Lawrence of Arabia in World War I celebrates his 90th birthday tomorrow.

Bert Creek's army career gained him a Distinguished Conduct Medal.

He was being official driver to the Prince of Wales, later Duke of Windsor, and Lord Louis Mountbatten during their 1920 Australian tour.

This week Bert recalled escorting Lawrence of Arabia in a gunboat across the Dead Sea in the blackness of night.

"We knew little about Lawrence of Arabia who lived with the Arabs.

PROVED

"He had great influence with them and proved useful to the Allies.

"Allied intelligence wanted him urgently.

"We were told to cross the Dead Sea to collect him and bring him across safely.

"I was one of three machine gunners on a small gunboat who picked him up by night and later returned him to the other shore."

Bert described Lawrence of Arabia as quietly spoken and dressed like an Arab.

Bert was an infantry man, later claimed by the 1st Armored Car Section because of his mechanical knowledge.

He held armored car regimental Number 5.

Bert said they chased many Germans and Turks around the desert in armored cars.

On May 26, 1919 ,while still in the desert, Bert received word of his DCM award.

The citation read: "On September 20, 1918, at

Mr Bert Creek decorated for bravery

Lawrence of Arabia

Ajule, Sergeant H. Creek, 1st Australian Armored Car Section, cut off three enemy motor lorries full of men and materials, causing them to surrender.

"The lorries were driven into the town intact and undamaged, and all occupants were taken prisoner."

Bert came back to Australia and was discharged in July, 1919.

Back in Horsham he was chosen as the official driver for the 1920 Australian tour by the Prince of Wales, and Lord Louis Mountbatten, then a Naval officer.

IMPORTED

Bert drove the Crossley cars imported for the visit in Victoria, NSW, Queensland and South Australia.

Bert has prized treasures to recall the visit.

He was given a framed autographed photo of the Prince of Wales and a gold tie pin carrying the Prince's crest to mark his work.

Bert also received an inscribed heavy silver cigarette case from the Crossley car firm in England.

He was presented with a civil decoration, the Royal Victorian Medal, for personal service to royalty.

On a later visit to Australia, Lord Louis Mountbatten sent an autographed service card to Bert.

It was arranged by the late Senator Harrie Wade, who met Lord Louis Mountbatten at a Canberra luncheon.

Senator Wade produced Bert's service pass authorising him to drive the official Crossley back in 1920.

Bert Creek drove cars for 60 years without an accident.

He was proud of his car licence No. 3570.

In fact he was driving before licences and car registrations became law.

"That's about 69 years ago. I believe they were first issued early in 1909," Mr Creek said.

Bert Creek was working in Horsham at Young's Garage when he enlisted in 1915.

His two brothers also served in the First World War and returned.

96. In his later years Bert Creek's war time experiences were the subject of newspaper special features. Roy Withell's piece appeared in the late 1970s. (Courtesy Creek family collection)

PART 2

"Grit"

Australia's First Tank.

TIMELINE

Australia's First Tank

1916

September   First use of the new 'tank' in warfare.

October   Australian infantry encounter the remains of tanks on the battlefield near Flers.

November   First scheduled attack of Australian infantry with tank support. Tank unable to participate due to ground conditions.

1917

11 April   First Battle of Bullecourt: first attack by Australian infantry with tank support. Tanks are soon disabled and the infantry lose faith in the new weapon.

May   Second Battle of Bullecourt: Australian infantry decline the offer of tank support, while the British 62nd Division advance on their left with ten tanks in support.

May   Australian newspapers report that Mr Andrew Fisher, Australian High Commissioner in London, has requested that the British government allocate a tank to Australia as a war relic.

1918

21 January   Lieutenant Norman Lovell Brown called to AIF HQ in London and placed in charge of a 'heavy motor' and crew to be sent to Australia.

23 January   Lieutenant Brown and a British Tank Corps Technical Officer choose 12 AIF candidates to undergo tank training at the Tank Corps Training Centre, Bovington Camp, Dorset. The top eight students will form the tank crew.

25 January   Australian newspapers report that a tank has been allocated to Australia.

19 March   HMAT A42 *Boorara* departs the UK with the tank, a veteran of fighting on the Western Front, aboard but the ship is torpedoed the next day and beached.

20 April   A replacement tank, serial number 4643, a newly build Mk. IV, plus a suite of spare parts, is loaded aboard HMAT C4 *Dongarra* at Glasgow docks, destined for Australia.

8 May	AIF Transport Section commences arrangements for the eight crew and Lieutenant Brown to return to Australia as the 'Special Tank Personnel'.
12 May	Special Tank Personnel embark aboard HT D8 *Ruahine* on their way to Australia.
4 July	Battle of Hamel: first successful cooperation between tanks and Australian infantry.
5 July	The Special Tank Personnel arrive in Sydney aboard HT D8 *Ruahine*
9 July	HMAT C4 *Dongarra* docks briefly in Adelaide en route to Melbourne. Lieutenant Brown takes the opportunity to inspect the tank, which is lashed to the foredeck.
12 July	HMAT C4 *Dongarra* arrives in Port Phillip Bay, drops anchor in Hobson's Bay and awaits allocation of a berth.
13 July	HMAT C4 *Dongarra* docks in Melbourne and the tank is unloaded on the wharf.
17 July	Tank 4643 is moved by haulage company Vaughan's to Victoria Barracks yard, St Kilda Road. 'Special Tank Personnel' commence maintenance and preparation for use.
27 July	Tank 4643, under its own power, accompanies a parade of French troops through the streets of Melbourne, the first official public appearance of a tank crewed by an Australian crew in Australia.
12-13 August	Tank crew discharged from the AIF and re-enlisted for Home Service as members of the Special Unit Tank Crew.
15 August	Lieutenant Brown discharged from the AIF and re-enlisted in the Home Service as OC Special Unit Tank Crew.
4 September	Tank 4643 arrives at Mitcham railway yard, Adelaide, South Australia, for 'War Tank Week'.
5–14 September	Tank 4643 performs for packed crowds at Unley Oval during 'War Tank Week'. A naming competition is held.
14 September	Lady Galway, wife of the Governor of South Australia, officially christens Tank 4643 'Grit'.
16-17 September	Grit takes part in the launch of the Seventh War Loan in central Adelaide.
18 September	Grit is loaded onto a flatcar for the rail journey back to Melbourne.

23 September	Grit is unloaded at the Royal Agricultural Showgrounds in Melbourne, where it is discovered that various items have been stolen from the vehicle while en route.
23–28 September	Grit is displayed at the Royal Agricultural Show, Melbourne, in support of the Seventh War Loan.
28 September	Grit is loaded onto a flatcar for transport to Sydney, NSW.
2 October	Grit is transhipped from the Victorian broad gauge to the NSW standard gauge at Albury, NSW.
3 October	Grit arrives and is unloaded at Sydney's Central Railway Station.
10–15 October	Grit and crew support the war loan rallies in Sydney.
24 October – 2 November	Mobility demonstrations at the Victoria Park Racecourse.
11 November	Cessation of hostilities.
12 November	Grit is loaded onto a flatcar for the return journey to Melbourne.
13 November	H.V. McKay of the Board of Business Administration passes formal administrative control of Grit to Colonel Dangar, Chief of Ordnance.
14 November	Grit arrives in Albury for transfer from the standard to the broad gauge railway.
16 November	Grit and crew give mobility demonstrations in Albury.
18 November	Grit is loaded aboard a broad gauge railway flatcar for shipment to Melbourne.
20 November	Grit arrives in Melbourne, is unloaded at the Spencer Street railway yard, and motors under its own power back to the Engineer Depot in Alexandra Avenue.
10 December	First of the AIF crewmen, Corporal Swain, is discharged.
26 December	Most of the AIF crewmen discharged. Only Captain Brown and Corporal Fleming remain in service. Members of the Royal Australian Engineers, PMF, allocated for training as tank crew.

1919

5 April	Grit and the newly trained RAE crew, under command of Captain Brown, depart Spencer Street railway yard bound for Brisbane, Queensland.
17 April	Grit arrives at Roma Street Station, Brisbane.
17–27 April	Participation in fundraising events in Brisbane, including mobility demonstrations at Exhibition Oval.

23 April	Official visit to Grit by various dignitaries, including the Governor and Lady Goold-Adams.
26 April	Lady Goold-Adams rides inside Grit as it performs a mobility demonstration around an obstacle course at Exhibition Oval.
27 April	Grit departs Brisbane for Melbourne aboard a railway flatcar.
10 May	Some members of the tank crew arrive in Melbourne.
12 May	Grit and the remainder of the crew arrive in Melbourne.
May	Sergeant Fleming discharged.
19 May	Grit participates in the Victory March through Melbourne.
May-June	Grit given an extensive overhaul by the RAE crew under the supervision of Brown.
23 October	Captain Brown discharged.
20 September	Grit placed on exhibition at the Royal Agricultural Show, Melbourne, for a week.
6 December	Grit placed on public display in central Melbourne before being driven to St Kilda for the St Kilda Carnival.
6–13 December	Grit on display at the St Kilda Carnival.
15 December	Grit driven from St Kilda to the Engineer Depot, Alexandra Avenue.

1920

	Grit remains in storage at the Engineer Depot, Alexandra Avenue, Melbourne.

1921

14 October	Grit makes its final journey under its own power from the Engineer Depot in South Melbourne to the Australian War Museum Annex housed in the Exhibition Buildings, Carlton.

1921-1936

	Grit on display at the Australian War Memorial Annex in Melbourne.

1936-1941

	In storage in Canberra.

1941

November	Grit transferred to the new Australian War Memorial building in Canberra and placed on public display in the lower gallery.

INTRODUCTION

During September 1916, Australians discovered a new meaning for an old word. The tank, once a large, mundane and often corrugated receptacle for liquids, would henceforth be a word whispered in awe — it was the name given to a new and terrifying super weapon.[1] To a war-weary public already horrified by the slaughter of Gallipoli and the Western Front, the tank appeared to offer a means of overcoming the enemy's defences and advancing to a decisive victory.[2] Australians were eager to learn more about the tank, and to actually see one was an opportunity that few members of the Australian public could resist.

Almost from their unveiling on the Western Front, moves were underway to secure a tank for Australia. The initial requests were for a veteran of the fighting on the front for inclusion in the growing list of acquisitions for the future Australian War Museum. However, with the success of public exhibitions and demonstrations of tanks in the UK and the US in support of events to raise money for patriotic causes, the proposal to send a tank on a lengthy journey to Australia acquired a new purpose. By the beginning of 1918 when the British War Office finally agreed to allocate a tank to Australia, its primary role was no longer simply that of historic war relic, but had become one of an object of such public interest and curiosity that it could be successfully utilised to raise money and lure precious recruits for the war effort.

As an item of curiosity rather than a war relic, it needed to be functional. To function, the tank needed a crew. These men were initially drawn from available invalid AIF personnel who were then trained in the UK and repatriated to Australia as the 'special tank personnel'. As such, this crew constituted the first officially trained and mobilised tank crew in the AMF. Subsequently, additional crewmen, drawn from Permanent Military Forces (PMF) RAE personnel, were also trained in the maintenance and operation of the tank. The tank was very successfully utilised on several occasions in Australia from July 1918 until it was formally transferred to the Australian War Museum in October 1921.

REALITY — THE FIRST EXPERIENCES OF TANK SUPPORT

The average Australian digger's first sight of the new weapon of war could hardly have been less inspiring. In late October 1916, infantrymen of the 55th, 56th and 53rd Australian infantry battalions were moved to an area close to Flers, scene of the first combat use of tanks the previous month. While making their way to their new positions, the Australians 'saw their first tanks, derelicts of the September fighting, in some cases with the crew still lying dead among the machinery.'[3]

Their first experience of tanks in combat was scheduled for early November, when the 7th Australian Infantry Brigade was to be supported by British tanks in an attack on the German lines east of the Bapaume Road. Unfortunately, the sole tank fit for action was not able to take part 'owing to the state of the ground'.[4] The new weapon — touted as impervious to enemy fire and with the ability to overcome enemy trenches — had been defeated by the mud of a northern European winter.

It was not until the First Battle of Bullecourt some five months later that Australian infantry were supported by tanks under fire, and it was far from an inspiring experience. The attack on the Hindenburg Line by the 4th Australian Infantry Division scheduled for the early morning of 10 April 1917 had to be postponed due to the late arrival of the supporting tanks at the jumping-off point.

The vehicles — early Mk. II tanks — were then concentrated in a leaguer at Noreuil, much closer to the front line and ready for the rescheduled attack the next day.[5] However the 11 tanks that took part in the attack on 11 April were all quickly disabled or suffered mechanical failure, the majority failing to reach even the first line of German trenches.[6] The tanks

> … attracted such a storm of small arms fire that men watching from close in the rear could at times see their shapes outlined by the sparks of the bullets that rattled against their sides. They were still short of the wire and the contingency deeply feared by the Anzac leaders, and so confidently rejected by the army commander, had happened. The 4th Brigade was facing intense machine gun fire all along insufficiently broken entanglements without a single tank ahead of it to clear a passage.[7]

Indeed, 'All the tanks – with the exception of the one that entered Bullecourt – had fought their short fight in the area in the rear of the Australian front line before 7 o'clock; their carcasses could be seen motionless, and in most cases burning, all over the battlefield.'[8] The tank crews suffered serious losses: of the 103 officers and men manning the vehicles, 52 were killed, wounded or missing.[9]

The 4th Infantry Division also suffered many casualties in the battle, including a number of men with a wealth of battlefield experience from Gallipoli and in earlier battles on the Western Front. Among them was the 16th Battalion's Major Percy Black, cited by some as the bravest man in the AIF, and extremely popular with his men. On seeing the unbroken wire entanglements and having left the crippled tanks behind, Black had yelled 'Come on boys, bugger the tanks!' and led his men forward. He was killed shortly afterwards, moments after his unit attained its initial objective.[10]

The tanks' perceived lack of reliability — and punctuality — made the Australians very dubious of their value in the attack. Official historian Charles Bean wrote that 'it is therefore hardly to be wondered at that officers and men of the 4th Division vowed never again to rely upon tanks, an attitude which was generally maintained in the AIF until 1918.'[11] Indeed, for the Second Battle of Bullecourt in May 1917, the British 62nd Division on the left of the Australians was to be supported by ten tanks 'but after the experience of April 11th the Australians preferred to attack without them.'[12]

1. Early tanks were neither reliable nor immune to shellfire, often ending up disabled on the battlefield (NLA 23478288 & NAA B4260.3).

That attitude was maintained until late in the war when, at the Battle of Hamel on 4 July 1918, tanks were successfully used in support of Australian infantry. With memories of their failure at the First Battle of Bullecourt still fresh in their minds, the infantry were given the opportunity to become acquainted with the newer, more reliable Mk. V tanks prior to the battle. Each battalion had a day's familiarisation which included mock attacks, joy rides and mobility demonstrations, all of which helped overcome their previous distrust of the vehicles. The attack achieved its objectives in just 93 minutes and was a model of combined arms cooperation.[13]

PERCEPTION — THE AUSTRALIAN PUBLIC'S VIEW

In Australia, the public held an exulted view of the value of the new 'super weapon'. From its first unveiling in September 1916, the daily newspapers provided seemingly endless promotion — and exaggeration — of the capabilities of the tank.

The first news of the tank was splashed across the pages of Australian newspapers as part of broader reports on the progress of the campaign that commenced in mid-September 1916. Although few Australians were directly involved, the newspapers talked in glowing terms of the 'new armoured car'. The *Adelaide Mail* was typical of the Australian newspapers that paraphrased a news piece from the London *Times*. Under the banner 'New Armoured Car Nonplussed Germans', it proclaimed that

> … lately there have been persistent rumours current that a new type of armoured car had been constructed …. Invulnerable to machine-guns, shell splinters and rifle-fire – everything in fact except a direct hit by a heavy projectile. When the secrecy can be lifted it may be possible to imagine the German feelings, when in the uncertain light of dawn, he saw advancing an array of unearthly monsters, steel cased, spitting fire and crawling laboriously and ceaselessly over trenches, barbed wire entanglements, and shell craters.[14]

The name 'tank' took a little time to become the accepted title — in the early stages, these vehicles were almost invariably described as 'armoured cars', such as in the *Argus* report of Wednesday 20 September 1916: 'The armoured cars gallantly led the action, knocking out enemy machine-guns and inflicting heavy losses by their own machine-gun fire. They enfiladed the German trenches and caused indescribable demoralisation in the enemy's ranks.'[15]

Certainly, the perception that the tank could readily break the deadlock of trench warfare was a recurrent theme — and one in which the public was apparently eager to believe. The *Launceston Examiner* reported on tanks dramatically breaking enemy strongholds too tough for infantry alone. In an article entitled 'Bring Up The Tanks!' the advance from Mouquet Farm was described as held up on the left where,

> … for a long time it was impossible to get near the chateau, but the cry was raised "Bring up the tanks!" The very idea was a firm tonic to the

attackers. Soon a tank lumbered along, lurching over the shell craters and momentarily sitting on broken parapets. Then it waddled forwards toward the infantry, and when it opened fire, it resembled a dragon with indigestion. It got over the enemy's trench and trudged down the whole length, sweeping it with fire. Soon, the German machine-guns were silenced.[16]

There were even some reports of Australians manning tanks, one of which claimed to be a first-hand account from the diary of an Australian soldier. While these may have made dramatic newspaper copy, their authenticity is, at the very least, questionable. Nevertheless, for the Australian public, such reports only helped to heighten expectations of battlefield success and a quicker end to the war.

Not content with reporting the Allied view, many papers also reported the German perception of the tank. The *Leader*, a Melbourne suburban newspaper, ran the headline 'German View of "Cruel Monsters"' in its Saturday issue on 23 September 1916, supposedly quoting an 'official paper found upon a German major who was taken prisoner' which stated that 'the cruelty of the new engines equals their efficiency. Steps must be taken to combat the monsters'.[17] According to one report the German government proposed to lodge a protest with the International Red Cross in Geneva at the use of tanks which was described as 'contrary to the recognised methods of civilised warfare' — a curious view given the Germans' widespread use of poison gas, flamethrowers and the indiscriminate bombing of civilian targets by long-range Zeppelins.[18] The rumoured German protest even inspired satirical English poetry:

> *Ach Himmel! England is unfair,*
> *On land, sea and in the air,*
> *She cannot fight us fair and square.*
>
> *With horrible, illegal "tanks",*
> *Of which she boasts (and even "swanks"),*
> *She decimates our serried ranks ...*[19]

Tanks certainly fired the imagination of the public, and were even the subject of schoolchildren's essays. Gerald Acraman, an 11-year-old fifth grader at Port Elliott, South Australia, had his 'Autobiography of a Tank' published by the local newspaper:

I am a tank. I was built last year by some clever men. I am a great help in this great war. One day I went right into the German trenches, and the Huns were very much afraid. One of them tried to stick his rifle into me, but I only made a noise, and he broke his rifle. He was soon killed by the deadly fire of the machine guns inside me. About a hundred Germans were killed by me today. I went out again in a week's time. A lot of Germans saw me coming and hid behind a bush. The men inside me saw them hide luckily, so I went right over them, killing and wounding them all. In a few minutes a shell landed on top of me. It made a terrific noise, but did not do much damage to me. I went back to my base again, and now I am being repaired.[20]

The description of violent death scribed so nonchalantly by young Gerald — doubtless condoned by his teacher and the local newspaper's editor — provides an insight into the public's attitude after more than two years of bloody warfare. The tank, as Gerald so naively believed, was almost impervious to the enemy's defences. Not only was the tank a 'super weapon', it was *our* super weapon. The public was enthralled.

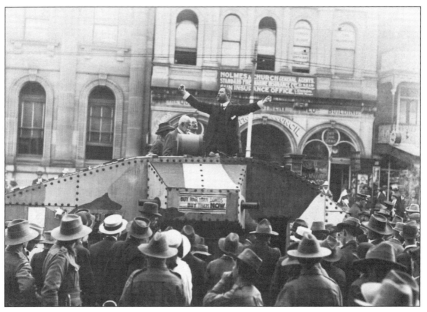

2. From Brisbane to Hobart, Sydney to Perth, replica tanks capitalised on the public's enthusiasm, becoming the focal point of many patriotic fundraising events. In Brisbane, Mr Frank Bowcher appeals to the crowd to buy war bonds (AWM H02152).

The poem *Tommy's Tank* by Thomas Edwin Holtham was cabled to Australia just after the first use of tanks on the Somme and appeared in several Australian newspapers in late September 1916. The editorial note in the the *Shepparton Advertiser* boldly states that 'the full narrative of the achievements of the new British armoured "tanks" shows that they have established one of the most dramatic and gallant records of the war.'[21] According to both the poem and the supporting editorial material, the tank was the weapon that would overcome the difficulties of trench warfare and was a uniquely British innovation:

TOMMY'S "TANK."
By Thomas Edwin Holtham

I.

They call me by different names,
On the fellow it all depends,
Whether its jam or mud he aims,
Just to suit his own private ends.
But I go on my way all the same,
Quite defiant of fence or foe,
For I'm iron encased in frame,
And iron all round and below.
Then ho! and hooray!
-To clearing the way.
For I'm ready to whistle and go.

II.

To Tommy I'm comedy quite,
His giggle expands to a roar;
To the Hun I'm tragedy's fright,
With devilish thirst for his gore.
And to all I'm the strangest thing
That ever the battlefield knew,
With fire-ball mouth and fiery sting,
In just where the tail should come through.
Then, heigho! my boys,
I'm one of the toys,
Come to put up a flutter for you.

III.

I crawl, but can jump and can dive,
My short legs can instantly grow;
And if Huns won't come out alive,
I make them all dead men below.
I can crash at the bombers o'er trench
And laugh at their fierce fusillade;
And with bullets their parapets drench,
For my barrels are all British made.
Then ho! and ha-ha!
This new armoured car
Will from them their battlements wrench.

IV.

Monster, dug-out devil, trench hog,
Fiend come from the furnace of hell;
Or dragon born of British bulldog-
Are some names the scooting Huns yell.
No ghost ever people so scared,
Why, they hadn't a tail left to wag;
No men demented ever so stared
As they came up to show the white flag.
Ha, ha, and heigho!
I laid them out low,
As they thought "Here's old Nick on his nag."

V.

But Tommy just calls me a "Tank;"
He thinks it is glorious fun,
That a tank should spank and take rank
As a devil that frightens the Hun.
But he knows I've the best of the game,
And that adds fiz to his mirth,
For says he "Why, what's in a name?"
When British brains have given me birth.
Then ho! and away
For the fray and the day
That's to bring lasting peace to the earth.

By the beginning of 1918, tanks were being used very successfully overseas as fundraising platforms by governments and charities. The British government's war bond drive in early 1918 raised millions of pounds, with British tanks and German war trophies as the centrepieces of the displays at major centres across the country. Thousands of citizens from all walks of life flocked to see the 'Tank Banks', hear the patriotic speeches and donate money.

It was a lesson not lost on Australian fundraisers. In the absence of a genuine tank and with only the vaguest of dimensions to work with, charitable committees across the nation built their own versions of 'tanks'. While the designs were many and varied —with some even resembling the real thing — the sentiment was always the same: the tank was a wonderful war machine, impervious to enemy fire and with the ability to overcome his defences; but just a few more pounds were needed for the push to final victory.

3. Many replicas bore only a vague resemblance to the real thing. This juggernaut is supporting Red Cross Day in Hobart, Tasmania (AWM H16150).

The replicas were certainly a successful enterprise, raising many thousands of pounds in donations to patriotic causes and in the sale of government war bonds. Newspapers heralded their arrival at each town and followed them as they toured country centres. Each town's successful fundraising event was reported in detail, promoting competition between towns, with each vying to raise the largest amount of revenue.

4. In Perth, Western Australia, a 'low profile' version is paraded in support of the Sixth War Loan (AWM H16156).

While the public showed its enthusiasm in attending rallies and listening to long patriotic speeches delivered by notable persons from the tops of replica tanks — and giving generously as a result — the poorly constructed models were no substitute for the 'real thing'.

5. In Sydney, speakers exhort the crowd to buy war bonds from a more compact version of the 'tank' (AWM H18494).

A REAL TANK FOR AUSTRALIA

With the growing public interest in tanks, it was widely reported in May 1917 that the Australian High Commissioner in London, Andrew Fisher, had requested the British War Office to allocate a tank to Australia. Fisher, it was reported, 'is establishing an Australian War Records branch to gather the accounts of the historic events in which Australian troops have been concerned, and to make a collection of picture films, photographs and of war relics illustrating the most recent war devices. In this connection, Mr Fisher has already put in a claim for a "tank".'[22]

6. The use of replica tanks was not confined to the state capitals. Here, the Lord Major of Harden, in country NSW, addresses the crowd, supported by Corporal George Julian Howell, VC, MM. The use of high profile diggers was a common theme in patriotic fundraising appeals. Howell was awarded the MM for his actions during the capture of the village of Dernancourt in April 1917, and the VC for gallantry displayed on 6 May 1917 during the Second Battle of Bullecourt. He was severely wounded during that action. After prolonged hospitalisation, he was repatriated to Australia in October 1917 and discharged on 5 June 1918 (AWM P08338.002).

While Australian newspapers continued to publish lavish reports on the effectiveness of 'tanks', no further reports of such a vehicle being earmarked for Australia were published for several months until, on 25 January 1918, confirmation appeared that the request had been accepted by the War Office. Under the heading 'Tank for Australia', the newspapers proudly announced that 'after the battle of Pozieres, Mr A Fisher, High Commissioner for Australia, applied for a tank for despatch to Australia. He has now secured one, and it will be shipped to Australia shortly.'[23]

7. The three replica tanks that toured Victoria in 1918, each one taking a different route across the state, before returning to Melbourne. Here, the three line up outside Melbourne Town Hall, with large banners proclaiming the success of their fundraising expeditions. Despite some disappointment that these were not 'real tanks', country Victorians welcomed their visit to each town, digging deeply and buying hundreds of thousands of pounds worth of war bonds (AWM H02146).

8. Despite their ungainly and less than accurate appearance, replica tanks were crowd-pleasers nonetheless (SLSA PRG 280/1/28/268).

A crew is chosen

As the tank was to be mobile, it required a competent crew. There is some indication that the British War Office originally intended to send a British tank crew to man the tank in Australia, but this was soon revised to training a crew comprising AIF personnel who were being invalided home for various reasons.[24] AIF Administrative Headquarters in London then began searching for a suitable officer and a group of likely candidates for tank crew training.

Sometime around 21 January 1918, Lieutenant Norman Lovell Brown was called to AIF Headquarters in Horseferry Road, London, and asked to take charge of a 'heavy motor' to be sent to Australia. Brown initially declined on the basis of ill-health but, as the only qualified motor transport officer readily available, Brown and a captain from the Engineers were interviewed for the posting. As the engineer captain had little experience with internal combustion engines, Brown was chosen.

Along with the Assistant Adjutant General, Brown interviewed a number of possible candidates on 23 January, eventually choosing 12 to undergo an interview with a British Tank Corps technical officer before being sent for final training at the Tank Corps Training Centre, Bovington Camp, Dorset. Of the 12, the top eight students would form the tank crew under the command of Lieutenant Brown.

The eight crewmen chosen by Brown were from diverse backgrounds and had widely differing levels of military experience. All the drivers passed the course with excellent grades — probably understandable given their previous experience with both military and civilian motor transport. Brown, as officer in command, was classed as 'VG1' — presumably 'Very Good Grade 1'. The two workshop personnel were not graded nor qualified for driving, but their mechanical work was noted as being of a high standard (see Table 1).

Table 1: AIF Tank Crew Course Results[25]

Service No.	Name & Rank	Driving	Lectures	% Overall
	Lt N L Brown			'VG1'
1929	L/Cpl D B Lord	96	100	98
9351	Pte R J Dalton	95	90	92.5
2904	Pte H D Swain	95	87	91
1255	Pte M G McFadden	90	90	90
1568	Pte A R Rowland	93	86	89.5
287	Pte J R Fleming	91	80	85.5

Service No.	Name & Rank	Driving	Lectures	% Overall
Workshop Personnel:				
1254	Cpl/Artif C R Jackson	'Their work has been of a high standard'		
2815	Artif F G Gifford			

On 8 May the AIF Transport Section was directed to make arrangements for the nine personnel to accompany the tank to Australia. Australia now had its first qualified tank driving and maintenance crew.

A tank is sent

That a tank had been allocated for transport to Australia was certainly true and a Mk. IV tank that had seen service on the Western Front was loaded aboard HMAT A42 *Boorara* in March 1918.[26] On 22 March 1918, with the tank safely aboard the *Boorara*, AIF Administrative Headquarters in London notified the Secretary of the Department of Defence in Melbourne that the tank was on its way to Australia. The ship headed first to an English port further south to pick up troops being repatriated to Australia.[27] The notification reached Australia several weeks later, and the authorities duly announced the shipment of the tank to Australia 'at an early date'.[28]

Unfortunately, the notification was a little premature. On 20 March, only a day into the voyage, the *Boorara* was intercepted south-east of Beachy Head by the German submarine *UB-31* which scored a single torpedo hit amidships. The explosion and flooding killed five seamen in the stoking room. Although severely damaged, the ship managed to limp into Southampton. It was then towed to Newcastle-Upon-Tyne for repairs.[29]

... and another

The damage to the *Boorara* meant that the tank destined for Australia 'was rendered unavailable for a long period', so a replacement vehicle was quickly allocated by the British War Office.[30] Rather than a veteran of the Western Front, the replacement tank was a new Mk. IV Female constructed by Coventry Ordnance Works in Glasgow, Scotland, with build number 4643. It was loaded aboard the cargo ship HMAT C4 *Dongarra* at Glasgow docks on 20 April 1918.[31] Several cases of spare parts were loaded aboard on 1 May 1918 shortly before the ship put to sea. As a cargo ship, it could not carry the tank personnel. They would follow later aboard another vessel.

With the tank loaded on the ship's foredeck, there was a strong possibility that it would be awash with salt water in rough seas. At the insistence of Lieutenant Brown, the officer in command of the tank and its AIF crew, this matter was brought to the attention of the Secretary of the Department of Defence in Australia in a letter dated 8 May 1918. Given the tank's exposed stowage position, it would therefore

> … be necessary to have all bearing parts looked over before the machine is moved any distance on disembarkation. It is wished to emphasise the desirability of not overhauling until the arrival of the crew on account of the special nature of the mechanism. It is suggested that, should it arrive before the personnel, it should be housed in a shed on the wharf until taken over by them. The magneto has been removed from the machine and placed in the strong room of the vessel in charge of the master.[32]

9. Nothing, however, could substitute for seeing the real tank once it arrived in Australia. Captain Norman Brown, seen here with his first wife Emma, poses for the photographer next to his charge, tank number 4643. The tank was later christened 'Grit' by Lady Galway, wife of the Governor of South Australia, following a public naming competition (AWM P05386.001).

The speed of events appears to have overtaken Defence Headquarters in Melbourne. Although it was announced by the Minister for Defence, Senator Sir George Foster Pearce, in early July that the first tank had been lost and another was being requested, the arrival of the tank aboard HMAT C4 *Dongarra* caught the authorities by surprise.[33] Lieutenant Brown had arrived in Sydney aboard the HT *Ruahine* on 5 July, and made his way to his hometown of Adelaide on leave. He took the opportunity to inspect the tank when the *Dongarra* docked in Adelaide on 9 July, prior to the final leg of its voyage to Melbourne where it was to be unloaded. He reported by letter on 11 July that he had '... found everything in good order. The tracks and rollers being the only part rusty' and advised that 'it will be necessary to see to these parts as early as possible to save renewals.'[34]

The ship departed Adelaide early on Wednesday 10 July 1918 and arrived in Port Phillip Bay late on Friday 12 July — evidently before Brown's letter had arrived and the portent of its contents realised. The newspapers in South Australia had reported the passage of the tank through the port of Adelaide in a small article entitled 'War Tank In Australia',[35] but neither this news nor Brown's letter had reached the authorities by the time the *Dongarra* docked in Melbourne early on Saturday morning, 13 July 1918, having sailed into Port Phillip Bay at dusk the previous evening and spent the night at anchorage in Hobson's Bay.[36]

The newspapers seemed to delight in the opportunity to report at length on the surprise of the Department of Defence at the tank's arrival, which was considerably earlier than anticipated. The Department, perhaps not unreasonably, had expected that it would take some time before a replacement would be made available. The *Argus* reported that,

> ... to the surprise of the military authorities, a battle scarred tank, fresh from many encounters on the battlefields of France, was landed in Melbourne on Saturday from a steamer which had arrived from Great Britain ... Practically the first intimation of the presence of the tank in Melbourne was the request of the shipping agents for a berth for the steamer alongside the largest crane in the port, situated near the Lower Yarra swinging basin. Here the Landship, which appeared to be in perfect working order, though having suffered some hard knocks, was hoisted ashore, and during Saturday morning attracted considerable attention. The attention of a number of boys was not confined to its exterior. They endeavoured to climb inside and, as the machine is easily set in motion, the military authorities placed a guard over it, and later, the tank was covered in tarpaulins.[37]

The tank remained at the wharf while authorities made arrangements for it to be moved to the ordnance yard at Victoria Barracks. With the 'special tank personnel' still on leave, and alerted by Brown's caution not to move the tank on its tracks until maintenance had been completed, the authorities contracted Vaughan's, a local heavy haulage firm, to move the tank from the wharf to Victoria Barracks.[38] The journey from the docks, which commenced at around

9.00 am the following Wednesday, proceeded along Flinders Street and turned right into Swanston Street before crossing Princes Bridge over the Yarra River and heading south along St Kilda Road to Victoria Barracks. The journey was evidently quite a spectacle. The *Leader* newspaper published this account the following Saturday:

On Wednesday morning[39] the tank moved into the ordnance yard at Victoria Barracks. After all the secrecy and comic opera tactics of the military authorities in regard to the tank it was hardly to be expected that the task of removing the tank from the docks to the barracks would be accomplished easily. On the contrary, the progress of the tank through the city was productive of scenes rarely encountered outside the pages of a "penny thriller". A guard of soldiers with fixed bayonets chased a camera man who had the audacity to endeavour to "snap" the tank as it passed through the streets. Threatened with the confiscation of his camera the photographer dramatically broke the plate in the presence of sternly accusing military officials. Later permission was given to photograph the tank. The rumbling juggernaut, 35 tons of tank, plus some tons of lorry and the weight of 23 horses used for haulage purposes, broke a plate on the tram lines when proceeding along Flinders street, and as a fitting climax to all the ridiculous officialism that has been displayed in regard to the tank, the huge war machine got jammed in the entrance to the ordnance yard at Victoria Barracks, and the fore wheels of the lorry sank six or seven inches beneath the surface of the yard. For four or five hours, workmen were busily engaged levering, tugging and hauling at the tank, which during the whole of this time was kept hidden in tarpaulins and guarded by armed soldiers. A newspaper reporter who had the temerity to enter the ordnance yard to gaze at the proceedings was promptly ordered away by the armed guard. Eventually the tank was dragged into the yard, where it will remain until it has been overhauled and cleaned.[40]

A large quantity of equipment and spare parts had been despatched from the UK with the tank, and these were also moved into storage at the ordnance yard. On 23 July 1918 John Sanderson & Company, the Australian Agents for the shipping company, requested that the Department of Defence endorse the bill of lading to the effect that the consignment had been received in good order and condition. However this request could not be met initially as one of the cases of spare parts was missing. The case was not located and delivered until much later, at which time the bill of lading was suitably endorsed and provided to the agents on 27 August.

Status and administration

With the tank safely secured at Victoria Barracks, attention turned to the control and administration of the vehicle and its AIF crew. The primary purpose of the tank was not as part of the military defences of Australia, but rather as an item of curiosity. It was to be used to capture as much of the enthusiasm over the new 'war-winner' as possible, and convert it into cash for the war effort, either as loans to the government or financial support for the various civilian patriotic organisations. The use of tanks for fundraising had worked very well overseas and, given the public's enthusiasm for them, there was every reason to expect that it would also work in Australia.

10. Members of the Military Board at the outbreak of war in 1914. Front row (L to R): Mr G. Swinburne, Civil Member; Brigadier V.C.M. Sellheim, Adjutant General; Senator E.J. Russell, acting Minister for Defence; Brigadier J.K. Forsythe, Quartermaster General; General J.G. Legge, Chief of the General Staff. Back row (L to R): Mr V.C. Duffy, Colonel H.W. Dangar, acting Chief of Ordnance, and Mr T. Trumble, Secretary, Department of Defence. Two would later play prominent roles in the story of Australia's first tank. General Legge was the Chief of the General Staff at the time of the tank's arrival, but recommended against the formation of a Tank Corps in Australia at that stage. Responsibility for the tank and its equipment and, later, the crew, was assigned to Colonel Dangar, by then confirmed as the Chief of Ordnance (AWM A03318).

The status of the tank was clearly defined by the Chief of the General Staff (CGS), Major General James Gordon Legge, on 16 August 1918, when he stated, 'I do not recommend the formation of any Tank Corps in Australia at present. As this tank is required for propaganda work principally,

I think its use should be as directed by the Business Board. The officer and crew should remain soldiers on the H.S. [Home Service] strength and under the Commandant of the State in which they happen to be.'[41] This was later modified slightly by the Minister for Defence, George Pearce, who placed the tank and all associated spare parts (physical assets) under the control of the Chief of Ordnance, Colonel Horace William Dangar.[42]

The day-to-day management of the activities of the tank and its crew were vested in Hugh Victor McKay of the Department of Defence's Board of Business Administration — essentially a civilian body within the Department responsible for overseeing and advising on defence contracts. The members were all well-established civilians within industry and commerce. McKay, of the Sunshine Harvester Company, was a member, and he volunteered to personally administer the operations of the 'war tank'.[43]

The crew was discharged from AIF service (most as 'medically unfit') and subsequently enlisted as Home Service personnel within the PMF. Home Service personnel enlisted under different terms and conditions to the PMF. They were employed for a specific period or purpose, with most taken on only for the duration of the First World War. In the case of the tank personnel, their Home Service enlistment was restricted to the period for which the tank was required. The enlistment for Home Service came with one singular benefit: all received a promotion.

Public appearances

Once the crew returned from leave, the men went to work to complete an extensive service of the tank after its long sea voyage exposed on the ship's foredeck. They also equipped it with its full complement of gear and a stock of spare parts likely to be needed when demonstrating the vehicle's abilities at interstate locations. The work proceeded smoothly, with McKay noting that 'the crew are being instructed to work from 8 a.m. until 12.30 – and from 1.30 p.m. till 5pm in order that no delay may take place in having the Tank ready for action.'[44]

While the crew laboured on the vehicle, McKay sought to deal with the flood of requests for the presence of the tank at various fundraising ventures. Prominent among them was the personal appeal forwarded directly to the Minister for Defence by the Governor of South Australia, Sir Henry Lionel Galway, for the tank to be exhibited in Adelaide for the Red Cross appeal during September.[45]

Cognisant of the level of public interest in the tank, McKay sought to satisfy as many requests at as many venues as possible. Not all could be satisfied. Some could not be met because of the difficulties of moving the tank to far-flung rural centres, while others could not be fitted into the tank's busy schedule. A few were refused because they did not fit the criterion of a patriotic fundraising event in support of the war effort.[46]

On 25 July, McKay reported to the Minister that the 'Tank is to be ready for action on Saturday morning, the 27th. Inst.' The Minister replied that 'if the tank can safely be taken through the streets, it would be a good idea to use it in the procession tomorrow.'[47] The news that the tank would join a parade of French troops through Melbourne on Saturday 27 July was released to the press late on Friday.[48]

So on Saturday 27 July 1918, the fully equipped tank, manned by its Australian crew, clanked out of the ordnance yard gates and turned north along St Kilda Road. It followed the parade of French troops as they marched through the city, with the CGS, Major General Legge, taking the salute on the steps of the Melbourne Town Hall. However subsequent reporting of the event concentrated on the tank rather than the more deserving French. The *Ballarat Courier* was typical of the reporting, proclaiming: 'Tank in the City' – 'Attracts Great Crowds' – 'Parade of French Troops'. The page 3 article went on to state that, in Melbourne on Saturday,

> … the armoured tank, which was presented by the British Government to the Commonwealth, made its first cruise through the principal streets of the city this morning. The lumbering engine of war attracted great crowds as it followed a parade of French troops who were about to take their leave. It came up from the Ordnance Depot under its own power and armed as it was with guns at the front and sides it presented a very real reminder of the mechanical genius that has been displayed in this war. The models of the tank that have served their purpose in various patriotic efforts will now be replaced by the real thing. As the tank proceeded along the city streets the crowds cheered, but they were not neglectful of the French soldiers who have played a part in big battles of recent date. In the absence of the Minister for Defence, the Chief of the General Staff, Maj-Gen Legge, took the salute at the portico of the Town Hall where, from the balcony above, people threw flowers on the Frenchmen in the procession.[49]

It was a day of 'firsts'. The Australian crew was handling this particular tank for the first time, having last crewed a tank during the training course at the

Tank Corps Training Centre at Bovington Camp several months before. Perhaps more importantly, it was also the first time that a tank had motored any distance under its own power in Australia. Saturday 27 July 1918 thus marks the day that Australia's first tank, crewed by the Australian Army's first tank crew, motored on Australian soil for the first time — and they performed flawlessly.

To Adelaide

Doubtless further encouraged by the public interest generated by a simple drive through the streets of Melbourne, the Board of Business Administration 'considered it wise to send the tank to both Sydney and Adelaide, and perhaps some other Capital cities when the itinerary can be arranged for it.'[50]

Moving the tank presented some formidable challenges to both Defence and state railways personnel in getting the 30-tonne monster around the country. There was little experience and minimal infrastructure to handle an item of the tank's size and weight. Temporary end-loading ramps had to be constructed at each end of a journey and a railway flatcar had to be specially modified to carry it safely and securely. This all came at a price that, in theory at least, was to be borne by whichever group was utilising the tank for fundraising purposes.

11. Tank Week in Adelaide, South Australia, was the first interstate outing for Australia's first tank. Thousands of 'British War Tank' buttons were sold in conjunction with the visit, raising a considerable sum for charity (AWM REL23902.099).

The tank's first major outing was to Adelaide in early September. Much had to be organised. The Victorian Railways agreed to modify a QB class railway flatcar for transport of the tank over the broad gauge line between Melbourne and Adelaide, and to provide an end-loading ramp in the Spencer Street railway yard. To confirm arrangements in South Australia, the newly appointed Captain Brown, Officer Commanding Tank, travelled to Adelaide by the overnight train arriving on 24 August, to confer with Robert Duncan of the organising committee on the program of events. He also discussed requirements with officers of the South Australian Railways concerning the offloading point and the provision of an end-loading ramp. Although some expenses were absorbed by the South Australian Railways, the overall cost of the round trip between Melbourne and Adelaide for the tank and crew still amounted to £124-11-6 — a considerable sum at a time when the average Australian earned around £5 a week.

In late August the tank motored under its own power from the ordnance yard at Victoria Barracks to the Spencer Street Station railway yard where it moved up an end-loading ramp and onto the specially prepared flatcar. It arrived at the Mitcham railway yard in Adelaide on 4 September, where it was unloaded by members of the tank crew and motored the 3.5 kilometres north to Unley Oval. Here it was prepared for a gruelling round of demonstrations and exhibitions to be conducted over the next few days.

'War Tank Week' was organised by the War Tank Demonstration Committee of The Motor and Allied Traders' Association. The net proceeds after expenses were to be divided between the Red Cross Society and the Repatriation Department. 'War Tank Week' ran from September 5 to 14 and was widely advertised in the daily newspapers throughout the state, the committee hoping 'to get a lot of country people in during show week.'[51] It also made good news copy, and was well reported by the newspapers such as the *Adelaide Register* which, under the headline 'War Tank In Adelaide', provided an extensive description of the tank's movement to the 'city of culture':

> The story goes that the tank when it learned that its first public appearance was to be made in the City of Culture, waddled down on its own to Spencer street, Melbourne and climbed on board a particularly strong truck. As this is not a war story the incident cannot be confirmed. As a bald outstanding fact let it be stated that there is a tank in Adelaide – not an ordinary tank which may have co-existed with the earliest days of settlement – but a real go-on-its-own war tank. Entrained at Melbourne, the tank – a before-the flood-looking object, with caterpillar

feet, an inquisitive nose, and a desire to climb over all sorts of forbidding obstacles such as dead-ends at railway stations and stumps of trees – arrived at Mitcham in the early hours of Wednesday morning. The hours were early because the goods train gets in early, and the military conductors of the tank did not want too many of the public to gaze upon it free of charge. The tank has come to make money for the local Red Cross and Repatriation Funds, and every penny counts. When the train drew up a few spectators who had long awaited the arrival of the stranger attempted to view it with "sparrow tickets" but they were repulsed. There were sentries, and it was of no use to argue with a sentry, as he carried all the main points. A ramp made of old rails and sleepers had been erected. The engineers who are "on the tank" put on a switch or two, turned on a lever or two, and their pet turned on its axis. Then it climbed down the ramp and by way of Mitcham road,[52] the Cross roads, and Cambridge terrace, it turned in a dignified way towards the gate of the Unley Oval, climbed up the clayey slope, dropped down the other side, and waddled towards what its crew called its stable. There it is now. Later in the day, a trial of the monster took place and "all well" was reported. The tank carnival will extend from today until September 14.[53]

The activities were centred on Unley Oval, a few kilometres south of the city centre, and included various sporting activities and demonstrations of motorcycles and military prowess. But undoubtedly the star of the show was the tank, which rumbled its way around a pre-set course of obstacles including trenches, steep gradients and a knife edge. The finale of each of the Saturday performances saw the tank nosing up to a specially constructed stone house with walls 750 mm thick, pushing its way through and reducing the house to a pile of rubble — to be rebuilt before the following Saturday's performance.

In addition to charging the public to see the demonstrations, the committee also sold 'War Tank Buttons' to commemorate the week and, for the particularly curious with money to spare, 'War Tank Bonds'. The bonds comprised 'a certificate (signed by His Excellency the Governor and the commander of the tank) authorising the holder to take a ride in the tank in return for the payment of £10 10/-. The certificate (or bond) can then be kept by the purchaser as a memento or souvenir of the first visit of a war tank to Australia.'[54]

There was also a 'name the tank' competition. The idea first came to light in late August, when Robert Duncan, a member of the organising committee in Adelaide, forwarded a telegram to McKay, requesting 'your permission official naming of tank ... would have competition for names … would submit names your final selection ...'[55] McKay telegrammed his agreement to Duncan on 26 August.

Competitors submitted names for consideration — and in the hope of winning a £10-10-0 prize — during the course of 'War Tank Week'. Unfortunately, the winner chose to have his name withheld, so his identity is lost to history, but he was evidently a very generous and patriotic person as he chose to donate the prize money — the equivalent of more than two weeks' wages — to the 'War Tank Week' fund.

During the tank's last performance at Unley Oval on Saturday 14 September 1918, the wife of the South Australian Governor, Marie, Lady Galway,[56] christened the tank by breaking the traditional bottle of champagne against the vehicle and 'wishing the huge engine every success.'[57] Tank '4643' would henceforth be known as 'Grit'.

Tank demonstration, 'War Tank Week', Adelaide.

The tank demonstrated its mobility at the Unley Oval, following a preset path across a series of specially constructed obstacles simulating the shell holes of no man's land and the enemy's fortified trenches. Similar obstacle courses were constructed for demonstrations in Sydney, Melbourne and later Brisbane. Thousands of spectators paid for the opportunity to see Grit in action.

12. The tank demonstrated its mobility at the Unley Oval, following a preset path across a series of specially constructed obstacles simulating the shell holes of no man's land and the enemy's fortified trenches.

13. Tank demonstration, 'War Tank Week', Adelaide.

14. Tank demonstration, 'War Tank Week', Adelaide.

15. Tank demonstration, 'War Tank Week', Adelaide.

16. Tank demonstration, 'War Tank Week', Adelaide.

17. The culmination of each Saturday's performance was the tank crashing through a specially-built stone house, much to the delight of the crowd (AWM A04992).

'War Tank Week' was a great success, raising well over £1000 after expenses. Many thousands of people flocked to Unley Oval to see the tank in action, with over 12,000 people in attendance at the first Saturday performance. Demonstrations and rides were conducted daily except for Tuesday 10 September, which the crew devoted to maintenance. The newspapers, always looking for a story, reported an unfortunate incident during the show the following day. Under the headline 'War Tank Sensation', the *Adelaide Register* reported that 'a battle scene in connection with the tank demonstration at the Unley Oval on Wednesday was rendered more realistic than the programme had anticipated by the premature occurrence involving the supposed explosion of a bomb as it was being prepared. It is stated that three members of the crew received burns which necessitated treatment. The incident was enveloped in official secrecy, and inquiries by the reporter were met with intimation that Capt. Brown, who was in charge of the machine, had instructed that nothing should be said about the affair.'[58]

At the end of 'War Tank Week', Grit clanked its way into the city centre to the garage of a member of the Motor and Allied Traders' Association. From there, its activities were for the benefit of the South Australian Central War Loan

Committee, which utilised it on Monday 16 and the morning of Tuesday 17 September to assist the launch of the Seventh War Loan.

At the opening of the loan on Monday 16 September, Grit led a 'monster procession' of military bands, large detachments of sailors and soldiers, and 1500 motorcars, six-abreast, along King William Street to North Terrace, where it was parked adjacent to the 'Bank of Thrift' constructed near Government House.[59] According to the *Advertiser*, 'the procession occasioned great public interest' and 'the tank and its crew had a demonstrative welcome all along the route.'[60]

Patriotic speeches were delivered from Grit's turret and the steps of the 'Bank of Thrift' calling for cash deposits into the 'bank'. The first deposit was made on behalf of the Returned Soldiers Association[61] by Captain Arthur Seaforth Blackburn, who had been awarded the Victoria Cross for conspicuous bravery at Pozieres on 23 July 1916.[62] Following the very successful launch of the Seventh War Loan, Grit was driven to Mitcham railway yard and loaded onto the flatcar for the return journey to Melbourne on 18 September.

Theft on the return journey

The Chief of Ordnance, Colonel H.W. Dangar had, by direction of the Minister for Defence, been given responsibility for the tank and all associated stores. On 12 September, while still in Adelaide, Captain Brown was ordered to undertake a complete inventory so that the items could be formally entered into the 3rd Military District's stores accounts. He planned to complete the inventory on his return to Melbourne several days later. Unfortunately, a number of parts and equipment were destined never to be taken on charge. During the return journey from Adelaide to Melbourne, the interior of the tank was rifled and an estimated £38-5-0 worth of items stolen.

The items were pilfered sometime between the loading of Grit onto the flatcar on 18 September, and the unloading at the Royal Melbourne Showgrounds in the early morning of 23 September. A Court of Inquiry was convened and both police and Army investigators tried to piece together the circumstances. Three of the crew provided statements — Captain Brown, Staff Sergeant Jackson and Sergeant Gifford. All provided essentially similar statements, with Jackson stating:

> On Wednesday September 18, I received from Captain Brown the following orders – load tank, swing sponsons in and couple them up; load all spares and machine guns, lash Tank and then sheet her down, making everything secure which was done and passed by Captain Brown.

On Monday, September 23, 6 a.m. I reported to Showground, Melbourne, to unload the tank. As soon as I saw the tank I saw that the sheets had been removed. I and Sgt. Gifford then made an inspection and found that one of the sponsons had been unfastened and pushed out into position. I found Captain Brown's overcoat on the floor of the tank, it had been stripped of badges and some of the buttons and his bag was lying open.

I reported same to Captain Brown and he gave me orders to go through the tools and Machine Guns. I and Sergt. Gifford did so and found that the Tools had been gone through and one King Dick Spanner missing. Tools in the Machine Gun replacement Bag had nearly all been taken.

I also found the door at the rear of the Tank had been opened and the trap-door on the petrol tank open, both of which can only be opened from the inside.[63]

The missing items included a number of Lewis machine-gun parts stripped from one of the weapons and from the spares bag. Less specialised tools such as spanners and screwdrivers — stored for convenience in one of the ammunition magazine boxes — were looted, along with six pairs of overalls, five pairs of boots, two sets of leggings and two lengths of carpet. Despite inquiries by the Criminal Investigation Branch of the Victoria Police and the listing of the items in police circulars, none was ever recovered. Detective F. Hawkins concluded that 'it is difficult to say if they were stolen at Adelaide or en route to Melbourne, however nothing was reported by the Railway officials in charge of the truck as to any irregularities. The Tank was a novelty and no doubt many people would like to have some of the parts as War Curios.'[64] Fortunately, the large stock of spare equipment imported with the tank provided replacements for most of the stolen tools and equipment, and the crew's boots and coveralls were replaced from the 3rd Military District Quartermaster Store.

At Melbourne's Royal Show

The unloading of Grit at the showground's railway station on 23 September marked the start of another busy week of fundraising for the tank and crew. The Royal Show was a week-long festival that regularly attracted tens of thousands of visitors from all over Victoria. It was a fundraising opportunity that had been on McKay's agenda from the beginning. His goal in capitalising on the tank's popularity was stated in no uncertain terms to the Secretary for Defence on 24 July, when he wrote that 'there is likely to be an immense crowd at the Melbourne

Show, which takes place about the last week in September, and as farmers come down with their pockets well lined and City people are in a spending mood at the same time, it would be a pity to miss the opportunity to rake in some money through the tank for patriotic purposes.'[65]

The Seventh War Loan was widely reported in newspapers across Australia, and 'visitors to the Royal Agricultural Show ... were not permitted to forget that the seventh war loan was on the market. At every point there was a reminder of the fact ...' It seemed that there were schemes and slogans everywhere exhorting patriots to 'Buy War Bonds'. However, 'the most successful advertising scheme on the ground ... was the war tank. Throughout the day returned soldiers spoke from the top of this monster, urging the people to subscribe and as an inducement, all those who applied for bonds of any denomination were permitted to inspect the interior of the war machine. So keen was the demand for this privilege that before the close of the day the bank officers had run out of the official receipt forms and had to issue interim receipts. Special provision is being made to meet the rush that is expected today [Thursday 26 September, the official Show Day public holiday].'[66]

On Saturday 28 September, the last day of formal events at the Show, Grit made the short run into the main arena to demonstrate its abilities. The *Argus* reported that

> ... the competitive events were many and varied but, from the point of view of popularity, all gave place to the demonstration of battle manoeuvres by the war tank, which had been on view at the show all week. When the tank, amid a skirl of bagpipes of the Collingwood Caledonian Pipe Band, climbed the mound near the wine kiosk, and moved down the slope into the arena, everybody was on tip-toe with excitement. Gliding silently over the level ground, it splashed through the water-jump and, to the delight of the onlookers, successfully negotiated a specially prepared obstacle composed of logs, the remains of the wood-chopping contests of the previous days. To those who had not seen the tank in action before, the feat seemed impossible.[67]

McKay's predictions had been correct, with almost 174,000 people attending the show during the week. The *Age* reported on the Monday following the close of the Royal Show that, 'as the result of six days' appeals at the show by a section of recruiting sergeants at the war tank, £10,000 has been added to the war loan subscriptions; £1,200 was netted on Saturday before the tank set out on its demonstration. The forcible and commendable oral efforts of the recruiting sergeants, aided by the war tank inspection "stunt", proved a great success.'[68]

To Sydney

But there was no resting on their laurels, and Grit and crew now departed for a round of fundraising events in Sydney. Loaded on Saturday 28 September 1918 immediately after the demonstration at the Royal Show was completed, Grit was transported as far as Albury on the broad gauge line. Decisions dating back to colonial times meant that the railway gauges were not standardised between the states. While Victoria and South Australia had both adopted broad gauge (which made the earlier trip to Adelaide relatively straightforward), the NSW railways ran on standard gauge tracks. Hence, trips between the two states required all passengers and freight to change trains at the state border. It was known as the 'break of gauge' and was a cause of constant delay and additional expense.

In the case of Grit, a specially modified standard gauge flatcar had to be brought from Sydney to Albury, and the tank transhipped to it. Unfortunately, the flatcar was delayed and arrived a day later than expected. Grit was unloaded from the Victorian Railways flatcar via a temporary end-loading ramp, moved a short distance across the railway yard to another temporary loading ramp, which it climbed to reach the NSW Railways standard gauge flatcar waiting on a parallel track. Transhipment was finally completed in the early morning of Wednesday 2 October, and Grit left on the final leg of its journey to Sydney as part of the regular 9.00 am freight train. It arrived at Sydney's Central Railway Station at around 2.30 pm on Thursday 3 October, and was immediately unloaded.

Grit's arrival in Sydney was reported in detail — and with some journalistic embellishments — in the *Sydney Morning Herald* the following day:

His Majesty's landship Grit crawled through some of the city streets yesterday from the Central Railway Station, and berthed its ponderous form in Moore street where the caterpillar legs will rest for some time while it is given over to the lofty mission of building up the war loan. The people of Sydney have had to be content merely with pictures of the British tanks that have been so profoundly impressing the enemy and bringing chaotic terror into the hearts of the German soldiers. They now have an opportunity to see one of these British monsters, for the Grit was one of a fleet of 200 in France. Its full battle weight is 29 tons. Stripped, it weighs 28 tons. It is 30 ft long and stands 10ft 6in in height, and carries a crew of eight, all invalided men, and the majority of them 1914 men. Captain Norman L. Brown, who is in charge of it, has also seen service. It is a British tank of the latest pattern, and looks precisely the thing of terror that it has proved to be in the din of battle. It was conveyed from Albury in a 40-ton truck, and was welcomed, along with the crew, at the station by Mr A S Jones, one of the joint organising secretaries of the central war loan committee, in the unavoidable absence of the Lord Mayor. With a war loan flag triumphantly aloft, Grit left the station at about 4 p.m. and excited the curiosity of crowds of people as it trundled along. Four eyes that peered through two apertures in front were the only visible part of the crew. Ahead of it strode two policemen to clear the way for it, although as a matter of fact, the tank cleared its own way. It held complete dominion over the traffic. "Take this thing out of the way" bawled a lorry driver. But the tank just moved on. Some of the horses, used probably to the throb of city traffic, passed it by contemptuously, but others could not understand the monster in their presence. They eyed it curiously, pricked up their ears, and timidly snorted; others threw up their hind legs and had to be patted and coaxed into the belief that it was something quite harmless. By the time it reached Moore Street it had a large crowd around it. Men and women vied with small boys to get a close look at it.[69]

However, it appears that the Seventh War Loan Committee made limited use of Grit from 10 to 15 October, using it primarily as a static drawcard and a platform for patriotic speeches. In the meantime, the Motor and Allied Traders' Association sought to have Grit undertake a series of mobility demonstrations at the Victoria Park Racecourse once the Seventh War Loan Committee had completed its fundraising efforts. Arrangements were made with the organising committee, and it was clearly stated and agreed from the outset that the expense of transporting Grit and her crew to and from Melbourne would have to be met by the committee. Funds raised, after expenses, were to be divided equally between Jacks Day — the fund to assist Navy and mercantile marine personnel — and the Dependants' Day Fund.

Grit commenced demonstrations at the Victoria Park Racecourse on Thursday 24 October 1918 and these continued every few days until Saturday 2 November. Based on attendance figures, they were a major success, with 20,000 paying spectators in attendance on Saturday 26 October and 'large groups who gathered on the hills and sand hummocks overlooking the park and had a free view of all that went on.'[70] Over 10,000 children were present for the demonstrations the following Tuesday, and double that number were expected to see the tank perform on Thursday 31 October, thanks in no small part to the granting of a half-holiday to schools located south of Sydney Harbour and the provision of special public transport to carry them to the venue.[71]

Grit performed what by now was a well-rehearsed demonstration, carrying paying passengers over an obstacle course similar to the one built at Unley Oval in September. The *Sydney Morning Herald* reported on the demonstration in eloquent terms:

> At one moment it could be seen climbing snail-like over a stiff barrier of wood and earth; it would then almost disappear from view in a shell hole – or what was intended to be such; then it would ascend and cant ominously on top of a series of trench embankments; but no matter what task beset it, nothing was too difficult of accomplishment. Youngsters yelled with delight when the tank struck a wreck and brought the whole structure down upon itself like a house of cards. The tank upon emerging from the wreckage was lustily cheered.[72]

The demonstrations at the racecourse raised a total of £1363-15-0, the majority from gate takings (£933-3-9). Tank rides accounted for £89-5-0, while the sale of souvenir buttons raised a further £150. However, advertising the event, wages for racecourse staff, the musical bands that entertained the crowd — even the bricks for the 'house' that Grit wrecked at each performance, plus rectifying the damage caused to the racecourse by the tank's tracks — all had to be funded by the proceeds, reducing the amount to £670-1-8. This was duly divided equally between the two recipients.

Unfortunately, what had been overlooked was payment of the cost of transport to and from Sydney. The round trip from Melbourne to Sydney and return required two specially prepared flatcars — one for carriage over the broad gauge line to the Victorian border, and the other for carriage across the NSW standard gauge line to Sydney. The break of gauge at the border also incurred charges for loading and unloading, and the preparation of two sets of temporary ramps in the freight yard. The total cost was £168-17-6, but this was reduced to £151-11-10 by apportioning the conversion of the flatcar used on the broad gauge network into thirds, each third payable by the Department of Defence and the organising committees in Adelaide and Sydney. The organisers in Adelaide were happy to finalise their accounts promptly, but an approach to the leading representative of the Sydney committee, Alex McNeil of Garratts Ltd, was met with refusal as he 'declined to admit that he agreed to any arrangement whereby the Patriotic Committees using the Tank were to bear freight expenses.'[73] There followed an unfortunate series of exchanges between Departmental officers and McNeil concerning the arrangements for the use of Grit, with the end result that the Department of Defence was forced to bear the cost. It would not be the last time that such a divergence of memories regarding freight costs for Grit and her crew would occur.[74]

Grit was loaded onto the modified flatcar in Sydney on 12 November 1918. Up until just a few days before, the tank and its crew seemed destined to travel north to Brisbane for a round of demonstrations in the Queensland capital.

To Brisbane — first attempt

The Motor Traders' Association of Queensland first requested that Grit be railed north to Brisbane in a telegram to McKay on 3 October. This was followed by a visit to Melbourne by Mr G.W. Whatmore to discuss the matter in more detail. On his return to Brisbane, Whatmore was sufficiently confident to release details to the press. On Tuesday 8 October the *Brisbane Courier* reported that, 'while in Melbourne, Mr. Whatmore interviewed the military authorities and the outcome is that there is every prospect of the people of Brisbane being given the opportunity of seeing the "tank". Mr. Whatmore states that the tank will probably arrive in Brisbane within the course of the next week or two, the only difficulty at present in the way being the transportation over the railways of this huge piece of machinery weighing upwards of 28 tons. The main difficulty lies in the exchange of trucks at Wallangarra.'[75]

Yet again, the decisions made in colonial times that resulted in differing railway gauges were affecting the carriage of Grit. Queensland used narrow gauge, so the tank would need to be transhipped from the NSW standard gauge flatcar to a Queensland Railways narrow gauge flatcar at Wallangarra for transport over the final leg of the journey to Brisbane. The Queensland Railways worked diligently to ascertain whether the tank could be transported over the narrow gauge line and whether a suitable flatcar could be modified to carry it. On 6 November, Captain Brown was informed that a narrow gauge flatcar had been despatched from Brisbane to Wallangarra for modification.

However, other aspects of the proposed trip had already intervened. On 5 November, the sub-committee of the Motor Traders' Association of Queensland reluctantly concluded that the visit would have to be cancelled due to the lack of a suitable venue. The only site that could accommodate the anticipated crowds and provide open space for Grit's demonstrations was the main arena of the agricultural showgrounds — but this site was already committed to other functions. The Agricultural Society was also concerned about the amount of damage that was likely to occur.[76] Brown was informed by McKay on 6 November: 'Brisbane Trip abandoned. Arrange return Melbourne with tank and crew promptly.'[77]

Albury sojourn

On 7 November 1918, Mr T.W. Tietyns, Secretary of the War Chest Fund in Albury, requested that Grit and crew make a short stop in Albury on their way to Melbourne to support the efforts of the local War Chest Fund. While the presence of the tank was requested for the weekend of 9–10 November, difficulties in arranging for the modified flatcar to come from Sydney made this impossible, so the following weekend was chosen. Grit arrived in Albury on 14 November and performed its demonstrations on Saturday 16 November. It was loaded onto the broad gauge flatcar on Monday 18 November and arrived at Spencer Street railway yard in Melbourne on 20 November. From there, Grit trundled along Flinders Street, turned right into Swanston Street, crossed Princes Bridge and made its way to the wagon shed at the Engineer Depot, a 1.5 hectare site located in Alexandra Avenue some 200 metres east of Princes Bridge.

A change of management

During Grit's time in Sydney, decisions had been taken at Defence Headquarters in Melbourne concerning the vehicle's ongoing management. McKay, a civilian member of the Board of Business Administration, arranged to transfer control of the day-to-day administration of Grit's activities to the Chief of Ordnance, Colonel Dangar. Dangar was already responsible for Grit and all associated equipment and spare parts, so it made sense to transfer overall management to him once interest in the tank began to plateau. The formal handover was completed on 13 November 1918, just two days after the cessation of hostilities and while Grit and the crew were enjoying the brief stopover in Albury. Grit and her crew were now fully controlled by the Department of Defence. Captain Brown was also informed of the change in a simple note from McKay: 'I am handing over control of the Tank to Col. Dangar from to-day on – and understand you … will work in future under his direction.'[78]

… and crew

With the nation now at peace and interest in the tank beginning to wane, the decision was taken in late November to terminate the Home Service of the majority of the tank crew. Corporal Swain had already lodged a request for discharge during October while in Sydney, and this formally took effect on 10 December. Most of the remainder of the tank crew — Staff Sergeant Jackson, Sergeant Gifford and corporals Lord, Dalton and McFadden — were discharged on 26 December 1918 at the completion of a fortnight's accrued leave.

Captain Brown and Corporal Fleming were retained specifically to provide instruction to a selected group of PMF RAE personnel on the operation and maintenance of Grit. With the discharge of Staff Sergeant Jackson, Corporal Fleming was promoted to staff sergeant. Brown was permitted to take 28 days' accrued leave in late December. He and Fleming were directed to deliver a course of instruction to the selected RAE personnel on Brown's return to duty in January 1919. The RAE personnel detailed to become the new tank crew comprised Sergeant W. Nicholson and corporals E. McDonald, MM, A. Kubale, Lance Corporal F.A. Hosking and Sapper S.B. Cook.[79]

The YMCA appeal

The Victorian public's waning interest in Grit — the tank had been highly visible on several occasions since its arrival in July — and the change in mood since peace was declared is perhaps illustrated by the request from the Young Men's Christian Association (YMCA) for the use of Grit. The organisation sought to have the tank perform a series of demonstrations in support of its appeal for £150,000 for its Army and Navy work. To that end, the Secretary of the Entertainments Committee, Mr G.D. Portus, lodged a request with Colonel Dangar late in November 1918. Dangar replied positively, but with the usual proviso that all expenses for the tank and crew would need to be met by the YMCA. He apparently also suggested that Luna Park at St Kilda — a relatively short distance from where the tank was housed in Alexandra Avenue — might prove a suitable location for the demonstration.

On 5 December, having rejected Luna Park as unsuitable, the YMCA committee considered the Royal Showgrounds at Ascot Vale where Grit had been displayed and demonstrated in September. However, 'after careful deliberation, it was decided that the general expenses in furthering this proposal would be too heavy for our body to undertake [and] under the existing Peace conditions, my committee consider that it will be unwise to go further in this matter.'[80] Grit remained in the wagon shed until, early in 1919, a special shed was built to accommodate the tank.

To Brisbane

While many members of the South Australian, Victorian and NSW public had experienced the thrill of watching Grit's demonstrations, and a fortunate few had even ridden inside the tank, Queenslanders had yet to enjoy the tank's performance. The aborted attempt to deliver Grit to Brisbane in November 1918 had not dampened their enthusiasm to view the tank and another opportunity was sought in 1919.

In late February a request was made for Grit to be sent to Brisbane, where it would be used for fundraising in conjunction with the Anzac Memorial Day Celebrations on 23 April 1919. The request, from Lieutenant G.C. Hanlon, was initially lodged with Mr McKay, who immediately forwarded it to Colonel Dangar for attention. Colonel Dangar's initial response was that Grit was 'unavailable due to the great expense in sending it such a distance and further that on a previous occasion when the question of forwarding the Tank to Brisbane was raised, a doubt existed as to whether the Queensland Railway could arrange to transport it.'[81]

Hanlon repechaged on 7 March with a letter to the Secretary, Department of Defence, stating that Queensland Railways could transport Grit over the narrow gauge line from Wallangarra to Brisbane, and that the organising committee was prepared to meet all expenses. The matter was considered by the Minister for Defence, who was favourable to the proposal 'if they agree to bear all expense, of which they should be first advised.'[82] A telegram informing Lieutenant Hanlon that the estimated cost would be not less than £350 was sent to Brisbane on 22 March. The Chairman of the Anzac Commemoration Committee, Mr Maurice Baldwin, replied positively on 26 March, guaranteeing that the costs would be met by the committee, and requesting that Grit be sent to Brisbane. Colonel Dangar issued orders for Grit and the tank crew 'to proceed to Brisbane by rail at the earliest possible date, as owing to quarantine restrictions, the journey will take a number of days to complete.'[83]

No doubt with the financial difficulties experienced after the trip to Sydney still fresh in his mind, Colonel Dangar forwarded a minute to the Commandant 1st Military District on 28 March advising of the arrangements and requesting that he 'advise the Chairman of the Anzac Commemoration Committee, Brisbane, accordingly. As stated in the above telegram, all expenses in connection with the visit will be borne by the Anzac Commemoration Committee, and an undertaking to that effect should be obtained from them.' On 3 April, Grant Hanlon, as the committee's General Organiser, and Maurice Baldwin, the Chairman, jointly signed a guarantee 'to certify that the Memorial Day Celebrations Committee undertake to defray all expenses in connection with the visit of the Tank to Brisbane, in connection with the Anzac Memorial Celebrations.'[84]

Grit and crew left the Spencer Street Station railway yard at 4.00 pm on 5 April for the long haul to Brisbane. Quarantine and break-of-gauge at the state borders added significantly to the time taken to reach Wallangarra and effect the transfer to the narrow gauge line for the final leg to Roma Street Station in Brisbane. The Queensland Railways conveyed Grit on a special train at a maximum speed of 12 kilometres per hour, travelling only during daylight hours. The train reached Helidon on 16 April where it spent the night, and passed through Toowoomba on Thursday 17 April, reaching Roma Street Station at around 3.30 pm the same day. Once unloaded, Grit was driven along Roma and Adelaide streets to its destination.

The daily activities centred on Grit were covered in some detail by the newspapers, particularly the *Brisbane Courier*. Captain Brown and his staff of six assistants were present throughout Monday 21 April, explaining the workings of the tank while it was being shown to the public for a price 'quite within the reach of all'.[85]

On Wednesday 23 April a procession of returned soldiers marched through the city, the *Brisbane Courier* noting that 'Captain Norman Brown and his crew of the battle tank "Grit" will head the returned soldiers' while, on Thursday 24 April, Grit was paid an official visit by the Governor and Lady Goold-Adams and other dignitaries.[86] They were shown over the tank's internal mechanism by Captain Brown.

Late that night, however, Grit was attacked by 'persons unknown'. The *Brisbane Courier* proudly reported that 'those who carried out the onslaught were unable to do any damage to the great war machine, so they had their revenge on the woodwork around it. … it is satisfactory at least to know that the battle tank "Grit" is impregnable to their puny efforts.'[87]

Friday produced another fundraising event as Grit deployed to the Exhibition Oval where it thrilled the paying crowd with a mobility display over an obstacle course. The Saturday performance proved to be rather special. On entering the arena, Grit halted to allow Lady Goold-Adams to board, before proceeding around the obstacle course and stopping at the north-eastern entrance to permit its distinguished passenger to alight. Once Grit was parked, the general public was allowed to see the interior — at 5/- each.

Grit, safely loaded aboard the specially adapted narrow gauge flatcar, departed Brisbane on Sunday 27 April. Although a request was made for the tank to be unloaded for a week-long display in Toowoomba, the organisers considered the estimated cost of £120 to cover expenses prohibitive, and withdrew the request. Nevertheless, the special train did stop for a day at both Toowoomba and Warwick so that local citizens could view the vehicle. The majority of the tank crew arrived back in Melbourne on 10 May, while Grit and the remainder of the crew arrived at Spencer Street railway yard on Monday 12 May, and then proceeded along the now-familiar route to the Engineer Depot in Alexandra Avenue.[88]

The demonstrations and exhibition of Grit in Brisbane proved a great success, raising over £9000 after expenses, the funds subsequently donated to the Returned Sailors and Soldiers Imperial League of Australia. Unfortunately, the Army was extraordinarily slow in finalising the accounts for the trip, the penultimate account for £437-19-9 not being forwarded to the General Organiser of the committee until March 1920. Repeated attempts to reach Grant Hanlon over the ensuing months met with no reply. In August, the account was sent to the other signatory to the guarantee, Mr Maurice Baldwin, but by that time the committee was long disbanded and the recipients of the funds had distributed them to sub-branches across Australia. Considerable correspondence ensued, but neither the guarantors nor the recipients of the funds would accept any liability. On 15 November 1921, the Department of Defence Finance Secretary recommended that, as there was no chance of recovering the money owed, it should be written off as a public expense. The Minister for Defence and the Treasurer subsequently agreed, and Maurice Baldwin was informed by letter on 16 December 1921. It was a bitter ending to what had otherwise been a highly successful performance in Brisbane.

The 1919 Victory Parade

For the rest of May, June and the beginning of July, Grit was given an extensive overhaul, primarily because the working parts were sorely in need of attention, but also as a training exercise for the RAE crew. Captain Brown remained 'OC Australian Tank', but Staff Sergeant Fleming took his discharge in late May and was replaced by an RAE NCO, Sergeant Marnie. Grit's next public exhibition was on 19 May 1919, as part of the Victory March through Melbourne. More than 7000 returned service personnel took part, divided into 11 groups, each commanded by an AIF officer, with Commander 3rd Military District, Brigadier General Brand, CB, CMG, DSO, in overall command. Grit followed the second group, which comprised engineer and artillery units, and was ahead of the first group of infantry. The tank, along with considerable quantities of captured weapons and equipment, reportedly excited great interest among the crowds lining the route.[89]

18. Grit takes its place in the Victory March through Melbourne on 19 May 1919, between the second and third groups of veterans. The crew is careful to stay to the left side of Swanston Street to avoid damaging the cable tram tracks and guides. By this time, only Captain Brown of the original AIF crew remained in uniform, the others having been discharged and replaced by a crew of RAE personnel based at Swan Island (AWM DAX2080).

At the end of the march, Grit trundled back to the special shed at the Engineer Depot in Alexandra Avenue.

Captain Brown discharged

By the middle of 1919, Captain Brown was the last member of the group of AIF tank personnel still serving. Brown's future in the Army and the ultimate destiny of Grit the tank were regarded as being closely linked. In a report to the Secretary of the Department of Defence by the Chief of Ordnance in late June 1919, it was noted that Brown was an excellent engineer and manager, and a 'first rate man'. Obviously keen to retain Brown in some capacity that would ensure his ongoing availability for duties with Grit, the Chief of Ordnance was willing to accommodate Brown 'even though his physical condition will occasionally render him more or less unfit for duty.'[90]

The matter was subsequently referred to the Military Board for consideration. At its meeting of 29 August 1919, the Board recommended that, 'pending re-organisation and the possible creation of a Tank Corps, no further military work need be performed in connection with the Tank, and the Board therefore recommends that Captain Brown be demobilized and the Tank put into store.'[91] On 9 September, the Chief of Ordnance informed the Commandant 3rd Military District that 'it has been decided that the "War Tank" be stored, and crew dispersed, and that Captain Brown be demobilized. Please give effect to this forthwith, and report when action completed.'[92]

The RAE crew members were then returned to their stations, the majority to Parnell Barracks, the RAE depot on Swan Island. Brown remained on leave until 23 October. On his return, he was demobilised.

No tank for Geelong

Despite the placement of Grit in storage, requests for the participation of the tank in patriotic fundraising activities continued to arrive. The Commandant 3rd Military District supported a request from the Executive Committee of the Gala Day to be held in Geelong, Victoria, on 31 October, noting that the committee would pay all transport and running expenses, and that the funds raised were for the support of war widows. The Chief of Ordnance, however, had a different view, replying on 9 September that 'in view of the pressing need for strict economy, the services of the "War Tank" cannot now be regarded as available for public purposes. It is regretted that the request of the Executive Committee of the Gala Day conveyed in your DHQ 19/7431 cannot be complied with.'[93] Apparently, a brigadier general's support was insufficient to secure Grit in support of a worthy cause.

At the Royal Show again

The support of the Acting Minister for Defence, however, was another matter. The Central Peace Loan Committee made its application for the use of Grit directly to the top. Once the Minister had approved the exhibition of Grit at Melbourne's Royal Show in late September, the Secretary forwarded a minute to the Chief of Ordnance, explaining that

... an application has been made by the Central Peace Loan Committee for the use of the Tank in connection with the Committee's activities during Show Week. It is desired that the Tank be placed in position at the Show Ground on Saturday 20th September, and allowed to remain during the currency of Show (1 week). All expenses in connection with the movement of Tank, and personnel necessary, to be defrayed by Central Peace Loan Committee. The Acting Minister has approved of the foregoing application, and would like action taken accordingly.[94]

Accordingly it was, with Grit delivered to the showgrounds as directed, and two of the RAE tank crew attending each day to look after the tank.[95] An overnight military piquet was not considered necessary as the showgrounds were constantly patrolled after hours through show week, and Grit was 'securely locked up and it would take a considerable amount of work and the use of special tools to break into it.'[96]

At the completion of Show Week, Grit was returned to the special shed at Alexandra Avenue.

Luna Park — just for fun

Grit's last public appearance in aid of fundraising was at the St Kilda Carnival from Saturday 6 to Saturday 13 December 1919. The Carnival Committee's honorary secretary had first spoken with Major Locke at Defence Headquarters, and followed up with a written request on 28 October asking for Grit to be made available. The tank was requested to appear at The Block in Collins Street, Central Melbourne, for the morning of 6 December, before proceeding to Luna Park on the Esplanade at St Kilda, a distance of some eight kilometres.

The Commandant 3rd Military District was very supportive of the request. He stated in his minute to the Chief of Ordnance and the Secretary of the Department of Defence that 'the sub-branch in question is endeavouring to raise sufficient funds to build a Memorial Hall at St. Kilda for the use of the Returned Sailors and Soldiers of Victoria. This Memorial Hall will be, more or less, a seaside club house for all Victorians and Interstate Returned Sailors and Soldiers, and will perpetuate the excellent work which has been done at the

St. Kilda Lounge for all soldiers who have passed through Victorian Camps.'[97] The Honourable Mr Agar Wynne, Member of the Legislative Assembly of the Victorian Parliament, also voiced his support for the loan of Grit to the Carnival Committee.[98]

Approval was given provided that all expenses were paid by the Carnival Committee — a requirement reiterated several times in correspondence. It appears that the Department of Defence was particularly concerned that the problems encountered following the Sydney trip would not be repeated.[99] The total cost was estimated to be at least £35-12-0 as the appearance involved deploying the crew from the RAE depot on Swan Island on Friday 5 December, preparing and driving Grit into the city on Saturday morning, then to Luna Park at St Kilda in the afternoon. Two crewmen —Temporary Corporal Kubale and Sapper Cook — would remain with the vehicle while the remainder — Sergeant Marnie, Corporal McDonald and Temporary Corporal Hosking — returned to Swan Island for the week. The latter three would return on Monday 15 December and Grit would be driven back to the Engineer depot in Alexandra Parade. The three crewmen would then return to Swan Island by train the same day, while the others remained at the Alexandra Avenue depot to complete the process of returning Grit to storage.

19. Grit's final fundraising appearance was near Luna Park on the esplanade at St Kilda, during the week of 6 to 13 December 1919. Two of the RAE crew remained in attendance as both security and to answer questions from the public. The tank was adorned with posters and remained static behind a timber barrier, a far cry from the heady mobility displays that had so enthralled the public just over a year ago (Museum of Victoria MM6754).

Evidently, the display proceeded without any problems, and the expenses were paid in full. Grit, covered in posters exhorting the public to give generously, was displayed for the week behind a temporary timber barrier. It was the last time Grit was used as a means of fundraising.

An Imperial demand

December 1919 was a busy month for Grit, not only at Luna Park in Victoria, but also at AIF Administrative Headquarters in London, where a claim for payment was received for the tank and associated equipment. The claim was for a total of £6953-10-9, comprising £6315 for the tank and spares as delivered to Australia, and a further £638-10-9 for tank stores lost when HMAT A42 *Boorara* was severely damaged by a torpedo.

The Commandant was clearly under the impression that Grit and all associated stores and equipment had been provided to Australia as a gift, and returned the claim to the British Ministry of Munitions with a request that it be withdrawn. Late in April 1920, however, the Ministry resubmitted the claim on the basis that there was no evidence in Ministry records indicating that the tank was a gift. The Commandant consequently forwarded the claim to the Secretary, Department of Defence, in Melbourne, seeking clarification and direction.

Before a reply was provided, a claim for a further £657-16-7 was received from the Army Ordnance Officer, Royal Arsenal, Woolwich, for the five Lewis light machine-guns and associated equipment supplied to Australia with the tank. The claim brought the total to £7611-7-4.

In the meantime, a review of correspondence and requests for information from former AIF personnel was being undertaken in Melbourne. Since the end of the war, those involved with securing the tank had moved on — some to far-flung postings, while others had long since been demobilised. General Griffiths, the Commandant at AIF Headquarters in London during the period when the tank was secured, was by this time the Administrator in Rabaul. In reply to inquiries, he telegrammed that the 'tank was offered to and accepted by us on understanding it was without cost other than freight.'[100]

Based on General Griffiths' recollections, further representations were made to the War Office by AIF staff in London in an effort to have the claims withdrawn. On 10 February 1921 the Secretary of the Department of Defence was informed that those representations had been successful:

His Majesty's Treasury have now sanctioned the waiving of those charges against Australian funds, the Ministry of Munitions having withdrawn the three claims in question, the tank and the whole of the spares thus being a "free issue" to the Commonwealth.[101] It might be incidentally stated that the Imperial authorities were unable to confirm, or obtain any evidence whatever in substantiation of the arrangement understood to have been made between the Acting AQMG, Administrative Headquarters. As a matter of fact I ascertained from Colonel Hurley (while the latter was recently in London) that no definite arrangement of that nature was actually made, the question of payment or otherwise not being discussed with the War Office in the earlier negotiations for the supply of the tank, etc. The trend of my latest representations was therefore, more or less confined to the national character of the purposes for which the tank, etc, was required, viz. to stimulate Recruiting and Loan Campaigns, the result, whereby no charges will be borne by Australia, being very satisfactory.[102]

Given the expenditure in the lives of young Australians over the period of the Great War, it was perhaps the very least the British government could do.

Retired to the Australian War Museum

While officers of the Department of Defence were still wrestling with the British War Office over the question of payment for Grit, Sir Henry Gullett, Director of the Australian War Museum (then a part of the Home and Territories Department), made inquiries in February 1920 concerning the transfer of Grit to the museum.[103] Gullett's memorandum sparked a series of internal inquiries, with the CGS stating that the Army no longer required the tank for any purpose. Indeed, the ever-pragmatic Chief of Ordnance considered it desirable that Grit 'should be relegated to museum purposes as soon as possible in order that military responsibility for its maintenance in a serviceable condition may reach finality.'[104] The Director of the War Museum was then informed that Grit and equipment could be transferred as soon as the museum, at that time located in the Exhibition Buildings in Melbourne, was in a position to accept it. Further correspondence ensued with the War Museum requesting that the tank remain in storage at Alexandra Avenue for some time yet to allow suitable exhibition space to be finalised.

There was also the question of what to do with the extensive list of spare parts and equipment held on RAE charge with the tank at the Alexandra Avenue depot. Items with a ready application elsewhere, such as brooms, lights, tools, batteries and so on, were distributed to the RAE depots at Alexandra Avenue and Swan Island. Many of the remaining stores were retained to be transferred to the War Museum along with Grit, while the rest were returned to Ordnance stores for disposal.

20. Grit was transferred to the collection of the Australian War Museum in 1921, and was initially displayed in a semi-open area at the Exhibition Buildings in Melbourne. In 1941, Grit was installed in the lower gallery of the new Australian War Memorial building in Canberra, where it remained for many years (AWM P04425.001).

Time dragged on, and in February 1921, the Secretary inquired when the War Museum would be able to take delivery of Grit. The new director, John Treloar, replied in similar terms to his predecessor, indicating that it would be preferable for Grit to continue to remain at the Engineer depot until suitable long-term accommodation could be finalised. In August however, Treloar informed the Department of Defence that delivery could be made as soon as convenient.

As Grit had been maintained in a serviceable condition, the only questions remaining were the timing of the transfer and the cost. The crew had to be mobilised from the RAE depot on Swan Island, so there were expenses for travelling allowances and the petrol and oil required for the trip.[105] The costs amounted to £18-13-9, and were paid from the Museum's budget.

On Friday 14 October 1921, Grit was gently coaxed back to life by its RAE crew and trundled slowly from the Engineer depot in South Melbourne. The *Argus* reported the transfer — with typical literary embellishment — under 'Items of Interest – Tank for War Museum' in the Saturday edition:

> As it proceeded slowly through the principal streets of the city early yesterday afternoon, a British armoured tank, which during the war did service on the Western Front, attracted much attention. From the rear of Victoria Barracks, it crossed Prince's Bridge and went by way of Swanston, Collins, Elizabeth and Bourke Streets to the Exhibition. This tank will be included in the war museum. It arrived in Australia a long time ago, having been sent out as a specimen for exhibition. When in commission it was armed with Lewis guns. It travelled yesterday under its own power.[106]

Once settled into the open-sided exhibition annex, Grit was shut down for the last time.

On exhibition in Melbourne

The semi-exposed position in the Australian War Museum annex at the Exhibition Buildings was evidently not kind to Grit. On 8 December 1930, Major E.A. Wilton inspected Grit to see whether it was feasible to use the tank for fundraising purposes. Wilton, an experienced mechanical engineering officer, considered the engine and transmission in reasonable condition, and estimated it would take £50 to £100 to return the tank to running order.[107] However he also observed that, until the tank was started, it was not possible to say whether the tracks were too badly rusted for the tank to move. The proposal to use Grit was subsequently abandoned due to the cost and the short time-frame.

Pilfering and vandalism were also a problem. In January 1932, a somewhat exasperated John Treloar wrote an internal memorandum exhorting staff member 'Nich' to devise a way of preventing unauthorised entry into Grit:

> Yesterday afternoon when leaving this office I noticed that the local juvenile safe-breakers had managed to get into the tank again, and shortly afterwards noticed one of them making a hurried departure with a spanner in his hand. As he had nothing else I made no attempt to stop him, but the fact that he had a very serviceable looking spanner is suggestive.
>
> This is the third or fourth unsuccessful attempt to keep children out. I know the local youngsters are apparently very enterprising but I should

hate to think that they can outwit a man who served with distinction with that famous unit – the 3rd Pioneer Battalion. I wonder if you, in consultation with Comrades Baglin and Baxter, cannot think out a way of effectively closing the tank to trespassers once and for all. Even if we keep ourselves out this will not matter for the time being.[108]

A further request in March 1934 to have Grit lead a procession during the opening of the Melbourne Motor Show was declined on the basis that the tank was no longer in running order, and some of the parts required were no longer available.

A new place in Canberra

When the new Australian War Memorial was opened in November 1941, Grit was displayed in the lower gallery. Cosmetically refurbished for display, the tracks were no longer rusted and the exterior had been given a new coat of paint. In July 1977, Memorial staff repainted the build number '4643' and the name 'Grit' on each side of the tank.

21. The government transport service employees who moved Grit from the Canberra Railway Station to the Australian War Memorial pose on and around Grit in the area that later became the Western Courtyard. The tank has a number of fanciful claims chalked on the sides, and the paintwork appears to be rather shabby (AWM P08909.003).

22. The Mk. IV Female tank, known as Grit, is delivered to the Australian War Memorial. The tank arrived by rail from Melbourne and was towed by road from Canberra station to the Memorial by four government transport trucks. The steel towing cable is visible at the front of the tank and the original Parliament House is visible in the background (AWM P08909_001).

Grit remains in the collection of the Australian War Memorial, one of only a handful of surviving Mk. IV tanks. It is a tangible reminder of the rapid evolution in technology that war seems to bring. The Great War started with massed infantry and cavalry formations. None would survive in the face of the machine-gun, the aeroplane, ever more lethal artillery fire and, finally, the tank. The age of armoured manoeuvre warfare had arrived.

23. A newly repainted and conserved Grit in 2009. Memorial staff went to great lengths to clean and conserve the tank, one of only a handful of Mk. IV tanks in existence. Grit is arguably in the best and most original condition of the few survivors. Conservators and curators worked in close cooperation to authentically reproduce both the internal and external finish of the tank to reflect the condition in which it first arrived in Australia in July 1918, fresh from the manufacturer's works in Glasgow, Scotland (RELAWM05040.001).

DRAMATIS PERSONAE

of the
Tank Personnel, Special Unit Tank Crew, Home Service, 1918–19

Captain N.L. Brown
Corporal R.J. Dalton
Sergeant R.T. Fleming
Sergeant F.G. Gifford
Staff Sergeant C.R. Jackson
Corporal D.B. Lord
Corporal M.G. McFadden
Motor Transport Driver A.R. Rowland
Motor Transport Driver H.S. Swain

HOME SERVICES AND PERMANENT MILITARY FORCES

The men who manned Grit during its service in Australia came from two distinct groups. The first crew, trained at the Tank Corps Training Depot at Bovington Camp under the leadership of Lieutenant Brown, were members of the AASC Motor Transport Service. The other ranks were qualified motor transport drivers. On arrival in Australia they were all discharged from the AIF and re-enlisted in the Special Unit Tank Crew (Home Service). When these men finally discharged from military service in late 1918 and 1919, the responsibility for crewing and maintaining Grit passed to soldiers of the PMF stationed at the Swan Island RAE Depot. These men were technicians who garrisoned the forts that guarded Port Phillip Bay.

Returned to Australia for duty with tank

The traditional image of the AIF during the Great War was of units formed either in Australia or abroad for service overseas. Once a unit was disbanded, its members were generally returned to Australia in piecemeal fashion for demobilisation. The tank personnel of 1918 are possibly a unique example of a unit formed abroad for service in Australia.

The nine men gathered at Bovington Camp in January and February of 1918 all had relevant mechanical experience, both in the AIF as qualified motor transport drivers and before, with pre-war occupations including garage manager, four motor mechanics, one mechanical engineer and two chauffeurs. In terms of AIF service, three members had enlisted as early as 1914 and the average length of service was 32 months. The shortest service was no fewer than 16 months.

This group of men all came from the major urban centres and reflected the primary religious divisions within Australian society of the period: 33% were Roman Catholic while the remaining members belonged to the major protestant faiths. The majority were born in eastern Australia with the other 22% born in the UK. All members could claim Anglo-Irish roots. It is also apparent that these men came from predominantly skilled working class origins. The average age of the crew was a mature 28 years with the oldest 35 and the youngest 26.

Norman Lovell Brown

Norman Lovell Brown was born in Glenelg, South Australia, on 4 March 1883, the son of Israel and Emma Brown. He married Emma Monkhouse at Unley on 25 December 1902. By 1916 the couple had four children. At the time of his enlistment in the AIF, Brown was a garage manager residing in Rose Park.

Brown enlisted in Adelaide on 10 April 1916. His postings in Australia between April and October included: D Company, 2nd Depot Battalion, the Musketry School at Chatham, B Company Base Infantry, the 5th Reinforcements 50th Battalion and the NCO School. During this period Brown displayed leadership qualities and acted as corporal, sergeant and company sergeant major. On 16 September he applied for a commission which was granted on 7 October. Lieutenant Brown was posted to the 3rd Australian Army Mechanical Transport Company, AASC, on 16 October.

Lieutenant Brown embarked for overseas service on HMAT A34 *Persic* at Port Melbourne, Victoria, on 22 December 1916 and disembarked at Devonport, UK, on 3 March 1917. During this voyage an alarm was raised and Brown, rushing to the deck, suffered a head injury which caused concussion and saw him hospitalised aboard the *Persic*. Brown reported to the ASC Training Depot 6 March. On 31 March he was admitted to Delhi Hospital where a plate was inserted in his skull. He did not return to the training depot until 26 April. Lieutenant Brown embarked at Southampton and proceeded to Havre, France, on June 20 and joined the 5th Divisional Ammunition Sub Park, AASC. It was to be a short appointment. On 8 July he was posted to the 1st ANZAC Corps Supply Column.

The 1st ANZAC Corps Supply Column was engaged in support of the 1917 offensive around the Belgian city of Ypres. During this period Lieutenant Brown began to suffer pains in his head, caused chiefly by the gunfire. Despite this affliction, his Officer Commanding, Major Goddard, regarded Brown as a capable and efficient officer who performed the duties of Roads Officer particularly well. However Brown was medically boarded at Rouelles on 6 November and found to be unfit for general service for six months, but fit for home service. On 21 November, Lieutenant Brown was evacuated to the UK awaiting further appointment. The decision was made to return Brown to Australia and terminate his appointment due to his medical condition. At the same time, the Imperial government agreed to send a Mk. IV tank to Australia on public relations duties. An Australian crew was required, and it seemed logical that Brown, with his mechanical knowledge, should command the crew.

Lieutenant Brown reported to the Tank Corps School of Instruction at Bovington Camp, Dorset, for special duty on 27 January 1918 and was appointed officer in charge of tank personnel. On 12 May he embarked on the HT D8 *Ruahine* for Australia with eight Australian tank crew who were to maintain and demonstrate the Mk. IV on its tour of Australia. The Special Unit Tank Crew disembarked in Sydney on 5 July.

Lieutenant Brown's service with the AIF was terminated on 15 August 1918. The following day he was appointed a captain in the Home Service as Officer Commanding the Special Unit Tank Crew. Until his discharge he commanded the AASC crew that maintained and demonstrated Grit at various locations in eastern Australia. In early 1919 he supervised the training of the PMF engineers from the Swan Island detachment who took over the running of Grit until its final placement at the Australian War Memorial. This appointment was terminated on 23 October 1919.

For his service in the AIF, Lieutenant Brown was entitled to the British War and Victory Medals and the Silver War and Returned Soldier's Badges.[109]

Brown's later life illustrates his very complex personality. In 1923 Emma Brown wrote to the Base Records Office requesting her husband's medals as 'he has not and will not claim for the same. He has left me, and I understand he is living with another woman … My reason for this application is so that my young children may have them.'[110] In 1924 Brown returned his service medals. His service file also contains a 1933 letter from a family member that suggests that Brown's whereabouts were unknown to his family. In 1935 Brown visited the Australian War Memorial in Canberra where he claimed he was a major rather than a captain. By 1943 he had settled in Woollahra, NSW, and was working as an engineer.

Brown died suddenly at the Repatriation General Hospital in Concord, NSW, on 27 April 1949. His death notice in the *Sydney Morning Herald* added to Brown's mystique: 'Brown-Arroll Captain Norman April 27 (Suddenly), 3rd AAMTC and RNR at the Repatriation General Hospital Concord beloved husband of Edna, Thy will be done.'[111] In 1950 a memorial notice appeared: 'Arrol. In loving memory of my late husband, Captain. N.L. DSO and Bar, MC passed away April 27 1949, Love endureth forever and anon-yea even into Eternity. Inserted by his loving wife, Edna'.[112] These notices revealed a new surname as well as decorations and service that are not supported by his service record. Sadly, correspondence would continue for some time between Edna and the Imperial War Graves Commission as she attempted to substantiate her late husband's claim that he had been decorated at Cambrai.

Two of Brown's sons would serve in the AIF in World War II: Private Norman John Brown, 2/3rd Machine Gun Battalion, and Sergeant George Alfred Brown, 2/3rd Field Company.[113]

Richard John Dalton

Richard John Dalton was born in Essendon, Victoria, on 22 May 1891, the son of Martin and Mary Dalton. At the time of his enlistment in 1915, Dalton described his occupation as motor mechanic and driver, and his place of residence as Middle Park. Soon after enlistment he married Eileen Margret Houston of Punt Road, Windsor, Victoria.

Dalton's driving skills came to the attention of the police in June 1914 according to court report found in the *Port Melbourne Standard*:

Richard Dalton, chauffeur, drove a motor car along a section of Bay street at the rate of 30 & 1/2 miles an hour on 30 June 1914 and was fined £2 at the local court on Thursday last for travelling at a speed dangerous to the public. He did not appear, but the case for the prosecution was borne out by Constables Fitzgerald and Burke. Defendant told the latter that he was hurrying in order that he might be in time for a departing mail boat and that he had no idea that he was going so fast.[114]

Dalton enlisted in the AIF in Melbourne on 12 July 1915. His enlistment, unlike many of his contemporaries, was classed as special; he enlisted as a motor transport driver for service with the AAMC, thus employing his civilian trade and associated skills. While in Australia, Dalton served with the AAMC Transport Section and the 1st Motor Transport Base Depot. During this time he was promoted lance corporal.

Lance Corporal Dalton embarked for overseas service on HMAT A19 *Afric* at Port Melbourne on 5 January 1916 as part of a group of reinforcement AAMC motor drivers. On arrival in Egypt on 13 February he was taken on strength by the Australian Motor Transport Service. Dalton served in Egypt until he embarked at Alexandria for Marseilles, France, on 16 June. He was then posted to the 4th Divisional Ammunition Sub Park, AASC, on 5 August as a motor transport driver. It is unclear when Dalton reverted from lance corporal to motor transport driver. He served in France and Flanders between June 1916 and August 1917 when he was granted leave to the UK. While on leave he was admitted to the 2nd Auxiliary Hospital. Following his discharge from hospital on 1 November, he was posted to the Australian Motor Transport Service, London. He remained in London until 27 January 1918 when he marched into the Tank

Corps Depot at Bovington to attend a course. Having completed this course, Dalton embarked on the HT D8 *Ruahine* on 12 May bound for Australia as a member of the tank personnel. Dalton disembarked in Sydney on 5 July.

On 12 August 1918 Dalton was discharged from the AIF in Melbourne. The following day he re-enlisted in the AIF Home Service 'for service in Australia only' as a member of the Special Unit Tank Crew. Until his discharge he was part of the AASC crew that maintained and demonstrated Grit at various locations in eastern Australia. He was discharged at his own request on 26 December 1918.[115]

In August 1922 Richard Dalton was one of four men who faced the Williamstown Magistrate's Court for a breach of licensing laws. The publican, Mr Fyfe, pleaded guilty, arguing that, 'they were returned soldiers, celebrating a great battle on the Rhine. They were just having a "sing-song" and playing on the piano. It was 3 o'clock when they left. Why the bar door was open when the police entered was that the licensee had gone to it for some cigarettes. There was no intention to commit a breach of the law.' The ex-diggers asserted that they 'were celebrating the last engagement of the war, the battle of Villers Bretonneux.' The police prosecutor withdrew the charges under the circumstances.[116]

On 7 May 1940 Dalton enlisted in the CMF at Puckapunyal, Victoria. While serving with the Australian Army Canteens Service, Corporal Dalton died suddenly at Caulfield on 22 July 1942.[117] He is buried at the Williamstown General Cemetery.

For his service in the AIF Corporal Dalton was entitled to the British War and Victory Medals and the Returned Soldier's Badge. He was also entitled to the War and Australian Service Medals for his service in the Second World War.

Two of Dalton's sons served in the Second World War: Sergeant Geoffrey Dalton, 2/23rd Battalion, and Able Seaman Thomas Houston Dalton, HMAS *Lonsdale*.[118]

Thomas Richard Fleming

Thomas Richard (Montague) Fleming was born in Paddington, Middlesex, UK, in March 1893, the son of John and Emma Fleming. In the 1911 census, Fleming was residing at Maynard Road, Rotherhithe, and was employed as a van boy. Sometime between 1911 and 1914 Fleming arrived in Sydney. At the time of his enlistment in 1914, his next of kin was his mother who resided at Shirland Road, Paddington, London. Fleming described his occupation as a chauffeur; his attestation papers also stated that he had served for two years in the Portsmouth Division of the Naval Brigade, Royal Naval Volunteer Reserve.

Fleming enlisted in the AIF in Sydney on 22 August 1914 and was posted to the 2nd Infantry Battalion's C Company. Private Fleming embarked for overseas service on HMAT A23 *Suffolk* in Sydney on 18 October and disembarked in Alexandria on 8 December. After training in Egypt, Fleming embarked on the *Derfflinger* at Alexandria on 5 April 1915 with the 2nd Battalion to join the Mediterranean Expeditionary Force. On 25 April he landed on the Gallipoli Peninsula. Fleming was wounded in the foot in the week following the landing and was evacuated to Egypt. After convalescing at Mustapha Camp he rejoined his battalion on 8 June. This return proved short lived as, on 8 June, he was wounded a second time, hit by gunshot in the forearm. Fleming was evacuated to Egypt and admitted to the 1st Australian General Hospital and later the 2nd Auxiliary Convalescent Depot. On 25 April 1916 he embarked at Alexandria on the *Ansonia* for the UK, where he would remain for the rest of his overseas service. Having recovered from his wounds, Fleming was transferred to the Australian Motor Transport Service on 30 January 1917. In August he was mustered as a motor transport driver and medically reclassified as C1.

Fleming remained with the Australian Motor Transport Service at Chelsea until 27 January 1918 when he marched into the Tank Corps Depot at Bovington to attend a course. Having completed this course, Fleming embarked on the HT D8 *Ruahine* on 12 May for Australia as a member of the tank personnel. He disembarked in Sydney on 5 July.[119]

On 12 August 1918 Fleming was discharged as medically unfit from the AIF in Melbourne. The following day he re-enlisted in the Home Service 'for service in Australia only' as a member of the Special Unit Tank Crew. Promotion to staff sergeant would soon follow. Until his discharge he remained part of the AASC crew that maintained and demonstrated Grit at various locations in eastern Australia.

For his service in the AIF, Staff Sergeant Fleming was entitled to the 1914–15 Star, British War and Victory Medals, and the Silver War and Returned Soldier's Badges. In 1967 he claimed his Gallipoli Medallion.

Following discharge, Fleming lived in Adelaide and on the York Peninsula, South Australia, also spending some time in Queensland. He married Lorell Nobel in Maitland, South Australia, in April 1928. In 1967 he was living at Urania on the York Peninsula. Fleming died in Maitland on 21 November 1969 and is buried at the Maitland Cemetery.[12]

Frederick George Gifford

Frederick George Gifford was born in Exeter, South Australia, in 1889, the son of William and Ellen Gifford. At the time of his enlistment in 1916, his next of kin was his mother, Ellen Gifford, who resided in Glen Osmond Road, Glen Osmond. Gifford described his occupation as mechanical engineer; his attestation papers also stated that he had served in the Naval Reserve and had been rejected as unfit for service on a previous occasion.

Gifford enlisted in the AIF in Adelaide on 24 October 1916 and was posted to A Company of the 9th Depot Battalion. Private Gifford embarked for overseas service on HMAT A35 *Berrima* in Port Adelaide on 16 December with the 6th Reinforcements, 43rd Infantry Battalion, and disembarked at Devonport, UK, on 16 February 1917. In England, Gifford trained with the 2nd and 11th Training Battalions at Durrington. While at Durrington, Private Gifford was medically boarded and graded as C1. On 2 October he was transferred to the Australian Mechanical Transport Service, London, and mustered as a motorcyclist.

Gifford remained with the Australian Motor Transport Service in London until 26 January 1918 when he marched into the Tank Corps Depot at Bovington to attend a course. This also involved a change of mustering and an appointment as an artificer. Having completed the course, Gifford embarked on the HT D8 *Ruahine* on 12 May for Australia as a member of the tank personnel, disembarking in Sydney on 5 July.

On 12 August 1918 Gifford was discharged from the AIF in Melbourne. The following day he re-enlisted in the AIF 'for service in Australia only' in the Special Unit Tank Crew. Until his discharge he was part of the AASC crew that maintained and demonstrated Grit at various locations in eastern Australia. He was discharged on 26 December 1918. For his service in the AIF, Artificer Gifford was entitled to the British War Medal and the Returned Soldier's Badge.[121]

Following his discharge, Gifford settled in Mount Gambier, South Australia, and was initially employed by the British Imperial Oil Company. His marriage to Ellen Maloney on 2 July 1922 at St Paul's Catholic Church brought a significant change of fortune. Articles appeared in the *Border Watch* for the next 30 years portrayed a very successful life: he played cricket for the Standard Cricket and Kookaburras Clubs, was a patron of Gambier East Football Club, he became licensee of the Mount Gambier Hotel, promoted the local tourist industry, was a successful businessman, involved in the local aviation industry, and a supporter of many local charities and good causes. In the early 1940s the Giffords moved to Melbourne but retained a strong interest in the affairs of

Mount Gambier; again the *Border Watch* contains numerous references to visits and correspondence from the Giffords. In March 1954 the Hotel was sold for £100,000.[122] Gifford died in Albert Park, Victoria, in 1961.

Charles Robert Jackson

Charles Robert Jackson was born Newtown, Sydney, in 1890, the son of William and Meta Sophia Jackson. In 1914 his next of kin was his mother, Sophia Jackson, who resided at the Hospital, Great Victoria Street, Belfast, Ireland. On his enlistment Jackson stated that he was an engineer by occupation.

Jackson enlisted in the AIF in Sydney on 15 October 1914 and was posted to the 8th Company, AASC. This unit was also known as the 301st (Motor Transport) Company, 17th Divisional Ammunition. The 8th Company was to be one of the first motorised transport units in the Australian Army.[123]

Driver Jackson embarked for overseas service on HMAT A40 *Ceramic* in Port Melbourne on 22 November 1914 and disembarked at Avonmouth, Gloucestershire, UK, on 15 February 1915. In England, the 8th Company spent the spring of 1915 training and supporting the construction of the military camps being built on the Salisbury Plain. On 12 July Driver Jackson embarked on the SS *Saba* at Avonmouth and disembarked in France. The 8th Company and its sister company, the 1st Divisional Supply Column, became the first units of the AIF to arrive in France, almost a year before the infantry divisions. Jackson was transferred to the 23rd Ammunition Sub Park on 28 August. On 16 September 1916 he was posted to the Australian Motor Transport Service, London, thus ending his active service in France. In the UK Jackson was promoted corporal on 21 August 1917 and married Kathleen Alice Jackson at Winchester on 16 February 1918.

Jackson remained with the Australian Motor Transport Service at Chelsea until 26 January 1918 when he marched into the Tank Corps Depot at Bovington to attend a course. Having completed this course, Jackson embarked on the HT D8 *Ruahine* on 12 May for Australia as a member of the tank personnel. He disembarked in Sydney on 5 July.

On 12 August 1918 Corporal Jackson was discharged from the AIF in Melbourne. The following day he re-enlisted in the AIF 'for service in Australia only' in the Special Unit Tank Crew. Until his discharge he was part of the AASC crew that maintained and demonstrated Grit at various locations in eastern Australia. He was discharged on December 26.

For his service in the AIF, Corporal Jackson was entitled to the 1914–15 Star, the British War and Victory Medals and the Returned Soldier's Badge.[124]

Following discharge, Jackson returned to Sydney, where the 1930 electoral roll shows him residing in Matilda Street, Bondi, and employed as a motor mechanic. His marriage to Kathleen was dissolved in February 1931 on the grounds of his wife's desertion. In 1933 he married Annie Titterington and they eventually settled in Bellingen where he ran a garage. Jackson died at the Bellingen Hospital on 29 June 1953 and was buried in the Presbyterian section of the Bellingen Cemetery.[125]

Donald Bernard Lord

Donald Bernard Lord was born in Hanwell, Ealing, Middlesex, UK, in 1890, the son of James and Elizabeth Lord. Donald married Camille Dolly Cameron in 1912. At the time of his enlistment in 1914, his next of kin was his wife, Camille Lord, who resided in Millington Street, South Yarra, Victoria. Lord described his occupation as motor mechanic; his attestation papers also stated that he had served in the light horse in the CMF.

Lord and his elder brother Norman both enlisted in the AIF at the Albert Park Drill Hall on 17 September 1914 and were posted to the 9th Company, AASC, a unit also known as the 1st Divisional Supply Company. The 9th Company was to be one of the first motorised transport units in the Australian Army.[126]

Private Lord embarked for overseas service on HMAT A40 *Ceramic* in Port Melbourne on 22 November 1914 and disembarked at Avonmouth, UK, on 15 February 1915. He was promoted lance corporal on 21 December. In England, the 9th and its sister company, the 8th Company, spent the spring of 1915 training and supporting the construction of the military camps being built on Salisbury Plain. In June both units were warned for service in France with the British Expeditionary Force. On 3 June, Lord wrote to his wife, 'tomorrow I am going before a medical board that will decide if I am to be invalided home. I presume they will decide, as I cannot walk yet. I don't know what you will do with a cripple.'[127] Lord did not proceed to France with his company. Between June 1915 and September 1916 there is no indication as to where he was hospitalised or located. On 16 September he was taken on strength by the Australian Motor Transport Service, Chelsea. His brother, Driver Norman Lord, would move to France with the 9th Company in July 1915 where he would serve until January 1917 when he was invalided from France after a serious accident. The brothers would be reunited in the Australian Motor Transport Service, Chelsea.[128]

Donald Lord remained with the Australian Motor Transport Service in Chelsea until 26 January 1918 when he marched into the Tank Corps Depot at Bovington to attend a course. Having completed this course, Lord embarked on the HT D8 *Ruahine* on 12 May for Australia, disembarking in Sydney on 5 July.

On 12 August 1918 Lance Corporal Lord was discharged from the AIF in Melbourne. The following day he re-enlisted in the AIF 'for service in Australia only' in the Special Unit Tank Crew. Until his discharge on December 26 he was part of the AASC crew that maintained and demonstrated Grit at various locations in eastern Australia.

For his service in the AIF, Lance Corporal Lord was entitled to the British War Medal and the Silver War and Returned Soldier's Badges.

Following his discharge it is unclear whether Lord was reunited with his wife and child. The correspondence contained in his service record contains several letters from Camille enquiring about Lord's location or complaining that he had not maintained contact with her. By 1922 Lord had returned to the UK where he married Louisa Weldon at Melton Mowbray, Leicester. Lord died in Wells, Somerset, UK, in 1972.[129]

Michael George McFadden

Michael George McFadden was born in Sydney in 1891, the son of Michael and Kate McFadden. At the time of his enlistment in 1915 his next of kin was his father who resided in Latimer Road, Rose Bay, Sydney. He stated that he was a motor mechanic by trade.

McFadden enlisted in the AIF at Victoria Barracks, Sydney, on 22 November 1915. Prior to embarkation he served with Depot Battalion at Casula and the Mining Corps, Australian Engineers. Sapper McFadden embarked for overseas service with the 3rd Mining Company, boarding HMAT A38 *Ulysses* in Sydney on 20 February 1916. The *Ulysses'* voyage was delayed at Fremantle when it ran aground on rocks while leaving Fremantle Harbour on 8 March.[130] The Mining Corps was disembarked at Fremantle and transferred to Black Boy Camp outside Perth where it undertook a period of further training. On 2 April the Corps finally departed Western Australia on a repaired *Ulysses* for France via Egypt. On 5 May the miners disembarked in Marseilles. McFadden served with this unit until June when he was admitted to the 26th General Hospital. He was evacuated to England on 4 September and, after treatment at the Northamptonshire War Hospital and a period of leave, he returned to France on 13 February 1917. At the Australian General Base Depot at Etaples, McFadden was told that he would return to the UK to serve permanent base duty. After a period of hospitalisation in the UK, McFadden was transferred to the Australian Motor Transport Service on 19 May when he was mustered as a motor transport driver.[131]

Driver McFadden remained with the Australian Motor Transport Service at Chelsea until 27 January 1918 when he marched into the Tank Corps Depot at Bovington to attend a course. Having completed this course, McFadden embarked on the D8 *Ruahine* on 12 May bound for Australia. He disembarked in Sydney on 5 July.

In Melbourne, on 12 August 1918, McFadden was discharged from the AIF as medically unfit. The following day he re-enlisted in the AIF 'for service in Australia only' in the Special Unit Tank Crew. Until his discharge on December 26 he was part of the AASC crew that maintained and demonstrated Grit at various locations in eastern Australia.

For his service in the AIF, Driver McFadden was entitled to the British War and Victory Medals and the Silver War and Returned Soldier's Badges.

Following discharge, McFadden married Annie Hales in Sydney in 1928 and resided in Rose Bay and Kogarah. He died in Kogarah in August 1928 from war-related causes and was buried at the Woronora Catholic Cemetery. The Army added a memorial plaque and scroll to his headstone in 1929.[132]

Arthur Reginald Rowland

Arthur Reginald Rowland was born at Maryland Station, Tenterfield, NSW, in 1885 the son of John Edward and Mary Anne Rowland. At the time of his enlistment in 1915, his next of kin was his mother who resided in Locke Street, Warwick, Queensland. Rowland gave his occupation as a dentist; his attestation papers also stated that he had served in the CMF with the 5th Bearer Company, AAMC, for two years.

Rowland enlisted in the AIF in Toowoomba on 2 January 1915 and was posted to the AAMC as a motor transport driver for the field ambulance. Driver Rowland embarked for overseas service on HMAT A7 *Medic* in Brisbane on 2 June 1915 with the AAMC drivers. He disembarked in Egypt and was taken on strength by the 1st Australian General Hospital in July 1915. On 1 October, Rowland was transferred to the Australian Motor Transport Service at Gamrab. On 10 June 1916 he embarked at Alexandria, disembarking in Marseilles on

16 October. He marched into the Base Motor Transport Depot at Rouen on 6 August and was posted on the same day to the 4th Divisional Ammunition Sub Park. On 29 March 1917 he was evacuated to the 15th Field Ambulance with a hernia. He was medically boarded at Etaples and classified as permanent base staff on 4 April. In England, Rowland passed through Army Headquarters and the Command Depots at Perham Downs and Weymouth. He was medically boarded and graded as C1 in August. Between 22 June and 20 September he served with the 66th Dental Unit at Perham Downs and was then transferred to the Australian Army Mechanical Transport Service, Chelsea, and mustered as a motor transport driver.[133]

Rowland remained with the Australian Motor Transport Service in Chelsea until 26 January 1918 when he marched into the Tank Corps Depot at Bovington to attend a course. This also involved a change of mustering and an appointment as an artificer. Having completed this course, Rowland embarked on the HT D8 *Ruahine* on 12 May for Australia, disembarking in Sydney on 5 July.

On 12 August 1918 Rowland was discharged from the AIF in Melbourne. The following day he re-enlisted in the AIF 'for service in Australia only' in the Special Unit Tank Crew. Until his discharge he remained part of the AASC crew that maintained and demonstrated Grit at various locations in eastern Australia.

For his service in the AIF, Driver Rowland was entitled to the 1914–15 Star, the British War and Victory Medals and the Silver War and Returned Soldier's Badges.

Following his discharge, he married Lena Mary Smith on 16 June 1919. They settled in Fisher Street, Chifton, on the Darling Downs and he returned to dentistry. In around 1930 the family moved to Melbourne. Between 1930 and 1950 the electoral rolls show Rowland's occupation and residence as service station proprietor of Carlton, sales manager of Brighton, and fitter and garager of Hawthorn. He died in Kew, Victoria, on 8 October 1952 and was cremated at the Springvale Crematorium.[134]

Three of Rowland's sons would serve in the Second World War. Private John Herbert Rowland served in the CMF while Corporals Reginald Laurence Rowland, Central Flying School, and William James Rowland, Radio Development and Installation Unit, served in the RAAF.[135]

Harry Stewart Swain

Harry Stewart Swain was born in Strafford, Essex, UK, on 28 July 1891, the son of Henry and Elizabeth Swain. At the time of his enlistment in 1914, Swain was residing in Brunswick Road, Parkville, Victoria, his next of kin his mother, Elizabeth Cox of Greenvale. Prior to embarkation, he married Elizabeth Ruth Prebble of Grant Street, Clifton Hill. Swain gave his occupation as a chauffeur; his attestation papers also stated that he had served in the Royal Navy for two years and had received a free discharge.

Swain enlisted in the AIF at Victoria Barracks, Melbourne, on 24 August 1914 and was posted to Headquarters Section, the Divisional Ammunition Column. The Divisional Ammunition Column was part of the Australian Artillery and was responsible for providing ammunition and reinforcements to artillery units. Gunner Swain embarked for overseas service on HMAT A9 *Shropshire* at Port Melbourne on 20 October, disembarking in Egypt in December. He remained in Egypt until 26 May 1915 when he moved to the Gallipoli Peninsula. On 6 September he was transferred to the 5th Battery of the 2nd Field Artillery Brigade. Swain developed enteric fever on 25 September and was evacuated to the 21st General Hospital in Alexandria. On 25 October he embarked on HMT *Delta* at Alexandria and, on 11 November, he was admitted to Graylingwell War Hospital, Chichester.

On 24 January 1916 Swain was transferred to the Australian Motor Transport Service, Chelsea, and mustered as a motor transport driver. He remained with the Australian Motor Transport Service in London until 26 January 1918 when he marched into the Tank Corps Depot at Bovington to attend a course. Having completed this course, Swain embarked on the HT D8 *Ruahine* on 12 May for Australia. He disembarked in Sydney on 5 July.[136]

On 12 August 1918 Swain was discharged from the AIF in Melbourne. The following day he re-enlisted in the AIF 'for service in Australia only' in the Special Unit Tank Crew. Until his discharge he remained a member of the AASC crew that maintained and demonstrated Grit at various locations in eastern Australia. He served as a corporal until 10 December 1918 when he was discharged at his own request.

For his service in the AIF, Corporal Swain was entitled to the 1914–15 Star, British War and Victory Medals and the Returned Soldier's Badge. He died in Adelaide on 31 July 1957 and was buried at the Old Noarlunga Anglican Cemetery.[137]

Fortress Engineers of the PMF

Members of the PMF were confined to service in Australia and its territories. Under the Defence Act, members could not be forced to serve abroad. Those

PMF soldiers who sought service abroad had to seek permission to enlist in the AIF; once granted they were discharged from the PMF and could then enlist in the AIF. Of the six members of Grit's PMF crew, four followed this path. Second Corporal Marnie joined the AIF in September 1914 and served with the 1st and 5th Division Engineers at Gallipoli and in campaigns in France and Belgium, reaching the appointment of Regimental Sergeant Major before being commissioned. Sappers Hosking, Kubale and McDonald waited until 1916 before joining the AIF in field artillery and engineering units. Hosking and Kubale were both wounded while McDonald was awarded the Military Medal for bravery in the field. By the start of 1920 all had returned to Australia and rejoined the PMF as sappers. Sapper Cook and Artificer Nicholson remained in Australia during the Great War.

By the time these men began crewing Grit they had served an average of five years in the PMF and AIF, and all had significant experience in maintaining the mechanical and electrical devices in use within the fortress. The sappers came from a more diverse background than the AIF AASC motor transport drivers. They were evenly divided between rural and urban backgrounds, and between primary industry and trade occupations. Two were born in the UK, while the others were born in Victoria. All were protestant and all but one claimed Anglo-Saxon heritage. The average age was around 31, based on Artificer Nicholson's very flexible 45 years!

Grit's final crew comprised both experienced soldiers and technicians, qualities that kept the tank mobile until its transfer to the Australian War Museum in 1921.

Royal Australian Engineers Detachment,
Permanent Military Forces, 1919–1921
Sapper S.B. Cook
Corporal F.A. Hosking
Corporal A.H. Kubale
Sergeant W.K. Marnie
Corporal E. Mc. McDonald, MM
Artificer W.D. Nicholson

Stanley Brensley Cook

Stanley Brensley Cook was born in Williamstown, Victoria, on 29 March 1890, the son of Archibald and Mary Cook. At the time of his enlistment in 1912,

Cook was an engine cleaner who resided in Bridge Street, Queenscliff, Victoria. He married Ruby Ellen Barnard in 1916.

Cook enlisted in the PMF in Queenscliff on 9 May 1912 and served with the 3rd Fortress Engineers Company, RAE, at the Swan Island Depot. He served in many of the Fortress Engineer garrisons within Australia in various technical trades such as engine driver and machinist. He was also posted to the Alexandra Battery in Hobart, Headquarters Fremantle Fixed Defences, Fort Queenscliff, the Engineers School at Wagga and the 3rd Australian Engineer Stores Base Depot.[138]

His skills as an engine driver and machinist would have served Cook well in the aftermath of World War I when he joined the crew of the Mk. IV tank Grit as a temporary corporal and while stationed at the Swan Island Depot. He was promoted corporal in 1920 and sergeant in 1922. During his posting to the Fixed Defences in Hobart in 1932 he was awarded the Long Service and Good Conduct Medal. He was promoted staff sergeant on 3 March 1936, temporary warrant officer Class II on 14 April 1940 and temporary warrant officer Class I on 20 January 1942. Cook's posting to the Headquarters Fortress Engineers at Fort Queenscliff as Regimental Sergeant Major on 9 February 1942, almost 30 years after joining the same unit as a recruit, represents a significant achievement and milestone for any regular soldier. He was discharged at the age of 60 on 29 March 1950 after completing almost 38 years of service.

Tragedy would affect the Cook family while in Tasmania in May 1931 when Cook's wife Ruby disappeared from her Sandy Bay home while Cook was absent on military duties. Her body was recovered several days later at Bull Bay after an extensive search. The Coroner handed down an open finding and Cook was widowed with six children.[139] He would marry his second wife, Florence, in September 1933.

For his service, Cook was entitled to the War, Australian Service, Long Service and Good Conduct and the Meritorious Service Medal. He died in Heidelberg, Victoria, on 29 May 1974 and is buried at the Queenscliff Cemetery.

Frederick Alexander Hosking

Frederick Alexander Hosking was born in Flemington, Victoria, on 22 January 1890, the son of Richard and Helen Hosking. He married Francis Glover in 1916. At the time of his enlistment in the AIF in 1916, Hosking was a permanent soldier who resided at Swan Bay, Queenscliff, Victoria. His next of kin was his wife, Francis Hosking, of Richardson Street, Essendon.

Hosking enlisted in the CMF sometime in 1908 and served with the 38th Fortress Engineers in South Melbourne. In mid-1914 he enlisted in the PMF and served as a corporal with the RAE on Swan Island. In May 1916 he was granted permission to enlist in the AIF, joining on 8 May in Melbourne and was posted to the 10th Field Company. He was promoted to second corporal on 25 May and embarked for overseas service on HMAT A54 *Runic* in Port Melbourne on 20 June, disembarking at Plymouth, UK, on 10 August. Hosking was detached to the Engineers Training Depot at Christchurch on 7 November and promoted to temporary corporal. On 4 December he reverted to second corporal and proceeded to France where he rejoined the 10th Field Company on 19 December.

During 1917, apart from brief periods of hospitalisation and convalescence, Hosking would serve with the 10th Field Company in France and Flanders until 5 October when he was wounded in action. He suffered a gunshot wound to the left arm that caused a compound fracture. He was initially treated at the 10th Casualty Clearing Station and the 6th General Hospital in France. On 14 October he was evacuated to the UK and admitted to the Southern General Hospital, Birmingham, and later the 1st Australian Auxiliary Hospital. Following convalescence and leave, Second Corporal Hosking embarked on the *Durham Castle* on 10 March 1918 for South Africa. Hosking's voyage to Australia would continue when he boarded the *Orontes* on 19 April, disembarking in Melbourne on 10 May. On 17 June Hosking was discharged from the AIF in Melbourne, deemed medically unfit.

For his service in the AIF, Hosking was entitled to the British War and Victory Medals and the Silver War and Returned Soldier's Badges.[140]

In 1918 Hosking returned to the RAE's Swan Island detachment. During his service at the Swan Island Depot, he was a member of the RAE crew that manned the Mk. IV tank Grit. Later he transferred from the PMF to the newly raised Australian Air Force. Hosking's death was reported in the Melbourne *Argus* of 7 October 1925:

Fall From Motor Lorry. Inquiry Into Airman's Death. A fall from the top of a motor lorry, which resulted in the death of Frederick Alexander Hosking aged 36 years, an aircraftsman at Point Cook, was inquired into by the city coroner (Mr. D. Berryman, P.M.) at the morgue on Tuesday. Charles Seymour Vaughan an aircraftsman motor driver at Point Cook, said; "On the afternoon of September 22, I was one of a squad which included Hosking which was detailed to load some heavy rolls of canvas onto a motor wagon in No. 11 hangar. To lift the canvas we had to fix a block and tackle to a beam on the roof of the hangar and to reach the beam Hosking stood on the roof of the lorry just over the tailboard. I was standing on the floor of the lorry. I said to him 'look out, I am going to jump down,' and caught hold of the rope from the block and jumped to the ground. As soon as the whole weight was taken on the rope it broke, and I fell to the ground at the same time causing Hosking who had been steadying himself by holding the rope to fall. In falling he struck his head on the tailboard and was made unconscious." He was taken to the Caulfield Military Hospital suffering from a fractured skull and died on September 28. The coroner found that the fall was accidentally caused.[141]

Albert Henry Kubale
(Heinrich Albert Kubale)

Heinrich Albert Kubale was born in Natimuk, Victoria, on 2 May 1889, the son of Johann and Emma Kubale. Prior to joining the Army, Kubale worked at his uncle's foundry at Natimuk.

Kubale enlisted in the PMF sometime in 1911 and, by 1915, he had been appointed a second corporal at the Swan Island Depot. On 6 November he enlisted in the AIF in Melbourne and was posted to the 2nd Divisional Ammunition Column where he worked as a wheeler. On enlistment, Kubale anglicised his name to Albert Henry Kubale.

Gunner Kubale embarked for overseas service on HMAT A39 *Port Macquarie* in Port Melbourne on 16 November with the 2nd Divisional Ammunition Column and disembarked at Suez on 13 December. He was posted initially to the 105th Howitzer Battery of the 22nd Howitzer Brigade on 10 March 1916. He embarked at Alexandria on 18 March and disembarked in Marseilles on 22 March. On 13 May Kubale was posted to the 5th Field Artillery Brigade where he remained until 13 May 1917 when he suffered gunshot wounds to the right elbow and foot. He was evacuated to the 8th Field Ambulance and 2nd Stationary Hospital. Kubale was further evacuated to the UK on the HMHS *St Patrick* on 5 June. After treatment and convalescence at the Norfolk War and 1st Australian Auxiliary Hospitals, he was medically classified as unfit for further overseas service.

Gunner Kubale embarked on the *Suevic* on 27 September 1917 bound for Australia and disembarked in Melbourne on 18 November. On 31 December he was discharged from the AIF in Melbourne, having been deemed medically unfit. He was initially awarded a pension of 45/- per fortnight for his war wounds. For his service in the AIF he was entitled to the 1914–15 Star, Military British War and Victory Medals and the Silver War and Returned Soldier's Badges.[142]

Kubale returned to the RAE's Swan Island detachment in 1918. During his service at the Swan Island Depot he was a member of the RAE crew that manned the Mk. IV tank Grit.

Kubale married Ethel Dandel at St Andrew's Church, Queenscliff, on 16 March 1918 and, after his discharge from the Army, resided in Masters Street, Caulfield. He would later work for the Post Master General's Department. Kubale died suddenly on 22 November 1953 and was cremated at the Necropolis, Springvale.[143]

Kubale's son, Ronald James Kubale, served as a corporal with the 4th Aircraft Depot, RAAF, during the Second World War.[144]

William Kermack Marnie

William Kermack Marnie was born at Kerriemuir, Forfar, Angus, Scotland, on 29 July 1888, the son of David and Margaret Marnie. He was educated at the Dundee Technical College and completed an apprenticeship as a mechanical engineer in Scotland. Prior to arriving in Australia he had spent time in Waikato, New Zealand, working as an electrical and mechanical engineer. At the time of his enlistment, Marnie was a mechanical engineer and his next of kin was his father, David Marnie, of Myrtle Cottage, Kerriemuir, Scotland.

Marnie enlisted in the PMF on 18 May 1912 and served with the RAE at Swan Island, which was part of the Port Phillip Defences. By 1914 he had been promoted to second corporal. In August 1914 he was granted permission to enlist in the AIF. On 1 September he enlisted in Melbourne and was posted to No. 1 Section, 2nd Field Company. He was still in Melbourne when he was promoted second corporal on 24 September. Marnie embarked for overseas service on HMAT A3 *Orvieto* in Port Melbourne on 21 October, disembarking in Egypt in November. After training in Egypt, the 2nd Field Company embarked for service with the Mediterranean Expeditionary Force on 5 April 1915 and landed at Gallipoli on 25 April. On 15 May Marnie was promoted corporal; he would remain at Gallipoli until the evacuation in December. He disembarked from the HT *Caledonian* in Alexandria on 27 December.

On its return to Egypt in 1916, the AIF was reorganised as reinforcements were absorbed and new formations raised. Marnie was transferred to the 8th Field Company at Tel el Kebir and promoted sergeant on 10 January 1916; an appointment as acting company sergeant major followed on 13 March and promotion to warrant officer Class II on 19 April. The 8th Field Company embarked on the *Manitou* in Alexandria on 17 June and disembarked in Marseilles on 25 June. Marnie served with the 8th Field Company until 29 September when he was temporally attached to the Commander Royal Engineers 'Frank's Force'. On 11 October he was promoted warrant officer Class I and posted to Headquarters 5th Division Engineers as the Regimental Sergeant Major on 23 October. RSM Marnie remained in this appointment in France and Flanders until 8 August 1917 when he reported to the Royal Engineers Training School at Newark in the UK. After successfully completing his course, he was appointed as a second lieutenant on 17 November. He returned to France on 19 December and rejoined the 5th Division Engineers on 26 December. He was posted to the 15th Field Company Engineers on 30 December. On 31 January 1918 Marnie was promoted lieutenant. On 16 December he returned to the UK for 1914 leave and return to Australia.

Lieutenant Marnie embarked on the *City of Exeter* on 15 January 1919 for Australia and disembarked in Melbourne on 2 March. On 1 May Marnie's appointment in the AIF was terminated in Melbourne. For his service in the AIF, Lieutenant Marnie was entitled to the 1914–15 Star, Military British War and Victory Medals and the Returned Soldier's Badge. In 1969, while residing in Chatswood, NSW, Marnie applied for the Gallipoli Medallion.[145]

Marnie returned to the RAE's Swan Island detachment in May 1919. On return to the PMF, Marnie reverted to non-commissioned rank. During his service at the Swan Island Depot he was a member of the RAE crew that manned the Mk. IV tank Grit. By 1922 he had been promoted to warrant officer Class II. During his service in the PMF he served in the RAE Works Section which was responsible for the construction and maintenance of Army camps and fortifications. In 1932 Warrant Officer Class I and Honorary Lieutenant Marnie was detached from the 2nd Military District Base, where he held the position of works foreman, and assigned to the Darwin detachment. Marnie boarded HMAS *Australia* in Sydney on 24 August bound for Darwin, arriving on 6 September. On arrival in Darwin, Marnie was appointed Assistant Director of Works for the construction of the East Point Battery gun positions and magazines. On 13 October 1933 Marnie boarded the SS *Marella* and returned to Sydney.[146]

January 1939 saw Marnie promoted to quartermaster and honorary lieutenant with the Headquarters Eastern Command Directorate of Works. In February 1939 Lieutenant Marnie visited Port Moresby and the Mandated Territories to view the establishment of fixed defences and battery positions.[147] Promotion to captain followed in July 1939 and temporary major in September

1941. This promotion was confirmed in September 1942 and Marnie transferred to the second AIF on 12 April 1943. During the Second World War he served in a variety of RAE Works units within Eastern Command. He would attain the rank of major and retire on 7 April 1949 as an honorary lieutenant colonel after almost 38 years of service in the Australian Army.[148] Marnie was awarded the War, Australian Service, the Long Service and Good Conduct, and Meritorious Service Medals and the Australian Service Badge for his career in the PMF.

Marnie married Emily Gertrude Muir in Victoria in 1919. While he initially settled in Francis Street, Ascot Vale, he relocated to NSW sometime prior to 1930 when the Australian Electoral Roll recorded that the Marnies resided in Snape Street, Kingsford. At this point Marnie described his occupation as a clerk of works. He died in 1971 in Wahroonga, NSW.[149]

24. Sappers William Kermack Marnie (left) and Arthur James Crampton, both of 2nd Field Company Engineers, outside their dugout at Anzac Cove (P04173.010).

Ewen McColl McDonald, MM

Ewen McColl McDonald was born in Queenscliff, Victoria, on 18 September 1891, the son of Philip and Emily McDonald. Ewen McDonald enlisted in the PMF sometime in 1915 and served with the RAE at Swan Island, which was part of the Port Phillip defences. At the time of his enlistment in 1915, McDonald was a farmer who resided at Dunrobin in Swan Bay, Queenscliff, and his next of kin was his father, Phillip McDonald.

In mid-1916 Ewen was granted permission to enlist in the AIF. On 8 May he enlisted in Melbourne and was posted to the 4th Section, 10th Field Company Engineers. Prior to embarkation he married Hilda Ferguson of Ascot Terrace, Moonee Ponds, on 25 May 1916.[150]

Sapper McDonald embarked for overseas service on HMAT A54 *Runic* in Port Melbourne on 20 June with the 10th Field Company Engineers and disembarked in Plymouth, UK, on 10 August. While in training in England, McDonald was promoted lance corporal and proceeded to France on 23 November. He served with the 10th Field Company until November 1918 with only brief periods of leave and hospitalisation away from his unit. He was promoted second corporal on 31 March 1918 and corporal on 19 April. McDonald returned briefly to France between 29 January and 14 February 1919. On his return to the UK he was posted to the Australian Mechanical Transport Service, Chelsea, for duty with AIF Headquarters.[151]

In the 'Australians on Service' column of the *Argus* of 5 February 1918, a notice reported that:

Corporal Ewen McColl McDonald, the third youngest son of Mr and Mrs Philip McDonald, Dunrobin, Swan Bay, Queenscliff, [was] awarded the Military Medal for conspicuous bravery at the battle of Passchendaele. Corporal McDonald left Australia 18 months ago. Before enlisting he was a member of the Royal Australian Engineers, Swan Island. A younger brother, Sergeant Philip McDonald is serving with the Imperial Camel Corps in Palestine.[152]

On 3 September Corporal McDonald embarked on the *Barambah* for Australia and disembarked in Melbourne on 25 October 1919. On 17 January 1920 he was discharged from the AIF in Melbourne. For his service in the AIF, Corporal McDonald was entitled to the Military British War and Victory Medals and the Returned Soldier's Badge.

McDonald returned to the PMF and the RAE's Swan Island detachment in 1920. During his service at the Swan Island Depot he was a member of the RAE crew that manned the Mk. IV tank Grit. On 31 March 1921 Corporal McDonald transferred from the PMF to the newly raised Australian Air Force. He would attain the rank of flight lieutenant and retire on 30 June 1950 after almost 35 years of service in the AMF and RAAF.[153] McDonald initially retired to Moonee Ponds and later Eildon, Victoria. He died on 16 August 1969 and was buried in the Eildon Cemetery.

McDonald's son, Douglas Ewen McDonald, served as a corporal with the 7th Operational Training Unit, RAAF, during the Second World War.[154]

William Davidson Nicholson

William Davidson Nicholson was born at Byker, Newcastle upon Tyne, Northumberland, UK, on 14 April 1874, the son of Benjamin and Agness Nicholson.[155] The 1891 census records that the 16-year-old William was an apprentice in a sawmill in Northumberland. In early 1895 he married Charlotte Grieves at Horton, Tynemouth, and in 1911 the Nicholson family resided in Shields Road, Walker Gate, Newcastle upon Tyne. By this time the family had seven children. Sometime after Charlotte's death in 1911, William migrated to Australia and, by 1914, he appears on the electoral roll at a North Geelong address.[156] On enlistment in 1918, Nicholson was a bricklayer, his next of kin his son Corporal William G. Nicholson of the 12th Royal Lancers, Curragh Barracks, Ireland.

Nicholson enlisted in the PMF in Melbourne on 30 August 1918 and was allocated to the RAE. His postings included Fort Queenscliff, Swan Island and the Broadmeadows Camp. During his service at the Swan Island Depot he was a member of the RAE crew that manned the Mk. IV tank Grit. On 29 September 1924 he was transferred to the RAE Works Section as an artisan and appointed caretaker of the Broadmeadows Camp. He was appointed an artificer on 1 July 1920 and promoted sergeant on 7 October 1924.

Sergeant Nicholson died of injuries received on 31 December 1924, the Melbourne *Argus* reporting his death on 2 January 1925:

MYSTERIOUS DEATH. Camp Caretaker's Injury. Returning to his home at the Broadmeadows military camp on Wednesday night Sergeant William Davidson Nicholson, widower, aged 51 years who was employed at the camp as caretaker suddenly became ill. When a doctor was summoned he found that Nicholson was dead. The body was removed to the morgue where a post mortem examination was made yesterday. The examination disclosed that Nicholson had died from haemorrhage of the stomach, caused probably by an injury. The matter has been reported to the detective office and Detective-sergeants M. Davey and A. McKerral are making efforts to trace Nicholson's movements on Wednesday.[157]

The inquest into Nicholson's death was held on 20 January and was covered by the *Argus*:

Caretaker's Death. Owing to the absence of several important witnesses, Detective McKerral, who appeared to assist coroner (Mr. D. Berriman, P M), applied for the adjournment of the inquest which was commenced at the morgue yesterday concerning the death of William Davidson Nicholson, aged 51 years, a caretaker employed at the Broadmeadows

Military camp. Richard Hodges, of Edward street North Geelong, said: "On December 31 I was on holidays at Broadmeadows camp. About half past 9 o'clock, with Nicholson and a man named Williams, I went in hotel at Campbellfield. There I left my companions, and later, when I got back to the camp, found that Nicholson had preceded me. He was quite sober. At half past 3 o'clock Nicholson went away by himself and it not until half past 6 o'clock that I saw him again. He was returning to the camp in a spring cart, and lying in the arms of Williams, who was driving. I said to Williams, 'What is the matter with Bill (meaning Nicholson)?' Williams replied, 'I think he has taken a fit.' Finding him unconscious I telephoned for Dr. Deane of Essendon, who said on arrival that Nicholson was dead." Francis Kesson, Nicholson's daughter, of Barkly Street East Brunswick said: "On November 23 my father told me that he had been asked to bring a lorry driver named Giles from Melbourne to the camp. About 6 o'clock he came to the gate of his quarters and called out. I went and saw my father with Giles, leaning for support against the fence My father's face was covered with blood, and one of his eves was blackened. He said that the lorry driver Giles had knocked him down and put the boot into him as he was descending from the jinker. Dr. Deane attended later and directed my attention to a lump on my father's side, which it was said had been caused by a kick. On the following Tuesday, though the doctor indicated that haemorrhage had set in, he said that if my father kept quiet he would probably be all right."

Dr. Brett, Government pathologist, who conducted a post mortem examination of the body, said that death was due to internal haemorrhage.

Detective McKerral: "Assuming that Nicholson had received a severe kick on November 23 and that the injured part had been tender for about 14 days afterwards, could you say that the injuries found were consistent with the injuries he had received?"

Dr. Brett: "Not Directly. A man who could exist for so long with such a haemorrhage going on in the stomach would be abnormal."

Senior Detective Davey said: "Though Detective McKerral and myself have made inquires in connection with Nicholson's death we have been unable to obtain and evidence of his having sustained any recent injuries."

The inquest was adjourned to a date to be fixed.[158]

OLD SOLDIERS

The AIF AASC men and those from the PMF resumed their lives in the Australia of the 1920s. Of the AIF AASC men, all appear to have returned to their callings very quickly and settled into their civilian lives leaving scant evidence of their post-service careers. McFadden died in Sydney in 1928 from war-related causes and Dalton died of illness while serving with the Australian Army Canteen Service in 1942. The last survivor died in the UK in 1972 at the age of 82. Their average age at death was 64 years.

Of the PMF crew, Cook and Marnie had long service careers. Cook would rise to the rank of warrant officer Class I by the time of his retirement. Marnie had a distinguished career in the RAE Works Section and retired as a lieutenant colonel in 1949. Sergeant Nicholson died in mysterious circumstances at the Broadmeadows Military Area on New Year's Eve in 1924. In 1921 McDonald and Hosking became foundation members of the RAAF. Hosking died in 1925 as a consequence of a fall, while McDonald retired in 1950 as a flight lieutenant. Kubale would leave the PMF due to war-related illness and join the Post Master General's Department. Cook was the last PMF member to die, passing away in 1972 at the age of 84. The average lifespan of these men was identical to the AIF AASC men at 64 years.

Today Grit is a treasured exhibit of the Australian War Memorial in Canberra. Standing on the outside looking in, it is hard to imagine the noise, heat and discomfort the crew endured while driving and maintaining Grit. The sheer effort of just keeping it running must have been extraordinary and is testament to the efforts of the men of the AASC and RAE who operated Grit during its Australian odyssey from 1918 to 1921. It was their efforts that helped transform the sepia images and newspaper reports, providing the Australian public a better understanding of just what a tank was and what it could do. These men were truly the pioneers of Australian armour.

APPENDIX A

Honours and Decorations

1st Australian Armoured Car Battery and 1st Australian Light Car Patrol

1916–1921

Captain   James, E.H., MC & Bar   Member of Royal Victorian Order 15/10/1921
'For services as Commanding Officer Armoured Car Section AIF.'

Captain   James, E.H.   Military Cross   1/1/1920
'For continuous good work in command of his unit when he has shown marked zeal and ability, especially when acting with cavalry reconnaissances.'

Captain   James, E.H., MC   Bar to the Military Cross   8/3/1919
'At Aleppo, on 24th and 25th October 1918, he displayed great dash and perseverance in the way he attached and drove the enemy cavalry off the hills south of the town. He so disposed his cars that he held a strong force of enemy in check and denied them the crest and observation. All through the operations he displayed courage and resource.'

Captain   James, E.H., MVO, MC & Bar   Colonial Auxiliary Forces Decoration 1920
'For 18 years commissioned service to the Volunteer Forces.'

Captain   James, E.H.   Colonial Auxiliary Forces Long Service Medal   1918
'For 20 years service to the Volunteer Forces.'

Sergeant   Langley, J.H.   Distinguished Conduct Medal   14/3/1919
'For conspicuous gallantry and devotion to duty. When in charge of a Lewis Gun section he twice stampeded enemy machine gun section, enfiladed a trench causing many casualties and dispersed several digging parties. He captured a machine gun killing some of the gunners and putting the rest to flight. He showed marked skill throughout.'

Sergeant   Langley, J.H., DCM   Bar to the Distinguished Conduct Medal
20/5/1920
'On the 23rd October, 1918, at Khan Tuman, he pursued in an armoured car, over very rough ground, an enemy patrol, which he approached the armoured car position. His quickness and dash enabled him to kill one of the enemy and capture four. He set a brilliant example of determination and initiative.'

Sergeant   Creek, H.   Distinguished Conduct Medal   26/5/19
'For conspicuous gallantry and initiative. On 20 September 1918, at Ajule, he cut off three enemy motor lorries full of men and material, causing them to surrender. The lorries were afterwards driven into the town intact and undamaged and all occupants taken prisoners'.

Sergeant   Creek, H., DCM   Royal Victorian Medal.   1/1/1920
'For services as driver to His Royal Highness The Prince of Wales during the 1919 Royal Tour.'

Motor Transport Driver Harkin, H.L.F.   Royal Victorian Medal   1/1/1920
'For services as a driver during Prince of Wales's visit.'

Corporal Bisset, N.S.   Mentioned in Despatches   6/10/1919
'Mentioned in General Sir E.H.H. Allenby's Despatch 6th October 1918 for services rendered during the period from 19th September 1918 to 31st January 1919.'

Other Decorations and Awards

Mr. Cohn, L.R.   Order or the British Empire (Civil)   15/6/1974
'For services to the Community.'

1151 Trooper Arnott, F.   Military Medal   10/4/1918
'For bravery in the field with the 6th Light Horse Regiment.'

Lieutenant   Gibbs, A.C.   Mentioned in Despatches   14/6/1918
'Mentioned in General Sir E.H.H. Allenby's Despatch 3rd April 1918 for gallantry and devotion to duty.'

APPENDIX B

AUSTRALIAN IMPERIAL FORCE.
NOMINAL ROLL.

ARMOURED CAR SECTION.
(EMBARKED AT MELBOURNE, VICTORIA, PER H.M.A.T. A13, "KATUNA," 20TH JUNE, 1916.)

Regtl. No.	Name in full	Rank	Age	Trade or Calling	Married or Single	Address at Date of Enrolment	Next of Kin and Address	Religion	Date of Joining	A.M.F. Unit serving in at Date of Enrolment	Before Embarkation		After Embarkation				Remarks
											Rate per diem	Date to which Paid	Daily Rate, excluding Deferred Pay	Allotment in Australia per diem	Net Rate, not including Allowances or Deferred Pay	Daily Rate of Deferred Pay, only issuable on Conclusion of Service with Expeditionary Force	
											s. d.		s. d.	s. d.	s. d.	s. d.	
...	JAMES, Ernest Homewood	Lieutenant	36	Engineer	M.	Hawthorn, Victoria	Wife, Mrs. K. James, 174 Riversdale road, Hawthorn, Victoria	C. of E.	16.3.16	29th. Fort. Coy. (A.E.)	15 0	19.5.16	14 6	13 0	1 6	3 0	
...	CORNWELL, Percy Vernon Reginald	2nd Lieut. (Hon. Lieut.)	33	Pottery manufacturer	S.	Coburg, Victoria	Brother, J. Cornwell, The Grove, Coburg, Victoria	C. of E.	...	29th. Fort. Coy. (A.E.)	15 0	...	14 6	Nil	14 6	3 0	
3	LANGLEY, John Hudson	Sergeant	21	Electrician	S.	White Hills, Bendigo, Victoria	Father, J. H. Langley, Ocean, Ocean Island	C. of E.	12.7.15	66th Inf.	10 0	...	8 6	6 6	2 0	2 0	
4	YOUNG, Ivan Sinclair	Corporal	26	Motor driver	S.	Nhill, Victoria	Father, J. Young, Nhill, Victoria	Pres.	9.7.15	...	10 0	...	8 6	5 0	3 6	2 0	
5	CREEK, Herbert	Corporal	27	Motor mechanic	S.	Horsham, Victoria	Father, J. Creek, Coleraine road, Hamilton, Victoria	Pres.	2.7.15	...	10 0	...	8 6	6 6	2 0	1 6	
6	MILLAR, Leslie John	Corporal	36	Accountant and motor car expert	M.	Melbourne, Victoria	Wife, Mrs. L. Millar, 127 William-street, Melbourne, Victoria	Pres.	3.4.16	...	9 0	...	8 6	7 6	1 0	1 6	
7	THOMPSON, Walter Perrin	L/Corporal	41	Merchant	M.	Hawthorn, Victoria	Wife, Mrs. F. M. Thompson, 38 Berkeley street, Hawthorn, Victoria	Pres.	28.3.16	...	8 0	...	7 0	3 0	4 0	1 0	
8	BISSET, Norman Sinclair	M.T. Driver	28	Accountant	S.	Golden Square, Victoria	Father, G. S. Bisset, Wade - street, Golden Square, Victoria	Pres.	12.11.14	...	8 0	...	7 0	2 6	4 6	1 0	Previously served as No. 1401, 16th Bn.
9	HARKIN, Henry Lloyd	"	18	Motor mechanic	S.	Chiltern, Victoria	Father, Dr. C. F. Harkin, Chiltern, Victoria	C. of E.	13.3.16	...	8 0	19.6.16	7 0	3 0	4 0	1 0	
10	HARKIN, Oscar Henric Fitzmaurice	"	38	Motor mechanic	M.	Malvern, South Australia	Wife, Mrs. H. Hynon, 39 Winchester-street, Unley, South Australia	C. of E.	23.3.16	...	8 0	...	7 0	3 0	4 0	1 0	
11	JONES, Stanley George	"	25	Clerk and motor mechanic	S.	Albert Park, Victoria	Father, W. E. Jones, 61 Page - street, Albert Park, Victoria	Meth.	23.5.16	...	8 0	...	7 0	3 0	4 0	1 0	
12	McGIBBON, Robert Wilson	"	19	Mechanic	S.	Albert Park, Victoria	Father, J. McGibbon, 51 Moubray-street, Albert Park, Victoria	Pres.	27.3.16	34th Fort. Coy. (A.E.)	8 0	...	7 0	3 0	4 0	1 0	
13	McKAY, Gordon Alexander	"	29	Clerk	M.	Preston, Victoria	Wife, Mrs. A. McKay, "Elsym," Bruce-street, Preston, Victoria	Pres.	1.7.15	...	8 0	...	7 0	4 0	3 0	1 0	
14	MORGAN, George Foy	"	22	Motor mechanic	S.	Castlemaine, Victoria	Stepmother, Mrs. M. Morgan, Castlemaine, Victoria	C. of E.	31.3.16	60th Inf.	8 0	...	7 0	3 0	4 0	1 0	

APPENDIX C

Nominal Roll: 1st Australian Armoured Car Section, Battery and 1st Australian Light Car Patrol 1916-1919.

Number	Rank	Name	Taken on Strength	Previous Unit	Struck off Strength	Posted Unit	Comments
	Capt	James, E.H.	13/3/16	38th Fort Eng, AE.	13/3/19	AIF Details Camp.	Capt. MVO 15/10/21. MC 8/3/19, Bar to MC 8.3/19. VD 1920. RTA 16/5/19 HT *Kaiser-I-Hind.*
	Lt	Cornwell, P.V.R.	16/3/16	38th Fort Eng, AE.	6/2/19	AIF Details Camp.	RTA 21/1/19 HMAT A11 *Ascanius.*
4	Sgt	Young, I. S.	16/3/16	24th Depot Bn.	15/5/17	67th Sqn, AFC.	MT Dvr. Sgt 17/1/16. 2Lt AFC 15/5/17. RTA 12/8/17 HMAT A42 *Boorara.*
5	Sgt	Creek, H.	16/3/16	24th Depot Bn.	15/3/19	AIF Details Camp.	DCM 26/5/19. RMV 1/1/1920. MT Dvr. Cpl 17/1/16. Sgt 1/8/17. RTA 16/5/19 HT *Kaiser-I-Hind.*
12	Dvr	McGibbon, R.W.	27/3/16	34th Elec Coy AE.	6/8/17	67th Sqn, AFC.	Discharged in Egypt 11/2/1919. Commissioned into the Engineering Section, American Red Cross, Palestine.
10	L/Cpl	Hyman, O.H.	28/3/16	24th Depot Bn.	13/3/19	AIF Details Camp.	MT Dvr. L/Cpl 1/8/17. RTA 16/5/19 HT *Kaiser-I-Hind.*
7	L/Cpl	Thompson, W.P.	28/3/16	22nd Depot Bn.	4/8/17	AIF Pay Corps.	L/Cpl 17/5/16. RTA 19/5/18 HT *Port Sydney.*
9	MT Dvr	Harkin, H.L.F.	30/3/16	24th Depot Bn.	13/3/19	AIF Details Camp.	RMV 1/1/1920. MT Dvr. RTA 29/4/19 HT *Dorset.*
6	L/Sgt	Millar, L.G.	3/4/16	24th Depot Bn.	19/9/17	AIF Details Camp.	Cpl 3/4/16 L/Sgt & QMS 20/6/16. RTA 30/8/18 *Wiltshire.*
13	MT Dvr	McKay, G.A.	27/5/16	24th Depot Bn.	20/7/17	AIF Canteens Service.	ASgt 31/5/18. ER S/Sgt 10/11/18. ER WO1 11/11/18. RTA 13/3/19 *Ulimaroa.*
8	Cpl	Bisset, N.S.	20/3/16	24th Depot Bn.	13/3/19	AIF Details Camp.	Ex 1401 16th Bn 1914-16. Cpl 1/8/17. MID 6/10/19. RTA 16/5/19 HT *Kaiser-I-Hind.*
11	MT Dvr	Jones, S.G.	20/6/16	24th Depot Bn.	28/12/17	14th AGH (Patient).	RTA 28/12/17 HT *Tofua.*
3	Sgt	Langley, J.H.	20/6/16	24th Depot Bn.	2/1/19		Sgt 12/7/15. DCM 14/3/19. Bar to DCM 20/5/20. Died of Illness, 2/1/19.
14	Cpl	Morgan, G.F.	20/6/16	24th Depot Bn.	28/12/18	14th AGH (Patient).	MT Dvr, Cpl 1/8/17. RTA 29/1/19 HT *Marghs.*
3078	Pte	Gray, L.A.	20/5/17	1 ALH Trg Regt.	13/3/19	AIF Details Camp.	RTA 16/5/19 HT *Kaiser-I-Hind..*
3198	Pte	Christensen. G.	30/5/17	3rd ALH Trg Regt.	16/2/18	AIF Kit Stores.	(Correct name George Christian Christensen.) Cook. RTA 6/5/19 *City of Poona.*
3013	Pte	Riley, J.C.	30/5/17	6th ALH.	13/3/19	AIF Details Camp.	MT Driver. Brother of 2420 K.C. Riley. RTA 29/4/19 HT *Dorset.*

Number	Rank	Name	Taken on Strength	Previous Unit	Struck off Strength	Posted Unit	Comments
2814	Pte	Driscoll, J.A.	10/6/17	7th ALH.	20/7/17	2nd LHTR.	Batman to Lt Gibbs. RTA 26/6/19 HT *Madras*.
	Lt	Gibbs, A.C.	10/6/17	2nd ALH Trg Regt.	27/7/17	2nd LHTR.	RTA 3/7/19 MT *Malta*.
34A	Pte	Rhoades, F.	14/8/17	4th ALH Trg Regt.	1/1/19	AIF Details Camp.	(Correct Name Frank Hetherset Huntington Rhoades.) RTA 16/5/19 HT *Kaiser-I-Hind*.
2420	Pte	Riley, K.C.	21/8/17	6th ALH.	4/2/18	6th ALH.	Bother of 3013 J.C. Riley. Killed in Action, 27/3/18.
3138	Pte	Jarvis, B.C.	31/8/17	9th ALH.	13/3/19	AIF Details Camp.	RTA 16/5/19 HT *Kaiser-I-Hind*.
1039	Dvr	Cohn, L.R.	8/9/17	8th ALH.	13/3/19	AIF Details Camp.	RTA 16/5/19 HT *Kaiser-I-Hind*.
2996	Pte	Forsyth, S.C.K.	18/9/17	10th ALH.	19/11/17	10th ALH.	RTA 19/7/19 *Oxfordshire*.
2226	Pte	Eddie, A.	19/9/17	4th ALH.	13/3/19	AIF Details Camp.	RTA 16/5/19 HT *Kaiser-I-Hind*.
105	Pte	Somny, G.V.	23/9/17	Aust Trg Centre.	1/10/17	58th Sqn, RAF.	Artificer. RTA 22/12/18 HT *Somali*.
1327	Pte	McKay, J.B,	4/10/17	6th ALH.	13/3/19	AIF Details Camp.	RTA 29/4/19 HT Dorset.
1351	Pte	Pines, M.C.	4/10/17	6th ALH.	4/1/19	14th AGH (Patient).	RTA 15/3/19 Euripides.
1183	Pte	Richardson, C.L	3/11/17	6th ALH.	4/3/19	AIF Details Camp.	RTA 5/3/19 The Port Sydney.
1206	Pte	Simpson, R.J.	3/11/17	6th ALH.	13/3/19	AIF Details Camp.	RTA 16/5/19 HT *Kaiser-I-Hind*.
7720	Dvr	Holley, A.G.	4/11/17	1st Aust Pack Wireless Troop.	8/2/19	AIF Details Camp.	RTA 16/9/19 *Devon*.
35	Pte	Bosanquet, L.G.V.	24/2/18	7th ALH.	13/3/19	AIF Details Camp.	MT DVR. RTA 16/5/19 HT *Kaiser-I-Hind*.
1151	Pte	Arnott, F.	10/3/18	6th ALH.	4/3/19	AIF Details Camp.	MM 9/12/18 MG Gunner, RTA 4/3/19 *Port Sydney*.

APPENDIX D

Other Military Service: 1st Australian Armoured Car Section/Battery and 1st Australian Light Car Patrol 1916-1919.

Number	Rank	Name	Unit	Comments
355 N102148	Pte A/Sgt	Bosanquet, L.G.V.	A Company, 3rd NSW Imperial Bushman. 8th Garrison Bn. CMF.	1900-01. South Africa. 1940-42.
V360272	Pte Lt	Cohn, L.R.	68th Bn Senior Cadets, 21st BnVDC, CMF.	1942-45.
	Lt	Cornwell, P.V.R.	38th Fort Eng, AE, CMF. RO 3MD, CMF.	1915-16. 1921-42.
V80242	Pte Cpl	Christensen, G	Scottish Volunteer Militia. 15 Depot Bn AIF 12th Garrison Bn, 3MD Workshops , Area Signals 15 th Line Maintenance Land HQ Signals. CMF.	1915-16. 1939-44.
N70548 N274638 N409926	Pte	Driscoll, J.A.	2nd Garrison Bn CMF. 7th Garrison Bn CMF. VDC.	1939-40. 1941-2. 1942-43.
W34519	Spr	Forsyth, S.C.K.	88th Infantry, CMF 22nd Fd Coy RAE CMF	1915. 1941.
	Lt	Gibbs, A.C	1st ALH Regt, CMF.	3 & 1/2 Years.
	Cdt Tpr	Gray, L.A.	Senior Cadets. 22nd ALH Regt, CMF.	1914-15.
	Lt	Gray, L.A.	18th ALH & 3rd ALH, CMF. Reserve of Officers (Cavalry) 3MD	1921-25. 1939-44.
	Cdt Sgt	Harkin, H.L.F.	Senior Cadets, Melbourne Grammar School. 29th Bn Senior Cadets	1912-16.
	Lt Capt Hon Maj	James, E.H.	Senior Cadets, VMF. 5th Inf Regt, CMF. Reserve of Officers. 38th Fort Eng, AE, CMF. 38th Fort Eng, AE. CMF. Reserve of Officers.	c.1897. 1903-11. 1911-15. 1915-16. 1920-24. 1924-42.
	Tpr	Jarvis, B.C.	22nd LH Regt, CMF.	
V82705	Pte SSgt	Jones, S.G.	Home Service Pay Corps. Infantry Training Units and Vic Lines of Communication, CMF.	1940-44.
	Sgt	Langley. J.H.	Senior Cadets Trinity Grammar School. 66th Inf Regt, CMF.	1912-15.
	Spr Lt	McGibbon, R.W.	34th Electrical Coy AE, CMF. American Red Cross, Engineering Division, Palestine.	1915-16. 1919-20.
	Tpr	McKay, J.B.	Senior Cadets, St Ignatius College.	
502	Pte	Millar, L.J.	Senior Cadets. 3rd Victorian Imperial Bushman. Home Service Pay Corps	South Africa. 1900-01. 1914-15.
155 69	Pte Pte	Morgan, G.F.	66th Inf Regt, CMF. Ammunition Workers Company AIF	1912-16. 23/7/15 to 16/10/15.
N69851	Sgt	Pines, M.C	2nd & 12th Garr Bns, HQ E. Comd, 5th & 12th Sup Pers Coys, CMF.	1939-43.
N289165	Pte	Simpson, R.J	6th Bn, VDC, CMF.	1942-44.
	Cdt	Rhoades, J.F.	Naval Institute Cadets.	
	Cdt	Richardson, C.L.	Senior Cadets, The Kings School, Parramatta.	
	Lt	Young, I.S.	Reserve of Officers 3MD. B Squadron 19th Light Horse (Armoured Car) Regiment. Reserve of Officers 3MD. Australian Armoured Corps.	1920-1933. 1933-34 1934-1944

APPENDIX E

Nominal Roll: United Kingdom Personnel, attached 1st Australian Armoured Car Battery and 1st Australian Light Car Patrol 1916-1919. (Incomplete)

Number	Rank	Name	Comments
M2/116887	Fitter	Bell, George.	Fitter, ASC (MT). 12/9/15. Arrived Middle East. 17/8/17 posted to ASC, Ismalia.
M2/074638	Dvr	Bohan, Patrick. J.	Motor Transport Driver, ASC (MT). 17/8/17 posted to ASC, Ismalia.
345022	Cpl	Cock, John.	Dispatch Rider. 23/9/15 Arrived Gallipoli as L/Cpl (1805) with 1st Devonshire Yeomanry, 30/12/15 Arrived Egypt. 4/1/17 16th Bn Devonshire Regiment. 27/1/19 to 16th Bn Devonshire Regiment.
		Hick	Dispatch Rider
M2/187902	Dvr	Hockett. Gilbert.	Motor Transport Driver, ASC (MT). Address Red Hills Surrey, motor driver by occupation. 3/6/16, Enlisted ASC MT. 21/6/16 Embarked for Middle East. 7/10/16 Taken on strength with 1st Light Car Patrol. 17/8/17 Motor Transport Driver, ASC (MT) posted to ASC, Ismalia. 110/10/19 Discharged.
M2/131214	Dvr	Horton, Arthur.E.	Motor Transport Driver, ASC (MT). 11/11/15 Arrived France. 17/8/17 Posted to ASC, Ismalia. 27/1/19 Dicharged.
DM2/154309	A/Sgt	Lloyd, Sidney.	Motor Transport Driver, ASC (MT) 6/7/17 Mentioned in Dispatches London Gazette. 17/8/17 posted to ASC, Ismalia.
345168	Pte	Rees, William .J.	Dispatch Rider. 23/9/15 Arrived Gallipoli as Pte. (2380) with 1st Devonshire Yeomanry, 30/12/15 Arrived Egypt. 4/1/17 16th Bn Devonshire Regiment. 27/1/19 Spr. (515891) 1st Sig Coy (Devon Fortress Engineers RE (TF). 15/7/19 Transferred to reserve.
151532	Dvr	Williams, C.R.	Motor Transport Driver, ASC (MT) 17/8/17 posted to ASC, Ismalia.
	Dvr	Wright, A.	Motor Transport Driver, ASC (MT).

APPENDIX F

Vehicles and Vehicle Records of 1st Australian Armoured Car Section/Battery and 1st Australian Light Car Patrol 1916-1919.

1. The first Australian armoured vehicle was Daimler-based 'Gentle Annie', designed and built by its enthusiastic crew.

Daimler Armoured Car
"Gentle Annie"
1st Australian Armoured Car Section
Melbourne May 1916

The first Australian armoured vehicles were designed and built by enthusiastic amateurs. The Daimler-based vehicle, the first to be completed, was named 'Gentle Annie' by its crew and was armed with a .303 calibre Colt Model 1895 'potato digger' machine-gun mounted in a mid-mounted revolving gun shield. The car's bodywork comprised flat sections of armour plate bolted together to form a crude but functional box-type structure. As the plate was available in only one thickness, increased protection for vital elements of the car was achieved by doubling or tripling the plates. The result weighed in excess of 1.5 tonnes, which would later prove problematic in the soft sands of the Egyptian desert.

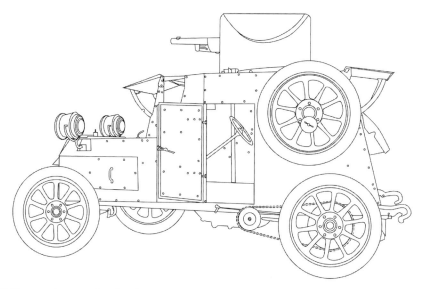

2. The second armoured car, based on a Mercedes chassis, was christened 'Silent Sue' by its crew who considered it the quietest of the unit's vehicles.

Mercedes Armoured Car
"Silent Sue"
1st Australian Armoured Car Battery
Egypt November 1916

The second armoured car, based on a Mercedes chassis, was christened 'Silent Sue' by its crew who considered it the quietest of the unit's vehicles. In contrast to the Daimler, the Mercedes had a fully enclosed turret with bevelled edges reminiscent of the type then employed on British Rolls Royce armoured cars. Both vehicles were equipped with the same Model 1895 Colt 'potato digger' machine gun in .303 inch calibre. Later, when operating in the desert, the turret was removed to improve air circulation and decrease the overall vehicle weight. Dual rear wheels were also fitted. Despite these changes, there was no appreciable change in 'Silent Sue's' mobility on the soft sands of the desert.

3. The Model T Ford was one of the most widely recognised vehicles of its time.

Model T Ford
Light Car
1 st Australian Light Car Patrol
Syria October 1918

The Model T Ford was one of the most widely recognised vehicles of its time. Mass produced in both the US and UK, it was ruggedly constructed, simple to operate and relatively easy to maintain. Its performance over soft ground was far superior to the two Australian-built armoured cars it replaced when the unit was reorganised into the 1st Australian Light Car Patrol. With all extraneous bodywork stripped away, the Model T Ford carried only the bare essentials for fast-moving operations in the desert — tools, spares, rations, water, fuel and ammunition. Each was equipped with two Lewis light machine-guns, one forward-facing mounted on the scuttle, and the other on a pedestal mount facing to the rear for defence against aerial attacks.

No.	Car	Height	Length	Width	Remarks	Chassis	Engine	War Dept. No.	Comments
1	Daimler	6'2"+2'4"	14'8"	5'8"	The 2nd measurement column is the height of the turret and gun mounting, which can be detached measurement in height.			LC 0726	Donated by Ivan Young, Melbourne 17/8/15. 50h.p. Carrying Capacity 4 men. Armoured conversion completed 7/2/16. Armoured Car accepted by Defence Department 28/4/16. Car converted with twin rear wheels 29/8/16. Returned to Stores 6/12/16 in Egypt. Re-valuation Board held on 17/12/16.
2	Mercedes	6'2"+2'2"	12'11"	5'3"	ditto.	2992	2994	LC 0727	Donated by Percy Cornwell, Melbourne 17/8/15. 60-80h.p. Carrying Capacity 4 men. Armoured conversion commenced 8/2/16. Accepted by Defence Department 28/4/16. Armoured Car. Car converted with "Stephney Wheels" 21/9/16. Returned to Stores 6/12/16 in Egypt. Re-valuation Board held on 17/12/16.
3	Minerva	6'10"	15'5"	5'10"		K 2081	2082	LC 0728	Donated by Sol Green, Melbourne 1916. 50h.p. Carrying Capacity 8 men or 10 cwt. Un-armoured tender. (Box Wagon). Returned to Stores 6/12/16 in Egypt. Re-valuation Board held on 17/12/16. This car apparently returned from the Middle East as part of a consignment of surplus captured stores and was sold at auction in Sydney in June 1921for 18 Pounds. (The Argus 23/6/21)
4	New Hudson Cycle with Side Car.	3'10"	7'2"	4'11"	Measurements includes side-car which is detachable.	5740	V952	LB 1250	Donated from Queensland.23/10/15. 6h.p. Carrying Capacity 2 men. Side Car detachable. Returned to stores 6/12/16. Re-valuation Board held on 17/12/16.

No.	Car	Height	Length	Width	Remarks	Chassis	Engine	War Dept. No.	Comments
	Ford Model T								4 vehicles taken on strength from 1st Light Car Patrol (UK) 8/12/16 other vehicles arrive by 7 Feb 1917.
								LC 488	RTS 10/12/17.
								LC 500	RTS 10/12/17. (Langley)
								LC 0545	RTS 10/12/17.
								LC 0554	RTS 10/12/17.
								LC 0577	RTS 10/12/17.
								LC 0580	RTS 10/12/17. Ration Car
								LC 1215	TOS 11/12/17. (New Vehicle), RTS 3/3/19.
								LC 1216	TOS 11/12/17. (New Vehicle), RTS 3/3/19. (Bisset & Cornwell)
									TOS 11/12/17. (New Vehicle), RTS 3/3/19. (Langley)
								LC 1217	TOS 11/12/17. (New Vehicle), RTS 3/3/19. (Creek)
								LC 1218	TOS 11/12/17. (New Vehicle), RTS 3/3/19. (Morgan)
								LC 1219	TOS 11/12/17. (New Vehicle), RTS 3/3/19. (Tender)
								LC 1220	(Individual cars were known as: ANZAC, Billzac, Otasel Silent Sue, Imshi and Bung.)
	Motor Cycle								4 Motor Cycles taken on strength from Light Car Patrol (UK) 8/12/16. 3 Motor Cycles transferred to 2nd Light Car Patrol.
									RTS 4/1/19.
								LBO 0552	RTS 3/3/19.
								LBO 496	RTS 3/3/19.
								LBO 040	
	German Loreley Touring Car								Captured 22/9/18. Trophy retained for transport purposes. E1722/87.

Prepared from the private papers of Capt. E.H. James MVO, MC & Bar, VD (Army Tank Museum) and War Diary (Australian War Memorial)

APPENDIX G

Notes on the establishment of a Light Car Patrol, 1941.[159]

Personnel.

Officers 2.		
Sergeants	2.	
Corporals	2.	
Drivers	6.	
Lewis Gunners	6.	
Cook	1.	
Batmen	2.	(also Drivers or Gunners)
Cyclist	1 or 2.	(Attached)

Transport.

Light Cars (fitted for machine guns.)	4.
Light Cars (for transport.)	2.
Motor Cycles (if cyclists attached.)	1 or 2.

Armament.

Lewis or other machine guns.	4.
Rifles.	14.
Revolvers (for machine gunners and officers.)	8.

Other equipment

Four cars are fitted with mountings for machine guns and boxes for ammunition, and each of the 6 cars carries a ration box, two-gallon petrol tin, two-gallons water tin, fire extinguisher, and ordinary tools and spares.

Two transport Cars carry reserve ammunition, oil petrol, water, rations also unit's kit, baggage, blankets etc.

A Light Car Patrol.

Is divided into two sections, each with two 'Gun' cars and one transport car, with the necessary personnel. In no case is any smaller formation than a section used, as cars always operate in pairs when on active service.

A Gun car is always in charge of an officer or sergeant. One transport car is in the charge of a Corporal who acts as Quartermaster. The other transport car is in charge of a Corporal who is a trained mechanic and is responsible for all running repairs.

APPENDIX H

5th Cavalry Division
Narrative of Operations
(19th September to 31st October 1918)

These Operations may be divided into four periods:

19th to 22nd September	NAZARETH Operations.
23rd September	HAIFA-ACRE Operations.
26th September to 1st October	DAMASCUS Operations
2nd October to 31st October	Advance to ALEPPO.

NAZARETH Operations.

The task of the 5th Cavalry Division was:

1st Objective.   The line TELL ED DHRUR – LIKTERA to the Sea.

2nd Objective.   NAZARETH and the capture of the German Commander in Chief.

3rd Objective.   EL MEZRAH, astride the EL AFULEH- NAZARUTH road, and to be ready to operate towards BEISEN and JENIN.

The first two objectives were the special task of the 13th Cavalry Brigade and the third objective was the task of the remainder of the Division.

September 19th.

At 0530, the 13th and 14th Cavalry Brigades were disposed along the beach, head of the 13th Cavalry Brigade at ARSUF. The 15th Cavalry Brigade and all the wheels of the Division, less 'B' Echelon at SARONA, were about EL JELIL; and B HAC and Essex Batteries were in action supporting the 60th Division attack.

At 0730, the 5th Cavalry Division moved forward and crossed the NAHR El FALIK at its mouth, opposition being very slight. The 'going' through the sand along the beach was very heavy.

At 0810, the 15th Cavalry Brigade and wheels of the Division began to move up to NAHR EL FALIK, picking up the batteries en route.

By 0900, the 13th and 14th Cavalry Brigades (less wheels) had crossed the FALIK and were moving towards the first objective – line TELL ED DHRUR- LIKTERA- to the sea.

The 13th Cavalry Brigade had by 1100 occupied their first objective taking

250 prisoners and 4 guns. By this time the 14th Cavalry Brigade had crossed the ISKANDERUNEH and the 15th Cavalry Brigade and fighting wheels were moving on MUKHALID with A.II Echelon and Divisional Train under escort some miles in the rear.

On arrival at LIKTERA, the General Officer Commanding decided to rest men and horse and continue his advance on NAZARUTH, via KH ED DUFEIS and JARAK, at 1815 with the 13th and 14th Cavalry Brigades (less wheels). The 15th Cavalry Brigade, who had reached LIKTERA at 1500 with the fighting wheels, to remain as escort to the guns and the fighting wheels, detailing one regiment to escort the A.II Echelon and Divisional Train.

Owing to reports of the bad condition of the JARAK route, permission was requested to move the wheels via BEIDUS and LEJJUN.

At 1815, Divisional Headquarters, 13th and 14th Cavalry Brigades, marched via KH ED DUFEIS and reached JARAK at 0100 on the 20th.

September 20th.

Here a Squadron of the 9th Hobson's Horse was left to guard the flank of the Desert Mounted Corps passing through the MESMUS defile.

On debouching into the Plain of ESDRAELON, the 13th Cavalry Brigade moved straight to its objective, while the remainder of the division turned east towards EL MEZRAH, which was reached at 0530.

The plain was found to be black cotton soil with large cracks and covered with thistles, which made it difficult to get horses across it.

The 13th Cavalry Brigade destroyed the AFULEH-HAIFA Railway and entered NAZARUTH after considerable opposition at 0530. It was reported that the German Commander in Chief had left the previous evening and, the Division was ordered to operate towards BEISEN and JENIN, the 13th Cavalry Brigade was ordered to withdraw from NAZARETH and rejoin the division about AFULEH.

The captures of the 13th Cavalry Brigade in neighbourhood of NAZARUTH were 1,200 prisoners.

The distance from the starting point near ARSUF to NAZARETH is about 50 miles as the crow flies and was covered in 22 hours.

Meanwhile the 14th Cavalry Brigade cleared the country around AFULEH taking many prisoners, and at 0730 were attacking AFULEH from the North.

No further fighting occurred during the day and, as soon as the 13th Cavalry Brigade had rejoined the Division (less the 15th Cavalry Brigade) bivouacked at EL AFULEH.

Sept 21st.

The 15th Cavalry Brigade, Guns, and Fighting Wheels, rejoined the Division at 0100. At 0400 the 14th Cavalry Brigade (less wheels) marched to JENIN to assist the Australian Mounted Division. At 1330 the 13th Cavalry Brigade re-occupied NAZARETH and the junction of the TIBERIAS-ACRE and TIBERIAS-HAIFA roads, after slight opposition.

Reconnaissance were pushed forward to KEFR KENNA and SEFURIEH; 26 German and 20 Turks being taken prisoner.

The 14th Cavalry Brigade re-joined the Division at 1530 and, during the night, they and the 15th Cavalry Brigade picketed the line SHUTTA STATION to AFULEH, in conjunction with the 4th Cavalry Division to the East and the Australian Mounted Division in the West and South; in order to cut off the enemy reported to be retiring from NABLUS.

September 22nd.

In the early hours of the morning a force of Turks, estimated at 700, which was marching from HAIFA to TIBERIAS attacked our outposts on the ARCRE-NAZARETH road, but were easily repulsed. In the counter attack by the 18th Lancers, 311 prisoners and 4 Machine Guns were taken.

During these operations 3,057 prisoners were taken.

HAFIA- ACRE Operations.

At 1230 on the 22nd orders were received for the Division to move at 0500 on the 23rd and occupy HAIFA and ACRE.

September 23rd.

At 0500, having been relieved by the Australian Mounted Division, the Division marched in two columns on HAIFA and ACRE, as follows:

Right Column.

13th Cavalry Brigade Group (B/H.A.C. Battery and Light Section B.A.C.; and plus No 11 L.A.M Battery, and No.1 Light Car Patrol, to march via NAZARETH-ACRE road on ACRE.

This column marched from NAZARETH at 0500 and at 1300, reported ACRE occupied after slight opposition, 9 officers, 250 O.R.'s and two guns captured.

Left Column.

Advanced Guard. 15th Cavalry Brigade Group (less Hyderabad Lancers and plus B/H.A.C. Battery).

Main Body in order. Divisional Headquarters, 14th Cavalry Brigade Group, A.I. Echelon in order of Brigade, and A.II. Echelon.

This column marched at 0500, via the JEBATA-JEIDA and main NAZARETH road, on HAIFA. At JEBATA at 0800 a contact patrol aeroplane dropped a message reporting 200 Turks holding the HAIFA Railway station, also machine gun fire from JIDRU. At 1015 the leading troops of the Advanced Guard cam under shell fire at Ref. L.6.b., and at 1300, when the main body had halted at Ref. Q.23.1. the situation was as follows:

Advanced Guard. One Squadron of Mysore Lancers about Ref. Z.15.c., Two Squadrons about Refs. Z.26. And J.2. and one Squadron about Ref. H.16.

Sherwood Rangers. One Squadron about Ref.J.13. on its way to join the Mysore Lancers, two Squadrons in reserve about Ref. J.16.d.

Jodhpur Lancers. About Ref. Z.29.a. Waiting to Gallop through the Mysore Lancers and attack.

The attack was postponed until 1445 in order to give time for the two squadron to get on the hilltop towards KARMELHEIM. B/H.A.C. Battery came into action at Ref. J.12.a.

Patrols reported two guns and eight machine guns along the North Side of Wadi in Ref.s Z.25. and Z19. They could not reach the Wadi because of enemy guns and machine guns in Refs. H.6 and Z.25.a., and in the palm trees near the shore. The enemy maintained a desultory fire to which B/H.A.C. Battery replied as target presented themselves. At 1400, the Jodhpur Lancers from a position of readiness 500 yards Northeast of BELEDESH SHEIKH, moved forward at a trot in 'column of squadrons in line of troop columns', their advance being covered by B/H.A.C. Battery at Ref. J.8.c and two Squadrons of Mysore Lances and two machine guns rom Refs. J.8.b. and J.2.d. Enemy machine gun and rifle fire became intense as they crossed the ACRE Railway. The Wadi through Z.25.a & c., which could not be properly reconnoitred owing to intense machine gun fire, was found to be impassable. Two of the ground scouts who jumped in disappeared instantaneously in quicksand. The regiment change direction left, the leading Squadron being directed on machine guns and riflemen in Ref.H.6.a. whom they killed, thus clearing the passage of the defile. The second squadron as then directed on the mound about Ref Y.24. Central, were they captured two machine guns and further on three guns. The remaining two Squadrons led by Colonel Holden charged straight through the town, where they were joined by the remainder of the Regiment. One Squadron passed South of the town along the lower slopes of MT. CARMEL, capturing two guns en route. Considerable street fighting occurred. Meanwhile, the detached Squadron of Mysore Lancers in Ref.Z.9.b., under Lieutenant Mein which had been held up, mounted and charged the Turks near the mouth of the MAHR EL MAKATTA, capturing two guns, two machine guns and 110 prisoners. The remainder of the Regiment (less two Squadrons) followed the Jodhpur Lancers through the town. Simultaneously with the mounted attack from the East, the Squadron of the Mysore Lancers, under Lieutenant Horseman, which has worked their way on to MT. CARMEL, charged the enemy position one mile south of KARMELHEIM. The total strength of the Squadron after the machine guns and Hotchkiss Rifle fire had come into action on the flank, was fifteen, and they charged over rocky ground in the face of heavy fire: taking one 6' Naval Gun, two mountain guns, two machine guns, and 78 prisoners. This attack was supported by a portion of the Squadron of Sherwood Rangers, who took a further 50 prisoners. This ended the fighting and the town was entered by the General Officer Commanding and the remainder of the Division at 1500. Steps were immediately taken to stop all looting by the Bedouins, and Brigades bivouacked outside the town, 14th Cavalry Brigade to the east and 15th Cavalry brigade to the west. Divisional Headquarters was established at the Austrian Consuls House.

The total captures during the operations were:

27	Guns	6	German Officers
20	Machine Guns	266	German Other Ranks
		352	Turkish Officers
		9314	Turkish Other Ranks

DAMASCUS Operations.
At 1440, on the 25th. The Division received orders to concentrate in KEFR KENNA Area by 1700 on the 26th. One Regiment was to be left at HAIFA and one Squadron at Acre, until the arrival of the 7th Division.

September 26th.
The Leicestershire Regiment relieved all guards and piquets, and at 0500, the Division (less Sherwood Rangers and one Squadron of the Gloucestershire

Hussars) marched in two columns to KEFR KENNA (24 miles) and concentrated there at 1700. Owing to the lack of sufficient water, the 15th Cavalry Brigade Group, Batteries and Fighting Wheels bivouacked near REINE.

September 27th.

At 0300 the Division marched, 14th Cavalry Brigade leading to TEBERIAS, which was reached at 0700. A halt was made till 1200 to allow the Australian Mounted Division to clear TIBERIAS, when the Division was moved on via the DAMASCUS road and bivouacked north of the road between MISHMAR HAYARDEN and MAHANAYIM. It had been intended to bivouac at KUSR ATRA, but the enemy was still holding up the Australian Mounted Division at the bridge over the JORDAN.

September 28th.

At 0600, the Australian Mounted Division reported two bridges over the JORDAN, three guns and about 50 prisoners taken and the enemy withdrawn northwards. At 1100 the Division moved to the JORDAN and concentrated in Refs. O23, O.36.b. & d. Considerable delay was caused by a lorry breaking down a temporary bridge over the JORDAN, ant it was not till 1500 that the Division commenced crossing the fords north and south of the bridge.. At 1800 all fighting troops and fighting wheels were across. The road north of the JORDAN was very bad in parts and caused considerable delay to the wheels. The Division arrived at KUNEITRA at 2030 and went into bivouac south of the village. Rear wheels did not get into camp until 0600 on the 29th.

Before leaving the JORDAN, tired horses, about 30 per Brigade, were left under an officer detailed from the 14th Cavalry Brigade, to report to the General Officer Commanding, Lines of Communication, as it was intended that the Division should be within striking distance of DAMASCUS by 0500 on the 30th inst.

September 29th.

At 1800 the Division moved off in the rear of the Australian Mounted Division. Order of march; 14th Cavalry Brigade, 13th Cavalry Brigade and 15th Cavalry Brigade Groups. 15th Cavalry Brigade detailed one Regiment as escort to the Guns and Fighting Wheels of Both Divisions, which followed in the rear of the Fighting Troops of the 5th Cavalry Division.

Desert Mounted Corps Headquarters marched at the head of the 5th Cavalry Division. The advance of the Corps was delayed about three hours by the leading Brigade of the Australian Mounted Division being held up by enemy with machine guns and two light field guns holding the high ground south of SASA. These were eventually captured and the Division reached SASA at 0830 on the 30th.

September 30th.
At 0845, information was received by aeroplane that a force of 2,000 Turks was retiring on DAMASCUS by the DERAA road, and the 14th Cavalry Brigade was ordered to intercept this force and to march on DAMASCUS, 13th and 15th Cavalry Brigades concentrated just North of SASA in Corps reserve. At 1200, after some opposition, the 14th Cavalry Brigade seized the hills JEBEL EL ASWAD astride the KISWE-DAMASCUS road thereby cutting off large numbers of Turks who withdrew on KISWE and endeavoured to break out to flanks and up the Wadi ZABIRANI. Further large numbers were streaming in a disorganized mob up the hills to the North East and down the main road to DAMASCUS. The former were shelled by the Essex Battery and the later pursued by Squadrons of the leading Regiment. At 1300, the 13th Cavalry Brigade advanced to KAUKAB, but on receipt of information from the 14th Cavalry Brigade that the enemy were breaking out West and East of KISWE, the Brigade marched on that village with the 15th Cavalry Brigade operating in its right astride the Wadi ZABIRANI. The Advanced Guard of the 13th Cavalry Brigade reached KISW at 1700 and, after slight opposition, captured 675 prisoners and four guns. As the Division had received orders to return to KAUKAB to bivouac and the 4th Cavalry Division had be advancing up the DERAA road two miles south of KISWE, the Advanced Guard was recalled and the Division returned to bivouac. The dispositions of Division for the night of 30th September to 1st October were: 14th Cavalry Brigade astride the KISWE-DAMASCUS road North of JEBEL EL ASWAD; Divisional Headquarters and 13th Cavalry Brigade at KUAKAB; and the 15th Cavalry Brigade about KHAN ESH SHEHA.

October 1st.
The task of the Division on 1st October was to surround DAMASCUS on the East and Southeast, in cooperation with the 4th Cavalry Division on the South and the Australian Mounted Division on the north.

During the early hours of the morning the 14th Cavalry Brigade had intercepted number of Turks who were endeavouring to reach DAMASCUS. The Division (less 14th Cavalry Brigade) concentrated at DEIR KHABIYE at 0600, and moved up the KISWE-DAMASCUS road to the 14th Cavalry Brigade, followed by the 4th Cavalry Division. From the 14th Cavalry Brigade it was learned that representatives of the Sherifian Forces had entered DAMASCUS the previous night and it was unlikely we should meet any opposition. The 13th Cavalry Brigade moved off to take up the outpost line allotted to it East of the town. The 14th Cavalry were proceeding to take their position on the Northeast, when 1t 1030, information was received from the Australian Mounted Division that the enemy were apparently escaping up the DUMA road.

Owing to the enclosed state of the country on the East of the town it was quicker to move straight through the town, and the 14th Cavalry advanced through the town of JOBAR, where they found a Brigade of the Australian Mounted Division had already blocked the road. They then took up the outpost line, joining with the Australian Mounted Division on the North and with the 13th Cavalry brigade on the NAHR BARADA. The 15th Cavalry Brigade meanwhile moved into Divisional reserve on the BELAT-DAMASCUS road, about two miles East of the town.

No more fighting occurred, but the Division collected during the day several hundred prisoners in the outskirts of the town.

The total prisoners captured during the period 19th September to 1st October was:

27	Guns	6	German Officers
20	Machine Guns	266	German Other Ranks
		352	Turkish Officers
		9314	Turkish Other Ranks

The Advance on DAMASCUS to ALEPPO
(2nd to 31st October.)
This period of the operations is divided into three stages:
The advance on RAYAK and ZAHLE.
The advance on HOMS, and
The advance from HOMES to ALEPPO.

The Advance from RAYAK and ZAHLE. (40 Miles)

On the 3rd of October the Division (less Sherwood Rangers and Hyderabad Lancers) was bivouacked about EL JUDEIDE, when orders were received that the 5th Cavalry Division, followed by the 4th Cavalry Division, would march on the 5th October on RAYAK and ZAHLE, so as to be within reasonable striking distance of the former place at dawn on the 7th. Reconnaissance of the track via KATANA to KHAN DIMEZ reported that it was not fit for wheels, so the wheels of the Division marched on the 4th to DAMASCUS where they bivouacked for the night. The Division marched on the 5th inst. Via KATANA to KHAN MEIZELUN (sixteen miles), which the track was found to be fit for wheels; the Sherwood rangers and wheels rejoined the Division that evening. No. 12 Light Armoured Motor Battery and No. 7 Light Car Patrol joined the Division. As reports were received that munitions depots and rolling stocks were being destroyed at RAYAK; orders were issued for the 14th Cavalry Brigade and Armoured Cars to march that night and seize RAYAK (24 miles) at dawn on the 6th inst. Remainder of the division to march at dawn, 6th. 15th Cavalry Brigade on ZAHLE (21 miles), 13th Cavalry Brigade in support of the 14th Cavalry Brigade. Later reports showed that the enemy had Evacuated RAYAK and the move of the 14th Cavalry Brigade was postponed till 0600 on the 6th inst. RAYAK was occupied at 1400, on the 6th inst. and ZAHLE at 1500, both without opposition. Two guns, two German other ranks, seven Turkish officers and 168 Turkish other ranks were captured in RAYAK and ZAHLE. Several munitions depots had been destroyed and many dead were lying about as the result of our bombing raids, but considerable Royal Engineers Stores, several engines and many trucks (broad and narrow gage) were captured. On the 7th inst. an armoured car reconnaissance was sent to BEIRUT to ascertain the state of affairs there. Reconnaissance of the railway to DAMASCUS and also BEIRUT were immediately undertaken. On the 8th inst. the Royal Engineers ran the first train from ZAHLE through RAYAK to the break on the RAYAK DAMASCUS line. Local French railway operatives were enrolled and breakdown gangs improvised to repair the breaks on both lines. The inhabitants of ZAHLE and neighbouring villages were instructed to elect and form local Governments and every assistance was given them in maintaining law and order.

The Advance on HOMs. (89 Miles)

On the 9th of October, the 5th Cavalry Division was disposed as follows:
13th and 14th Cavalry Brigade Groups at TELL ESH SHERIF.
15th Cavalry Brigade Group and Divisional Headquarters at MOALLAKA.

The division was ordered to be ready to leave BALLBEK on the 13th inst. and advance on HOMS, the Division to be clear of BAALBEK by 15th inst., when the 4th Cavalry Division would march to that place.

An armoured car Reconnaissance was sent to BAALBEK on the 10th inst. and reported that the place was unoccupied and that good order prevailed. On the 11th inst. the 13th Cavalry Brigade moved to BAALBEK and the 15th Cavalry Brigade to TELL ESH SHERIF. Divisional Headquarters Group Marched to BAALBEK (22 miles) on the 12th Inst.

The Division marched to HOMS in two columns. Colum A, Armoured Cars, 15th Cavalry Brigade Group and Divisional Headquarters Group. Column B 15th and 14th Cavalry Brigade Groups. Brigade Ammunition Column. Headquarters Divisional Train. Brigade Sections of A.II Echelon and Divisional Train Companies marched in order to facilitate requisitioning. Colum B Marched one day in the rear of the Column A. Stages were as follows: LEBWE (20 miles), EL KAA (16 miles), KHUSSEIR (13 miles, HOMS (18 miles). The road in parts was a good fair-weather lorry road with the exception of the WADI HARUN crossing West of ZERAA, an inundation South of KHUSSEIR and the first three mile North of LEBWE, which is very rough. Troops moved everywhere off the road. The 1/250,000 HOMS sheet proved entirely inaccurate. HOMS was entered by armoured cars on the 15th inst. and occupied by the division on the 16th. An Arab Governor had already been appointed and he gave every assistance in requisitioning supplies. Good order prevailed but considerable trouble was caused by Arabs cutting and steaming cable despite proclamations by the Arab Governor, it was not until severe measures had been taken with culprits that this ceased.

The Advance from HOMS to ALEPPO. (115 miles)

The Division was concentrated North West of HOMS by midday 17th October. A reconnaissance by armoured cars reported that that a body of Turks, reported to be at ER RASTAN, had left; but that the bridge over the river ORONTES had been blown. On the 19th orders were received to push on to ALEPPO and the 15th Cavalry Brigade with the 5th Field Squadron R.E. was sent to ER RASTAN (11 miles) to repair the bridge: bridging materials being sent with them in lorries.

No. 2 Light Armoured Motor Battery and No. 2 Light Car Patrol joined the Division.

The Armoured Car Column was now constituted as Follows: Nos. 2, 11 and 12 Light Armoured Motor Batteries and Nos. 1, 2 and 7 Light Car Patrols.

This Column and the Divisional Headquarters Group joined the 15th Cavalry Brigade on the 20th, by the evening of which day the bridge over the ORONTES was completed for all wheels and lorries. Column B remained at HOMS under Brig-General G.A. Weir DSO; with orders to follow one days march behind Column A. on the 21st, Column A and the Armoured Car Colum marched to HAMA and bivouacked three miles North of the town of ZOR DEFAI (20 miles). The 13th and 14th Field Troops R.E. were left behind to strengthen the bridge over the ORONTES and this was completed by the evening of the 21st. These Field Troops re-joined their Brigades on arrival, leaving a small party for the up keep of the Bridge.

A halt had been ordered at HAMA but these orders were cancelled on the evening of the 21st. Two routes were available to ALEEPPO, (a). The old caravan route., (b). The railway route. The latter, according to the map, promised a better supply of water but from agents and inhabitants reports it was decided to follow the caravan route. At 0700 on the 22nd the Armoured Car Colum was sent forward to gain touch with the enemy and harass his retirement. The Colum reached MAARIT EN NAAMAN about 1230 without meeting with any enemy but during a short halt at that place information was received from contact aeroplanes of a small force of Turks with Motor Transport about KHAN SEBIL. This report was shortly afterwards confirmed by some Arabs who had travelled through that village on a motorcar on their way from ALEPPO. KHAN SEBIL was reached about 1430 but the enemy had seen the advance of the cars from a distance of five or six miles and at once withdrew in six lorries, covered by fire of one armoured car and machine guns in the lorries themselves. Armoured Cars and Light Car Patrols were at once sent in pursuit and in less than one mile from KHAN SEBIL the armoured car and its crew of seven Turks had been captured. Two hostile aeroplanes appeared from the North West and at once dived and machined gunned their own retiring lorries. Four miles further North then rear lorry was brought to a standstill my machine gun fire of a Light Car Patrol and those occupants who had not already become casualties ran away into the hills East and West of the road. About 25 were killed and wounded and five captured. The pursuit of the remaining five lorries was pressed for a distance of fifteen miles over a very rough and rocky road before darkness made it impossible for the Rolls Cars to proceed further, the Colum bivouacked about four miles North of SERAIKIN for the night. Throughout this pursuit the Light Car and Light Armoured Motor Batteries kept up a heavy fire on the retreating lorries causing many casualties in killed and wounded, besides compelling one lorry to be abandoned. Despite the fire of the machine guns from the lorries and rifle fire of the occupants we suffered no casualties. The German iron-tyred lorry was found to be better suited to rough road than the Rolls or Ford cars and several times during the pursuit this advantages saved the convoy from capture. The Column started early on the morning of the 23rd and near BANIS overtook a seconded abandoned lorry with a machine gun and much equipment. Four of the occupants of this lorry and the German driver were subsequently taken prisoner.

On reaching KNAN TUMAN Turkish cavalry were seen to leave the village but on being pursued they left the road by routes, which were impracticable for the cars. Reconnaissances were then sent out through the hilly country North of KHAN TUMAN into the plain South of ALLEPPO up to within five miles of the town. These and air reconnaissances discovered that the enemy were holding short lengths of trench astride the HAMA-ALEPPO road about three miles south of the town and the ridges running South West from the town, with rifles and machine guns with a force that was variously reported from two to three thousand, while six or seven thousand more were in ALEPPO.

At 1000, Captain MACINTYRE, 7th Light Car Patrol, was sent in to the town under a white flag to demand its surrender. He returned at 1600 after being most courteously treated by the Turkish officers with the following reply: 'the Commander of the Turkish Garrison of ALEPPO does not find it necessary to answer your note'. Signed MAHMED HEZATI, C.G.S., ALEPPO. While waiting for Captain Macintyre's return a Turkish cavalry patrol approached the village from the South West getting within 500 yards from the cars before realizing what the pass held. Eventually they saw us and turned North West at a gallop. They were fired on and scattered.

1	Armoured Car	1	Turkish Officers
2	Lorries	1	German Other Ranks
2	Machine Guns	15	Turkish Other Ranks

Immediate pursuit by No. 1 Light Car Patrol over country that appeared impossible for cars resulted in the capture of four out of patrol of eight. At 1715 the Colum withdrew into the plain South of KHAN TUMAN in order to bivouac for the night in a position, which would give freedom of manoeuvre, should the enemy attack.

At 0700 on the 24th, the column again moved forward to KHAN TUMAN, sending reconnaissance towards ALEPPO and TREMANIN. The object of the later reconnaissance was to find a road by which the cars could attack the town from the North West and threaten the enemy's retreat along the ALEXANDRETTA road. The reconnaissance towards ALEPPO found the enemy in the same position as the previous day with cavalry outposts pushed forward into the hills north of KHAN TUMAN, while the cars, which had reconnoitred towards TERMANIN, reported that there was no track running in the required direction, which would take cars. It was then decided to withdraw to the village of ZIBRE. N the morning of the 25th the Car Colum again went forward to the hills North of KHAN TUMAN and further reconnaissances were sent forward towards ALEPPO. Each of these was met with considerable fire from light filed guns and by rifle fire from positions astride the road.

On the 15th Cavalry Brigade coming up in the afternoon the cars were relieved by cavalry outposts and the Colum withdrew to bivouacs in support of outposts North West of KHAN TUMAN.

The total captures of the Light Car Column were:

The 15th Cavalry Brigade Group and Divisional Headquarters Group followed one day's march behind B Column, camped as follows:

KHAN SHAIKHUN (21 miles),

MAARIT EN NAAMAN (16 miles),

SERAIKIN (18 ½ miles)

KHAN TUMAN (20 miles).

The road is little more than a fair-weather track, very rocky in places, but improved after passing SERAIKIN. No running water was encountered until KHAN TUMAN, but well water and cisterns were plentiful at each stage. Grain meat and bread were requisitioned easily, except at MAARIT EN NAAMAN where certain sections of the inhabitants displayed covert hostility. Groceries, petrol and some grain reached the troops daily by lorry.

Meanwhile the Sherifian Forces had been advancing up the railway route driving small bodies of Turks in front of them. On the 25th inst. they moved east of ALEPPO ready to attack the town from the flank in co-operation with us on the 26th. They with assistance of Arabs in the town, gained entrance into ALEPPO on the night of 25th-26th. After considerable fighting in which the Turks suffered heavy casualties.

The disposition of the Division at 0600 on the 26th was: Armoured Car Column, 15th Cavalry Brigade (less Hyderabad Lancers) and Divisional

Headquarters Group at KHAN TUMAN, remainder of division marching from SERAIKIN and due at KHAN TUMAN about noon.

At 0700 on the 26th the 15th Cavalry Brigade moved off to clear the hills on the west of HOMS-ALEPPO road to get astride the ALEXANDRETTA road. Armoured Cars followed the Divisional Headquarters Group after reconnaissances had been made entered the town sat 1000.

Meanwhile the 15th Cavalry Brigade moving West of the town found about 2,500 enemy infantry, 150 cavalry with numerous machine guns, and eight to ten guns, in a position astride the ALEXANDRETTA road, 1,000 yards South East of HARITAN, The enemy was charged by the Mysore Lancers and two Squadrons of the Jodhpur Lancers, who endeavoured to envelop the enemy's left flank. About 60 were killed and 20 prisoners taken, but owing to the weakness of squadrons there was not sufficient depth in the attack and after surrendering, enemy again took up arms and shot into the rear of the attacking Squadrons; and the attack could not be pushed home. The 15th Cavalry Brigade then took up positions astride the ALEPPO-ALEXANDRETTA road about EL HUSSEINE. Two more Armoured Car Batteries and the Light Car Patrols were placed under the orders of the General Officer Commanding 15th Cavalry Brigade and the 14th Cavalry Brigade was ordered forward through the town and support the 15th Cavalry Brigade at EL HUSSEINIE, and the 13th Cavalry Brigade to march at 0500 to ALEPPO. The 14th Cavalry Brigade left KHAN TUMAN AT 1645, and passed through ALEPPO at 2330 and moved out, less wheels, to take over the portion of the line held by the 15th Cavalry Brigade. New was received during the night that Turks were withdrawing and had retired Northwards. The 14th Cavalry Brigade relieved the outpost of 15th Cavalry Brigade at 0600 and an armoured car reconnaissance reported the Turkish rearguard, with two small guns, holding a ridge about two miles just North of BIANUM. The bridge over the road about two miles North of HARITAN had been blown but the cars managed to pass it and remained in observation. At 1200 the 15th Cavalry Brigade was withdrawn to bivouac North of the town and defence of the line astride the ALEXANDRETTA and KILLIS road was taken over by the 14th Cavalry Brigade on the Right of the 13th Cavalry Brigade on the Left. The Turks had withdrawn to a position about KHAN NARISTA-NUBBAL. A reconnaissance to the water supply at AIN TELL reported no mining or damage there. All hospitals and Government Stores were taken over and guards placed by the Sherifian Forces.

Eighteen Guns, 821 prisoners, consisting of one German Officer, nine German other ranks, seven Turkish Officers and 804 Turkish other ranks; and much rolling stock and materials of all kinds were captured.

Touch was maintained with the enemy by armoured cars and patrols and on the 28th it was reported that a further retirement had been made. The enemy were discovered to be holding a position in considerable strength commanding the main ALEXANDRETTA road about 1,000 West of DEIR EL JEMEL. On the 28th inst. Sherifian Forces occupied the MUSLIMIE JUNCTION. The Station, permanent was and points had been destroyed and engines and rolling stock damaged. The following day the 13th Cavalry Brigade relieved the 14th Cavalry Brigade and took over the whole position covering the ALEXANDRETTA road. The 14th Cavalry Brigade then took over the defence of the MUSLIMIE JUNCTION from the Sherifian Forces.

At 1000 on the 31st inst. a message was received by wireless from the General Headquarters to the effect an armistice had been concluded and that hostilities would cease between the Turkish Government and the Allies at 1200 on that day.

Since the commencement of operation on the 19th September to the 26th of October the Division has marched just over 500 miles. During this period 52 Guns, 6 German officers, 273 German other ranks, 371 Turkish officers, 11,191 Turkish other ranks and 151 Bedouins have been captured and the following towns occupied: NAZARETH, HAIFA, ACRE, DAMASCUS, ZAHLE, MOALLAKA, HOMS, HAMA and ALEPPO.

H.J.M. MACANDREW
Major General
Commanding, 5th Cavalry Division
Headquarters 5th Cavalry Division
2nd November 1918

Statement of Casualties.
(19 September to 31 October)
Personnel.

	British Officers	British ORs	Indian Officers	Indian ORs	Total
Killed	4	8	1	26	39
Wounded	11	23	13	113	160
Missing	-	3	-	6	9
Sick	55	778	8	493	1,334
Total	70	812	22	638	1,542
Establishment	236	2,955	131	2,954	6,276

Percentage 25%

(Many shown as sick have since re-joined the Division.)

Animals.

	Riding	Draught	Pack	Total
Killed	152	-	5	157
Died	265	57	5	327
Destroyed	179	44	14	237
Wounded & Evacuated	63	-	-	63
Evacuated	735	129	38	902
Missing	169	57	8	234
Total				1,920

Establishment 8,971, Percentage 21.41%

APPENDIX I

Nominal Roll: Tank Personnel 1918.

Number	Rank	Name	Taken on Strength	Previous Unit	Discharged	Comments
	Capt	Brown, N.L.	27/1/18	1st Aust Corps Supply Col.	15/8/18	Discharged Medically Unfit, AIF. Reenlisted Special Unit Tank Crew HS.
9351	MT Dvr	Dalton, R.J.	27/1/18	AMTS, London.	12/8/18	Reenlisted Special Unit Tank Crew HS.
287	MT Dvr	Fleming, R.T.	3/2/18	AMTS, Chelsea.	12/8/18	Discharged Medically Unfit, AIF. Reenlisted Special Unit Tank Crew HS.
2815	Art	Gifford, F.G.	26/1/18	AMTS, London.	12/8/18	Reenlisted Special Unit Tank Crew HS.
1524	Cpl	Jackson, C.R.	3/2/18	AMTS, London.	12/8/18	Reenlisted Special Unit Tank Crew HS.
1929	L/Cpl	Lord, D.B.	3/2/18	AMTS, Chelsea.	12/8/18	Discharged Medically Unfit, AIF. Reenlisted Special Unit Tank Crew HS.
1255	MT Dvr	McFadden, M.G.	27/1/18	AMTS, Chelsea.	12/8/18	Discharged Medically Unfit, AIF. Reenlisted Special Unit Tank Crew HS.
1568	MT Dvr	Rowland, A.R.	26/1/18	AMTS, Chelsea.	12/8/18	Discharged Medically Unfit, AIF. Reenlisted Special Unit Tank Crew HS.
2904A	MT Dvr	Swain, H.S.	26/1/18	AMTS, Chelsea.	12/8/18	Reenlisted Special Unit Tank Crew HS.

Nominal Roll: Special Unit Tank Crew, Home Service, 1918-1919.

Number	Rank	Name	Enlisted	Discharged	Comments
	Capt	Brown, N.L.	16/8/19	23/10/19	Discharged Medically Unfit.
V79671	Cpl	Dalton, R.J.	13/8/18	26/12/18	Discharged at own request.
V79672	S/Sgt	Fleming, R.T.	13/8/18	5/19	
V79673	Sgt	Gifford, F.G.	13/8/18	26/12/18	
V79674	S/Sgt	Jackson, C.R.	13/8/18	26/12/18	
V79675	Cpl	Lord, D.B.	13/8/18	26/12/18	
V79676	Cpl	McFadden, M.G.	13/8/18	26/12/18	
V79677	MT Dvr	Rowland, A.R.	13/8/18	26/12/18	
V79678	MT Dvr	Swain, H.S.	13/8/18	12/12/18	Discharged at own request.

Nominal Roll: Permanent Military Forces, Royal Australian Engineers, Detachment, 1919-1921.

Number	Rank	Name	Enlisted	Discharged	Comments
VP 991	Spr	Cook, S.B.	9/5/12		LSGCM Awarded as a Sergeant in Hobart 1932. Still serving 1949.
351	Cpl	Hosking, F.A.	1914	1921	Also referred as Hoskin. Transferred to Australian Air Force. Died of Injuries 28/9/25.
890	Cpl	Kubale, A.H.	1911		
505	Sgt	Marnie, W.K.	1912	11/4/43	RAE Works Section. To 2nd AIF 12/4/43.
373	Cpl	McDonald, E. Mc.	1915	30/3/21	Transferred to Australian Air Force.
1027	Art	Nicholson, W.D.	30/8/18		To RAE Works Section, Broadmeadows Military Camp 29/9/24. Died of Injuries 31/12/1924.

Australian Imperial Force Service, of Permanent Military Forces, Royal Australian Engineers, Detachment, 1919-1921.

Number	Rank	Name	Enlisted	Unit	Returned to Australia	Discharge	Comments
10187	2nd Cpl	Hosking, F.A.	8/5/16	10th Fd Coy Eng.	10/3/18	17/6/18	WIA 5/10/17. Discharged Medically Unfit.
8927	Whlr	Kubale, A.H.	11/6/16	5th Fd Arty Bde.	29/9/17	31/12/17	WIA 23/5/17. Discharged Medically Unfit.
157	Lt	Marnie, W.K.	1/9/14	5th Div Eng.	26/11/17	1/5/19	RSM 5th Div Engs 23/10/16. 2Lt 17/11/17. Lt 31/1/18.
10318	Cpl	McDonald, E. Mc.	8/5/16	10th Fd Coy Eng.	3/9/19	17/1/1920	MM London Gazette 30507, 4/2/1918.

Other Military Service: Tank Personnel, Special Unit, Tank Crew, Home Service 1918-19 and Permanent Military Forces, Royal Australian Engineers, Detachment. 1919-1921.

Number	Rank	Name	Unit	Comments
3677	WO1	Cook, S.B.	Australian Regular Army.	
V84042	Cpl	Dalton, R.J.	Australian Army Canteens Service.	1940-42, Died of Illness 22/7/42.
		Fleming, R.T.	Royal Naval Brigade, Portsmouth Division.	Time Expired.
		Gifford, F.G.	Royal Australian Naval and Military Department.	3 Months.
351 692	Spr AC	Hosking, F.A.	38th Fortress Engineers, RAE, CMF. RAAF.	1909-1914. Died of Injuries 28/9/25.
		Lord, D.B.	Light Horse, CMF.	
NX166405 2/60	Major Hon Lt Col	Marnie, W.K.	Royal Australian Engineers (Engineering Board). Australian Regular Army.	Enlisted 2nd AIF 12/4/43. Discharged 7/4/1949.
O3470	Ft/Lt	McDonald, E.Mc.	RAAF.	Enlisted 31/3/1921, Discharged 30/6/1950.
		Rowland, A.R.	5th Bearer Corps, Warwick, Queensland.	
		Swain, H.S.	Navy.	2 Years *"Free Discharge"*.

APPENDIX J

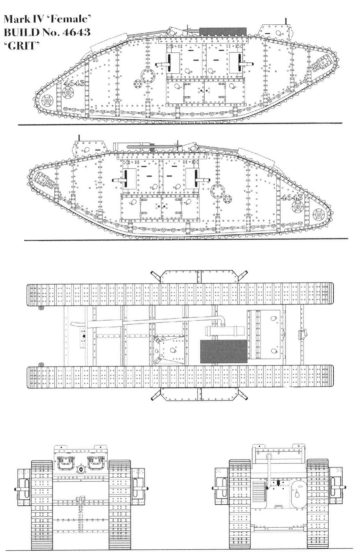

Mark IV 'Female'
BUILD No. 4643
'GRIT'

4. The Mk. IV (Female) tank sent to Australia was a standard early 1918 vehicle produced by the Coventry Ordnance Works in Scotland, one of several manufacturers of British tanks. As such it incorporated the latest design changes, including additional armour at the rear and a shorter exhaust pipe. Its configuration did not include operational modifications such as the de-ditching beam and rails which were so characteristic of tanks on the Western Front.

Mk. IV (Female) Tank
Technical Details

Length	8.05 metres
Width, Fighting Trim	3.20 metres
Width, Sponsons retracted	2.65 metres
Height	2.49 metres
Height to top of tracks	2.25 metres
Ground Clearance	0.32 metres
Weight Fully Stowed	27.4 tonnes
Centre of Gravity	2.44 metres from front, 0.91 metres from ground
Horse power per ton	3.75
Engine	Daimler 6-cylinder conventionally aspirated, water cooled, sleeve valve petrol engine developing 105bhp at 1,000rpm
Engine Ignition	Magneto
Engine Firing Order	1-5-3-6-2-4
Carburettor	One Zenith 48mm
Engine Lubrication	Gravity from 34.05 litre oil tank, pump return
Fuel Type	Aviation Spirit
Fuel Quantity	317.8 litres
Fuel Consumption	6.09 litres per kilometre on flat, hard ground
Fuel System	Pressurised by air from engine-mounted pump
Clutch	Ferrodo cone type
Gear Box (Driver operated)	Two forward, one reverse gears, selected by gate change
Differential	Worm and Crown Wheel with differential lock
Secondary Gears (Gearsmen operated)	High and Low, selected by Striking Levers and Interlocking Forks.
Speed at 1,000rpm: 1st: (1st + Low)	1.2 km/hour
Speed at 1,000rpm 2nd: (2nd + Low	2.1 km/hour
Speed at 1,000rpm 3rd (1st + High)	3.4 km/hour
Speed at 1,000rpm 4th (2nd + High)	5.9 km/hour
Speed at 1,000rpm Reverse	1.5 km/hour

Radius of action in 4th gear	56 kilometres maximum
Internal Lighting	Lucas system powered by engine-mounted dynamo to a 12-volt DC storage battery.
Track Width	520 mm
Track Shoes	90 of 6 mm thick armour plate shoes per track.
Track Rollers	12 heavy weight pairs beneath each track, plus 14 light pairs
Track Pressure Hard Ground	1.95 kilograms per square metre
Track Pressure Soft Ground	0.91 kilograms per square metre when sunk to depth of 152 mm
Track in Contact Hard Ground	1.4 metres
Track in Contact Soft Ground	3.4 metres when sunk to belly plate
Armament	Five Lewis Light Machine Guns
Ammunition	.303-inch (7.7 x 56R mm), 47 rounds/magazine
Ammunition Stowage	12,972 rounds stowed in 276 Lewis magazines
Armour – Front, sides, rear	12 mm
Armour – Roof and Belly	8 mm
Crew	Eight: One commander, one driver, two gearsmen, four Lewis gunners.

APPENDIX K

Notes on Tank Driving

(Extract from *Training Note No.2: Tank Driver's Handbook Marks I, II, and IV Tanks*.)

1. To steer slightly to the right, pull on the right hand brake. To steer slightly to the left, pull on the left hand brake.

2. To turn quickly to the right (Differential unlocked) put in the "High" Secondary Gear on the right and "Low" on the left and apply the right hand brake if necessary. To turn quickly to the left, do the opposite.

3. To "swing" the tank to the right, lock the differential put the secondary gear in "neutral" and left in "Low", put your change-speed lever in 1st or "Low" gear, and pull right hand brake on hard. To swing to the left, do the opposite.

4. Before negotiating a difficult obstacle, always lock the differential. It may not be possible to lock it when stuck. Remember to unlock it afterwards, otherwise the tank cannot be steered.

5. To make a steep ascent, lock the differential and change down to the lowest gear in gear box and Secondary gears, and open the throttle wide.

6. To descend a steep decline, lock the differential, thereby ensuring an even braking effect with the foot brake on both tracks. Go dead slow, gently de-clutching and apply the foot brake as may be necessary.

7. Drive straight at any real obstacle whenever possible so as to get the tracks squarely on to it. Small obstacles may be taken obliquely with careful driving.

8. Take the greatest care not to get "side-tracked" in a trench. If one track gets down a trench the tank will have to be dug out.

9. Be very careful of tree stumps, fallen timber, and any hard projections. If one gets under the belly of a tank it will probably force the bottom plating up against the engine flywheel and the tank will stop dead. Drive so as to get such obstructions under the track if it is impossible to avoid them altogether.

10. Drive as fast as possible over soft or muddy ground. The slower the tank goes the more likely is it to sink and get "bellied". If this happens the weight of the tank will be on its "belly" instead of the tracks, and these will go around without moving it.

11. Never use the footbrake with the clutch engaged.

12. Never reverse except in "Low" secondary gears, and then not for a longer period than is absolutely necessary.

13. Avoid hard macadam roads as much as possible to reduce wear, and avoid flints and stones if possible, as they may get in the track links and cause trouble.

14. Never attempt to change the Secondary gears when on a long steep slope. With these gears out of mesh, the powerful foot brake is useless, and the tank may take charge. The hand brakes will probably not be sufficiently powerful to stop it. Remember, therefore, before starting to climb a steep slope to change into "Low" Secondary gears.

15. So long as obstacles can be seen, drive straight at them, and do not pause on them. If, however. A high parapet hides the ground beyond a pause must be made when the parapet has been mounted to see if there is anything beyond which cannot be crossed. If so, reverse the tank and cross at a more suitable point.

APPENDIX L

Crewing a Mk. IV Tank: Martin Pegler's Account.

There are few people alive today who have had the experience of travelling in a tank dating from the First World War. In 1987, the Mk. IV (Male) tank belonging to the Royal Armoured Corps Tank Museum at Bovington Camp, Dorset, was moved to Aldershot for a display. The tank was driven under its own power from inside the storage building out into the museum's yard and onto a low-loader. British historian and author Martin Pegler was fortunate to be 'volunteered' to be one of the two gearsmen while the tank was driven by the museum's research officer, David Fletcher. Martin subsequently recounted the experience in 'The British Tank Crew's War, 1916-1918', first published in the magazine *Military Illustrated* No. 40, September 1991. The following extract from the article appears with the kind permission of the author. Martin's first-hand account provides a graphic insight into the experiences of the first Australian tank crewmen operating 'Grit':

At first sight, a Mk. IV (Male) viewed from the exterior appears gargantuan, being as high as a tall man can reach, and as wide as a bus. However, once you have clambered inside, the interior seems disproportionately small and appears to have been designed around a special breed of midget. One's credulity is further strained when, having successfully negotiated the narrow, awkwardly placed sponson door, one attempts to stand upright – an act that gives forceful reminder of the very low roof and the solid properties of armour plate.

The gloomy interior is dominated by the massive 105hp six-cylinder Daimler engine squatting like a malevolent animal in the centre of the vehicle, surrounded by a weblike network of exhaust, water and fuel lines. The clutch and primary drive behind it effectively bisect the tank, and every inch of wall and floor space is occupied by shell racks and cupboards. Comfort for crew members is purely incidental. Two solid and uncomfortable bucket seats are placed at the front of the tank for the driver and commander. The gearsmen perch on a narrow plank at the rear of the sponsons from where they can reach the pairs of secondary gear levers. Most of the space in the sponson is already occupied by the breeches of the 6-pounder gun and machine guns. Lighting is by dynamo through half a dozen dim bulbs, which are extinguished when in action.

A narrow gangway runs either side of the engine around which the crew perform an awkward ballet, barking shins, scraping knuckles and, in moments of forgetfulness, cracking skulls.

Starting up is an art in itself. In the Mk. I the fuel was gravity fed from tanks in each of the front 'horns'. In the case of a direct hit, this more or less guaranteed that the driver, commander and most of the crew would be immolated by the high-octane aviation spirit. In the Mk. IV the 70 gallon tank was armour-plated and moved to the rear with an Autovac suction system (that frequently didn't) for the fuel feed. With cylinders primed, mag retarded and petrol pumped through, a crank handle the thickness of a man's wrist is turned. This is located behind the engine block, where there was just sufficient room for three of us, sweating and straining, to crank for all we were worth. In terms of sheer effort, it felt like trying to wind up an ocean liner. With a splutter, the engine fired – and died. The whole laborious procedure was then repeated.

After more hernia-inducing straining, the engine rumbled into life. The sound is absolutely paralysing; imagine half a dozen steam hammers in a steel box, and you are halfway there. In addition, the stink of the exhaust mingles with the heady aroma of fuel, hot oil and sweat. Shouted conversation, even from a distance of inches, is impossible. We took up our stations, and the driver signalled with his finger for first (low) gear.

Steering demands considerable skill on the part of the driver, who must control clutch, brakes and throttle, all working through a two-speed gearbox, worm drive, differential, secondary gears, output shafts and chain final drive. It took four men to steer the tank. Turning involved locking the differential, putting one track into neutral and applying the handbrake to it, then allowing the vehicle to rotate around the locked track. This required smooth synchronisation on the part of the commander, driver and gearsmen. We managed it in a series of kangaroo hops accompanied by much inexpert graunching of gears.

As the tank lurched forward and we grabbed for handholds, every ripple in the ground could be felt through the 26 unsprung track rollers. Gradually the light became hazy as grey fumes filled the interior. With streaming eyes and burning throats we hung out of the sponson doors for fresh air. After 15 minutes the heat of the engine and coolant had turned the interior into an oven – and it was a cool day. Working temperatures on a summer's day could reach 120 degrees F (45 degrees C) with heat exhaustion, dehydration and vomiting the usual side effects. As the nose of the vehicle climbed the ramps onto the transporter we were flung backwards. (It was at this point, as we frantically clutched at handholds, that one realised that everything inside the tank is hot, sharp or both.)

In our Mark IV, the final drive chains were at least enclosed – in earlier Marks they were not, and would spray the inside with liquid mud until it was inches deep, adding to the over-whelming impression of being in a greasy slow-cooker. As we climbed the low-loader ramp our engine stalled, and we struggled against gravity to insert the dislodged crank handle and restart the engine. With all the hatches open, the tank looked from the outside as though it was on fire, with exhaust fumes streaming from every orifice. Eventually, safely loaded, we wearily levered ourselves out of the cramped cabin, red-eyed and coughing. We had been inside for a little over an hour. No one was trying to kill us; the tank was un-stowed; the ground had been basically level; and the interesting cocktail of fumes inside didn't include the throat-parching stink of cordite, or the smell of blood.

ABBREVIATIONS

Abbreviation	Meaning
3MD	Third Military District
AAMC	Australian Army Medical Corps
AAMTC	Australian Army Motor Transport Corps
ASC	Army Service Corps (British)
AASC	Australian Army Service Corps
AE	Australian Engineers
AFC	Australian Flying Corps
AGH	Australian General Hospital
AIF	Australian Imperial Force
ALH	Australian Light Horse
am	ante meridiem
AMF	Australian Military Force
ANZAC	Australian and New Zealand Army Corps
ARC	Australian Racing Club
Artif	Artificer
Arty	Artillery
ASC	Army Service Corps
ASgt	Acting Sergeant
Aust	Australia or Australian
AWM	Australian War Memorial
Bde	Brigade
Bn	Battalion
Bros	Brothers
C	Celsius
CB	Companion of the Order of the Bath
CBE	Commander of the Order of the British Empire
Cdt	Cadet
CGS	Chief of the General Staff
CMF	Citizen Military Force
CMG	Companion of the Order of Saint Michael and Saint Gerorge
Co	Company
CO	Commanding Officer

Col	Colonel
Comd	Command
Coy	Company
Cpl	Corporal
DC	Direct Current
DCM	Distinguished Conduct Medal
Div	Division
Divl	Divisional
DSO	Distinguished Service Order
Dvr	Driver
Elec	Electrical
Eng	Engineers
Fd	Field
Ft/Lt	Flight Lieutenant
Garr	Garrison
GCMG	Knight Grand Cross of the Order of Saint Michael and Saint George
H. Quarters	Headquarters
HMAS	His Majesty's Australian Ship
HMAT	His Majesty's Australian Transport
HMHS	His Majesty's Hospital Ship
Hon	Honorary
hp	Horse Power
HRH	His Royal Highness
HS	Home Service
HT	Hired Transport
Inf	Infantry
Inst	Instant
JP	Justice of the Peace
KCB	Knight Commander of the Order of the Bath
KCMG	Knight Commander of the Order of Saint Michael and Saint George
km/hr	kilometres per hour
L/Cpl	Lance Corporal
LC	Light Car
Lieut	Lieutenant

LSGCM	Long Service and Good Conduct Medal
Lt	Lieutenant
Lt Col	Lieutenant Colonel
Ltd	Limited
Maj	Major
Maj-Gen	Major General
MC	Military Cross
MG	Machine Gun
MID	Mentioned in Dispatches
Mk	Mark
MLC	Member of the Legislative Council
MM	Military Medal
mm	Millimetres
MOV	Museum of Victoria
MT Dvr	Motor Transport Driver
MVO	Member of the Victorian Order
NAA	National Archives of Australia
NCO	Non-Commissioned Officer
NLA	National Library of Australia
No	Number
NSW	New South Wales
OBE	Order of the British Empire
OC	Officer Commanding
Pers	Personnel
pm	post meridiem
PMF	Permanent Military Force
Pte	Private
Pty	Proprietary
RAAC	Royal Australian Armoured Corps
RAAF	Royal Australian Air Force
RAE	Royal Australian Engineers
RAF	Royal Air Force
RAN	Royal Australian Navy
RE	Royal Engineers
Regt	Regiment
RFC	Royal Flying Corps

RMS	Royal Mail Ship
RN	Royal Navy
RNR	Royal Naval Reserve
RO	Reserve Officer
RSM	Regimental Sergeant Major
RTA	Returned to Australia
RTS	Returned To Store
RVM	Royal Victorian Medal
RVO	Royal Victorian Order
s	shilling
SAJC	South Australian Jockey Club
Sig	Signal or Signaller
SLQ	State Library of Queensland
SLSA	State Library of South Australia
SP Bookie	Starting Price Bookmaker
Spr	Sapper
SS	Single Screw
SSgt	Staff Sergeant
St	Street
TF	Territorial Forces
TOS	Taken On Strength
Tpr	Trooper
Trg	Training
TV	Television
UK	United Kingdom
US	United States
VD	Volunteer Decoration
VDC	Volunteer Defence Corps
VRC	Victorian Racing Club
WDA	Water Dump A
Whlr	Wheeler
WIA	Wounded In Action
Xmas	Christmas
YMCA	Young Men's Christian Association

ENDNOTES

Part 1

1   Second Lieutenant Stewart Ridley and Air Mechanic 1st Class J.A. Garside of the 17th Squadron, Royal Flying Corps, died in mid-June 1916 and are commemorated at the Cairo War Memorial Cemetery. The original newspaper cutting was found in Ivan Young's photo album. This tragic incident provides some indication of the dangers posed by the desert.

2   In fact Bisset was not awarded the DCM, but Mentioned in Despatches.

3   Letter from Gunner L.R. Cohn, 20 July 1918.

4   Transcript of original operation orders from Captain James' papers at the Army Tank Museum.

5   In fact, the rescue of the sailors occurred in 1915 and the members of the Armoured Car Section did not participate. The original text has not been amended.

6   The unit title is variously referred to in official documents as the Armoured Car Section, 1st Armoured Car Section and 1st Armoured Car Battery. For clarity, the name '1st Armoured Car Section' will be used throughout.

7   The Citizen Military Force has been variously referred to over time as Citizens Forces, Citizen Military Forces, Militia and, more recently, the Army Reserve. For consistency, reserve forces of volunteers for service within the Commonwealth and territories will be called Citizen Military Force throughout, abbreviated to CMF.

8   NAA: B2455, James E.H., item barcode 7365498.

9   The *Argus*, 13 August 1919, p. 10.

10   The *Coburg Leader*, 14 December 1895, p. 4.

11   The *Coburg Leader*, 29 October 1904, p. 1.

12   The *Coburg Leader*, 20 March 1909, p. 4.

13   NAA: B2455, Cornwell, P.R.V., item barcode 3424461.

14   The *Argus*, 24 November 1913, p. 12.

15   The *Sydney Morning Herald*, 26 January 1914, p. 12.

16   The *Leader*, 7 February 1914, p. 23.

17   The *Leader*, 21 August 1915, 'Motors and Motoring', p. 21.

18   The *Brunswick and Coburg Leader*, 16 June 1916, p. 2.

19   The Heidelberg Conservation Study declared the home a historically important building in 1985. See the Victorian Heritage Database place details, Banyule City Council.

20   *The Cyclopedia of Victoria*, Vol. III, p. 225.

21   The *Nhill Free Press*, 22 January 1907, p. 2.

22   The *Nhill Free Press*, 28 August 1914, p. 2.

23   The *Horsham Times*, 7 December 1915, p. 3.

24   The *Nhill Free Press*, 21 September 1917, p. 3.

25   The *Horsham Times*, 6 July 1917, p. 5.

26   The *Horsham Times*, 2 October 1917, p. 3.

27   NAA: B2455, Young, I.S., item barcode 1911675.

28   K.M. Curkpatrick, *Saddle to Boots. A history of the 19th (Aust) Machine Gun Battalion*, self-published, Clifton Hill, Victoria, 1990, p. 6.

29   Reserve of Officers List 1946, Part 2, p. 1607.

30   The *Nhill Free Press*, 7 December 1917, p. 2.

31   The *Nhill Free Press*, Editorial, March 1920.

32   The *Nhill Free Press*, 16 November 1933, p. 2.

33   A number of Young's early home movies are held in the National Film and Sound Archive, Canberra.

34   The Victorian Government *Gazette*, 1 September 1943.

35   The *Horsham Times*, 15 February 1916, p. 6.

36   The *Hamilton Spectator*, 28 December 1919, p. 4. For some unknown reason Creek's rank was reported as private.

37   NAA: B2455, Creek, G., item barcode 3462415.

38   The *Horsham Times*, 31 August 1919, p. 5.

39   The *Advertiser*, 16 February 1954, p. 4.

40   An 'SP bookie' was a starting price bookmaker who accepted bets on horseraces away from the racecourse. It was a common but illegal form of fixed-odds gambling. SP bookies often established themselves in easy to access places such as hotel bars and those caught faced criminal charges.

41   The *Horsham Times*, 9 September 1930, p. 5.

42   NAA: B2455, McGibbon, R.W., item barcode 1944094.

43   The *Cumberland Evening Times*, 7 January 1942, p. 14.

44   The *Cumberland Evening Times*, 14 April 1941, p. 9.

45   J. Devany, australianfootball.com

46   The *Barrier Miner*, 9 September 1905, p. 2.

47   The *Barrier Miner*, 21 November 1905, p. 2.

48   The *Mail*, 27 December 1953, p. 9.

49   The *Advertiser*, 28 June 1920, p. 12.

50   The *Barrier Miner*, 3 April 1916, p. 4.

51   The *Port Pirie Recorder* and *North Western Mail*, 7 April 1916, p. 4.

52   The *Adelaide Register*, 19 February 1917, p. 6.

53   NAA: B2455, Hyman, O.H., item barcode 7361031.

54   The *Adelaide Register*, 10 April 1922, p. 5.

55   The *Advertiser*, 15 January 1926, p. 19.

56   The *Adelaide Chronicle*, June 1948.

57   The *Argus*, 18 November 1920, p. 4.

58   NAA: B2455, Thompson, W.P., item barcode 1836411.

59   Index of Wills and Administration 1858–1966; 1935, p. 90.

60   Notes provided by the Chiltern Historical Association.

61   Interview by D. Finlayson for *Ironsides* 2006.

62   NAA: B2455, Harkin, H.L.F., item barcode 4968963.

63   R. Droogleever, *That Ragged Mob*, Trojan Press, Melbourne, 2009, p. 483.

64   The *Argus*, 21 November 1911, p. 5.

65   The *Argus*, 10 November 1913, p. 12.

66   NAA: B2455, Millar, L.J., item barcode 1906034.

67   NAA: B2455, McKay, G.A., item barcode 1948011.

68   *Canowindra Star* and *Eugowra News*, 5 May 1922, p. 5.

69   NAA: B883, McKay, K.R., item barcode 1948154.

70   NAA: A9301, McKay, A.M., item barcode 5522452.

71   The *Bendigonian*, 8 March 1917, p. 27.

72   The *Bendigonian*, 10 June 1915, p. 9.

73   The *Bendigo Advertiser*, 24 November 1914, p. 14.

74   The *Bendigonian*, 30 March 1915, p. 19.

75   The *Bendigo Advertiser*, 29 April 1916, p. 11.

76   NAA: B2455, Bisset, N.S., item barcode 3086220.

77   The *Argus*, 26 December 1940, p. 5.

78   NAA: B2455, Jones, S.G., item barcode 1822184.

79   NAA: B884, Jones, S.G., item barcode 6278439.

80   See A.J. Sweeting, 'Langley, Hudson John Watson (1894–1919)', *Australian Dictionary of Biography*, Vol. 9, Melbourne University Press, 1983.

81   The *Nhill Free Press*, 30 November 1915, p. 2.

82   The *Mitre* (Trinity School Magazine), May 1919, p. 40.

83   NAA: B883, Langley, J.H., item barcode 11976488.

84   The *Mount Alexander Mail*, 22 July 1916, p. 2.

85   NAA: B883, Morgan, G.F., item barcode 7986680.

86   NAA: B883, Gray, L.A., item barcode 4671769.

87   NAA: B883, Christensen, G.C., item barcode 6284786.

88   NAA: B2455, Riley, J.C., item barcode 8032615.

89   The *Nepean Times*, 4 August 1955, p. 2.

90   Driscoll's postings mirror those of Lieutenant A.C. Gibbs and it is likely that Driscoll was his batman.

91   NAA: B2455, Driscoll, J.A., item barcode 3522293.

92   The *Sydney Morning Herald*, 1 December 1934, p. 14.

93   The *Sydney Morning Herald*, 22 February 1935, p. 6.

94   NAA: B884, Driscoll, J.A., item barcode 6184472.

95   The *Newcastle Morning Herald* and *Miners Advocate*, 19 July 1944, p. 6.

96   The *Newcastle Morning Herald* and *Miners Advocate*, 16 November 1944, p. 5.

97   The *Cumberland Argus and Fruitgrowers Advocate*, various dates.

98   The *Sydney Morning Herald*, 25 May 1904, p. 4.

99   The *Cumberland Argus and Fruitgrowers Advocate*, 5 October 1907, p. 8.

100   The *Daily Herald*, 19 September 1918, p. 5.

101   NAA: B2455, Gibbs, A.C., item barcode 4104617.

102   The *Sydney Morning Herald*, 25 March 1928, p. 13.

103   The *Sydney Morning Herald*, 29 August 1931, p. 10.

104   The *Sydney Morning Herald*, 24 September 1931, p. 4.

105   The *Sydney Morning Herald*, 26 September 1931, p. 10.

106   The *Sydney Morning Herald*, 21 November 1931, p. 10.

107   The *Sydney Morning Herald*, 9 June 1932, p. 9.

108   The *Sydney Morning Herald*, 25 June 1932, p. 14.

109   On enlistment he used Frank rather that Francis Hetherset Huntington Rhoades.

110   NAA: B2455, Rhoades, F., item barcode 8028561.

111   The *Sydney Morning Herald*, 17 September 1919, p. 8.

112   NAA: B2455, Riley, K.C., item barcode 11989288.
113   The *Sydney Morning Herald*, 5 December 1918, p. 7.
114   NAA: B2455, Jarvis, B.C, item barcode 7336521.
115   On several documents Sydney's name is spelled Sidney, clearly a clerical error.
116   NAA: B2455, Forsyth, S.C.K., item barcode 31849909.
117   NAA: B2455 Eddie, A., item barcode 3534085.
118   ancestry.com.au
119   NAA: B2455, Somny, G.V., item barcode 8088744.
120   The *West Australian*, 12 December 1935, p. 21.
121   NAA: B2455, McKay, J.B., item barcode 1948154.
122   NAA: B2455, Pines, M.C., item barcode 8014906.
123   NAA: B2455, Riley, J.C., item barcode 8032615.
124   *Cairns Post*, 3 May 1941, p. 6.
125   *The King's School Magazine*, December 1979. The King's School Archive Collection.
126   NAA: B2455, Simpson, R.J., item barcode 6157585.
127   The *Muswellbrook Chronicle*, 26 May 1940, p. 6.
128   The *Muswellbrook Chronicle*, 21 June 1940, p. 7.
129   The *Muswellbrook Chronicle*, 18 July 1941, p. 6.
130   The *Singleton Argus*, 22 February 1952, p. 1.
131   NAA: B2455, Holley, A.G., item barcode 5827676.
132   The *Argus*, 10 October 1925, p. 15.
133   The *Argus*, 21 September 1926, p. 1.
134   *Australian Town and Country Journal*, 1 June 1904, p. 35.
135   The *Cumberland Argus and Fruitgrowers Advocate*, 4 April 1900, p. 2.
136   The *Richmond River Herald and Northern District Advertiser*, 8 February 1916, p. 3.
137   NAA: B2455,Bosanquet, L.G.V., item barcode 3099579.
138   The King's School Archive Collection; e-mail November 2014.
139   NAA: B2455, Arnott, F., item barcode 3036152.
140   Cohn, L.R., letter, 12 February 1919.
141   Ibid., 28 April 1919.

Part 2

1.   The term 'super weapon' was used during the First World War, but only rarely. It came into more general use in the 1930s and rose to particular prominence during and after the Second World War. However, within the context of the First World War, the tank can be described as the 'super weapon' of that era.

2.   Australian casualties during the Gallipoli campaign in 1915 exceeded 26,000 and, in July and August of 1916, the AIF suffered more than 28,000 casualties in just three battles on the Western Front: Fromelles, Pozières and Mouquet Farm. While casualty rates rose, enlistments declined; only 12,515 enlisted during July–August 1916. The AIF was literally bleeding at an unsustainable rate. Although conscription was introduced in other Commonwealth countries, the first conscription referendum in Australia in October 1916 was soundly defeated. Figures from A.G. Butler, *Official History of the Australian Army Medical Services 1914-1918*, Vol. III, *Problems and Services*, AWM, Canberra, 1943. Additional information supplied by Brad Manera, Manager, Anzac Memorial, Sydney.

3. C.E.W. Bean, *Official History of Australia in the War of 1914-18*, Vol. III, *The AIF in France 1916*, Angus & Robertson, Sydney, 1929, p. 900. The diorama 'Somme Winter 1916' at the Australian War Memorial includes several tank hulks lying bogged and wrecked forward of the Australian trenches.

4. Bean, *Official History*, Vol. III, *The AIF in France 1916*, p. 905.

5. At least two, build numbers 586 and 799, were training tanks built of plates without case-hardened armour and never intended for combat use. Their capture and testing misled the Germans into the belief that their current issue armour-piercing small arms ammunition would penetrate British tank hulls. Jack Sheldon, 'Bullecourt: Day of Disaster', *Wartime*, Issue 63, winter 2013, p. 17.

6. Twelve were allocated, but one had suffered mechanical failure and was withdrawn.

7. C.E.W. Bean, *Official History of Australia in the War of 1914-18*, Vol. IV, *The AIF in France 1917*, Angus & Robertson, Sydney, 1933, p. 295. Although the lack of tank support was regarded as a failure by the Australians, the Germans under attack took a different view, the after-action report explicitly stating that 'the Australian troops exploited the momentary confusion and uncertainty which seized the fighting troops when the tanks appeared.' Sheldon 'Bullecourt: Day of Disaster', p. 18.

8. Bean, *Official History*, Vol. IV, *The AIF in France 1917*, p. 316.

9. Ibid.

10. Ibid., pp. 295, 297.

11. Ibid., p. 353.

12. Ibid., p. 421.

13. It was the Battle of Hamel that the Royal Tank Corps chose to commemorate with the presentation of a Silver Mk. V tank to the Australian Tank Corps in February 1935. See David Finlayson, 'Kinship and Co-operation. The Silver Mark V Tank' in *Ironsides*, Royal Australia Armoured Corps, March 2012, pp. 14–15.

14. The *Adelaide Mail*, Saturday 16 September 1916, p. 1 (Ref. A7375).

15. The *Argus*, Wednesday 20 September 1916, p. 9 (Ref. A7383).

16. *Launceston Examiner*, Saturday 30 September 1916, p. 7 (Ref. A7386).

17. The *Leader*, Saturday 23 September 1916, p. 32 (Ref. A7285).

18. The *Adelaide Register*, Saturday 16 December 1916, p. 11 (Ref. A7392).

19. W. Hudson Burnet, first published in *London Opinion*, partial quote from the complete poem reprinted in the *Adelaide Register*, Saturday 16 December 1816, p. 11 (Ref. A7392).

20. Gerald Frederic Dunning Acraman, 'Autobiography of a Tank', *Southern Argus*, Thursday 5 April 1917, p. 3. SX3183 G.F.D. Acraman served with an artillery unit in the 9th Australian Infantry Division during the Second World War, attaining the rank of bombardier.

21. 'Tommy's Tank', the *Shepparton Advertiser*, 28 September 1916.

22. 'A "Tank" for Australia': the *Argus*, Melbourne, Wednesday 2 May 1917, p. 9 (A7430). The report was published widely in, for example, the *Brisbane Courier*, the *Daily News* (Perth) and *The West Australian*, with most publishing the same text under different headlines. The *Ballarat Courier* in Victoria and the *Barrier Miner* in NSW embellished the story, however, by stating that the request was for 'the armored "tank" which supported the Australians in the attack upon Pozieres last year …' (*Barrier Miner*,

Tuesday 1 May 1917, p. 4). The Australian attacks on Pozières occurred during July-August 1916, well before the first combat use of the tank in mid-September, and several months before the first Australian operation which included tank support, the First Battle of Bullecourt, in April 1917. Placing the word 'tank' in quotation marks was common during the early years of reporting on the vehicle.

23. 'Tank for Australia', *Bendigo Advertiser*, Friday 25 January 1918, p. 5.

24. As would be the case when the Mk. IV tank 'Britannia' was sent to the Allied War Exposition in the US in mid-1918.

25. 'Report on Australian Personnel' by General Officer Commanding the Tank Corps Training Centre, Bovington Camp, UK (undated), appended to Minute from Assistant Adjutant General, Administrative Headquarters, AIF, to Transport Section, 8 May 1918. The ranks shown are as listed in the course report (Ref. A2147).

26. The *Boorara* was a historically significant ship. Built as the SS *Pfalz* in 1913 in Germany, the 6570-ton steamship was in Port Phillip Bay, Victoria, and heading for the open seas on 5 August 1914 when war with Germany was declared. The Royal Australian Garrison Artillery battery on Point Nepean was ordered to prevent the ship's departure. The ship initially ignored signals to stop, so a 6-inch round was fired across her bows as she approached Port Phillip Heads. This was the first shot to be fired in the First World War. The Commonwealth pilot aboard the *Pfalz* convinced the ship's master that the next round would likely be at the ship, rather than cautionary. Realising that any attempt to flee would probably end with the sinking of his ship, the master turned about and berthed at Portsea, where the crew was interned. The ship was then taken on charge by the RAN and converted to a troopship. Presumably, the ship's bell of the *Pfalz* was removed during the conversion. According to David Finlayson, it was still in daily use in the 1970s as the school bell at Ivanhoe Grammar.

27. Letter to Secretary, Department of Defence, Melbourne, from Commandant, AIF Administrative Headquarters, London: 'Tank for Australia', 22 March 1918 (Ref. Ab17186; A2226).

28. For example, The *Horsham Times*, Friday 17 May 1918, p. 5 and the *Leader* (Melbourne), Saturday May 18, 1918, p. 36.

29. HMAT A42 *Boorara* was put back into service, but suffered damage from another torpedo strike on 23 July 1918 during a British coastal voyage. The torpedo, fired from *UC-70*, caused damage but no casualties. Repaired again, the ship continued in Commonwealth service until sold to Greek shipping interests in 1926, when it was renamed the SS *Nereus*. It was wrecked off Vancouver Island, Canada, on 8 August 1937.

30. Letter to Secretary, Department of Defence, Melbourne, from Commandant, AIF Administrative Headquarters, London: 'Tank for Australia', 8 May 1918 (Ref. Ab4337/8/1; A2240).

31. HMAT C4 *Dongarra* was also a captured German vessel, the 5566-ton SS *Stolzenfels*. The *Dongarra* survived the war and remained in Commonwealth service until 1925, when it was sold and renamed the SS *Kotka*. In 1927 it was sold again, becoming the SS *Benvrackie*. The ship was broken up in 1931.

32. Letter to Secretary, Department of Defence, Melbourne, from Commandant, AIF Administrative Headquarters, London: 'Tank for Australia', 8 May 1918 (Ref. Ab4337/8/1; A2240).

33. See, for example, 'Tank for Australia' in the *West Gippsland Gazette*, Tuesday 2 July 1918, p. 2.

34. Letter to Assistant Adjutant General, Victoria Barracks, Melbourne, from Lieutenant Norman L Brown, OC Australian Tank, Eastwood, South Australia, 11 July 1918 (Ref: A2147).

35. See 'War Tank In Australia' in *The Register*, Adelaide, South Australia, Thursday 11 July 1918, p. 6.

36. The British Mk. IV Female was the first of three First World War tanks to arrive in Australia. On 22 July 1918, the 26th Infantry Battalion, AIF, with the assistance of the 1st Gun Carrier Company, retrieved the German A7V 'Mephisto' from no man's land in the Monument Wood area of the Western Front. It was claimed by Australia as a war trophy and landed in Brisbane in June 1919. In late 1921, the French government gifted several relics to the Australian War Museum, including a French Renault FT-17 Light Tank. Both the A7V and FT-17 were battle-damaged war relics and were not in operable condition.

37. 'War Tank In Melbourne': the *Argus*, Melbourne, Monday 15 July 1918, p. 4.

38. Vaughan's was a well-known local haulage company, though it is somewhat ironic that they were contracted for the task. Fiercely pro-Irish and anti-war, members of the Vaughan family were 'embroiled in the struggle against conscription' (Bruce Scates, *A Place to Remember*, Cambridge University Press, Melbourne, 2009, p. 99). Vaughan would later form a partnership with the stonemasons Lodge Brothers to form Vaughan and Lodge Pty Ltd, the builders of the Victorian Shrine of Remembrance in St Kilda Road, Melbourne.

39. Wednesday 17 July 1918. Curiously, the authority issued to 'Mr. Vaughan, Carrier' authorising him to move the 'military tank' from the wharf to the Victoria Barracks yard was dated 18 July 1918. All newspaper accounts, however, agree that the date the move took place was the Wednesday 17 July (Ref. A2240).

40. 'British Fighting Tank from the West Front Arrives in Melbourne': the *Leader*, Saturday 20 July 1918, p. 38 (Ref. A7302). The arrival and move from the wharf were widely reported. See, for example, the *Gippsland Times*, Thursday 18 July, p. 3; The *Argus*, Monday 15 July, p. 4; the *Adelaide Register*, Friday 19 July, p. 6; and the *Sydney Morning Herald*, Monday 15 July 1918, p. 7.

41. Minute from Adjutant General to Secretary, Department of Defence: 'Tank Personnel', 16 August 1918. The Minute was annotated by the CGS as quoted, with both the Chief of Ordnance and Quartermaster General noting their concurrence.

42. Minute from Secretary, Department of Defence to Minister for Defence: 'Tank Crew', undated reference A498/1/435. The minute was annotated by the Minister on 28 August with the direction to place the tank under the control of the Chief of Ordnance (Ref. A2148). Colonel Dangar also served on the Commonwealth Military Board throughout the First World War.

43. Hugh Victor McKay was awarded a Commander of the Order of the British Empire (CBE – Civil) on 15 March 1919 for services to war industries. His services included management of Grit and her crew until November 1918.

44. Minute from H.V. McKay, Member, Board of Business Administration to Finance Member, Melbourne: 'Tank Crew', 22 July 1918 (Ref. A2240).

45. Letter from Governor of South Australia to Minister for Defence, 19 July 1918 (Ref. A2240).

46. For example, the inability to exhibit the tank in aid of the Bridgewater-on-Loddon Red Cross Appeal, scheduled for 21 August, due to transport and scheduling difficulties, and the refusal to provide the tank for the 'Back to Ararat' Diamond Jubilee festivities from 24 to 31 December 1918 because the activity was not being held for patriotic fundraising purposes.

47. Minute from H.V. McKay to Minister for Defence: 'Tank', 25 July 1918, and Minister's annotated reply of 26 July 1918 (Ref. A2240).

48. The press release was included in many weekly papers the Monday after the event. See, for example, the *Launceston Examiner*, which reported on Monday 29 July under the heading 'The Armoured Tank', with the date-line 'Melbourne, Friday' that 'tomorrow morning the armoured tank … will make its first trip through the streets of Melbourne' (Ref. A7317).

49. 'Tank in the City', the *Ballarat Courier*, Monday 29 July 1918, p. 3 (Ref. A7304).

50. Minute from H.V. McKay, Member, Board of Business Administration to Secretary, Department of Defence: 'Tank', 30 July 1918 (Ref. A2240).

51. Letter from War Tank Demonstration Committee to H.V. McKay, 10 September 1918 (Ref.A2236). The Royal Adelaide Show was in full swing at the time, located on a site just four kilometres north of Unley Oval.

52. .Now Belair Road.

53. 'War Tank in Adelaide', the *Adelaide Register*, Thursday 5 September 1918, p. 8.

54. 'War Tank Bonds', the *Mail*, Saturday 31 August 1918, p. 13.

55. Telegram from Duncan to McKay, 25 August 1918.

56. Baroness Marie Carola Franciska Roselyne d'Erlanger became Marie, Lady Galway when she married Sir Henry Lionel Galway, KCMG, DSO. Sir Henry Galway was the 17th Governor of South Australia, serving from 18 April 1914 to 30 April 1920.

57. The ceremony was reported on page 7 of the *Advertiser* on Monday, 16 September 1918.

58. 'War Tank Sensation', the *Adelaide Register*, Thursday 12 September 1918 (Ref. A7321).

59. Possibly on or adjacent to the site of the current war memorial on North Terrace. The 'Bank of Thrift' was a physical expression of the South Australian Central War Loan Committee's slogan 'Thrift in the Home and Victory in the Field'.

60. 'The Seventh War Loan', the *Advertiser*, Tuesday 17 September 1918 (Ref A2770).

61. The Returned Soldiers Association evolved into the Returned Sailors, Soldiers and Airmen's Imperial League of Australia, today's Returned and Services League of Australia.

62. 'The Seventh War Loan', sub section 'In Other States', the *Age*, Tuesday 17 September 1918, p. 5. Blackburn was famous even before the award of the VC, as he was reputed to have been the Australian who made the deepest penetration into Turkish territory immediately following the landing at Anzac Cove on 25 April 1915. Brad Manera, personal communication, August 2013.

63. Witness Statement of Staff Sergeant C.R. Jackson, proceedings of the Court of Inquiry, convened at Sydney, 12 October 1918 (Ref. A2149).

64. 'Larceny of Tank fittings on the Defence Dept. between Adelaide – vide the attached file', F. Hawkins, Detective, CIB Melbourne, 23 January 1919 (Ref. A2149).

65. Memorandum from H.V. McKay, Member, Board of Business Administration to Secretary, Department of Defence, 24 July 1918 (Ref. A2240).

66. 'War Loan at The Show', the *Age,* Thursday 26 September 1918, p. 18 (Ref. A2770).

67. 'The Royal Show – Last Day's Events – War Tank Demonstration', the *Argus*, Monday 30 September 1918, p. 4 (Ref. A7341)

68. 'Seventh War Loan – Subscriptions at Royal Show', the *Age*, Monday 30 September 1918 (Ref. A2770).

69. 'A British Tank', *Sydney Morning Herald*, Friday 4 October 1918, p. 7 (Ref. A7319).

70. 'The Tank in Action', *Sydney Morning Herald*, Monday 28 October 1918, p. 6 (Ref. A7318).

71. The precedent of a school's half-holiday for major public events had been set in 1911 when the American Great White Fleet visited Sydney. It was repeated in 1941 when the crew of HMAS *Sydney* paraded through the streets following the ship's return from operations in the Mediterranean. Brad Manera, personal communication, August 2013.

72. 'The Tank in Action', *Sydney Morning Herald*, Monday 28 October 1918, p. 6 (Ref. A7318).

73. Letter from Mr Macquire, Department of Defence, to Mr H.V. McKay, 9 January 1919 (Ref. B411/5/46; A2234).

74. Apparently the finalisation of the tank's use in the Sydney area was also beset with difficulties. Captain Brown was sent to Sydney in late November to arrange for the return of stores and equipment used in conjunction with the displays, and subsequently held in the Ordnance Store, to their private owners, and to 'assist as far as possible in clearing up points under dispute between representatives of Jacks Day and Dependants' (Chief of Ordnance instruction to Captain Brown, 28 November 1918, Ref. A2233).

75. 'Tank Coming To Brisbane', *Brisbane Courier*, Tuesday 8 October 1918, p. 6 (Ref A7311).

76. Letter from Mr Longbottom, Secretary, the Motor Traders' Association of Queensland, to H.V. McKay, Business Board of Administration, 5 November 1918 (Ref. A2238).

77. Telegram H.V. McKay to Captain N.L. Brown, 6 November 1918 (Ref. A2238).

78. Letter from H.V. McKay to Captain N.L. Brown, 13 November 1918 (Ref. A2233).

79. The Mk. IV Female crew normally comprised eight personnel, four of whom were Lewis machine-gunners who were not required for crewing the tank in Australia. Hence, Brown and Fleming instructed four men under the command of a sergeant.

80. Letter from Mr. G.D. Portus, YMCA, to Colonel H.W. Dangar, 5 December 1918 (Ref. A2233).

81. Letter from Colonel H.W. Dangar, Chief of Ordnance, to Commandant, 1st Military District, 25 February 1919 (Ref. 411/5/53; A2235).

82. File Note, 21 March 1919 (Ref. A2235).

83. Minute from Colonel H.W. Dangar, Chief of Ordnance, to Commandant 3rd Military District. 27 March 1919 (Ref. B411/5/60; A2235). Quarantine restrictions were in place at each state border, adding several days to the trip.

84. Undertaking by Hanlon and Baldwin to Assistant Quartermaster General, 1st Military District, 3 April 1919 (Ref. 411/5/62; A2235).

85. 'Memorial Day Celebrations – Inspection of the Battle "Tank" – Arrangements for the Procession', *Brisbane Courier*, Tuesday 22 April 1919, p. 6.

86. Ibid.

87. 'Wanton Attack on the Battle "Tank"', *Brisbane Courier*, Saturday 26 April 1919, p. 4.

88. References conflict on the date the crew returned to Melbourne. While one states that the crew returned on 10 and 12 May, the travelling allowance summary states that Hosking returned to Melbourne on 28 April, McDonald on 7 May, Cook on 8 May, and

the remainder on 10 May. This seems to be at odds with the requirement to piquet the tank during its rail journey, which concluded on 12 May.

89. 'March through the City', the *Argus*, Monday 21 July 1919, p. 7 (Ref. A7432).

90. Minute from Chief of Ordnance to Secretary, Department of Defence, 'War Tank – Retention of Services of Captain Brown', 28 June 1919 (Ref A559/11/205; A2148). Norman Brown had been seriously injured in an accident aboard his troopship and a steel plate had been inserted in his skull. He suffered debilitating headaches as a result.

91. Military Board Agenda Number 176/19: War Tank – Retention of Services of Captain Brown.

92. Minute from Chief of Ordnance to Commandant 3rd Military District, 9 September 1919 (Ref. 411/5/71; A2148).

93. Ibid., Ref. B411/5/70; A2148.

94. Minute from Secretary, Department of Defence to Chief of Ordnance, 18 September 1919 (Ref. 411/5/73; A2148).

95. There is no indication of how this was achieved, but it is likely that Grit was driven the 8.5 kilometres.

96. Minute from Commandant, 3rd Military District to Secretary Department of Defence, 22 September 1919 (Ref. 411/5/75; A2148).

97. Minute from Commandant, 3rd Military District, to Chief of Ordnance and Secretary, Department of Defence, 29 October 1919 (Ref. 411/5/98; A2231).

98. Letter from Mr Agar Wynne, MLA, to Secretary, Department of Defence, 29 October 1919 (Ref. A2231).

99. The problem with the non-payment of the Brisbane trip accounts was not evident at that time.

100. Telegram from Administrator, Rabaul, to Secretary, Department of Defence, Melbourne, 23 August 1920 (Ref. B411-5-102; A2228).

101. The three claims were: £5500 for the tank, £1453-10-9 for equipment and £657-16-7 for the five Lewis light machine-guns with spares, totalling £7611-7-4. This was a slightly different itemisation to the original claims.

102. Letter from OIC AIF Cadre, Administrative Headquarters, London, to Secretary, Department of Defence, Melbourne: 'Tank and Accessories, etc, supplied by the Imperial Government for use in Australia', 10 February 1921 (Ref. 411/5/117; A2228).

103. Memorandum from Henry Gullett, Director, Australian War Museum to Secretary, Department of Defence, 23 February 1920 (Ref. 411/5/90; A2228).

104. Minute from Chief of Ordnance to Secretary, Department of Defence, 'War Tank – Transfer to Australian War Museum', 2 March 1920 (Ref. B411/5/90; A2228).

105. A roll of tape was also required to temporarily secure the water connections for the short trip through Melbourne to the Exhibition Buildings. The tape was sticky-backed and made of cloth which was wrapped around the radiator hose connections to prevent leakage during the short journey: a temporary 'fix'.

106. 'Items of Interest – Tank for War Museum', the *Argus*, Saturday 15 October 1921, p. 20 (Ref. A7414).

107. Major E.A. Wilton was the inventor of the Wilton trailer for the carriage of field artillery guns and limbers when towed behind a mechanical tractor. This was one of the earliest attempts in Australia to mechanise field artillery. Wilton died suddenly in early 1932.

108. Internal memorandum, J.L. Treloar to 'Nich', 12 January 1932 (Ref. A2225). A footnote indicated that action had been taken to close the tank, and that pilfering was indicated as there were some minor parts left loose inside the tank, but that it was 'impracticable to see whence they came'.

109. NAA: B2455, Brown, N.L., item barcode 1800629.

110. Ibid.

111. The *Sydney Morning Herald*, 27April 1949, p. 14.

112. Ibid., p. 24.

113. www.ww2roll.gov.au

114. The *Port Melbourne Standard*, 10 February 1914, p. 3.

115. NAA: B2455 Dalton, R.T., item barcode 3484504.

116. The *Williamstown Chronicle*, 12 August 1922, p. 2.

117. www.ww2roll.gov.au

118. www.ww2roll.gov.au

119. NAA: B2455, Fleming, F.G., item barcode 3912451.

120. ancestry.com.au

121. NAA: B2455, Gifford, F.A., item barcode 5033507.

122. The *Border Watch*, various dates 1920–61.

123. H. Fairclough, *Equal to the Task. The History of the Royal Australian Army Service Corps*, F.W. Cheshire, Melbourne, 1962, pp. 9–10.

124. NAA: B2455, Jackson, C.R., item barcode 7373005.

125. ancestry.com.au

126. Fairclough, *Equal to the Task*, pp. 9–10.

127. NAA: B2455, Lord, D.B., item barcode 8204867.

128. Ibid.

129. ancestry.com.au

130. D. Finlayson, *Crumps and Camouflets, Australian Tunnelling Companies on the Western Front*, Big Sky Publishing, Newport, 2010, pp. 61–62.

131. NAA: B2455, McFadden, M.G., item barcode 1943168.

132. ancestry.com.au

133. NAA: B2455, Rowland, A.R., item barcode 8072228.

134. ancestry.com.au

135. www.ww2roll.gov.au

136. NAA: B2455, Swain, H.S., item barcode 8070783.

137. ancestry.com.au

138. NAA: B4717, Cook, Stanley Brensley, item barcode 30107584.

139. The *Mercury*, 2 June 1931, p. 9.

140. NAA: B2455, Hosking, F.A., item barcode 5821871.

141. The *Argus*, 7 October 1925, p. 17.

142. NAA: B2455, Kubale, A.H., item barcode 7375558.

143. The *Argus*, 24 November 1953, p. 9.

144. www.ww2roll.gov.au

145. NAA: B2455, Marnie, W.K., item barcode 8213727.

146. R.J. Rayner, *Darwin Detachment, A Military and Social History*, Rudder Press, Wollongong, 2002.

147. The *Sydney Morning Herald*, 20 February 1939, p. 12.
148. www.ww2roll.gov.au
149. ancestry.com.au
150. *Queenscliff Sentinel*, 3 June 1916, p. 2.
151. NAA: B2455, McDonald, E.Mc., item barcode 840129.
152. The *Argus*, 3 February 1918, p. 4. His Military Medal was gazetted in the London *Gazette*, no. 30507 of 4 February.
153. www.ww2roll.gov.au
154. www.ww2roll.gov.au
155. NAA: B4717, Nicholson William Davidson, item barcode 4169586. Nicholson's enlistment documents give his year of birth as 1879. However, other evidence indicates that he was actually born in 1874.
156. ancestry.com.au
157. The *Argus*, 2 January 1925, p. 5.
158. The *Argus*, 20 January 1925, p. 3.
159   These notes were part of a presentation to a meeting of Volunteer Defence Corps by Captain James in 1941. They provide brief insight into the organisation and operation of a Light Car Patrol as recalled by James.

BIBLIOGRAPHY

Primary source collections

Cohn Collection

A chance conversation led to the eleventh hour discovery of Leo Cohn's letters and a series of photos. Leo joined the 1st Light Car Patrol in Palestine in 1917 and wrote a series of detailed observations on the patrol's experiences in the closing period of the war and the period of occupation in Syria. These letters were preserved by Leo Cohn's daughter Helen Bruinier and, thankfully, transcribed by granddaughter Shelley Cohn.

Cornwell Collection

Held by the Army Tank Museum. It consists of two photo albums which were donated to the Museum by Cornwell's grandson. The photos show the day-to-day life of the unit and the officers of the British Armoured Car units.

Creek Collection

Access provided by the Creek family in 2014. A series of photo albums, individual images, souvenirs and press cuttings relating to Herbert Creek's life.

Harkin Collection

Held by the Army Tank Museum. Donated to the Museum by Henry Harkin's great nephew, Henry Harkin Junior, in 2005. Artefacts include personal items, a Royal Victorian Medal and a series of commercial photographs of the unit.

James Collection

Held at the Army Tank Museum. Consists of Captain James' personal papers from the period 1916 to 1919. They include various original documents, random papers, photos and a series of exercise books that contain the day-to-day existence of the Armoured Car Section, 1st Australian Armoured Car Battery and 1st Light Car Patrol periods. It is evident that these papers were the primary source for *The Motor Patrol*. In 2013 additional material was added to this collection by the James family.

Morgan Collection

Access provided by Henry Morgan's family in 2014. Contains a series of individual images relating to Henry Morgan's life and service.

Young Collection

Access provided by the Young family in 2014. Extensive photo albums and individual images outlining the Royal Park, Egyptian and early Sinai periods, these albums proved invaluable as most images were captioned. Combined with Ivan Young's letters from the *Nhill Free Press* they effectively document the unit's history in a comprehensive manner.

The descendants of the 'Pioneers of Armour' have certainly inherited their ancestors' sense of comradeship and pride as all material has been shared without hesitation or reservation. Copies of these collections can now be found at the Army Tank Museum.

Books

Bean, C.E.W., *Official History of Australia in the War of 1914-18*, Vol. III, *The AIF in France 1916*, Angus & Robertson, Sydney, 1929.

——, *Official History of Australia in the War of 1914-18*, Vol. IV, *The AIF in France 1917*, Angus & Robertson, Sydney, 1929.

Butler, A.G., *Official History of the Australian Army Medical Services 1914-1918*, Vol. III, *Problems and Services*, AWM, Canberra, 1943.

Cohn, A.A., Cohn, J.M. and Cohn, L.J., *Tablets of Memory. The Bendigo Cohns and their Descendants 1853-1989*, Antelope Press, Doncaster, 1990.

Curkpatrick, K.M., *Saddle to Boots. A history of the 19th (Aust) Machine Gun Battalion*, self-published, Warracknabeal, 1990.

Droogleever, R., *That Ragged Mob*, Trogan Press, Melbourne, 2009.

Fairclough, H., *Equal to the Task. The History of the Royal Australian Army Service Corps*, F.W. Cheshire, Melbourne, 1962.

Finlayson, Damien, *Crumps and Camouflets, Australian Tunnelling Companies on the Western Front*, Big Sky Publishing, Newport, 2010.

McGuirk, Russell, *The Sanusi's Little War*, Arabian Publishing, London, 2007.

Perrett, Bryan, *Megiddo 1918. The last great cavalry victory*, Osprey, Oxford, 2005.

Rayner, R.J., *Darwin Detachment, A Military and Social History*, Rudder Press, Wollongong, 2002.

Scates, Bruce, *A Place to Remember. A History of the Shrine of Remembrance*, Cambridge University Press, Melbourne, 2009.

Williams, C. and McGuirk, R., *Light Car Patrols 1916-19. War and Exploration in Libya with the Model T Ford*, Silphium Press, London, 2013.

Smith James. *The Cyclopedia of Victoria*, Vol. III. The Cyclopedia Company Melbourne 1903.

Reserve of Officers List 1946, Part 2.

Journals

Cecil, Michael, 'Grit, Australia's First Tank', *Ironsides*, Journal of the Royal Australian Armoured Corps, 2001.

Coady, Mr 'The First Australian Armoured Cars', *RAAC Bulletin*, 1972.

Finlayson, David, 'I'm sitting at Uncle Henry's Desk', *Ironsides*, 2006.

——, 'Kinship and Co-operation. The Silver Mark V Tank', *Ironsides*, 2012.

——, 'Australia's First Mechanized Arms Officer', *Ironsides*, 2013.

——, 'Serviens. Australia's First Mechanized Sergeants', *Ironsides*, 2014.

Finlayson, David and Cecil, Michael, 'Pioneers of Australian Armour. The Armoured Car Section and 1st Light Car Patrol', *Ironsides*, 2005.

Sheldon, Jack, 'Bullecourt: Day of Disaster. The Assault seen from the German side of the wire', *Wartime: The Official Magazine of the Australian War Memorial*, Issue 63, winter 2013.

Sweeting, A.J., 'Langley, Hudson John Watson (1894–1919)', *Australian Dictionary of Biography*, Vol. 9, Melbourne University Press, 1983.

The Victorian Government *Gazette* (various).

Websites

ancestry.com.au
australianfootball.com
www.cv.vic.gov.au
www.ww2roll.gov.au

Newspapers

The *Adelaide Mail*
The *Adelaide Register*
The *Advertiser*
The *Age*
The *Argus*
The *Australian Town and Country Journal*
The *Ballarat Courier*
The *Bendigonian*
The *Bendigo Advertiser*
The *Barrier Miner*
The *Border Watch*
The *Brisbane Courier*
The *Brunswick and Coburg Leader*
The *Canberra Times*
The *Coburg Leader*
The *Cumberland and Fruitgrowers Advocate*
The *Cumberland Evening Times*
The *Daily Herald*
The *Egyptian*
The *Hamilton Spectator*
The *Horsham Times*
The *Mail*
The *Launceston Examiner*
The *Leader*
The *Mercury*
The *Newcastle Morning Herald and Miners Advocate*
The *Nhill Free Press*
The *Port Melbourne Standard*
The *Port Pirie Recorder and North Western Mail*
The *Register*
The *Shepparton Advertiser*
The *Sydney Morning Herald*
The *Queenscliff Sentinel*
The *West Australian*
The *Williamstown Chronicle*

INDEX

Index

Adoption After
a Biological Child

Holly Marlow

Paperback ISBN: 978-1-7399168-6-2

DEDICATION

To my husband, Jon. I'm so glad I'm going through these wild and wonderful parenting adventures with you. You are the best Dad and husband imaginable, and you make every day better. Now for goodness' sake, would you please call that plumber?

CONTENTS

DISCLAIMER

This is a true autobiographical account of my experiences as I remember them, and I believe my memories to be accurate. Although I occasionally mix up my children's names in the moment, or search for the car keys that are in my pocket, I have always found my long-term memory to be fairly reliable. Some chapters have been written while referring to old diary entries.

I have changed the names of social workers, and of my son's birth and foster family, to maintain privacy, and I have used general labels such as "a friend" and job titles such as "the social worker" (some of whom were family support workers, social work assistants, managers, etc), to preserve anonymity... and partly because I never really pay much attention to job titles.

ACKNOWLEDGEMENTS

Many thanks to Jon, Mum, Dad, Suzy, Marie and Chris, for your help and encouragement throughout the editing process. Thank you to all of my wonderful family and friends, Mama Lynn and her team at the orphanages in Tanzania, the amazing online community of adopters who have supported me, especially in the "You've Adopted. What Now? (YAWN)" and "Adoption or Fostering after a Biological Child" Facebook groups, and all the social workers and support workers who we met throughout the adoption process.

MY STORY

I am a Mum to a biological daughter (aged 7 at the time of writing) and an adopted son (aged 4 at the time of writing), who joined our family when he was 13 months old. It feels a little self-indulgent to give my own story so much attention, when my son is the one whose life was the most radically affected by adoption, but the details of his story are not mine to tell, so the emotions and experiences shared within this book are mine.

If you're a parent considering adopting your next child and wondering what it will be like to adopt when you already have a biological child (or more than one), I hope that you find this helpful, relatable and reassuring. It's worth noting that although I will talk about how I handled certain situations, I do not claim to be a parenting expert, and this isn't intended as advice for how you should parent your children. I've done my best, but that doesn't necessarily mean that my way is the best way, or that I disapprove if you've parented differently!

A note for my readers who are used to reading non-British variations of English:

I'm British, so I have used British English spellings and terminology (which include more "u"s than American English, for example, and there's often an "s" where you might expect a "z"). These are intentional! I'm afraid that you'll just need to ignore the "u"s, but here are some "z"s that you can mentally switch for "s" wherever you see fit: ZZZZZZZZZZZZZZZZZZZ.

FIRST THOUGHTS OF ADOPTION

When I was 17, I had an adventure in Africa with a group of friends and a teacher from school. We went on safari, climbed Mount Hanang and Mount Kilimanjaro, then spent a week helping at an orphanage. When we weren't fixing things, building play equipment or helping in the kitchens, we played with the children. The first lunchtime, as I finished handing out bowls of beef and rice to the children, Mama Lynn, the amazing lady who founded the orphanage, explained that there weren't enough adoptive families around, so she had recently needed to set up a second site, to expand the orphanage. I looked in disbelief at the gorgeous, chuckling children tucking into their beef and rice in front of me and wondered how it could be possible that people weren't fighting to be their parents. Mama Lynn told me about some of the children.

One little boy with beautiful eyes and a cracking sense of humour had been brought to her at 3 years old, addicted to various drugs. His father was in prison for attempted murder, and his mother (who was responsible for his drug addiction) had died. A few months later, he told Mama Lynn that he wanted to change his name, because he wouldn't be hurt any more if he was someone else. Another beautiful boy had inverted eyelashes that were destroying his sight. Mama Lynn winced as she told me that she didn't have parental rights for him, so his aunt was required to approve any medical procedures. The team at the orphanage were trying to persuade the little boy's aunt to allow them to pay for surgery to save his sight, but so far, she had refused to authorise it. They were struggling to understand why, or what they could do to change her mind before it was too late.

After the meal, we went to the second orphanage site, where there were a lot of new children who had been brought in from another orphanage that closed down the week before. Laughing and smiling, the children rushed up to shake hands with us, then they gathered together and sang some welcome songs in English and Swahili. I felt overwhelmed that our visit was so exciting to them.

We helped the orphanage staff to prepare food packages to take to the local Maasai tribal village, where many of the children had come from. The kindness of this organisation touched me. Looking back now, I see that it was a smart move, as well as kind. Perhaps a weekly food delivery might mean that the local community would be better able to take care of their children within their families. While we were decanting a huge sack of rice into smaller portions to be given to each family, there was a commotion. A little girl, perhaps six or seven years old, was brought in. I felt sick with horror when I saw the burns on her face and arms. One of the orphanage staff explained that she had just been brought in by a family friend who wanted her to be protected, because her parents had badly burned her whilst drunk. My friends and I gasped in unison, revealing our sheltered childhoods. How can that happen? How can parents burn their children? Many things have become clearer to me with age and experience, but that remains a terrible mystery.

We camped in the grounds of the orphanage, but cooked and ate separately to the people living and working at the orphanage, so that we wouldn't be a drain on their resources. My friend Harriet and I were in charge of making dinner for the volunteer group that night. We were making rice and a packet of freeze-dried camping food mix that purported to taste like beef hotpot. Several weeks into eating these packets, I knew they all tasted like vegetable mush, regardless of what flavour they claimed to be. I felt weary, as I stirred it into some boiling iodine-cleansed water. I was physically exhausted from the previous weeks, which we had spent climbing mountains and camping, but that was nothing compared to the emotional drain. As I stirred, I pictured the smiling children, laughing over dinner and singing their welcome songs so joyfully. Many of those children had HIV or AIDS. Some had been mistreated by the people who should love them most. They seemed so happy, despite their trauma and health struggles. Mama Lynn and her kind and nurturing team must be incredible. I wondered where they found their strength.

A huge pink locust jumped into the pot and plunged deep into the boiling mixture. I looked up. My eyes met with Harriet's, and I could tell she'd seen it too. I sighed pathetically. "Protein," she said, with a wink. Relieved, I kept stirring. Fishing a locust out of the soupy sludge didn't feel important. It wouldn't have survived anyway. I let my mind go back to processing this strange world, where babies didn't have the safe, nurturing beginning in life that I had been so privileged to experience.

TRYING

Several years after marrying my husband, Jon, we felt ready to expand our family. Ever since my experiences in Tanzania, I had been keen to adopt "one day," but we decided to have biological children first. Even with my limited knowledge of trauma at that stage, I thought that adopting would be harder and that I'd be better at adoptive parenting if I had experienced biological parenting. I also wanted to experience pregnancy. It's one of life's big experiences that lots of people have been through and I didn't want to wonder if I'd missed out.

I coped terribly with not getting pregnant for the first couple of months. I felt heartbroken and let down by my body. I didn't have the ability to "just see how it goes and if we get pregnant, it will be a nice surprise," which was the approach many of our friends took. That's not me. We had decided we were trying, so I needed it to happen. It was all I thought about. I took pre-natal supplements for 3 months before we even started trying, to make sure my body was ready. I had an irregular and long cycle, so I didn't know when my fertile window was. I was deeply frustrated when after 7 weeks I was still getting negative results on pregnancy tests, thinking that my period was 3 weeks late. I've always been quite practical and keen to problem-solve, so I started taking some additional supplements to regulate my cycle. I bought ovulation tests to figure out when I had the best chance of conceiving and every morning, I tracked my basal temperature (the temperature under

my tongue within a minute of waking up, before sitting up –
apparently these details count!), having learned that it would
increase for several days after ovulation. This charting enabled me
to calculate when would be the right day to take a pregnancy test,
which was hugely helpful for my mental health, as I wasn't
convincing myself I'd been pregnant for weeks before I'd even
ovulated. I took better care of my body than ever. I gave up alcohol,
caffeine, chocolate and all kinds of takeaway foods. I ate kale!

They say it's important to avoid stress while pregnant. Well, I
certainly didn't manage that at the start. I had recently taken on
additional responsibilities at work, having fallen for that "prove
yourself in this role and you'll get that promotion" con. One
Thursday morning, I turned off the car engine and checked my
phone before going in to the office. I saw that my sweet friend had
sent a message to let all her friends know that her long battle with
cancer had almost reached its end. She asked friends to give her
space, because she wanted to spend her last few days with her
husband. Distraught, I drove home to work from there, so that I
wouldn't need to face anyone except my own husband. I grieved
the strange sort of pre-grief that happens when you know
something miserable is coming, although it hasn't technically
happened yet.

After splashing my sore eyes with cold water, I bitterly looked
at the ovulation test kits and pregnancy tests in my bathroom and
felt like the universe owed me some happy news. The test was
negative, but I knew that pregnancy tests are most effective in the
morning, so the next morning, I tested again and was greeted with
two pink lines, confirming that I was pregnant. I was shocked!
Knowing the high risk of loss in the first few months of pregnancy,
I felt that I ought to be trying to stay calm, not getting my hopes
up, but I've never been much good at that. I rushed into our
bedroom and woke Jon up, squeaking "I'm pregnant!" at him.
"That's great," he muttered, rolling over sleepily. I stood frozen
for a few seconds, wondering if I should wake him up properly and
make sure he understood, or let him sleep, but his sleepy brain
processed it and woke him up before I decided. He rolled back over
and looked at me. "Are you sure?" he asked, rubbing his eyes. I

showed him the pregnancy test and he gave me a hug. I don't think he dared to believe it was true either!

At the weekend, a pick-pocket acquired my phone, bank cards and driving licence while I was shopping. Normally, I would be really stressed, but I didn't care. I was growing a baby! Nothing could bring me down! Then, when I was back at work on Monday, Jon called my work phone.

"Don't panic, but... don't come home."

"What, why?"

"The police have just picked me up. Apparently, some angry lady sent a death threat to the guy who used to live here and it included our address. She thinks he still lives here and she's threatened to come round with a gun."

"WHAT?!"

"Yeah... I'm just working from the police station and the police are going to watch our house for a few days, but they've suggested we find somewhere else to stay for a while."

We stayed with my sister and her husband until the police tracked down the person who made the threat and were satisfied that the threat was empty. My sister kept offering me wine, knowing how rough my week had been. I persuaded her that I was avoiding wine just in case I got pregnant soon. I have no idea how I resisted the urge to tell her I was pregnant for the rest of the week! We saw my parents and my other sister at the weekend and I told them all at once. It was very early on, but I didn't really share the popular mindset that you should wait until the 12-week scan to share the good news. I was raised in a family of celebrators. Mum once said "we celebrate the opening of an envelope in this family!" I also knew that, if something tragic happened, I would share that news with my family anyway, because I would want their support to help me through it. They were all thrilled for us, and after such an intense couple of weeks, it was wonderful to be surrounded by joy!

IN MY BLOOD

In June 2015, I was three months pregnant with my daughter, when my midwife advised me that the standard pregnancy blood tests had shown that I have rhesus-negative blood. I'd never heard of it! The midwife assured me that it would be fine. "There's no risk to your first pregnancy, and you will be given anti-D injections during pregnancy that keep your antibody levels down, to ensure that there is no risk to future pregnancies."

But it wasn't fine. There was a risk. The midwife went on to say that I would need to go to hospital for an extra injection within 48 hours if I had a bleed or any accidents, such as bumping my bump on a door handle, having to brake too hard in the car and feeling the seatbelt squash my bump, or falling over and landing on it. I panicked. I had experienced a bleed a few weeks earlier and had an ultrasound to check that everything was ok, but that was before anyone knew I had rhesus-negative blood.

The midwife advised against looking it up on the internet, to avoid unnecessary stress during pregnancy, but obviously as soon as I left the appointment, I looked it up on my phone. That was a window into a world of paranoia that I couldn't have imagined. It seems there are countless groups of conspiracy theorists who believe that people with rhesus-negative blood can shape-shift, or that they are aliens. While I am normally intrigued by the weird and wonderful conspiracy theories some people believe in, the worry for my baby was stronger than any curiosity. I quickly became irritated at the preposterous websites making it difficult for me to find scientific explanations of the risk to my pregnancy and any future pregnancies.

Eventually, I managed to find some informative websites that clarified things. If my baby's normal rhesus-positive blood somehow made its way into my rhesus-negative bloodstream, I would need an anti-D injection. Without the injection, my blood would treat Zoe's blood as a virus and develop antibodies to it, then attack any future baby that had rhesus-positive blood. Jon's rhesus-positive blood is the dominant blood type, so there was an 85% chance that future babies Jon and I created would have his blood type. The anti-D injections would prevent my body from generating any antibodies though, so it should all be fine.

A few months and three anti-D injections later, my incredible daughter, Zoe, was born. Labour was slow and horrible. Jon and I discussed during the three days of contractions that we would adopt any future babies. When Zoe was born, doctors tested the umbilical cord, then Zoe's blood. A matter-of-fact paediatrician advised that not only had our blood mixed and my body become ready to attack any future babies with Jon's blood type, the antibodies had also travelled through the placenta into Zoe's bloodstream and were attacking her. When I gasped, she reiterated that this is rare in the Western world, as the anti-D injections usually prevent antibodies from developing. Zoe would need medicine for 3 months to ensure that my blood didn't damage her and cause health conditions to develop, such as brain damage, deafness and blindness. I was speechless. We'd been reassured repeatedly that my blood posed *no risk* to the health of our first child.

When we were eventually discharged, I sat in the back of the car while Jon drove us home. I looked at the tiny little bundle in the car seat next to me and felt overwhelming responsibility. I must keep this beautiful child safe, healthy and happy. Breastfeeding was painful and relentless, but doctors told me that it would help her body in the fight against my rhesus-negative blood, so that was the only motivation I needed. My body had hurt her, so my body had to save her. My days (and nights!) were consumed with feeding her, changing her and getting her to sleep. We found ourselves in a repeating three-hour long cycle, trying to snatch little stretches of sleep. I heard Jon on the phone, telling a friend, "There are so many days, but they're all three hours long."

On one of those early days, a letter arrived from the hospital. It said "Your child has been diagnosed with Haemolytic Disease of the Newborn" and explained in medical terms what had happened and the importance of the medicine that we were already giving Zoe daily. Although we knew this, we hadn't heard the term "Haemolytic Disease of the Newborn." Somehow that made it seem even scarier.

The medicine worked well, so Zoe didn't develop any symptoms, but I still feel sick remembering how it felt waiting for her 3-weekly blood test results to check that the medicine was working... to check that my body wasn't destroying my baby. I have had a lot of health problems over the years, but I have never felt so betrayed by my own body. The doctors asked me with great concern whether it had been difficult to get her to swallow the medicine, and whether I was confident that she hadn't vomited it up. They didn't need to keep telling me how important it was to remember her medicine – I was too terrified to forget! - but they reminded me in grave tones at every appointment, just to be sure. Every time they pricked her heel and squeezed the blood out, she screamed, and I inwardly cursed my blood for making my little baby need extra blood tests. Finally, after 12 weeks of medicine and testing, a doctor confirmed that Zoe's blood had won in the fight against mine, and she no longer had Haemolytic Disease of the Newborn. I wept with relief!

Doctors told us that we could still have more children biologically, but that I would need to have regular blood tests to check antibody levels and might need blood transfusions into the womb. The baby might also need to be delivered early, by caesarean, to reduce the transfer of blood through the placenta. One doctor explained, "the risk was low with your first child, because the antibodies weren't there for the whole pregnancy, but now those antibodies are there. Your body is READY. Your blood is waiting to attack." That thought filled us with terror, so we considered other options. Adoption was already on our minds, but friends and family encouraged us to consider other ways to build our family, so we spent some time researching other possibilities. We just didn't feel excited about any of the other ways to build our family. They felt medical, scientific, and stressful. We kept coming back to adoption.

OF OUR OWN

When we started to tell other people about our plans to adopt, we were often asked, "don't you want a baby of your own? Are you sure you can love someone else's child as much as you love your daughter?" I was always bemused by that question. Nobody had ever suggested that I should marry a relative, so why would I need to be biologically-related to a child to love them? It's not genetics that make me love my family! Love is complicated, but as far as I'm concerned, shared DNA is not an essential requirement.

We had some very close friends who had children of a similar age to ours, and some had younger siblings. I loved those children, and looked after some of them for the odd day here and there. I felt that the more time I spent with them, the stronger our bond grew, so I knew that I would grow to love any child who joined our family. I could tell that they felt the same way too. At birthday parties for the children in our friendship group, if the children I'd babysat before couldn't see their parents, or if their parents were in the middle of a conversation, they'd ask me to get them food or a drink, or to come and play with them. Some would let me comfort them if they hurt themselves and I got to them before their own parent. They obviously didn't love me as deeply as they love their families, but after just a few days of babysitting, they clearly trusted that I could meet their needs. That gave me confidence that a child would grow to love me too and, at the very least, I could make a child feel safe and help them to understand that I'd always feed them and look after them.

Others asked "won't your adopted child resent Zoe?" and the truth was, I didn't know. I hoped we could avoid that and make both of our children feel immensely loved. I know plenty of families where the siblings are biologically-related and there are resentments there, so perhaps we would even be in a better position to avoid that because we'd be more vigilant to notice and prevent resentments between our children than we might have been if they'd both joined our family biologically.

Several people tried to talk us out of it, or gave advice about what we should and shouldn't consider. It was interesting and, at times, irritating. It's a rite of passage, I suppose. Pregnant women receive abundant unsolicited advice, so why should adopters be any different?

"Is there NO WAY that you can have another baby?" people asked. We could have tried, but the extra anti-D injections, transfusions and early caesarean section all sounded horribly stressful, not to mention the fact that none of these were guaranteed to fully protect our next child from my blood. I tried to explain this to a friend one day and as I spoke, I felt that my argument seemed weak. The doctor hadn't actually advised us against having more children. I wobbled. Maybe we should consider it more seriously?

I went to a chiropractor appointment, feeling confused. Zoe was with me, now toddling and babbling merrily at everyone in the waiting room. A lady in her fifties smiled at her. "I'd have loved to have a girl," she sighed. She went on to explain that she had rhesus-negative blood and had a similar experience to me during her first pregnancy and that her son was healthy after several weeks of medicine. She had then lost three baby girls just after the twenty-week scan and four other pregnancies too early to know the gender, before she eventually had a baby boy who shared her rhesus-negative blood type, so was able to grow safely in her womb. She spoke lightly, in the way you do when there are little children around, not really conveying what I assume was absolute devastation. I was horrified. When trying to get pregnant in the first place, I had felt miserable at the sight of a negative pregnancy test. There was no way I would cope with the heart-breaking losses that woman had faced. I didn't want to risk even one loss. I felt it would destroy me beyond emotional repair.

A few days later, I heard that an old friend had rhesus-negative blood too and her child had also had haemolytic disease of the newborn, but the medicine had not been as effective as it was for Zoe. She had brain damage and was partly deaf, partly blind and had some other problems with her muscles. These stories gave me renewed certainty that I didn't want to risk the heartbreak of losses, or the guilt of knowing that my child's health problems were because of my blood.

People asked what our other options were, to have a biological child using the wonders of modern medicine. It would have been scientifically possible to remove the rhesus-negative blood risk by using a surrogate with rhesus-positive blood, but who knows what other medical risks we would have introduced by going down that road? Alternatively, we could have used a sperm donor who had rhesus-negative blood like me, so that the antibodies in my blood wouldn't attack the growing baby.

We considered briefly whether there might be some clever doctor out there who could select rhesus-negative embryos and implant those into my womb, which would be a safe environment for a rhesus-negative baby. That felt cruel though, as it would be passing on the rhesus-negative gene intentionally, and potentially making it harder for our child to have their own biological children. As one doctor pointed out, at least we know Zoe won't have the same issue if she has children biologically, because her rhesus-positive blood won't behave in the same way.

More to the point, I just didn't feel comfortable with the idea of creating a baby scientifically. I still felt a pointless and unhelpful guilt because my body had made my daughter sick, even though she had been symptomless. I knew that I would never forgive myself if we used science to create a baby who had any medical problems, just as I would never forgive myself if we knowingly tried to get pregnant again and caused a baby to suffer from the medical risks my blood posed.

A friend of mine had adopted 9 years previously, so I confided in him that we were considering adopting our next child. He warned me that it could be really, really tough. We talked about attachment issues, trauma and the stressful nature of the adoption process itself. I didn't feel put off, perhaps because, despite his warning, I could see that he really loved his children and they sounded wonderful. I felt excited at the thought of adoption. It felt right.

SIGNING UP

A few days after Zoe's first birthday, Jon and I went to a "drop in" adoption information event, to find out more about the adoption process. We were the only prospective adopters who turned up that month, and it seemed like the social workers had forgotten all about the event and were having some sort of festive celebration, so we were ushered into a little office and sat on armchairs facing a social worker. I had my heart set on adoption and was terrified that Jon would hear the warnings about how tough adoption is and decide that he didn't want to do it. The social worker told us tragic tales of traumatised children and asked us why we were considering adoption. We talked about the scary time we had been through, worrying that my blood was putting Zoe's health at risk. I was already quite emotional, because I had dropped Zoe off at a friend's house before the meeting and I wasn't used to being apart from her, so it wasn't long before I turned into a sobbing, incoherent mess. The social worker kindly passed me some tissues and suggested that we should come back in a year if we still wanted to adopt. Her parting words to us were "in a way, I hope I don't see you again, because I hope you make peace with your life as it is." I wondered if I seemed like I didn't have what it took to be an adoptive parent.

We actually ended up leaving it for two more years, mostly because we moved house. We were happy, enjoying our busy life with our wonderful daughter and it would have been easy to just carry on as we were, but I kept thinking about adoption. I had more love to give. I kept looking at my incredible family. Jon is amazing with children and Zoe is so full of love, joy and kindness. I kept thinking how much they would enrich the life of a child.

Zoe wanted our family to be bigger too. When she was three years old, several of her friends' Mums were pregnant. It seemed like her nursery friends were gaining new baby brothers and sisters all the time. At least once a day, she asked me for a baby brother or sister to play with. Zoe has always enjoyed role play and kept bringing me dolls and asking me to put them under my top, to pretend that I was growing a baby. I felt like my heart tore a little each time she asked me to do that. Even if we did apply to adopt, I didn't know if we would be approved or if we would find the right match. I didn't know if I would ever be able to give her the younger sibling she desperately wanted. The role play became quite depressing for me, so I ended up explaining to Zoe that my tummy was a bit "broken" now, so I couldn't grow another baby. I explained that it sometimes made me sad to think about it, so I didn't want to pretend to be pregnant. It was a tough conversation and she was disappointed at the thought of never having a baby brother or sister. I wasn't sure whether I was doing the right thing, but the questions and role play were really getting me down.

In November 2018, we finally felt ready to start the process. We were settled in our home and Zoe was sleeping better, so we were all happier and coping well with life. We filled in the forms online to register our interest. A social worker called a few days later and booked a home visit. I've always been quite house-proud, but there's no cleaning incentive like knowing a social worker is coming to your home! On the other hand, I didn't want the house to look sterile and unfriendly! Before every social worker visit, I overthought the tidying, to the extent that I once got some of my daughter's toys back out again after I had tidied them away! For the first social worker visit, however, I barely had time to prepare. It was the day after Zoe's 3rd birthday party and the living room had been full of balloons. Her actual birthday was a few days later, so I had promised we could keep the balloons for a while, so they were hastily shoved into the playroom after I dropped her off at the

grandparents' house. Two social workers came to this meeting –
apparently standard protocol for a first visit. They were greeted
with "Happy Birthday" banners that I had promised Zoe I would
keep up until after her birthday. Unfortunately, it wasn't the warm
reception I had hoped to provide, because our heating had broken
the night before and the temperature was below freezing outside,
so not much higher in our unheated home! We all huddled round
the fireplace, as I apologised and we laughed about how bad the
timing was, which broke the ice, in more ways than one!

Jon and I had taken the day off work. I was glad Zoe wouldn't be
there in case I was an emotional wreck as I had been during that
first visit to an adoption agency when she was a year old.
Thankfully this meeting wasn't nearly as emotional. I knew that
Jon was on board with adopting because we'd been talking about it
for so long, so I didn't have that same concern that he might hear
what the social workers had to say and then change his mind.
Besides, he'd already heard the standard pitch a couple of years
ago. We talked about our reasons for wanting to adopt and one of
the social workers gave us an overview of the process. Then we
gave the social workers a tour of the house to see where we were
proposing our adopted child's bedroom would be and to check that
it seemed generally safe and suitable for a child. They didn't have
any concerns, so one of the social workers told me she'd be in
touch once she had completed the paperwork required for us to
progress to "Stage 1!"

Stage 1 of the adoption process is largely about checking that
you're "alright" to adopt. We had DBS checks done to show that
we had no criminal convictions. Jon's check was completed a
month quicker than mine, and my form turned up just as I was
beginning to panic that perhaps there might be a criminal Holly
Marlow out there who might cause problems for me due to
mistaken identity!

We were required to fill in a form with details of all loans and
"significant monthly income and outgoings," to show that we
could financially provide for a child. I asked what "significant"
meant. I was expecting to have to declare things over a certain
value, but the social worker advised that there was no specific

threshold. I suppose a "significant" expense varies, depending on your perspective. Perhaps it helps social workers to get a feel for how financially strained you are when they see what you feel is significant. We listed nursery fees, car insurance and tax, approximate fuel costs, food shop, household bills and phone contracts. We also had to show the social worker our bank statements and recent payslips. It felt like we were getting a mortgage! Jon worked for himself at the time and took a relatively low salary, topped up with dividend payments of varying amounts, depending on how well the company was performing. We calculated his approximate average salary and provided an explanation of this. The social worker was satisfied that we were not in financial peril and could indeed afford to have another child.

The social worker completed a Health and Safety assessment of the house and asked us questions about the garage and car. The Health and Safety check was eye-opening. I expected her to check certain things - that medicines, knives and cleaning products were out of reach, that the fire alarms were functional, that the staircase spindles were a safe distance apart, so that a child couldn't fall through them. I didn't expect to be asked, "do you keep dressing gowns on hooks on the back of bedroom doors?" Well, I don't any more! The social worker wasn't sure why this question had been included in the questionnaire, but surmised that a child must have become dangerously tangled in the belt of a dressing gown. It was good for us to have to think about a fire exit strategy which I must admit we hadn't discussed since moving into our new home. We were also asked to get the local fire brigade to come out and assess our home, as it was a 3-storey house, but the fire brigade advised that they no longer provide these assessments for adoption. We weren't sure then if we'd need to arrange some other sort of assessment in lieu of that but, after consulting with her boss, our social worker confirmed that we could proceed without that assessment and she just checked our fire alarms were operational before ticking that box on her checklist.

I wondered what she would have said or done if we had been in financial straits, unable to provide for our daughter, or if our house had been deemed unsafe for a child to live in. Does anyone begin the adoption process and then trigger red flags that result in their family receiving additional support from social services, or the removal of their child? I'd like to think that anyone who needs help is already known to social services, but there must be people who aren't on their radar. Do they always have the self-awareness to know they can't adopt? How often do they reach out for help? This process was making me think about things I'd never considered before.

We had to complete very thorough medical questionnaires and go through physical medical examinations with our doctor. We were poked and prodded, weighed and measured. We had to answer questions about our mental health history and our reproductive health, including whether we were using contraception and whether we could physically have more birth children if we wanted to. I was generally unfazed by the intrusive nature of the process, but something inside me caught fire when the doctor advised that I would need to go to the optician and get a copy of my glasses prescription to attach to the application. "FOR GOODNESS' SAKE! What a RIDICULOUS box-ticking requirement that delays me sending off this paperwork, while adding absolutely no value!" I ranted to Jon on the way home. Although good eyesight is undeniably useful for a parent, the fact that I had to actually provide evidence of my glasses prescription felt absurdly excessive, considering that nobody had ever questioned my sight since my driving test 15 years ago! Thinking about it, maybe all drivers should be required to get an eye test at regular intervals to maintain the validity of the driver's licence. That's not the case, however, and there's certainly no official body who keeps track of how well parents can see.

The requirement seemed utterly pointless. It wouldn't prove that I actually wear my glasses, and they weren't even checking that I actually had glasses with the right prescription. If I was severely visually impaired, then of course I would expect a social worker to quiz me as to how I would adapt my life to deal with certain challenges of parenting. Surely there should be a threshold though, some logic, rather than a blanket request for glasses-wearers only to submit evidence of their prescription. Jon didn't wear glasses but wasn't required to provide proof that he didn't need them. He could have had appalling eyesight, but just never had it checked out! It was frustratingly illogical, but of course I provided the evidence requested without objection, because adopting was so important to us.

The social worker wrote to our employers and asked for references to confirm that we weren't trouble-makers! She also wrote to two of our friends and my Mum, and asked them questions about our ability to adopt and how they felt we would approach adoption. The questionnaire responses were of course kept confidential, but we were told that they included questions such as, "do you think the couple would share with the child that they are adopted? How do you think they would approach staying in contact with the birth family?" Fortunately, everyone who was interviewed had discussed adoption with us at length and knew that we felt strongly that any adopted child should know their own story and that it is important to a child's identity to know as much about their birth parents as possible (in an age-appropriate way, of course).

One of the stranger parts of Stage 1 is that the social worker has to spend a certain number of hours with you, to be able to say that they've got to know you and that you seem like good people, who could handle the stresses of adopting a child. Our social worker brought round paper copies of "homework" activities for us. This included questions that we had to answer about our motivations to adopt, key milestones that had shaped our personalities, and creating a family tree and a spider-diagram of our support network. Each time she visited, she showed us a new document and then explained that she would email it over. The first couple of times, I thought, "just send through all the forms at once and let me blast through them, so we can do this quicker!" Then it dawned on me that the form was something to discuss while spending time with us, so that she could legitimately say that she had met with us several times and we seemed to have what it takes. I enjoyed doing the homework activities. It was good to have something to *do*. Each social worker visit completed and each form returned brought us one step closer to our child.

TRAINING

Towards the end of Stage 1 of the adoption process, we were invited to go to a "prospective adopters preparation course." This was three full days of training with other prospective adopters, plus a "Carousel Evening" to speak to experienced adopters. I was so excited to be doing something constructive to make progress towards our future child!

The training was HARD. Not in the sense that it was difficult to understand or to complete the tasks, just emotionally tough. There was a lot of information about the kinds of trauma and neglect that children can experience. We watched some emotive videos with sad piano music that made me well up, and we did exercises in groups.

It was strange being one of the few couples there who already had biological children. In some ways we were the experts in the group exercises, but I was very conscious that we had to show that we weren't making assumptions based on our experiences with Zoe, who hadn't experienced the trauma of a removal from her birth family. We were given scenarios to discuss with very limited conversation-starters, such as "Your child is terrified of going in the bath. What are your thoughts?" Some people who didn't have children immediately said, "sounds like the child has been abused and had a bad experience in the bath." The other people in our group nodded enthusiastically. "Yep, that's got to be it," one of them said. Jon and I looked at each other. I could tell he wasn't going to say anything, so I decided to bite the bullet. "I don't want to rule out the possibility that it's to do with abuse, but it could just be that they hate having their hair washed, because water gets in their eyes, or something like that. Zoe used to scream at the thought of having her hair washed."

Throughout the training, we had a few similar conversations with each other and the other prospective adopters and realised that it is all too easy to attribute everything to trauma. Knowing how much of an overthinker I can be, I kept wondering if I'd be able to tell the difference between a trauma-based behaviour and the weird and wonderful things that children do. *Will I overthink every single thing my child does?* It seemed likely I was in for a future of second-guessing myself.

We were given a copy of the sort of checklist that social workers use to determine which family is the best match for a child. It was a list of criteria, with columns for comments on up to four families. First on the list was "physical match," followed by "trauma-informed" and "supportive of proposed contact plan with birth family." We did an exercise where we worked in small groups to evaluate two fictional families, to decide which would be best-matched to a fictional child's profile. I was quite methodical and used the form to guide my decision. Both families shared the birth family's ethnicity and faith. One family was more trauma-informed and more open to contact than the other, so I felt they would be the better adoptive family. Jon came to the same conclusion. The other prospective adopters we were working with felt that the other fictional family would be a stronger match because one parent was a doctor and the other a teacher. We all felt strongly that we were right, which was in itself eye-opening. This must happen in real life when social workers are deciding which family would be the best match for a child. In other groups, some people had strong opinions and others didn't. Some groups came to a consensus. I was relieved that in real life, I will never be required to decide which family is matched with which child. What a responsibility!

The best part of the adoption preparation course was that there were people with experience of adoption there to talk to us. First off, a birth mother spoke to us about her experiences. It was eye-opening to hear her perspective, and wonderful to hear how lovingly she spoke about her daughter. That was a really valuable part of the training, as it humanised birth parents for all of us. The term "birth parent" is so cold really. It implies that all they do is produce a child and doesn't convey the strength of their emotions, their pain, or the way that they may have been set up to fail, because their support network was poor or non-existent. I had read several memoirs written by birth parents and watched TV programmes about adoption, but listening to a birth mother in person was much more powerful. I'll always be grateful to her for sharing her experiences, as I'm sure her talk has made me a better adoptive parent. When she finished talking, we struggled to ask questions. The whole room was sobbing or on the brink of tears. A couple of people managed to thank her for sharing her story and ask some questions, then we were released for a break. I stood in the queue for the Ladies toilets with the other sobbing and barely-holding-it-together women. After a moment, I burst out sob-laughing and said "I think they need to get this ceiling checked, because it's raining on all of our faces!" and the other women sob-laughed in agreement. We chatted briefly about how amazing but tragic the birth mother's talk had been, splashed our faces and generally pulled ourselves together, wondering what else the social workers had in store for us.

Next up was an adoptee! After a harrowing morning learning about the effects of trauma, then the emotional speech from the birth mother, it was a relief to hear from this happy, emotionally-stable adopted woman. Her key messages were the importance of making sure that a child knows about their birth family, and reassurance that wanting to meet their birth parents later doesn't detract from the relationship that a child has with their adoptive parents. Later in the course, we heard from a foster carer and from two adoptive mothers, who shared their varied experiences. Each talk broadened our minds and made it all feel more real.

The training also involved learning about Maslow's hierarchy of needs, attachment disorders, life story work (talking to children about what happened to them) and theraplay. We even got to see some profiles of children who were in need of adoptive families. That was emotional, but very helpful. We knew it was unlikely that we would be approved in time to be considered as adoptive parents for any of those children, but seeing those profiles gave us a feel for the kind of questions we would need to ask when we were looking for a match.

We didn't exchange phone numbers with any of the adoptive families on the same training sessions as us, which I later regretted. It felt awkward, especially as many of us were in similar positions and likely to be matched with children of a similar age. That is of course exactly why we should have befriended them, but we worried that we'd feel uncomfortable if we ended up being shown the same profiles and getting into a situation where we were in a competitive match, so I didn't ask anyone for their number. Thankfully, we have since built a strong support network of adopters and we've connected with some of those families again at events organised by the adoption agency.

The following week, we went to the "Carousel Evening," which was basically a speed-dating kind of set-up, so that we could talk to eight sets of adoptive parents and ask questions about their experiences. Each of those people shared at least one piece of wisdom that was worth hearing. I felt in awe of these people who had been through the whole adoption process and were coping with a range of attachment issues, trauma and various different contact arrangements with the birth families of their children. One adoptive dad spoke in hushed tones, as one of my favourite social workers walked past. "Watch out for that one," he warned. "She tries to get you to adopt the difficult-to-place children. She'll tell you there are no other children, to make you panic. She'll say this is the best you're going to get, the least traumatised child she's ever met on the job. Don't believe it." I gulped. Jon nudged me and said "remember that!" I didn't really want to. I hoped it wasn't true. It occurred to me that if that really was her approach, she was using a strategy that would get more children families. I could see why she might. It's not enough to just find families for children, though. Those families have to be able to cope and to parent the children well. Adopted children don't deserve for their parents to feel overwhelmed, or worse, regretful, because they've taken on too much.

Another adopter showed us his child's "Life Story Book," which was a ring-binder full of brightly-decorated pages that explained why that child was removed from their birth parents and some details about their experiences in foster care. One couple talked about how they felt that they were adopting more than just the child, and saw adoption as their family connecting forever with their son's biological family. They were huge advocates for face-to-face contact with birth families and felt that it really benefitted their son. They told us enthusiastically about their six-monthly meet-ups with their son's biological grandparents. An adoptive dad told us that he and his wife were required to send letters to their child's birth parents once a year, but they had requested an update to the letterbox agreement and now sent one every six months, because annually felt cruel. We hadn't really thought about it before, but instantly resolved to request six-monthly contact if we found ourselves in the same position. The people who kindly shared their experiences with us that evening gave us a lot to think about. Some of my preconceived notions started to shift. I became more open to contact of all forms, and hoped that we would be able to develop a positive relationship with our future child's birth family.

INTERVIEWS

Zoe loved it when the social workers came to visit. Our first social worker had snazzy patterned socks with animals on, which Zoe thought was brilliant. Zoe spent the duration of the appointments running between the playroom and the kitchen, bringing different toys to show the social worker, oblivious to the questions we were answering. The conversations were all relatively "safe," answering questions about topics such as our health, financial stability, job history, how much time we each expected to take off for adoption leave and a very top-level discussion of what our support network looked like.

Stage 2 was more intense, with more personal questions, so we made sure Zoe was at nursery for some of those appointments, or took it in turns to play with her in a different room. We had six interviews with a new social worker. We were advised that our adoption agency's policy is for different social workers to handle Stages 1 and 2. I assumed that this was so that more people have met the prospective adopter(s) and evaluated their suitability. A lot of the process seems to be about ensuring that each decision is reached by committee, so that there's more chance of it being the right choice, and perhaps so that no one person is fully to blame if things go wrong.

Our new social worker was just as lovely as the first, and managed to put us at ease. She asked us about our childhoods, our relationships with family and friends, our marriage, our jobs, hobbies, interests, views, beliefs, prejudices and priorities. Despite the nature of the questions, it somehow didn't feel too intrusive.

A somewhat uncomfortable part of the process was when the social worker asked us about "what sort of child" we would be willing to consider adopting. We were asked about a long list of disabilities and about varying levels of disability. I was surprised at how specific some of these questions were. "Would you be open to adopting a child who couldn't hear?" "How about a child with partial hearing loss?" "What about if they had some risk of hearing difficulty developing later in life?"

In contrast, we were also asked some very open questions, such as "would you feel able to adopt a child who had a mental illness?" which felt very vague, as mental illnesses vary so much. We found ourselves saying things like "it depends on the situation, but we wouldn't want to rule out any children based on that. We'd want to know more." We were more comfortable with some risks than others, but we knew that we would decide whether we wanted to adopt a baby based on their overall story, and it seemed silly to narrow the search unnecessarily.

We were relatively confident that we could cope with most health risks and disabilities, though we were clear that we didn't want to adopt a child who we knew had a medical condition that meant that they would need life-long, full-time care. I didn't think it would be fair to Zoe if we made her a carer when we die or become too old to look after her sibling, and I also felt that she deserved to have a sibling she can play with, not to effectively lose one parent to lengthy hospital stays with her younger sibling. We also expected to both need to work for a living, so it wasn't really practical for one of us to become a full-time carer to a child.

We said we wouldn't be comfortable with adopting a child who had a known health condition that significantly reduced their life expectancy, or a child with a contagious disease that might affect our daughter. That wasn't something we had even considered until we heard about a child who had an infectious, incurable skin condition. It would be one thing to take on that risk ourselves, but we couldn't put Zoe in that position, especially as children are so much more likely to share germs than adults!

It felt really awful to specify any criteria because the children who need families can't make stipulations about the kind of family they have. We knew that once we had adopted a child, we would find a way to cope with whatever life threw at us, just as we would have if we'd had a birth child with health problems, so I felt guilty for having any limitations at all, but we were also quite nervous about the impact on Zoe. I kept thinking that if we didn't have Zoe, we'd probably be a lot more open to adopting children with significant disabilities. But life without Zoe is unimaginable, and she is one of the main reasons why I felt we would be a great adoptive family. Zoe is warm, fun and kind. I knew she'd be a fantastic big sister and bring joy to her sibling's life.

There were some types of disabilities that we felt we were particularly strong candidates to support a child with. In pursuing diagnoses for my own chronic health issues, I've seen lots of different types of specialists. I understand the sort of medical jargon used and have a pretty good feel for what sort of questions to ask of a cardiologist, neurologist or rheumatologist. I have developed strategies for coping with chronic pain in lots of different joints and muscles, so I felt that I'd be a strong candidate to support a child with a chronic pain condition. My Mum has diabetes, and I felt that I understood it well enough to help a child to manage their symptoms. It might also be a comfort to a child to know another person who shared their medical condition. The social worker enthusiastically noted this down.

We were asked whether we would consider adopting a child who had other siblings in long-term foster care or who had been adopted into other families. That's a strange situation when you have a birth child, because you know that your adopted child may have additional siblings that aren't your birth child's siblings. We were asked how we would manage Zoe's feelings if her younger brother or sister had other siblings. Did we think she'd feel threatened, jealous, left out? Would we be affected by her feelings and perhaps not try as hard as we should to support the contact between our adopted child and their biological siblings? Obviously, it would be simpler to say we'd rather adopt a child who doesn't have any biological siblings, but that's not really practical, because in most cases there's still a chance that the birth parents may have more children after you've adopted. We knew it was something we would need to be open to, and that contact with their birth relatives would most likely be hugely beneficial to our adopted child, so we resolved to get our heads round it and make it work. We assured the social worker that we'd support whatever contact was possible with our future child's extended family, and we'd help Zoe to understand the importance of it, and to cope with however it made her feel.

We were limited by Zoe's age, as the adoption agency we were going through stipulated that the adoptive child must be the youngest child in the family by a minimum of 18 months, and preferably at least 24 months. There is psychological research behind this; essentially the requirement is so that they receive the increased level of attention that the baby in the family should receive and apparently it is also psychologically better for children who are already in the family if the adopted child is younger. So, we knew we would be looking to adopt a child under 2-ish years old, depending on how long it took to find a suitable match, as of course the acceptable age range would widen as Zoe got older. I was keen to adopt a child under 18 months old anyway, as my experience with Zoe and her little friends had shown me that that can be a very challenging age and I was keen for our future child to be settled and confident that we loved them before they started to have the big emotions and nightmares that are common from around 18 months old.

This age restriction meant that we weren't asked the full set of questions, but I had read a list online so that I could mentally prepare for the meeting and the question that shocked me most, although we didn't need to answer it, was "Would you consider adopting a child who was pregnant?" I often think about that even now, years later. *There are pregnant children in this world, who need to be adopted.* I imagine most must end up in long-term foster care placements because, even if there are adopters who are open to it, the children will be old enough to have a strong sense of identity and not want to be officially adopted out of their birth families.

We were asked how we would keep Zoe safe if a child had been subjected to sexual abuse and acted out their experiences towards Zoe. I was horrified at the thought of my precious daughter being in that position, but we felt that the risk of that happening was relatively low, due to the likely age of the child we would adopt. I reasoned that, although a baby might be emotionally affected by that sort of trauma, they were unlikely to remember what physically happened to them and try to re-enact it. I also felt comfortable that Zoe had a strong understanding of acceptable boundaries, so she would know if something wasn't right. She's always been very good at communicating, and I felt confident that she would be comfortable sharing any concerns with us.

We confirmed that we didn't have any preference about gender, race, religious background or language spoken by birth parents. I love learning languages and explained that I would learn whatever language the birth parents spoke, so that I could teach it to both of our children.

In hindsight, although we were open to it, I don't think we would have been seriously considered to adopt a child from a different race or nationality because we hadn't been saying that we specifically wanted to do that, whereas apparently some adopters do. We had also learned during the training that the social workers try as often as possible to find a "physical match," so that the child doesn't feel like the odd one out. We were asked about the diversity in our support network and the social worker noted down that we have Chinese friends, so that would be a positive for a Chinese child as they would feel less alone. The social worker told us that it was unlikely that we'd be matched with a Chinese child, however, as there are usually more Chinese adopters than children needing to be adopted in the UK foster care system, and they would be a better physical match and better able to support the child's cultural identity. We have some family links to Africa and South Africa, and the social worker asked us some questions about race and how we could support the identity of a child from various different cultural and ethnic backgrounds. There were some more general questions on racism in the UK, which seemed to be more about our character and values than our network. It was clear that the social worker was trying to figure out how much we really understood the challenges of adopting a child from another race and how we would support our child if they experienced racism. At the time, I thought we gave strong answers, but I've learned more about anti-racism since, and in hindsight, some of my responses were quite naïve.

Religion was another discussion point. I'm a Roman Catholic and Jon is an atheist. The social worker asked if I would be disappointed if my child didn't share my faith. I suppose in some families this could be an issue. For me, it's not really about the specific faith. I married Jon knowing he doesn't believe in the same things I do and never having any particular hope or expectation of that changing. I love him because he's kind and puts other people's needs before his own. I hope that my children will be kind too, but that doesn't need to be because they're trying to do God's Will. I talk to them a lot about how it's important to "make good choices" and "do the right thing," and it's not really my style to include God in those reminders. I want them to become intrinsically motivated to be kind, rather than behaving because they think God is a scary judge. That's not how I see God. I reassured the social worker that I will not feel disappointment if my children don't share my faith, and I would support them if they felt a connection with a different faith than mine. We were asked questions about our beliefs about homosexuality and I felt like I was under a little extra scrutiny when answering these questions, in case I was "that kind of Christian." We reassured the social worker that we would love and support our children, whatever their sexual orientation and gender identity.

The social worker also raised a concern that Jon and I are both university graduates and she worried that we might have unreasonably high academic expectations of our children, which might be especially difficult for some adopted children to achieve if they have learning disabilities or if trauma affects their development. We assured her that we know university is not for everyone and that we won't be disappointed in our children if they are not interested in academic learning. I told her, "I don't have ambitions for my children to be lawyers and doctors. I just want them to be happy." It wasn't just something I said to get a tick in the box. This is something I've felt quite strongly about for a long time. Although my parents didn't put unreasonable pressures on me to perform well academically, I put a lot of pressure on myself as a child. I grew up with undiagnosed hypermobility and fibromyalgia, which was quite scary at times. Every few months, another joint would start to hurt. I didn't know why I was in so much pain and I didn't have any effective treatment for it, so I worried that I would eventually become terribly disabled and be unable to work. I pushed myself to do well in school, telling myself that I needed to get strong qualifications, so that I could secure a job that paid well enough that I could survive on a part-time salary if I needed to. Thankfully, I was eventually diagnosed in my twenties, and having names for my conditions has enabled me to find more effective coping mechanisms, so the pain is now mostly under control. I have found it hard though, to cope with the misplaced ambition that once felt necessary to my survival. My career became a large part of my identity, especially as I wasn't physically able to handle many hobbies alongside it. At the time, I had a high-pressured job working for a large defence company, managing major subcontractors who were making some very technical stuff. It involved a lot of problem-solving, which was demanding, but intensely rewarding. A couple of my friends died very young, one of them completely unexpectedly, so I had been given a couple of harsh reminders that I should be making the most of life, and not prioritising work too highly. I wasn't sure what else to do with my life at that stage, but I knew that I wanted to change careers at some point, when I found something more rewarding that suited me. I didn't want my children to make the same mistakes that I had and to end up in highly stressful jobs.

The social worker interviewed some of our friends and family who had completed the initial reference questionnaires, and asked them more detailed questions about us. Some were asked if they felt that my job was too demanding. Our friends and family were asked about how my health affects my ability to parent, our parenting styles, whether they thought we would manage the needs of an adopted child and whether we would ask for help if we were struggling. They were asked if they thought we would be supportive of contact with our child's birth family and whether we would be good at managing attachment issues and supporting a child who might have different needs than Zoe. One of my friends told me that the social worker said she'd been relieved that I was warm and easy to talk to because she'd expected a more intimidating vibe when she read my job title, "Subcontract Programme Manager," in our Stage 1 paperwork. That made me laugh! I was definitely more formal at work, but my management style and my parenting style do have a lot of overlap.

ZOE'S INTERVIEW

Towards the end of the interviews, we had one extra meeting during which the social worker interviewed Zoe, who was 3 at the time and thrilled to be included in the process! Zoe's interview was very sweet. The social worker had brought some Play-Doh with her and asked Zoe to help her to make some families. They talked about how families look, and the social worker casually asked Zoe if she thought that everyone in the family needed to look similar. Zoe, who has been told countless times that she's a carbon copy of Jon, laughed and said "no, I just look like Daddy! Mummy's the only one in our family with blue eyes!"

The social worker explained, "I work with some children who can't stay with their mummies and daddies, and part of my job is to find new families for them. Do you think there's room in your family for another child?" Zoe answered enthusiastically, "Yes, I'd like to adopt LOADS of baby brothers and sisters!" The social worker smiled at this cute response, but I'd seen something she hadn't. Zoe's face had frozen for a second when she'd heard the words "some children who can't stay with their mummies and daddies," and I realised that, although I'd been working to normalise the concept of adoption through play and stories, we hadn't yet talked about *why* some children needed to be adopted. Zoe didn't mention it and kept making Play-Doh people and chatting to the social worker, who asked her, "is there room for another child to sleep in this house?" and "is there room in your car for another car seat?" Zoe happily told the social worker about the bedroom we'd decided would be for her sibling, and assured her that her sibling would sit in a car seat in the back of the car with her and she'd chat to them in the car. They talked about how some toys are too small for young children, so might need to be put away up high or kept in Zoe's room and we'd play with those toys while her brother or sister napped. I'd been talking to Zoe about all of this, so she was reeling off brilliant answers that showed she understood what we were getting into. It was all wonderfully adorable and anyone who wasn't Zoe's Mum would have been oblivious to the question on her mind. Sure enough, shortly after the social worker left, Zoe's eyes welled up, as she asked me, "why can't some children stay with their parents?"

Zoe was understandably distressed at the mere thought of being separated from me and Jon, and I felt I needed to help her to understand that there's no risk of her being removed for adoption. I needed to somehow explain to her how I am not the same as a birth mother whose child needs to be removed. At the same time, I didn't want to create a monstrous view of birth parents in her mind, which would have been easy to do, but unfair to birth parents. Children can view things in a very binary way, and I didn't want to imply that birth parents are bad and adoptive parents are good. That would damage our future child, who might grow up thinking they came from something bad.

I wanted to support Zoe's empathy for birth parents and I did my best to answer her questions, but felt that I hadn't quite done the topic justice. She kept asking more questions, or the same questions again, so it was clearly still bothering her. We typically used stories to talk through big worries, but I couldn't find anything that was quite right. There were lots of books that talked about a lost, abandoned child or baby animal, who needed a family, then found one and lived happily ever after. There were a few about couples who wanted a child, but couldn't have one, so they adopted. Some were done better than others, but a few made me uncomfortable, because the primary focus seemed to be how the child filled the void in the lives of those adults, rather than explaining what was best for the child. I couldn't find any books that explained why a child needed to be removed from their birth family in the first place, so one morning, while Zoe was watching TV, I sat on the sofa next to her and thought up a story to explain it to her. It poured out of me into the "Notes" app on my phone, and within about twenty minutes, I'd written "Delly Duck," my first children's book. I read it to Zoe, and asked what she thought. She sighed and said, "I understand why now, but I do wish that the duckling had been able to stay with his birth mother. I think it's a bit sad that he couldn't." I fine-tuned the story and eventually published it, so that Zoe and other children in her position could understand that social workers do a lot to support birth families before removing a child. I made sure that the birth mother character remained likeable, despite the fact that she didn't keep her child consistently safe. When I wrote it, we didn't know which child we'd end up adopting, so the story wasn't based on my son's life, but I was conscious that I'd one day use this story to explain things to whoever we adopted, so I worked in lots of metaphors that I could interpret in the most appropriate way to represent my future child's specific life story.

A LICENCE TO PARENT

Finally, when the interviews were all completed and typed up, the social worker sent us her Prospective Adopters Report for review, minus the reports of her interviews with our friends and family. Those were kept confidential, though our referees each chose to give us a debrief! We read through the report countless times, requested some tweaks and minor corrections, suggested some additional context in areas that we thought sounded weak, and then signed to confirm that everything we had told her was true. The 80-page summary of us was sent off to the review panel, who had several weeks to review it, ahead of the "Approval Panel" interview.

I was disproportionately nervous about the Approval Panel, although we had been reassured that it was pretty much a sure thing, because the adoption agency's policy was to only take adopters to panel when they are highly confident that they will be approved. We were taken into a small room by our social worker and shown a booklet that included photos and short biographies of all of the twelve panel members. These biographies stated impressive qualifications, such as "ex-foster parent of fifteen years and adoptive parent of two," "adoptee with twenty years of experience working with looked-after children" and so on. These people sounded amazing! Although we had no chance of remembering who was who, seeing their faces ahead of time and knowing a little about the sort of people they were, somehow made it much less daunting than it usually would be walking into an interview with twelve interviewers.

A friendly man came into the room and introduced himself as the Chair of the Approval Panel. He told us that he would be running the meeting, and outlined how it would be structured. First, the panel would list what they perceived to be our strengths and the reasons why we should be approved to adopt. He assured us that there were a lot of these, which made me blush! Then they would go on to talk about any concerns. Each member of the panel would ask us one question, then they'd have the chance to ask follow-up questions after we had responded. Then we would have the opportunity to tell them anything else that we felt they ought to know. Finally, we would leave and return to the little waiting room while they discussed the interview and voted as to whether or not we should be approved as "Prospective Adopters."

The Panel Chair guided us and our social worker into a much larger room where the tables were laid out in a square. He gestured to the three empty seats. I noticed that there was a large box of tissues strategically placed in front of me and Jon. I joked, "I hope you've not put those there because you're expecting me to need them!" and everyone laughed politely. The interview went smoothly and without tears! The Panel Chair read out a list of bullet points of strengths that the panel had identified from the Prospective Adopters Report that our social worker had sent them, then they asked her if she had anything more to add. I fully expected her to shrug, because they'd essentially reeled off all the positives from the report she had created, but she elaborated on some of the strengths mentioned. I managed to squeeze out a slightly croaky "thank you."

The focus shifted from our social worker to us, and we answered a lot of questions about how we planned to support Zoe, such as "How will you prepare Zoe?" "How will you know if Zoe is struggling emotionally during the introductions?" "How will you manage the fact that Zoe won't receive letterbox contact like your adopted child?" and so on. We were also asked how Jon would manage working from home while I was on adoption leave with our future child, and what we would do if we needed support. Jon's a naturally private person, so I knew he'd hate answering the questions and I was desperate to answer all of them to protect him from feeling uncomfortable, but the social worker, who knew us pretty well by this point, had advised us to make sure we each answered some of the questions, so I resisted the urge to answer for him.

We were escorted back to the waiting room and after a few minutes, the Chair of the Approval Panel came back and happily told us that we had a unanimous "Yes" vote. At that point, both of us welled up and I wondered why they didn't keep a box of tissues in the waiting room! That's where you really need it! The next step was for the report and recommendation from the panel to be sent to the adoption agency's "Independent Reviewing Officer," for yet another review, and the decision could theoretically be overturned at that stage. We were reassured that it is rare and extremely unlikely for there to be any issue after a unanimous "Yes" vote and sure enough, we received a letter ten days later confirming that we were officially approved as Prospective Adopters. Phew!

We had a licence to parent!

THE LINKING MEETING

The hardest part of the adoption process was without a doubt the linking and matching process. A couple of weeks before the approval panel, our social worker had told us that there was a little boy who she thought was perfect for us, whom I'll refer to here as baby "R." We couldn't believe our luck! It was so soon! We couldn't receive much information about him before we were approved, so we were just sent a couple of paragraphs referring to him as his first initial only, with basic information about his health, development and risks in terms of hereditary health conditions that he may later develop. We tried to imagine what his name might be, and pictured a baby with one of the possible names and did what all parents do when they have a second child – sounded out possible names with our eldest child's name, to see how they sound together. "Zoe and Robert! Zoe and Rupert! Zoe and Ray!" We had already talked about the importance of a name as part of a child's identity and agreed that we wouldn't change their name, unless social workers advised us that it was necessary to do so for safety reasons.

Everything sounded manageable and positive, so we asked for more information, which we received a few days after we were approved as Prospective Adopters. This was a much larger document, called the "Child Permanence Report," and it included far more detail about the reasons why this child was not able to stay with his birth family.

The Child Permanence Report included his name, which we'd never heard of before. I wasn't sure if it was a "real" name or something his birth parents had made up. It's rare, so I won't share it here, but I liked the sound of it and the way it looked. I searched for it online, to see if it was more common than I thought. It's a name of Arabic origin, though the child and his birth family were all white. I searched on Facebook and found just two profiles, both based in the middle-east. That confirmed my concern, that keeping that name would make this little boy very easy to track down if he uses his name on social media websites, particularly as he was likely to be the only white boy in this country with that name. I started to feel less conviction about keeping his name. It felt risky. I didn't want my son's birth family to contact him unexpectedly. I wanted him to have a relationship with them, but on his terms, or at least under the terms of the contact agreement drawn up by the social worker until he was old enough to decide how he felt about it. I imagined a teenage boy receiving confusing messages on social media.

I ran through several scenarios. I thought about changing R's name – we could choose a name that sounded similar, so that it was easier for R to adjust to his new name. Or we could choose a name that had a similar meaning, a name that began with the same letter, or a name that looked similar, though all of those sounded quite different. Then I thought perhaps we could just keep his name, but persuade him to use a nickname on social media when he was old enough to use it. I really liked his actual name, and would feel guilty changing it. Jon doesn't overthink like I do, and joked, "don't tell me we have to change it! I thought adopting meant I wouldn't have to come up with name suggestions!"

Our social worker arranged a "potential linking meeting" at our house. She told us they were considering other families, so they would be meeting with those families earlier in the week. I understood that it's their responsibility to find the best match for each child, but knowing other families were being considered added a layer of anxiety to the situation. This was about whether we were good enough for this child. Jon was unfazed. He shrugged and said "well, if there's a more suitable match than us, he should be matched with them and we'll be matched with a different baby. There's no point getting worked up about it." I just stared at him, completely baffled at his faith that it would all work out in the end.

On the day of the meeting, I dropped Zoe off at nursery and when I got home, Jon still had to work for the rest of the morning, so I was left alone with my thoughts. I was so excited that I frantically cleaned the whole house, including the insides of cupboards that I knew they'd never look in, then used my excess energy to do a litter-pick down the last couple of roads that the social workers would see as they drove up to our home. I knew this was complete overkill, but I needed to get rid of my nervous energy somehow. Just before they arrived, mid-afternoon, I noticed the fire alarm had somehow become unsecured from the ceiling and was dangling from a cable. I slightly hysterically asked Jon to fix it, feeling like I might explode with nerves.

A trio of social workers arrived shortly after; our social worker, the little boy's social worker, and his family finder. We have one long sofa in the living room, so the social workers sat in a line, Jon sat on the large foot stool that matches the sofa, and I sat awkwardly on a kitchen chair that I'd brought through, feeling a bit silly as I was higher up than everyone else. Usually, I sit on my yoga ball, as it helps my back, but I couldn't bring myself to do that for such an important meeting! I'd been to the chiropractor the day before, so that I wouldn't be fidgeting and clicking my joints.

First, our social worker asked the family finder to give us an update on how the little boy was doing, because the Child Permanence Report was a couple of months out of date. It sounded like he would have some developmental delays, but nothing too unmanageable. We had researched schools in the area that could help children with severe developmental delays, and my Mum was a teacher, so I knew she'd have some great ideas to help support a child. I had some questions about the biological family's medical history, and wanted to understand more about why R's extended family were unable to care for him. I have a very supportive family and know that if anything happened to Jon and me, there would be lots of family members keen to care for our children. I imagined my future son asking, "but why didn't my biological grandparents, aunties or uncles look after me?" and I wanted to be able to answer that. We'd been warned by other adoptive parents that social workers don't typically stay in the same job for long, so it was important to gather as much information as we could, as early as possible, in case they left and took that knowledge with them. We tried to imagine all the big questions our future son might have.

We also wanted to know for our own peace of mind, that all kinship care options had been thoroughly explored. We didn't want to find out several months into placement that there was a blood relative somewhere who was able to parent him and wanted to contest the adoption. We knew there would be some uncertainty for us until the Adoption Order was granted, but we wanted to know that that risk was low. I couldn't bear the thought of having to tell Zoe after a few months that actually her brother wasn't going to be her brother after all, because someone in his birth family was going to raise him. If we hadn't had Zoe, maybe we would have been less concerned about that. I needed to protect my own heart a bit too though, and I needed to know that the right thing had been done for the child, so I would still have wanted that reassurance that the extended family members had been fully vetted and ruled out as viable kinship carers.

The family finder's first question for us was "so, why this child?" I didn't feel we had a strong answer to that. The truth was his was the first and only profile we had seen, aside from in the training sessions! We gave an interview-worthy explanation of how we felt we could support the little boy based on the developmental delays that had been discussed. They nodded. I felt like we had ticked the boxes with a satisfactory answer.

The next question was, understandably, "what do you think of his name?" so we explained that we loved the name, but had concerns that it might make him very easy to track down and that we'd probably try to persuade him to use a nickname on social media when he was old enough to use it. We asked about contact, our logic being that if a birth parent was to engage in contact and we exchanged letters regularly, so they knew he was safe and happy, they would probably be less likely to try to track him down anyway. The child's social worker confirmed that R's birth mother was very keen to engage in letterbox contact and that she would have liked to have face-to-face contact, but that wasn't on the cards, regardless of how open we were to it, as it "wouldn't be in the child's best interests." That's a very social-worky phrase we had been hearing a lot and it was far from the last time we heard it. R's social worker was very keen to make sure we'd consider meeting his birth mother as a one-off, without R, because his birth mother had expressed that she wanted to meet her child's adoptive parents. We were open to that and hoped it would give us some more personal anecdotes to share with our son one day to balance out the formal reports from social workers about the reasons why his birth family couldn't care for him.

"And how did you feel when you first saw the photo of him?" the family finder asked. I felt a bit awkward at this point. I didn't want to lie to the social workers, but I hadn't really felt anything. I'd really just thought "huh, so that's what he looks like." I didn't expect to feel an instant connection though. I expected it to grow gradually while caring for him. I just said that he looked very sweet. I wasn't sure if the lack of gushing about a rush of maternal feelings made the rest of my thoughts clear or if it made me seem uncaring. Jon gave a similarly vague response and I wondered how enthusiastic the other prospective adopters had been when asked that question.

We were asked a few more questions about our support network, and my health, then when the questions came to an end, R's social worker asked to see the bedroom that we planned to have as our adopted child's bedroom. It was set up as a guestroom at that point and it's a very small room, so the single bed took up most of the room. Zoe had a bigger room, so I felt quite apologetic that we would be giving our adopted child a smaller one. I explained that he'd start off in the small room, as it is next to our bedroom and I'd want him to know that we're close, and to be able to get to him quickly if he had nightmares and for safety reasons such as if there was a fire. Longer term, I expected to move the rooms around to give him a bigger bedroom when he could get out of bed himself. I enthusiastically talked through where his bed would be and where we would put the chest of drawers. The child's social worker smiled patiently and said, "to be honest, I just need to see that you have a room that's suitable for a child." I realised I was over-explaining things.

The family finder and child's social worker left soon after this, and we were glad to have some slightly less intense time to talk to just our social worker. She explained that the next step was for us to decide whether we wanted to proceed with the match and, if we did, then the three social workers plus a few more would gather for a meeting the following week and decide whether they agreed that we were the right family for this child. We would then be assessed at a "Matching Panel" in about 8 weeks, so that there was time for the paperwork to be completed. She also explained that the family finder and child's social worker had decided to meet just with our family for now and would only meet with other families if we didn't want to proceed or if they felt it wasn't as good a match as they had thought when they read our profile. She assured us that we had come across well, and she couldn't see any reason why we wouldn't be matched with R, if that was what we wanted. You'd think I would have been relieved to hear that actually we weren't "competing" with any other families at this point. Instead, I felt a weight of responsibility. What if we weren't the right parents for this child?

When the social worker left, all my nervous energy seemed to go with her, and I just felt drained. I sat on the sofa and wrapped myself in a blanket. Jon picked up a ball and threw it to me. We threw it back and forth while we talked through everything we'd learned, analysed our abilities to parent R, and came to the conclusion that we could be a good family for him. We felt a bit nervous, but assumed that was normal. It is a massive, life-altering decision, after all!

LINKED

The morning after the linking meeting, I emailed our social worker, confirming that we wished to be considered as an adoptive family for R. A few days later, we received confirmation that the social workers had held their meeting and officially "linked" us, which meant that they would no longer pursue any other possible families for R, and we could proceed to matching panel. We were sent a copy of his latest medical report. That's when things started to unravel.

The report included a list of actions recommended by a doctor, including some blood tests and a referral to a paediatrician to investigate some abnormal measurements. When we asked if the blood tests had been completed, the response was, "we don't normally do that." We felt uncomfortable with that, as the doctor had recommended it, so we asked again if it could be done, as the doctor must have recommended it for a reason. The next response was along the lines of, "It really isn't necessary. There's nothing to indicate a higher risk of these diseases than normal."

We persisted, thinking that there must be a reason why the doctor had written it on the form as an action. This time we were told firmly that "it's too expensive" and would not be done. Exasperated, I asked if I could pay for the tests, to alleviate our concerns, but apparently that wasn't an option. One of the social workers commented that this was something no other adopter had ever insisted on and that it seemed unnecessary to put little R through these blood tests. I couldn't believe it. Surely we couldn't be the only adopters to have asked for the actions in the medical report to be completed! Surely the child's social worker should be insisting on the completion of all actions from the doctor to ensure that he got any treatment needed as early as possible! I was livid at the implication that I was cruel to ask for a child to have blood tests. The doctor was the one who requested them, not me. I was advocating for the child to have the testing that a medical professional had recommended, and I was being told by non-medical professionals that it wasn't necessary. I will never forget the horrible experience of taking baby Zoe for blood tests and I didn't want to be the reason that a child had to go through that, but the distress of a blood test is relatively brief, and I felt sure that the right thing to do was to make sure we caught anything as early as possible.

The majority of this communication was by email. We sent our questions to our social worker, who forwarded them on to the family finder, who contacted R's social worker. R's social worker usually then had to seek the answers from his foster carer, who sometimes had to contact the Health Visitor for more information. Responses came back through the same, convoluted chain of contacts, some of who worked part-time. Communication was slow and frustrating and the responses didn't always address our questions. We started to feel that we didn't know enough about this child. I felt concerned instead of excited.

It was clear we were not going to change the mind of whoever in the social worker chain thought the testing wasn't necessary, so we researched every health condition that the contentious blood tests were to check for. We determined that most of them would have presented symptoms by now, some would have been resolved by antibiotics that he'd had for a chest infection, so that only left a few possible illnesses on the list. These weren't highly contagious diseases and we felt that we could support a child who had any of those conditions. We decided to drop it. Perhaps we would take him to our doctor and ask for the blood tests when he was our son, so that we would know for sure that we had done our due diligence and not left any untreated illnesses to develop for years.

I felt that I was irritating the social workers, but continued to ask for updates on the referral to a specialist about the "abnormal" measurements. The matching panel was drawing nearer, and we kept receiving responses full of generalities like, "All children are different. These measurements Health Visitors use are just based on averages. Someone has to be at the upper and lower limits of these ranges!" While that were true, we didn't know how far out of the normal ranges these measurements were. The lack of detail was making us nervous. We were eventually told that a consultant appointment had taken place and was inconclusive. The abnormal measurements were indicative of a range of genetic conditions, including the one that had rendered his birth mother unable to care for him. It seemed most likely that he had that condition, but he would need to be monitored for a year or so before any doctor would make a conclusive diagnosis.

It was a condition that we felt would require a lot of time and focused care. It felt like too much to put on Zoe and, if I'm entirely honest, it felt like too much for me. I wished I felt able to take in all the children who need help and care for them all at a high standard, but I have physical and emotional limits. I felt that I would be overwhelmed if I was caring for a child with that health condition, and that I wouldn't be the Mum either of my children deserved. I asked if we could have a copy of the measurements ourselves, so we could understand the magnitude of the risk. As I emailed that request to our social worker, I wondered whether we were the most frustrating prospective adopters these social workers had ever met. I reminded myself of how we'd been told in training to "advocate for your child," and wondered if they saw my questions as advocating or annoying.

I don't think the social workers were intentionally holding back information to trick us into adopting a child we may not be best placed to support, though at times it did feel like that. I think they were just busy juggling lots of cases, struggling to get the information, maybe not sure how to get all of it, and feeling that it was outside of their normal processes to get hold of the information I was asking for. I'm sure they thought that I was probably worrying about nothing. I really hoped I was worrying about nothing, but the fact that it was so difficult to get more information completely destroyed our confidence in the match.

Eventually, I sent an email saying, "I'm sorry, I really don't want to be difficult, but we don't feel comfortable proceeding to panel without that information." Evidently this sounded an alarm. Within an hour of the email, I was sent a photo of the measurements. We did our own research, plotted the measurements on graphs and came to the conclusion that it was highly probable that he had the genetic condition we were worried about. One of the social workers booked us a call with a doctor, who confirmed our assessment of the medical information available to us and agreed that it seemed likely that R had the genetic condition. She found the measurements very concerning and talked about possible procedures that may be needed in the future.

It was all very overwhelming and we didn't feel we could adopt him knowing what we then knew. I felt wretched. "What kind of person says they won't adopt a child because their medical conditions are too difficult for them to handle?" I asked myself. I knew that we weren't the best placed people to handle his medical conditions and in fact I felt that he really ought to be an only child so that his parents could devote more time and attention to him if he developed the symptoms we expected. Oh, but the guilt was intense! The worst thing for me was knowing that the child would one day see this on his file and might feel that he wasn't good enough for us. I spoke to a friend who had adopted previously, needing the reassurance of someone who had been through the process. He had said "no" to profiles earlier in the linking/matching process, so he understood my guilt and the concern that social workers might think us heartless. My friend warned me that if we pulled out of the match, we might be seen as timewasters and put "to the back of the queue" for future matches. Our dream of adopting felt even further away.

I contacted the social workers and told them that unfortunately we didn't feel able to adopt R, based on the new medical information that we had received. I worded the email carefully, conscious that R might one day read it. I wanted to make sure that my words were on the record first. My social worker phoned me the next day to talk it through. Much to my relief, she was hugely understanding, and when we talked more about the medical risks, she said that she'd ensure R's social worker and family finder updated his profile so that they could find a more suitable match for him. She agreed that he should be an only child, as it seemed likely that his needs would significantly affect any siblings.

Although the guilt was hard to bear, the relief was strong too. We knew we'd made the right decision. I just prayed that it wouldn't result in us being passed over for future possible matches. Our social worker emailed me the "pen picture" we had created in Stage 2, to confirm that it was still accurate, then she sent it to all the family finders at the agency, explaining that we were still available. She updated me a couple of days later, saying that she'd not had any responses yet. I wondered if family finders were put off because we'd pulled out of a match.

I was relieved that we hadn't told Zoe about baby R. She kept asking me if the social workers had found a brother or sister for her yet. I explained that it was about finding the right family for the child, not the right child for our family, and we talked about how we'd be a great family for a child who needed a big sister. It had been so tempting to tell her about R when we were first linked, but the urge to tell her had faded as we waited for answers and gradually came to accept that we weren't the right family for R.

Years later, I saw R's family finder and asked how he was doing. She assured me that he had been adopted and was thriving. When I shared my relief and alluded to the guilt I had felt about pulling out of the match, she smiled and said, "Matches falling through are a part of the process. Every child ends up with the family that's right for them. It's lovely that you still wonder how he is, but you really don't need to worry about him. He's happy."

FAMILY FINDING

My friend who had warned us that we might end up at the "back of the queue" suggested we go along to some adoption matching events. We registered for one that sounded good, but when we received the event tickets, the words "complex needs" were added to the event title. That hadn't been in the event name advertised online! I wondered if we were just going to see profiles of more children like R and would feel awful for "saying no." Still, I thought we should go along and see who they were trying to find families for. "Complex" is open to interpretation. I have a lot of medical conditions myself, that some people might consider complex, but I could definitely parent a child with those health conditions.

Unfortunately, we all came down with a sickness bug, so couldn't make it on the day, but our profile was shared with all of the family finders at the event anyway. One of them sent a child's profile to our social worker who passed it on. We knew instantly that his medical needs were far too "complex" for us. He would need a lot of lengthy hospital stays and most likely a full-time carer. Our social worker was unsurprised when I explained that his needs were too much for us and said that she'd fully expected that to be our response, but she hadn't wanted to withhold the profile from us just in case something in it spoke to us.

Soon after, she sent us another profile. The two-paragraph summary didn't raise any red flags so we asked for more information. It went quiet for a few days, then our social worker advised that they'd made an assessment based on our profile and another family's and the other family was a stronger match. She didn't elaborate and, when I asked if there was anything we needed to do to improve our appeal as an adoptive family, she assured me that we were strong candidates but the family chosen for that child were just a better match for that specific child. It hurt a bit, but wasn't as distressing as having to pull out of the match with R.

Reading profiles was very emotional. It must be impossibly difficult for a social worker to summarise a child in a few paragraphs. The lengthier Child Permanence Reports were 40-odd pages about the reasons why a child was removed from their birth family and some of those made for tear-jerking reads. In several cases, the birth parents should probably have been adopted or taken into foster care as children, which might have set them on a better path, but their cases had sadly come to the attention of social services too late.

While waiting for our match, I read a lot of books about playful parenting and therapeutic parenting, which we had learned were the parenting styles most often recommended for traumatised children. Fortunately, these styles overlap with the gentle parenting style that we had stumbled into and found helpful for Zoe, so it didn't require a significant shift in our approach. In the evenings, I watched TV shows and films about adoption, and I listened to audiobooks and podcasts while driving to and from work each day. It was impossible to keep my mind off adoption. I couldn't bear the waiting and uncertainty, so I needed to feel like I was doing something useful. Learning how to be the best possible parent to a traumatised child was a positive way to keep busy.

I realised what a wonderfully sheltered life I had led as a child, and started to look at homeless people differently. I don't think I'd ever wondered before if a homeless person had children, but now every time I saw someone on the street, I wondered if they'd had any children removed. It just wasn't something that was on my radar until I watched a documentary about adoption and saw that some homeless mothers didn't accept the accommodation offered by social services and ultimately their babies were removed.

When I was pregnant with Zoe, we went to antenatal classes run by the National Childbirth Trust (NCT). In theory they were for learning about parenting, but the main appeal for me was that we'd meet people who were having babies around the same time as us. Having a support network who understood exactly what we were going through turned out to be invaluable. We had a constantly busy WhatsApp chat, asking each other questions and sharing tips we'd learned. All of us had a common goal; to be the best parents we could be to our babies. We were excited together about becoming parents, and supported each other through the traumas of childbirth, through sleep deprivation, colic and breastfeeding struggles. We'd only known each other for a few weeks before the first of the group had her baby, but we bonded fast and our children were friends before they had any concept of what friends were.

While we were going through the adoption process, three of our NCT friends had their second child, all boys. We were still very close to those families and spent a lot of time with them. Zoe loved playing with her friends' little brothers, and they adored her. Seeing Zoe making the babies smile and giggle was a regular reminder that she was going to be a wonderful big sister. While cuddling and playing with those babies, I often wondered if my own baby was out there somewhere already, and if they were with their birth parents or a foster family.

I felt a new respect and gratitude towards my friends for protecting their precious babies and keeping them safe, healthy and happy. I suppose I had taken it for granted before that parents look after their babies properly. I was now seeing profiles that made it painfully real that some parents don't keep their babies safe. One day, I was tickling my best friend's giggly little baby and marvelling at how full of joy he was. I felt overwhelmingly proud of her for being an incredible Mum. I welled up and told her how wonderful it is to know that she makes her son happy every day, and that he's safe. She hugged me and told me I'm a good Mum too, and I realised how silly I must sound. We had become Mums within two weeks of each other and learned how to do it together, along with our other antenatal Mum friends. I will never take it for granted again that a parent looks after their child properly though. If I'd been born into a different family and not had my NCT friends for support, things could have been much, much harder.

THE ONE

I was beginning to feel as if we would never be the right family for a child when I got an email from our social worker. It was another 2-paragraph profile about "Baby J." With each sentence, I felt more certain that he was "The One." I forwarded the email to Jon, but he didn't reply immediately. I texted him and he replied that he was in a meeting and would read it properly when he could concentrate. "I think this is our son!" I replied. "Don't get your hopes up too much," he warned. I laughed, imagining him tutting at his phone. He and I both knew that I had absolutely no chance of not getting my hopes up! I was buzzing with excitement. I bounced around the office for the rest of the day and, when I got home, Jon said, with what felt like comical levels of calmness, "yep, looks like a good match. Let's ask for more information. PLEASE try not to get your hopes up though." I did no such thing, excitedly racing off to hit "send" on the email I'd drafted hours ago, requesting more information.

It was only a few days until we were sent more information, but the hours felt like days, and the days felt like weeks! We soon learned that this little boy's name was Jake, which had coincidentally been one of my top name choices for if Zoe had been a boy. I was instantly reassured when the email came through, because Jake's social worker and family finder shared the information with us differently. Instead of a lengthy chain approach to communication, our social worker was copied into the conversation, while Jake's social worker and family finder sent us documents and asked us questions directly. We received information quickly and our questions didn't need to go through multiple people to be answered. When there were delays, Jake's social worker dropped us quick emails to let us know that she was going to be in meetings, but would get back to us later in the week. We were sent a copy of the updated medical report and, again, the doctor had recommended some blood tests. *Uh-oh, here we go*, I thought. I asked if all of the recommended actions had been completed. Jake's social worker replied straight away, saying she was pretty sure they had been and she would get back to us soon with confirmation. It seemed too good to be true, but within a few hours, she sent through a scan of the test results.

At this point, the Covid-19 virus (Coronavirus) was taking the world by storm and lots of countries were starting to shut down, entering various forms of "lockdown." The rules in the UK changed on an almost weekly basis, while the government tried to figure out what was safe. Every household in the country was sent a copy of the Prime Minister's "letter to the nation," asking people to stay at home to minimise the spread of the virus. Jon and I worked from home and kept Zoe off nursery to reduce our family's exposure to germs. It was a very stressful time. Jon works in healthcare, so his work became busier than usual and my job was constantly intense anyway. Thankfully, I had condensed my hours into 4 days, so I had Fridays off with Zoe. She was used to playing with her nursery friends Monday to Wednesday, and with my parents on Thursdays, so the lockdown was a massive shock to her system. She wasn't really used to playing alone, and we were conscious that it was all very unsettling for her, so we wanted to keep her happy and tried to make it as much fun as possible.

We worked in shifts as much as we could, comparing work calendars to find the best plan that allowed us to keep Zoe entertained, without missing any important meetings. This meant long, fragmented work days, interspersed with random hours of play. It felt like Jon and I hardly had time to talk, apart from giving each other quick handover notes about whether Zoe would need to eat soon, what activities we'd already done and what time we would need to switch over again. The long days quickly became unsustainable, so I tried to work more during the day and to encourage Zoe to play by herself. I moved my laptop around the house, so that I was at least in the same room as her, but it wasn't the same. She enjoyed being allowed more screentime at first, then became fed up that I was with her but not engaging properly in play. I felt like I was failing at work and, more importantly, I was failing Zoe.

I booked some time off so that I could enjoy the time with her instead of being constantly stressed that I was away from my laptop. It was a huge relief to have a week off and the weather was gloriously sunny, so we made the most of it and made kites (which fell apart), and played in the sand-pit and paddling pool. I tried to fully switch off for the week and just enjoy my wonderful daughter. I was also conscious that, if things went well, this could be our last decent chunk of time together before Jake joined us, so I wanted to shower her with attention for a while, before my focus would inevitably be divided. In a way, I'm glad I was pushed to take that time with her. I think that I would have otherwise saved up my holiday and added it onto my adoption leave, but it was really lovely to have some quality time with Zoe.

The lockdown restrictions meant that we had to have our linking meeting with Jake's social worker and family finder virtually, instead of the usual face-to-face approach. Jon joked that it was a shame I wouldn't be incentivised to blitz the house and do a litter-pick of the neighbourhood this time. Jon and I sat side-by-side in front of his computer for the video call. Jon laughed and told me to calm down as I hassled him to hurry up and sign in quickly. We couldn't send Zoe to nursery or to family or friends to babysit, so it was a bit of a juggling exercise to hold the meeting. We took it in turns to pop out and check on Zoe so that she wasn't on her own for long. She was watching a movie and was amused that we kept checking on her while she was just sitting still, but we weren't really used to leaving her in a different room. I felt strangely guilty that she didn't know we were talking to social workers about her potential future brother. I hadn't felt this way during our first linking meeting, but she'd been at nursery then.

This time, she was just a couple of rooms away from a conversation about something that I knew she'd be desperately excited about! We knew it was too early to get her hopes up, so we just said we had some important meetings. Sadly, by this point in the lockdown, she was getting used to hearing that.

The meeting was similar in format to the linking meeting about R, and with each bit of information shared, I felt more confident that we were the right family for Jake. Jon felt the same way, so I confirmed by email that we'd like to be officially linked with Jake. To my dismay, my social worker called and told me that although everyone was relatively convinced, they'd thought of a few extra questions after the call, so we had a follow-up call a couple of days later. Those days passed painfully slowly! During the second call, Jake's social worker asked us a lot of questions about our training on attachment and therapeutic parenting and Jake's family finder asked if one of us would be prepared to meet Jake's birth parents a few weeks after placement, but before the adoption order was granted. For various reasons, including the fact that we didn't think it would be helpful for our attachment if we got a babysitter so soon after Jake had moved in, we agreed with the family finder's suggestion that just one of us should meet them. Of the two of us, I was the one who most wanted to meet them, and Jon was happy for me to do it. I kept imagining our little boy asking me questions about his birth family and I wanted to have the answers. I was keen to get to know them a little, so that I could tell Jake humanising facts about them, to balance out the explanations about why they couldn't parent him. I wanted to be able to tell him their favourite colours, animals and hobbies. I wanted to know their favourite children's books, so I could read them to him, their favourite songs so I could play them to him and their favourite foods, so I could casually normalise talking about them, through questions like "hey, you know who else loves blueberries?"

Jake's social worker told me that his birth parents were keen to meet us too. They'd read that statistically, adopted children are more likely to be abused than children who aren't adopted, so they told the social worker that they needed to "look me in the eye" to reassure themselves that their boy was safe. That made me feel a bit nervous. I was going to have to convince them that I wasn't an abusive parent. I knew I wasn't, but how could I prove that to strangers in an hour or less? I wondered what they thought an abusive parent looks like. Did they expect to see something in my eyes? Did they think they'd hear it in my voice? Maybe they were just hoping for a general sense of warmth and kindness. I wasn't sure if I would come across as warm and kind. Maybe I'd just seem awkward and nervous. I'd probably ramble too much, which might seem insincere. I wondered if they'd threaten me or ask me to take good care of him.

I found myself worrying about how easy I would be to recognise if they saw me again. Should I dye my hair? Maybe I could curl it so I look different? I hardly ever curl it and, with two children to look after, it seemed unlikely I'd have the energy to do that again for a long time. I could do my make-up differently and wear clothes I don't normally wear. Should I hire a car, so that they don't know what mine looks like? I overthought the visit long before it was even time to book a date.

Thankfully, Jake's social worker confirmed at the end of this second call that she'd like us to be his family and felt we'd be a great match. The lockdown restrictions caused delays at various stages in the matching process. The first hurdle was the "chemistry meeting" that the agency would normally organise so that prospective adopters could meet the child before going to the matching panel. I already felt certain that I wanted to adopt Jake, but I also thought that the chemistry meeting was a sensible step in the process to give us extra confidence after everything we'd been through with R. Jake's social worker suggested that we have a virtual chemistry meeting while we were waiting for the Covid lockdown rules to be relaxed, though none of us really expected it to be particularly beneficial. Most ten-month-old babies don't really engage with people on the phone! At least we would have the opportunity to ask his foster carer some questions. I felt quite moved when Jake's social worker said, "I feel that you're the right family for Jake and I really want to make sure you stay engaged, so I think it's important that we do what we can to progress forwards."

The following week, we had a stroke of luck when Zoe fell asleep just before the chemistry meeting started. Jon was in a work call and I thought I might explode as the clock drew closer to the start of the meeting. He was totally relaxed as always and calmly finished his work call and got signed into the call bang on time. When I saw Jake's little face on the screen, I gasped and looked at Jon, whose eyes had welled up. I felt that he was our son and I could tell that Jon did too. I really hadn't expected to feel such a strong bond so quickly, but he was magic. I smiled for the rest of the call, watching this amazing little boy giggling and playing with his foster family. I wished I could reach into the screen and cuddle him. His laugh was infectious and he was amazingly interactive with the phone, peering at us and giggling. His foster carers, (who I'll call Karen and Sam to protect their identities), explained that he'd had a few calls with his birth family, so he was used to seeing faces on Karen's phone and was interested in them. I could have looked at his smiley face all day! We also learned more about Jake's routine, his development, and his likes and dislikes during that call, which made it all feel more real. I started to picture him as a part of our little family and I couldn't have been more excited.

After the call, Jon and I both felt that waiting for the lockdown rules to allow a face-to-face meeting wasn't necessary. We knew without a doubt that we wanted to be Jake's parents, so we were keen to get officially approved to be his family, so that we could start introductions as soon as possible. Matching Panels were on hold, but we asked for all paperwork to be completed so that we were ready to move forward as soon as possible.

The uncertainty was incredibly frustrating. I felt like the foster carers had my son and, while I'd been told by the social workers that Karen and Sam were brilliant foster carers, I found it unbearable that he wasn't with me. It reminded me of when I first dropped Zoe off at nursery towards the end of my maternity leave. I had felt panicked that she was in the care of someone I didn't know. I'd rationalised with myself that these were well-trained nursery staff who might not do things in the same way I would, but would look after her properly and had lots of experience. That didn't actually stop the tight feeling in my chest, though and I felt that tightness again, despite reassurances that Jake was the eighth baby Karen and Sam had looked after, so they definitely knew what they were doing!

The Matching Panel was held virtually and chaired by the same friendly man who had been the Chair of the Approval Panel. I felt instantly relieved to see his kind face and a few other familiar faces in the twelve boxes on the screen. The Chair spoke about how glad he was to see us again and asked our social worker, Jake's social worker and Jake's family finder to share their thoughts on the match. They all said lovely things about why they felt it was a good match. I started to well up when the family finder explained why she thought we were well-suited to be Jake's parents. It was moving to hear her listing all the reasons why I thought we'd be a good match and a few more reasons I hadn't thought of. It was a very humbling experience. With each comment they made about how we seemed to understand trauma and attachment well, I felt the weight of that responsibility. We had to live up to their expectations and be the wonderful parents we were promising to be. This little boy deserved the best.

We were asked a few questions about how we had prepared Zoe and our views on the proposed agreement for letterbox contact. Finally, we were asked to sign out of the virtual meeting so that the panel members could discuss us, then our social worker would call us back. Thankfully, we only had to wait for about 20 minutes for that call, and our social worker excitedly told us that we'd been unanimously approved. I didn't know what to do with myself! I was so excited, but we didn't know when we would actually get to meet him or bring him home, so we didn't know when the right time would be to tell Zoe. We started to drop hints that the social workers had mentioned a little boy who needed a big sister and told her that we were hoping to get more information soon.

The government continued to review and amend the lockdown regulations every couple of weeks and finally someone thought to amend the list of permitted activities to include adoption introductions. I excitedly rang our social worker to ask if that meant we could meet Jake soon, but she sighed and told me that she was waiting for advice on that to filter down the management chain, but that she expected there to be some new risk assessments required before introductions. The social workers did a paperwork risk assessment and determined that it wasn't safe to start introductions yet. Almost pleading, I listed all the precautions that we were taking to stay safe. We weren't going to supermarkets. We got home deliveries and disinfected everything that was coming into the house or quarantined it in the utility room for three days so that any germs would die off before we touched it. We were keeping Zoe at home from preschool, although we were now technically allowed to send her in. We offered to stay inside our home and garden for a couple of weeks so that we could be confident that we didn't have Covid-19. The social worker politely commended me on my enthusiasm, but told me it wasn't happening. We just had to wait.

On the plus side, we were allowed to have video calls with Jake as he was sort of our son now. It's a strange time between the matching panel and receiving the final adoption order (typically several months after the child moves in with you). Sometimes the child is "yours" and sometimes they're not, depending on the situation. We couldn't have the video calls too frequently as it was a lot to expect a child so young to sit in front of a phone and he was still having calls with his birth family, though those started to decrease once we were approved by the matching panel. We had a video call with Jake and Karen every couple of weeks. I asked one of the social workers supervising the call to take a screenshot so that I could one day show Jake the bizarre way in which we "met."

TELLING ZOE

In the hopes that things would change soon and suddenly, we started to prepare some "transition toys," intended to help Jake with the move from the foster home to ours. Our social worker had suggested that we give Jake a teddy that played a message from us when he squeezed it, to help him get used to our voices. I was browsing the teddies on my phone and asked Zoe which one she thought the baby would prefer, pointing out two tasteful brown bears. She wasn't impressed. "Oh no, these are too boring, Mummy. Get a rainbow one!" I didn't have a good reason for picking a tasteful one, so I let Zoe choose a garish rainbow bear, which in hindsight was absolutely the right choice for Jake, who loves anything colourful. Still having no idea whether it would be weeks or months until we met Jake, we were resisting the urge to tell Zoe all about him. I was finding the wait even more unbearable now that I knew whom I was waiting to meet. I couldn't put her through that.

When the bear arrived, Zoe was keen to record a message to "the baby" and I figured she could always record over it if she wanted to when she knew Jake's name, so we went for it. She told me she was going to say, "Hello baby, I'm your big sister and I can't wait to play with you," but she got distracted or excited and ended up saying "Hello baby! I'm your best sister! Do you want to know how the whole world is made?" Her little voice was so cute! Of course, being me, I overanalysed the situation and worried that

Jake's foster sister might think that Zoe referring to herself as his "best sister" instead of "big sister" was a slight against her. Zoe was thrilled with it though and told me she didn't want to record over it, because it was funny and it would make the baby laugh. Hushing the overthinking voice in my head, I smiled and told Zoe the baby would love hearing her beautiful voice and it would be nice for him to get used to it. Zoe corrected me, "but Mummy, we don't know if it will be a HIM yet!" Ohhh, I felt guilty lying to her, but it still felt like it was best for Zoe if she didn't know yet, so I let her think I'd just forgotten to say "or her." I deliberately said "he" and "him" whenever Zoe asked me about "the baby we're going to adopt" over the next few days, and said I had a feeling it might be a boy. I hoped that would help her to adjust to the thought that it would probably be a brother. Zoe chuckled and said "well, I think it's going to be a girl!"

Jake's first birthday was coming up and, although we had initially expected to have him home by then, we had sadly come to realise that that wasn't going to happen. Thankfully, Karen recognised that it was a big milestone and we'd want to be involved, so she contacted her social worker and offered to host a "socially distanced birthday party" in her garden. She outlined some stipulations to make sure no germs were passed from one household to another. We'd have to bring our own picnic blanket and our own food and drink. They had a caravan that would be parked on their drive and we could have access to it, if one of us needed to go to the toilet. If we wanted to give Jake a birthday present, we could drop it off a few days before, so that Karen could quarantine it in her home to ensure any germs on the gift or wrapping paper had expired before Jake touched it. As absurd as this all sounds now that the Covid-19 pandemic is over, at the time, it all sounded very fair and sensible. We gratefully accepted the invitation, and then, as we had a date to meet him, it finally felt like the right time to tell Zoe.

We had one photo of Jake at this point, showing him in a highchair at the foster home, with a huge smile on his face. It's still one of my favourite photos of him, as it really portrays his cheeky personality, so I can see why it's the photo that was chosen to send to us. I pulled the photo up on my phone and said to Zoe, "the social workers have found a baby who needs a family like us, with a big sister. It's a little boy called Jake." Zoe looked confused. "I thought it would be a girl." Clearly my hints that it was a boy hadn't broken down that preconception enough. I started panicking internally, wondering if she was going to be disappointed. She didn't say anything else, so I pressed on and explained that we'd be able to meet him soon, from a distance, but I wasn't sure when he'd be able to actually move in. I showed her the photo and she looked at it for a couple of minutes and said, "he looks very jolly," then went back to her dolls. I sat on the sofa, not sure what to do with myself. "Do you want to talk about it?" I asked, but Zoe shook her head and carried on playing. A few minutes later, she asked, "can we go and get him now then?" so I reminded her that the introductions would be gradual (we'd talked about this many times before), and explained about the socially-distanced birthday picnic. Zoe seemed a bit underwhelmed. I could relate. I was also finding it hard to get excited, having no idea when he'd actually move in. I'd literally told her that she would have the thing she wanted most in the world, but I didn't know when. It was a lot for a four-year-old to process! I let her play for a bit, then we called my Mum and sisters on video calls and Zoe told them about Jake. Their enthusiasm gave her a boost and we all felt more excited.

Now that Zoe knew about Jake, I brought out the rest of the transition toys that I'd been resisting the urge to prepare for so long! I had some recordable "buttons" that I'd found online, which were just the right size for a toddler to bash. We each recorded a short message so that he could get used to our voices. Mine was something along the lines of "Hello Jake, I'm Mummy! I love you very much and I'm so excited to play with you!" We all felt quite silly recording ourselves in front of each other and ended up ridiculously giggly! I'd also ordered some photos of all of us and a soft book that had slots for photos to slot into and lots of different textured bits for a child to squeeze, shake and pull. Zoe helped me to choose the photos to go in the book. I had also ordered a copy of the one photo we had of Jake, which I was planning to put in the living room so that he'd see it there with photos of the rest of us and, hopefully, feel on some level that he was part of our family and belonged here. Zoe gently picked up the framed photo and asked if she could have it in her bedroom, so of course I agreed, and ordered another photo for the living room. She hugged and kissed the photo, as though it was the most precious possession she'd ever had, then spent a while trying it out in different places in her room, finally settling on a place where she would be able to see his sweet face from her bed. I felt like I might burst with happiness!

That weekend, the three of us painted Jake's room together. It was such a wholesome experience, it felt like something from a movie. There should have been an uplifting soundtrack playing to a montage of us painting and smiling together, to signify that our "happily ever after" was on the horizon. Jon built a new toy box in Zoe's room, and Zoe and I filled it with all the toys that weren't safe for Jake. Zoe took great pride in this, knowing that she was helping to protect her brother and that she was responsible enough to have the small toys in her room. We talked about how he'd probably put things in his mouth a lot, so she could always go and play in her room if she wanted to play with something that wasn't safe for him, or we could get those toys out and play with them together during his naps. I also suggested that Zoe should put any toys in those toy boxes that she wouldn't feel comfortable sharing, but she insisted that she loved Jake so much that she wouldn't need to do that. "I'll even let him cuddle my special penguin!" she assured me.

MEETING MY SON

It was somewhat surreal choosing a birthday present for the son I'd never met. I'd bought gifts for my friends' sons over the past few months, as several of them turned one and I was torn about what to buy for my own. At such a young age, these children already had favourite toys and were beginning to show specific interests. I didn't really know what my own son liked! We'd seen him play with a few toys in the video calls and I knew that he liked balls, but he couldn't walk yet, so a football seemed ridiculous. I also didn't know what he already had. I asked my trusty Mum-friends what they thought and one of them suggested a push-along toy she'd seen that played music and popped out balls. He wouldn't be able to walk along with it yet, but he could still push it a bit and enjoy the balls and the various buttons on the side of it that played music and made lights flash. I ordered that and a toy phone that also had lots of buttons that made noises and lights flash. I wondered if the foster family would consider those appropriate gifts for my "child-who-wasn't-yet-quite-my-child." If he'd been living with us already, I'd have given him more gifts on his birthday, but Karen had said "a present" and I felt that I shouldn't give her too much stuff to look after for what was hopefully going to be a short time until he moved in with us anyway. I ordered a few other toys that I thought he'd like, but decided to keep them for when he moved in. I figured we might need some new and exciting distractions when he was living with us and missing his foster family.

A few days before Jake's birthday, Zoe and I drove over to the foster family's home to drop off the gifts to be quarantined ahead of the socially-distanced picnic. We also took the transition toys we'd prepared, so that the foster family could start showing Jake photos of us and letting him listen to our voices. We weren't sure if we'd actually get to see him, but it was a bright, sunny day and the foster family had some benches in the garden, so Karen suggested we sit on them, as they weren't too close together. It was wonderful and surreal! Jake was just waking up from a nap in the pram, so Karen picked him up and held him on her lap. Jake was smiley and giggly, especially when Karen tickled him. He looked tiny in real life! He seemed really excited to see Zoe and kept grinning at her. We talked about how she was the smallest person he'd seen for months, so he was probably amazed to see someone closer to his size than the family he was living with. Karen apologised that we couldn't cuddle him, but I wasn't upset. I hadn't expected to cuddle him that day. I was so grateful to be allowed to see him, even from a two-metre distance! I was soaking up every gorgeous smile and giggle! The rest of the foster family came back from a walk and we got to chat to them a bit too. I could see that Jake's foster brothers were particularly dreading him moving out. They all clearly loved him, but his foster brothers hadn't been in the family long enough to be used to babies being moved on. I made a point of saying, "I can see Jake is really going to miss you! We'll have to stay in touch and make sure we meet up a lot."

One of Jake's foster brothers brought a football over, which Jake pounced on, hugging it and then trying to roll it along the bench, even though it was almost as big as him. It rolled onto the floor, and he started to cry. Zoe leaned over to me and commented "not so jolly now! Are you sure we're at the right foster carer's house? He looked much jollier in the photo!" Thankfully Jake was all smiles again when the ball was handed back to him, so Zoe decided it probably was the right child after all!

I assured Karen that we were keeping Zoe off nursery until after Jake moved home so that we would be ready to do introductions as soon as we were allowed to. It was June and we knew by this time that the government planned to keep gradually relaxing the rules up to September, when they were aiming for all children to be back in school as normal. Karen explained that the older foster children and the birth child in her family were in three different schools, so she felt that we may as well do introductions in September when we'd have to accept the germ risk in all areas of our life anyway. My heart sank. I really, REALLY wanted to bring Jake home before then. Not just for the obvious reason that I wanted to hold him, cuddle him and properly be his Mum as soon as possible, but because my Dad was having chemotherapy and I hadn't been able to see him or my Mum for months. I was hoping that, once Jake moved in, we could quarantine for a while until my parents were convinced that we hadn't caught Covid from the foster family during introductions, then see my parents for socially-distanced picnics and walks before Zoe started school in the September. I didn't know when we'd see them after our germ pool was drastically expanded by school.

I was also really keen for Zoe to have as much time as possible to bond and play with Jake over the summer before she started school. She'd been at home with us for over three months already. If she was finally forced to leave us all day every day around the same time that her new brother moved in, I was sure she would feel like we were replacing her.

I found it quite terrifying that Karen's three children would be at different schools. Our germ pool would be widening significantly with Zoe starting school, but Jon would continue to work from home and I'd be on adoption leave with Jake. Three schools' worth of germs sounded utterly petrifying. I shared my concerns, but could understand why Karen was in no rush to increase her potential exposure to germs any earlier. She also explained that it would be easier for her if the other children were all at school during the introductions. They'd be out of the way, distracted from their sadness about their adorable little foster brother moving out.

I kept checking the weather forecasts over the next few days and it was looking promising for our picnic on Jake's birthday. But when the day came, the forecasts turned out to be all wrong and it absolutely poured down. We had quite a drive to get to Karen's home, so I wasn't sure if the weather was as bad there. We couldn't get hold of her, so we decided to chance it and head over anyway. Fortunately, Karen knew someone who had access to a large village hall, and she borrowed the key so that we could meet in there instead. We kept the windows open and sat on picnic blankets a few metres apart. A social worker sat further away and told us to pretend that she wasn't there while she did some work on her phone. Karen had organised some personalised first birthday decorations and made a phenomenal cake in the shape of a number 1, so it all felt very special and like a "real" party, despite the social distancing!

Jake took one look at Jon and was besotted. It was absolutely magical! He lit up! He started to crawl over to Jon, with a cheeky grin on his face. Karen tried to keep him over on their picnic blanket, so that we stayed at least 2 metres apart. I was a bit concerned that it would set us back if he picked up on a vibe that it wasn't safe to come too close to us. It seemed like nothing could put him off Jon though! Karen spent most of the two-hour party pulling Jake back or distracting him with food and toys so that he'd stay put. Watching Jake eat, I made mental notes of all the foods he was enjoying, so that I could order them in. Karen brought out the gifts and transition toys that we'd given her to quarantine, and Jake unwrapped them. It was so wonderful to see his gorgeous little face full of excitement and, for the first time, to feel like we were the reason for that incredible smile! We had brought along Zoe's toy phone, so when Jake opened his and put it to his ear, she did the same, and pretended to talk to him. He was fascinated! Then he looked at me taking a photo of the moment with my phone and his face was expectant, so I dutifully pretended to answer my phone too! It was a wonderful moment.

I found it all very strange trying to engage with Jake from a distance, with an audience, but fortunately the foster family were all lovely, friendly people. We all sang "happy birthday" and I had brought cake so that Zoe wouldn't be upset that the birthday cake was behind an invisible two-metre social distancing barrier! It was lovely to see Jake playing with his toys and with his foster family. After the birthday presents, Karen gave Jake the transition toys to play with. He was mostly interested in the buttons with the recorded messages, but we hadn't realised that it would be quite easy for him to inadvertently record over them, and within minutes, he sat on one and recorded over my voice with 20 seconds of the party conversation. One of Jake's foster brothers listened to the messages on the remaining two, and then recorded his own message over the party noise, "Hello Jakey, I'm your big brother!" That made me smile and, at the same time, break a little inside, knowing I was going to take this lovely boy's little brother away from him! I was glad that they felt like he was truly family, because that meant they'd been showering him with love, but it definitely made me feel guilty. Karen's Mum popped by with a gift for Jake too, and I realised that he'd been a sort of grandson to her. I hadn't really considered the wider members of the foster family who didn't live with Jake. I felt increasingly guilty about taking him away from this family that he so clearly loved, and who loved him.

THE TRANSITION PLAN

A couple of weeks after Jake's birthday, our social worker (who I'll call Lianne for privacy) phoned and told me that the agency had done another risk assessment based on the latest advice from the government. They had decided that we could start the transition for Jake to get to know us over the course of a week, at the end of which, he would move in. Lianne had spoken to Karen's social worker already and Karen had said she wasn't happy to start proper "contact" introductions until September. I was expecting that and understood her perspective, but I was gutted at the thought of having to wait until September. I also wondered if it would even really happen in September, or if we'd end up with more delays from the children bringing Covid home from their various schools.

Lianne already knew I was worried that things would be higher risk in September and would make it harder for Zoe and my parents to spend time with Jake. I asked her, "if Covid ramps up again when the schools re-open and the rate of infection stays high for another six months, a year, or more, and we don't find a time when everyone feels happy to proceed with introductions, what happens then? Do we just wait indefinitely? Do we have to be re-approved after a year or something, to stay matched with Jake? At what point should we accept that he's just going to stay living with the foster family?"

Lianne cut me off, which was probably just as well. I was

starting to sound a bit shrill. "No, Holly. He is going to move in with you. We have no reason not to do this now and Karen can't refuse. This is her job. She has to support his transition into your family." I tried to find my normal voice again. "But presumably the agency can't force her to let us into her home if she's saying she doesn't feel that's safe?" I was feeling a bit worried now. Could they force her? Would this damage our relationship with the foster family? I really wanted to stay in touch with them, for Jake's benefit. "We aren't going to keep paying for him to be in foster care when he has an approved adoptive family waiting for him", Lianne explained. "There's no legal reason why we can't go ahead with introductions now and we think the risk is low enough. We have a duty of care to Jake, and the panel decided that he should be with you, so we should be doing that as soon as possible. More children than ever are going into foster care. We can't have that space taken with a child who doesn't need it."

That all made sense to me, but I still didn't see how anyone could force Karen to let people into her home when there was a virus going around that could potentially make her family very sick. Lianne went on, "You're right, we can't force her to allow us access into her home, but we've come up with an alternative transition plan. You've both got big enough gardens that we can do it all outdoors, socially distanced, and then on the last day, Karen can put him in his car seat and step back, and you can pick him up, and take him with you." I gasped. We wouldn't be able to physically touch Jake until the last day! "He's going to feel like we've kidnapped him, isn't he?" I asked. "I mean, the whole point of the introductions is for him to see his foster carer allowing us to gradually take over his care so he feels safe with us. I don't want to sound ungrateful. You know I desperately want to bring him home! I'm just so worried this is going to damage our attachment and he'll be terrified of us." Lianne reassured me that we had had enough theraplay training to help him to cope with the trauma of the removal. "It's not ideal, but think about it. For most children, when they're removed from their birth family, they're moved without any warning at all and the foster family help them to adjust. You can help Jake in the same way." It was a good point.

Maybe it was better to help him through that, than to wait for who knows how many months when he'd be even more bonded to the foster family. Lianne listened patiently to my worries and told me she'd send through the proposed transition plan by email later and we'd have a call the next day to talk it through with the family finder, Jake's social worker, and Karen. After the phone call, I burst into tears. This didn't feel like the best thing for Jake, but waiting wasn't the best thing for him either. Jon and I talked through the transition plan that Lianne emailed over and we both felt miserable about it. We reluctantly agreed that we'd call the social worker back the next day and ask if we could wait until September, so that we could do introductions properly.

Thankfully, we weren't the only ones who were worried that the proposed plan would traumatise Jake. Karen phoned me, completely outraged at the proposal. She and her husband wanted Jake to have the best chance to bond with his new family, so they had also been agonising over the best way forward and had decided that they were willing to do introductions properly in order to avoid that. She proposed that we added in some video calls and socially-distanced meetings. These would start almost immediately, then we'd start "proper" introductions a week later than the latest transition plan proposed. We were so relieved that we could do introductions in a way that would minimise the trauma to Jake and thrilled that this would be in July rather than the dreaded September, so we gratefully agreed to the proposed changes and the one-week delay. I also suggested that we should tweak the part of the plan where Karen was supposed to bring Jake to our house and drop him off for a few hours. I wanted the foster family to know that he'd be in a nice, safe house, so I asked if Karen would like to bring the whole family over to see where we live. She thought that was a great idea, as she was worried that the children would struggle with the transition. I wondered if the social workers and family finder would mind that we'd come up with these plans together. If they did, they didn't show it. When we had the call the next morning, they just seemed pleased that we were all ready to move forward and they agreed to all of our proposed changes to the plan.

Now that we finally had an agreed transition plan, it was time to tell work! Jon was the owner of a small business at the time, working with a few of his closest friends, so he'd been keeping them posted and I had been keeping my boss in the loop too. As the socially-distanced intros would be starting right away and I happened to have a holiday booked for the following week, my adoption leave would be starting almost immediately. I had told my close friends at work, but now it was time to explain to more people that I was about to disappear for a year. Some of the reactions made me cringe.

Several people said things along the lines of "You're so inspiring!" and "That's a very noble thing to do!" They meant well, but we weren't being noble. It wasn't an act of charity. We wanted to have another child. On two separate occasions, I was asked whether we would tell Jake that he's adopted or try to hide it from him. For starters, hiding it would have been impossible, because Zoe was old enough to know and would have told him. Furthermore, his birth certificate would at some point be replaced by an adoption certificate, so that would be a bit of a giveaway. Those practicalities aside, I was surprised that at least two highly-educated men, who I had a lot of respect for, thought that hiding such a massive part of a child's identity from them might be the way forward. I explained that hiding it could make my son feel that he couldn't trust us, or worse, that we didn't fully accept him for who he is.

Several people asked, "what kind" of baby we'd "gone for," which was uncomfortable. I explained the process a bit, as it was clear that most people expected that we'd have a catalogue of photos and information to flick through. One even joked, "you should have gone for a Chinese one, then get a black one next time! You could get all different kids, like Angelina Jolie!" Ugh. I didn't know where to begin with that one, but I tried to educate him about how the process was about finding the right family for the child, not finding a child for the family. He also asked "couldn't you get a newborn? Then you'd have had a blank slate." In fairness, at some point, I had also assumed that adopting a child as young as possible would be an effective way to avoid trauma. That felt like a lifetime ago though. I'd had so much training and read so many books about the ways in which the body remembers trauma, even when the mind doesn't. I'd also once assumed that there were lots of babies relinquished by mothers who simply didn't want to parent. Looking back, that seems so ignorant. That hasn't been the norm in the UK for decades. Before we decided to adopt, I also didn't really consider how traumatic it must be, to learn that your parents chose not to parent you.

One friend was shocked that I was planning to take the full year of adoption leave and couldn't understand why I'd need more than a few days off to hang out with my new son. I couldn't help but laugh when he asked "but if he's over a year old, can't you stick him in nursery? Zoe went at that age, didn't she? Mine were all in nursery by the time they were one!" It was silly that I had to explain that I'd actually like to get to know my own child and that we needed that time for all of us to form healthy attachments to one another. My friend tried to reassure me, "You won't need that long. You'll bond in no time and forget you even adopted him!" What a disservice it would be to my son if I were to forget his life story and neglect to keep him aware of his birth family as he grows and develops his own sense of identity.

These friends and co-workers mostly meant well. One of them had always been a bit of a jerk, if I'm honest, but the majority of them were good eggs. They just hadn't been taught anything about trauma or attachment. These questions made me feel quite disappointed that so many people had no idea about the realities of adoption and foster care. My son is going to grow up in a world where people have these ignorant and outdated views of what happened to him. It would soon be my job to help him to find ways to deal with this ignorance.

INTRODUCTIONS

The new transition plan included two video calls, so that we could see different parts of Jake's routine and he could get used to our voices. One was his bath and bedtime routine, and it was adorable to see him splashing about excitedly and getting all snuggled up in his pyjamas. I was amazed that Karen had established a routine where she could simply put Jake in his cot and walk out of the room and he would fall asleep happily! Zoe was four by this point and I had been sitting in the rocking chair next to her bed until relatively recently, because she hadn't been happy to go to sleep without me there. Over the past few months, we'd been working on that and she was now happy for me to sit there for just a few minutes, but when she was Jake's age, I had to cuddle and rock her to sleep. I crossed my fingers that we'd be able to replicate Karen's routine, which would make bedtime with two children so much easier than I'd dared to hope!

The second video call in the introductions process was to show us how Jake got on during mealtimes. Karen found them the most frustrating part of the day and suspected that we would have issues at mealtimes too. We called one lunchtime and saw Jake in his highchair, with a roast dinner cut up in front of him. He rejected everything on his plate and got irritated when Karen tried to encourage him to eat it. Zoe was excited to see him but, when she could see that Jake was pushing the food away and Karen was persisting in trying to persuade him to eat it, she was furious! "He doesn't want to eat that!" she shouted. "He's pushing it away! Stop! That's my brother and he doesn't want it! Leave him alone!" She turned to me and said scathingly, "they don't seem like a very kind family." Totally mortified, I hissed, "Zoe! They can hear you!" I tried to explain that Karen just wanted to coax him into trying some of the food in front of him. At the same time, I was filled with pride because she was already feeling so protective of her little brother! It reminded me of the fiercely protective instincts that I felt for my own sisters when we were growing up. Karen graciously acted as though she hadn't heard it. I suppose after years of foster care of all different ages, she must be used to children speaking their minds!

A few days later, we had our first socially-distanced introduction session, so the three of us went over to the foster family's home again and sat in their garden. Zoe brought her toy phone and a few dolls. Jake was fascinated by her Ken doll, who had ginger hair, a similar shade to his own. He was clearly desperate to get to it but, unfortunately, as we were still socially-distancing, Karen had to pull him back when he was trying to crawl to us. Jake was visibly thrilled to see Jon again, giving him massive smiles, giggling at him and playing peekaboo. He smiled at all of us, but it was clear that he already thought Jon was amazing. The foster family were very friendly, but it was still hard not to feel slightly awkward while I was pulling faces and playing peekaboo in front of them! That soon wore off, as we spent more time together. We had three socially-distanced meetings in the garden, each an hour and a half long in the plan, but one had to be cut short as it started raining. It was quite tough for Zoe to sit still for such a long time, so the youngest of the foster children kindly told Zoe that she could play on his swings in the garden, saying "It's fine, I just won't play on them for two days, so any germs die off... you know, in case you have Covid." It was surreal hearing children talking about the pandemic in such practical terms! It felt like Covid was everywhere and I was so worried that someone would come down with Covid and delay introductions even further. Thankfully everyone stayed healthy and finally the day came when we'd be allowed to cuddle our boy!

It was also the first day we were allowed to set foot inside the foster home. We arrived after Jake's morning nap and he seemed happy to see us! Karen and her daughter sat on the sofa, so that Jake knew they were still close. Jon, Zoe and I sat on the floor with Jake and played with his toys. He giggled happily, as we rolled balls around the floor together and he tried to catch them. When a ball rolled under the sofa, he made a sad little noise until Zoe retrieved it for him. His foster sister asked, "Aw, do you want a cuddle from Mama?" I wasn't sure if she meant me or her own Mum, but for some reason, I assumed it was probably Karen. I didn't know whether I should cuddle him and risk looking like I was asserting my position as his "Mama," or not cuddle him, and risk looking like I was uninterested in cuddling and comforting my own son. Introductions are not a comfortable situation for an overthinker! Jake was giggling again before I could decide what to do.

I asked Karen if she could take a photo of us all playing together, and Zoe went to put her arm around Jake. As soon as Zoe's arm touched him, Jake burst into tears. Zoe pulled her arm away and Jake stopped crying. Zoe looked at me, clearly worried. I reassured her that he was just nervous because nobody had touched him for months apart from the foster family, and he didn't know that we're safe people yet. "But I'm his big sister!" she objected. The same thing happened a few minutes later when I picked Jake up to stop him from hurting himself on the door, and again when Jon picked him up for the first time to put him in the baby bouncer. We managed to make him laugh by tickling him and bouncing him up and down, but he was clearly not fully comfortable with us making physical contact yet.

As the week went on, we spent a little more time at the foster family's home each day, arriving and leaving at different times, so that we could see different parts of his daily routine. Aside from his refusals to eat, he seemed like a much easier baby than any other baby I'd ever met! On the second day, when we arrived, he was playing with some toys on the floor. I knelt down next to him and said "Hello, Jake!" He reached his hand out to touch my cheek. I froze with his hand on my cheek, not wanting to do anything that might make it stop. We stayed there for a magical moment, looking at each other's faces. Years later, he still touches my face like this sometimes, and I'm always taken back to that special moment when I felt like he was peering into my soul and trying to figure me out.

It was so special watching Jake interacting with Jon and Zoe. He was absolutely smitten with Jon and soon wanted Jon to hold him a lot of the time. Zoe dipped in and out of playing with Jake. She got on really well with the youngest of Jake's foster siblings, so she kept going off to play with him for a while, then coming back to play with Jake. It worked really well, because she didn't want to play with the baby toys all day, and it meant that Jon and I had some time to focus on Jake. Zoe coped really well for the most part, but she crumbled when I said, "Aw, look at that sweet face" and stroked Jake's cheek. I don't think she'd really processed that Jon and I were going to love Jake and he would be our child. She'd been focused on him being her brother, whom she would love. I saw her face crumple and scooped her into a hug, reassuring her that she'll always be my special girl. She sobbed, "I wish I was still small and cute!" I was careful to make more of a fuss of her after that and babied her a little, offering to help with things I knew she could do herself, like putting her shoes on. Every time she protested, "I don't need you to do that, I'm a big girl," I said, "Aw, but you'll always be my sweet little baby, even when you're bigger than me!" It seemed to help her to accept that she wasn't being replaced by a new baby.

The next day, Jake was a bit frustrated during dinner and he banged his head on the highchair tray. His lip split open and he screamed. I still felt like a bit of an imposter, as if I wasn't really his Mum yet, and I automatically assumed that he would want Karen to comfort him. I picked him up out of the highchair and cuddled him, but then immediately passed him to Karen, explaining, "I think he'll want you to comfort him after that!" Karen gave him a quick jiggle and passed him back to me, happy. I couldn't believe how quickly he'd calmed down! I immediately regretted not trying harder to soothe him myself. I'd assumed it would take a lot longer for him to recover from that, and that he'd want the comfort of the woman who had been his Mum for the past ten months. I kicked myself mentally for not showing him that I could comfort him too.

It felt like Jake was having more fun with Jon and Zoe than with me. I wasn't sure if I was overthinking things, or if the foster family were seeing that too, and worrying that the little boy they cared about might not bond with his new Mum. It was a really unnatural situation to be in, spending so much time in the home of people we hardly knew. I was loving every smile and giggle from Jake, but feeling an underlying stress, despite the foster family doing everything they could to help us feel comfortable there. Every day when we got home, I felt utterly exhausted!

On the fourth day, we took Jake out for a walk with the foster family, so that he'd see that we were safe people to leave the house with, then the next day, we took him out for a few hours by ourselves! It felt liberating to know that nobody was watching us. I wondered if the foster family were worried about Jake, or if they knew us well enough yet to feel comfortable with us taking him out of their sight. Obviously, they'd have to get used to it soon, but I kept wondering how they were coping. We got Jake and Zoe into their car seats and drove to a lake nearby, to feed ducks and have a picnic. Jake's car seat was rear-facing and Zoe was forward-facing now, so they could see each other really well. I'd given Zoe a jingly ball toy to pass to Jake if he got bored in the car. She shook it first, so that he understood that it made a sound, then handed it to him. Jake shook it excitedly, then passed it back to her. They kept taking it in turns, and it was utterly adorable. Jake was so excited to be with Zoe, and started singing a happy little song, "de-de-den, de-de-de-deeee." Zoe joined in, and it was the merriest little combination of random sounds I've ever heard! Our plan was for Jake to have his nap in his buggy, but he nodded off just before we arrived at the lake. I had never had much luck at transferring Zoe from the car seat to the buggy without waking her, but I had a feeling this baby would be different! Jon shook his head, saying "We should just wait in the car. He's going to be miserable if you wake him up!" I persuaded him that it would be alright, and went for it. I got Jake's dummy (that's a pacifier to my American readers!) out of the bag and got the buggy (stroller) set up with the shade up, before risking the transfer. Jake opened his eyes and mouth for one terrifying second, but I popped the dummy in and he went straight back to sleep. Magic! That would never have worked with Zoe! Our whole afternoon would have been ruined! Jon and I looked at one another in disbelief. "This baby is so easy!" I squealed.

Walking along, pushing the buggy, I felt like I was doing role-play with Zoe, pretending to be "the Mummy one." It had taken such a long time to get to this stage, it felt too good to be true. We had a lovely walk in the sun, finding grasshoppers in the long grass a few metres away from the lake, while our sweet boy slept. I kept peeking at his serene little face. He slept with his hands behind his head and I felt so honoured that he had fallen asleep with us, and even more so that he'd gone back to sleep after that split-second when he saw that I was lifting him out of the car seat and into the buggy. "He must feel safe with us, to allow himself to sleep," I told Jon, happily.

After about half an hour, Jake woke up, smiley as ever. His skin was much fairer than the rest of us, and I felt a huge sense of responsibility to not let him get sunburnt! Karen had joked the day before that she was relieved they'd made it through the recent heatwave without Jake getting sunburn. Obviously, I would never want either of my children to get sunburn, but I felt that this was probably the worst possible time for me to fail at that, so after we'd fed the ducks, we sat on a picnic blanket in the shade, far from the reflections of the lake. It was so much fun! I'd brought all of Jake's and Zoe's favourite snacks and some toys for when they'd finished eating. We had lots of lovely cuddles and took some photos of the four of us. I felt so content. We were a family at last and our little boy was happy with us.

We went back to the foster family's home after the picnic, where we all had dinner together, then we stayed for Jake's bedtime routine. As we'd seen the routine on the video call, Karen and Sam stepped back so that I could take the lead. We hoped that Jake would be reassured that I could give him a bath and put him to bed. He had a fab time splashing in the bath, then I got him dressed and brought him downstairs. At this point, Karen would normally pass Jake to Sam, then go off and prepare his milk, which Sam would give to Jake. In an attempt to recreate this routine ourselves, I passed Jake to Jon. Jake burst into tears, pointing at Sam! Sam leapt up and left the room, saying "I think it'll be better if he can't see me! Don't worry, it's part of the process!" Karen rushed off to prepare the milk, and I took Jake back from Jon, saying "It's OK, Daddy's going to give you your milk! Karen's just making it!" It was as though we had rewound and paused the routine, so Jake stopped crying and just looked at me, his little face worried. I cuddled him until Karen came back with the bottle and passed it to Jon, then Jake was happy for me to pass him over to Jon. He drank the milk slowly, clutching the bottle with white knuckles and suspiciously eyeing everyone in the room. We knew from Karen that Jake didn't even really like milk that much, but the change to his routine obviously unsettled him, so presumably he wanted to make sure that as much as possible stayed consistent.

After Jake finished his milk, I took him up to bed, following the same routine that Karen had shown us. I was relatively confident that Jake would be happy, as I'd put him down for naps a couple of times during the day, and he'd just happily gone to sleep. I put him in his cot, then started to walk away, but he cried. I instinctively scooped him back up and cuddled him, not knowing quite what to do. Karen had told me that she never, ever picked him up after she'd put him down, but she'd also said that he'd always just happily snuggled his teddies and fallen asleep. I couldn't leave him crying. I held him until he calmed down, then tried again and he cried again. I started to panic. He wanted his normal bedtime routine, but he wasn't going to get many more of those. How distressed would he be when he moved in with us? After a few more failed attempts to put him in his cot, Karen came to see if I needed help. I burst into tears. Karen hugged us both and reassured me that Jake was probably just sensing that some things were changing and feeling unsettled by it all. She thought we were doing brilliantly and it would all be fine. We chatted for a while and I sobbed some more, then I said goodbye to Jake and handed him to Karen. She put him in the cot and he didn't make a sound. I was conscious that Zoe was going to need to get to sleep soon, so I hurried downstairs and we got ready to go. Sam kindly commented that perhaps Jake was just upset because he'd been having such a lovely time with us and didn't want it to end. I thanked him with a wobbly voice, and we headed home.

The next day was the 6th day of introductions. Karen came to drop Jake off at our house for a few hours after his first nap. She stayed for a bit, and I asked her to come up to Jake's room while I showed him it, so that he could see that she thought it was a safe place. Karen was enthusiastic for Jake's benefit, but he wasn't looking to her for reassurance as much as I'd expected. He was mostly beaming at Jon! Karen shot off quickly when I was about to give Jake some lunch. I had expected him to cry, but he was excited to see the food, and he was loving every second of Jon's attention, so it was OK. After lunch, he had a nap in our cot. I was terrified that it would go wrong, after the night before, so I decided to stay in the room until he'd fallen asleep. I sat on the floor next to the cot, where he could see me without turning his head. He lay completely still, watching me for a few moments, then fell asleep. I was so relieved! I snuck out and told Jon it had worked. He tutted when I said I'd stayed in the room. "Now he'll expect you to do that every time! You should have left, like Karen does! That's his routine!" I didn't care if I had to stay with him from now on. I just needed my precious boy to feel happy and safe.

When Jake woke up, Zoe gave him a full tour of the house. We'd been gradually bringing some of his things home, so there were familiar toys dotted round the house. I'd read that children can feel more at home if they are surrounded by familiar smells, so I'd asked Karen which washing powder she used for Jake's clothes. I hadn't bought him a lot of clothes yet, because I wasn't sure what he'd bring with him, but I'd washed his bedding in the same washing powder that he was used to. I also washed some of the blankets and towels around the house in that washing powder. I hoped that he'd feel an overall sense of familiarity. I figured it probably wouldn't make a huge difference, but it was easy enough to do, and I was painfully aware that his life as he knew it was about to change, so I wanted to do whatever I could to make him feel at home. I was gobsmacked at how effective it was. When we went back into the lounge for the first time after his nap, he was crawling around happily. When he went close to one of the blankets that I'd washed in that washing powder, he stopped moving, sniffed the air, and smiled. He buried his face in the blanket, with a satisfied little "mmmmm!" As the day went on, he did the same thing in other rooms, and I marvelled at the power of that adorable little nose!

Zoe and Jake had a wonderful time exploring the toys together, and it was glorious to see them playing happily. Zoe hadn't been able to have a playdate for over three months. Of course, Jon and I had been playing with her, but it was doing her so much good to play with a child again. She was the happiest I'd seen her for months. A few hours later, at the agreed time, I drove Jake back to the foster family, so that he could have dinner and sleep there. It was a long drive for Zoe and we'd done a lot of driving earlier in the week, so Jon and Zoe stayed at home. In the rear-view mirror, I could see Jake was holding his little hand out towards Zoe's car seat. I reassured him that she'd be in the car seat again next time and chatted to him the whole way back to the foster family. When I took him inside, he was quite unsettled again and he cried when I tried to put him down. Karen's daughter said, "Oh dear, do you want a cuddle with Mama?" and for a split second, I thought she meant her Mum, then I saw she was nodding encouragingly at me and realised she must have meant me the other day too. I kept cuddling him for a while and chatted to the foster family about how the afternoon had been, then I handed him over to Karen, which he was happy with.

Karen gave me a few last things to take home, including some photo albums and a list of all of Jake's possessions and who had given them to him. It was moving to see that lots of his clothes and favourite toys were from his birth parents. I had assumed that he would have grown out of everything they'd bought for him, but the cute little red jumper I adored was from his birth parents. I wished his birth parents could know that he enjoyed those toys and wore that jumper a lot. I made a mental note to take photos of him wearing the clothes they'd given him and playing with those toys. Our contact agreement stated that we would exchange letters and artwork. For reasons I won't go into, Jake's social worker felt that it would not be safe for Jake's birth family to be given photos to keep, but we could send photos and videos to the post-adoption team, which Jake's birth family could view in the council offices.

Another precious item was the contact book. Karen had used a little notebook to share messages with Jake's birth family back when he'd been visiting them for contact sessions in a contact centre. They were mostly informative messages back and forth, letting each other know how he'd been, if he'd napped and when he'd last had milk or food. There were a few more personal gems in there, where one of the birth parents had shared some information about themselves, and anecdotes about sweet or funny things that had happened during their contact sessions. The messages also mentioned a couple of Jake's "firsts" that hadn't been documented elsewhere, such as his first trip to the zoo and first time going swimming. That book remains one of the things I value most in this house. It's the thing I'd grab first in a fire, after getting the family to safety, of course! I know that Jake will treasure it when he's older.

The next day the whole foster family came to drop Jake off for a longer stretch. I'd explained to Zoe that they were all coming so that Jake's foster siblings would see that it was a nice, safe house, with lots of toys and hopefully then they wouldn't worry about him. She took this very seriously and asked if she could help me to clean the house. I'd already cleaned it, so we did some serious deep-cleaning! I've never seen Zoe like that before or since. Her energy was intense! We scrubbed the tiles in the bathroom, hand-washed the cushions for the garden chairs, dusted every skirting board and cleaned every door in the house. This must be what it was like for Jon to watch me blitzing the house before a social worker visit! Before they arrived, Zoe changed into her fanciest dress and stood in the hallway, holding a friendly-looking teddy that she'd chosen. When I asked why she was waiting there like that, she said "so they feel welcome!"

When the foster family arrived, I opened the door and Zoe grandly announced, "Welcome to our home! We hope you feel very welcome here!" She led a tour of the house, which worked really well, because she pointed out all of the things that a child would be interested in. Jake's foster siblings seemed satisfied that Jake would be happy and safe in our home, and I tried my best to reassure them that they weren't losing him completely. I had put the photo albums Karen had given me on top of his chest of drawers. When we showed Jake's foster brothers his bedroom, I made sure to point out the albums and tell them, "We'll look at those whenever Jake misses you. Even though we'll still see you a lot, I'm sure he'll miss you loads!" When we'd finished the tour, we all posed together in the lounge for one big group photo.

Jake was a bit more concerned about the foster family leaving without him this time, but we managed to distract him with a snack. Jake stayed with us until bedtime and we did the whole bedtime routine at our house. When we put him in the bath, he started to cry. Maybe he thought that having his bath there meant that he was staying with us, and it was a bit much. Or maybe he just didn't know me well enough yet to feel confident that I could keep him safe in the bath without Karen in the room. I got him straight out and wrapped him up in a towel, then got him into his pyjamas. Jake was fascinated to see Zoe brushing her teeth, and thrilled when I gave him his own toothbrush to hold. He didn't have many teeth to brush, but was keen to do whatever Zoe was doing! Jon took Jake back to the foster family and I read Zoe a story and put her to bed, wondering how that part of the routine would work with a wriggly one-year-old around. Karen had told us that they hadn't really read him stories yet. I'd read him a few during the day and he'd enjoyed it, but I knew from my experiences with Zoe that all bets are off when a child is tired!

The next morning was moving-in day. Karen dropped Jake off after lunch and told us he'd had his favourite foods, so he'd eaten a decent amount, then gave me a few last documents, including Jake's passport, birth certificate and the "red book" that recorded all of his vaccinations and birth information. She also gave me a letter she'd written for Jake to read when he was older, some cards his foster siblings had made for him, and a card that her daughter had written for me, Jon and Zoe. That card was beautiful, speaking about how she'd miss Jake, but was so glad that we were going to be his family. I was overwhelmed by her kind words.

Karen and I were both on the verge of tears, as she gave Jake a quick ruffle and a kiss goodbye, hugged me and wished me luck, then darted off, so that she wouldn't cry in front of him. I was full of emotion. I was so happy to finally have my son home, but I knew his lovely foster family were going to miss him beyond measure, and it was only a matter of time before he realised he wasn't going back to them, and he'd miss them too. I passed Jake to Jon and nipped off to have a little cry.

SETTLING IN

Jake's social worker came over the morning after "moving in day," to finalise some paperwork with us. We had a meeting in the garden, two metres apart. She had a list of instructions that she had to share with us, about how to look after Jake, and apologised in advance for how patronising some of the advice might seem, chuckling that it felt absurd to tell us how to parent a one-year-old when we already had a four-year-old and had been through this age. She reeled off the list of bullet points, including reminders that children need regular checks with dentists and opticians, then asked us to look after his emotional needs. We hugged him and promised to look after him. We had to read and sign a document that clarified which things we were allowed to do before the adoption order was granted, and which things we would have to get approval for from the local authority. It was a comprehensive document, even stating that we must not get his ears pierced before the adoption order was final, not that we had any plans to pierce his ears! The social worker advised that we'd have weekly meetings with her or another social worker for the next couple of months, to check that we were all adjusting well to being a family, then the frequency of meetings would decrease, stopping only once the adoption order was granted.

We spent the next two weeks mostly outdoors. Our new little poppet enjoyed long buggy walks, pointing out with great excitement any birds, cats, dogs and squirrels that we passed. He couldn't say many words yet but enjoyed "woofing" at any animals he saw, shouting "oof, oof!" enthusiastically. Cats were entranced by him! Every time I opened the door to the garden or the front door to leave the house, a cat or several seemed to appear within seconds and strike up a conversation with him. Jake would repeat "oof" over and over, while the cat miaowed. One even followed us round the block once, miaowing at him for the duration of our walk. It was really adorable to see Jake chatting to them, though I had to be vigilant, as cats would shoot into the house as soon as the door opened, looking for Jake. It was July, so the weather was mostly dry and sunny. We had countless picnics and went on a lot of walks. We spent a lot of time in the garden, watching caterpillars demolishing my broccoli. We played with the sand-pit, water table and paddling pool. It was fabulous!

The lockdown restrictions were still easing gradually, and we were allowed to visit outdoor parks again. Jake loved being pushed on the swings, especially if Zoe was in the swing next to him. He was thrilled whenever they could do the same thing! Ever since the start of introductions, we'd been pointing each other out to Jake, so that he'd learn our names. He soon got the hang of "Daddy," and as we'd been saying "that's Zozo, your big sister," he soon started to call Zoe "Dodo Dister." Jake didn't seem to make any attempts to call me "Mummy," but he definitely recognised the word. Karen had been "Mummy" to him. He was full of joy for the majority of the day, but whenever Jon or Zoe referred to me as "Mummy," he pointed at the front door and cried. I didn't know how to say, "Not that Mummy! You'll know her as Karen now!" It was quite emotionally wearing, but all I could do was keep doing my best to show him that I was worthy of the title. I couldn't ask Zoe to stop calling me Mummy, when she had all this change going on. I didn't think she'd be able to break the habit, even if I'd decided I wanted to be "Mama" or something else from then on. When someone came to the door, Jake cried. Sometimes, it felt like he was disappointed because it wasn't Karen. Other times, he seemed scared to see someone new. Maybe he wasn't sure if he'd be moved on again.

Video calls frightened Jake, which was surprising, because he'd loved having video calls with us when he lived with Karen, and he had been really smiley towards the screen. I wondered if the anxiety was because the last time he'd spoken to people on a phone, he'd ended up moving to live with them. Could a child that young understand that? It felt like he did on some level. The social worker agreed that that was probably the issue but unfortunately she still needed to see him on the calls so that she could tick the box on her reports to say that she'd seen him.

One afternoon, we were out for a walk round a lake, when a little girl shouted "Mummy, isn't that Jake?" and pointed at us. I tensed up, but tried not to react outwardly. The Mum glanced at all of us, then said "no, of course not" and they kept walking. We had a lovely time feeding the ducks and having a picnic by the lake, but I felt on edge for the rest of the day, and kept running through scenarios in my head, planning what to say and do if Jake is ever recognised by someone who knows his birth family.

After two weeks, Jon had to go back to work full-time. Jake was devastated. Jon was working from home upstairs in his office and Jake knew he was there. He didn't want to be with me when he knew Jon was so close. Sometimes Jon would pop down to play with Jake for a bit, which was lovely, but then Jake would be miserable when Jon left again, so it didn't really help overall. He didn't want me to comfort him, which was really distressing and quite difficult practically. He was just learning to walk so was quite wobbly on his feet. If he fell, or bumped into something, he'd scream for Jon, slapping my hands away if I tried to pick him up or cuddle him. Zoe found the sound of him crying really upsetting and sometimes she'd burst into tears too. Her crying was even louder, which frightened Jake. Sometimes Zoe and I could cheer him up by being silly but in the first couple of weeks he was often too upset for that to help. He just wanted Jon. I tried to keep him distracted as much as possible, taking the children out on various adventures and hoping that he'd start to see me as fun!

It was a period of adjustment for all of us and Zoe was brilliant at keeping Jake busy and happy, but the changes to her routine were understandably a bit frustrating for her at times. They were normal frustrations that you'd expect a big brother or sister to struggle with, though the impact on her life would have been more gradual in some ways if Jake had been with us since before he could crawl. Sometimes Zoe wanted to play with small toys that he might have put in his mouth, or things that were too fragile, such as her paper dolls. He loved ripping anything made of paper that he could get his hands on, so we knew that wouldn't be a good activity for him! Zoe was sensible enough that I could let her play with those toys in her room, but she wasn't really a fan of playing alone. She understood why Jake couldn't be the one left to play on his own, but that didn't stop her from feeling that it was unfair. Jake needed a morning nap and an afternoon nap, so Zoe had to play quietly during those times. I'd never noticed just how loudly she moved! Even her quiet role-play games with Barbies seemed excruciatingly loud when I knew that Jake was upstairs. At first, she was hugely frustrated that we couldn't go anywhere while he was napping, but she soon started to look forward to those times, because we could play with the paper dolls, play card games, build Lego or make things with small beads. I could have done with the free time to tidy up some of the growing chaos, to get on top of the washing, or to just sit and rest, so some days I persuaded her to watch a movie during one of his naps, but I was also really grateful to have some one-on-one time with Zoe.

I've always tried to be a responsive parent, to ensure Zoe knew that I'd always meet her needs. I ran to her whenever she woke in the night. I breastfed on demand, cuddled and rocked her to sleep, and generally tried to make sure that she knew I was always there for her. I would have wanted to parent my second child in the same way, regardless of how they joined our family, but knowing that I was Jake's third Mum, and feeling that he was upset with me for trying to replace his foster Mum, it felt crucial to show him that I will always be here for him. When Jake woke up from his naps, he shouted or cried, and I would race into his room and scoop him up immediately. The only problem was, this time round, I had another child to think of! Zoe was quite put-out that I'd essentially run away to get Jake the instant he woke up. She took it well, but I could see she was frustrated by it and understandably so. It wasn't fair to her that we had to stop playing cards mid-game, because he'd rip them up if he got his hands on them. We soon figured out a better routine. We started to do any activities Zoe wanted to do immediately at the beginning of his nap time, then we'd spend any extra time watching a TV show that she could finish watching on her own if Jake woke up before it was finished.

We had some of the typical "sibling issues" that you'd expect. Jake thought Zoe was amazing, so he wanted whatever toy she was holding. We adapted by playing with toys that we had multiples of, and Zoe became expertly skilled at pretending she preferred the toy that she wanted him to use, so that she could still have her real favourites. It helped that Jake had a couple of naps each day, because Zoe knew that she wouldn't have to share during that time, so she was able to summon up more generosity when Jake was asking for the toys she wanted to play with, so long as I reassured her that he wouldn't be taking them with him when he went for his nap. We had to think creatively in a few instances, as he didn't have the patience yet for sharing, as Zoe was getting fed up of always being the one to let Jake have the thing they both wanted. I realised that taking it in turns to have "the purple cup" wasn't working, so I took the lid off that cup and swapped it with a green one that was the same shape, so that both children had a part of their beloved purple cup. Zoe was fascinated to learn that this was a "compromise," and started throwing her newly-discovered big word around whenever there was a compromise to be made.

I'd always managed to avoid cooking multiple dinners, not because Zoe was a brilliantly diverse eater, but because Jon and I just ate whatever she would eat. We often included one or two new things to try alongside things we knew she'd eat, but we were pretty relaxed about whether or not she tried the new things. With two children in the family, it was absurdly difficult to find meals they would both eat. I wanted Jake to feel at home, so I made some of his favourite meals. Zoe was appalled at having to try so many new things. I felt that she was going through so much change, I ought to be more flexible, so I soon ended up making multiple options for the family.

Mealtimes were a bit fraught, because Jake wasn't confident yet that we would feed him enough food, or often enough. It was really difficult to actually get food into him, because he would cram as much as he could into his mouth, then spit it out in frustration, because he couldn't chew or swallow properly with his mouth so full. He would then be distressed that it was all chewed up and soggy, so he wouldn't eat it. Sometimes he'd throw it on the floor, then scream for Zoe's remaining food, which she found very upsetting, because she was so desperate to make her little brother happy, but she wanted to eat her own food! It seemed like the very thought of food was triggering a primal panic and he felt unsafe. If a story or TV show mentioned food, he cried, and the only thing that would cheer him up was food, even if he'd eaten recently. I once set Zoe's plate down on the table a second before Jake's, and he absolutely sobbed. It seemed like he was worried that I'd forget to feed him.

We adapted quickly, but it took a lot of little steps for Jake to trust that we would feed him. In the early weeks, he couldn't cope with any sensation of hunger at all. I made sure I always had lots of quick snacks around, so that he didn't have to wait. To start with, I gave him a snack about every hour, and it seemed like all I did was pass him food and clean up the mess after meals. If we went out, I brought a picnic, even if we'd just eaten a meal. If he saw someone eating when we were at the park, or even if someone's parent called out "time to go home for lunch," he would quickly become hysterical and I would have to whip out a snack. One time, we saw a child with a picture of a monkey holding a banana on their tee-shirt and that was enough to cause Jake huge distress. One of our most upsetting outings was when we got stuck in a traffic jam, and the driver in the car next to me pulled out a chocolate bar and proceeded to eat it. She had no idea what misery she was causing! Whenever we went to a new place, Jake immediately demanded food, even if he'd eaten just before we left home. It felt like he was testing my ability to look after him in each new location.

I tried a few different approaches at home, while figuring out how to help him best. The health visitor suggested putting just a few pieces of food on his plate at a time, but it felt like that was fuelling his concern that I wouldn't give him enough food, so then I tried putting the rest of his food on a second plate that he could see, but not reach. That infuriated him, but fortunately he did understand that that was his plate. I had to keep up with him and pass him one thing at a time, so that he didn't get upset. The problem with that approach was it wasn't really slowing him down. He was still shoving it all in, then storing it in his cheeks until he had too much to chew and swallow. He was just trying to get through it quickly, so that I'd pass him the rest of the food. I decided to try some foods that were naturally slow to eat, and the first thing that came to mind was brioche. It worked brilliantly. He could hold the whole brioche, and because it was so chewy, he ate it relatively slowly. For months, it felt like all he wanted was brioche. I was somewhat mortified at the volume of brioche he was eating compared with fruit and veg, but he was very small for his age, so I was glad he was eating carbs that contained some dairy. He would still eat fruit, but I had to be careful not to give him too much in one go. Larger items, like a whole banana, worked best, and he was excited to hold a whole banana like Zoe. Picnics outdoors seemed to work better than sit-down meals. I did find that he'd raid the picnic bag and eat a bit of everything straight away, but he didn't usually get as upset. We had a lot of picnics in our own garden and he enjoyed watching the squirrels and cats so perhaps that distraction is what made it easier as well as the immediate nature of picnic food. We didn't eat many cooked meals in the first few months. When we did, one of us would cook while Jake was on a walk with the other parent. When we got back from the walk (which almost always involved a brioche, because we'd see a bird eating a worm, or another child with a snack), we'd take his coat and shoes off speedily, sometimes even before opening the front door, then rush to get him to the table before he could smell the food and become too upset to actually eat it.

I found that Jake could cope a little better if I was holding him for the moment or two that it took me to organise his food. He liked to see that the food was coming and needed that visual reassurance. Me saying, "I'm just getting some food out for you" wasn't enough. I had to hold him with my other arm while I was opening the fridge, and sometimes he would frantically try to lunge into the fridge to grab things. He didn't actually eat a lot, but it was extremely often.

I soon learned which of our children's books mentioned or depicted food, and hid them away for a while. Sometimes it wasn't even a main feature of the story, but a scene set in the kitchen was problematic, as were pictures of fruit trees in the background. We changed our TV watching habits to avoid programmes that heavily featured food. Zoe was very aware of his anxiety around food, so if we were on a walk and she clocked someone eating, she'd quickly nudge me and say, "Look! I think you need to get something out of the bag, before Jake sees that!" Zoe helped in other ways, too. When we were all eating together, she'd say things like, "See Jake, Mummy did feed you. She always feeds us. She's never forgotten to feed me, and she won't forget to feed you, because she's your Mummy too." I felt incredibly proud of her for being so supportive and understanding of his fears, but at the same time, it was heartbreaking that my two sweet children were aware that some parents don't remember to feed their children.

I was worried that Jake wasn't learning to trust his own body's hunger signals, because we were giving him so many snacks to prevent him from getting hungry. We'd done baby-led weaning with Zoe and it had worked brilliantly. She has always been very in tune with her body, and recognises when she's hungry and when she's full. I hadn't expected to be in a situation where I was preventing my child from experiencing or noticing any sensation of hunger at all, but it was more urgent for him to learn that I, his mother, will meet his needs. Learning how to listen to his own body would have to come later, when the sensation of hunger didn't send him into a panic. Gradually, Jake became less frantic around food, so we slowly increased the amount of food on his plate. We were also able to give him smaller items of food, once he was eating more calmly and less likely to choke.

Something I really hadn't been prepared for, was that Jake's birth parents were constantly on my mind. I kept wondering how they were coping. Were they more upset now that he'd been moved to our family? Had they thought there was still a chance he might end up back with them, or had they expected this and resigned themselves to it? I hoped they were looking after themselves. When Jake did the boundary-testing things that toddlers do, I wondered how they would have handled it. When he giggled, I felt so lucky that I was the one who got to make him laugh, but so sad for his birth parents that they missed it.

I was asked to write a "settling-in letter" for Jake's birth parents, which would kick off our letterbox contact. Writing the letter was therapeutic. It took the edge off the irrational guilt I was feeling about being the one who gets to raise this wonderful boy. I found it surprisingly enjoyable to write. There aren't enough excuses in life to write pages and pages about how brilliant your child is. Jake had reached lots of milestones and was starting to talk, so I shared lots of sweet and funny anecdotes that reflected his cheeky sense of humour. I tried to make sure it didn't sound like I was taking credit for any of his achievements and included some reassurance that we talk regularly about his birth family and plan to continue to do so, so that he'll always know that they love him. I asked lots of questions, hoping it might help them to reply if they had something to answer. I asked, "What's your favourite food? We'll let you know if Jake likes it!" and "What stories did you enjoy as a child? We'll try to get hold of them and read them to Jake!"

I picked out some of Jake's drawings and paintings, and sorted them into piles for each birth parent. I tried to give them similar artwork, in case they were still in touch and compared what they received. Then I selected some photos and videos, which I sent to the post-adoption support team, so that Jake's birth parents could go into the office to view them. As those meetings were temporarily on hold due to the Covid restrictions, I also sent copies of the photos to a social worker, so that she could meet them outdoors and show them on her phone.

When Zoe was little, I used to cuddle her in the rocking chair next to her cot. It helped her get to sleep and comforted her when she had colic. During my first year as a parent, I spent more time in the rocking chair than in my bed! When Jake joined us, I was grateful that he had a well-established bedtime routine, but at the same time, I was a little sad to think that we'd missed out on those lovely bonding times in the rocking chair. Sometimes, when he woke from a nap, if I picked him up quickly and shushed while rocking him, he fell back asleep in my arms. It was a light sleep that wouldn't last if I put him back in his cot, but I found that he'd stay asleep for a while if I carried him through to Zoe's room and sat in the rocking chair, cuddling him. It usually only lasted for 20 minutes or so, but each of those "cuddle-naps" was wonderful. I gazed at his serene little sleeping face, feeling as though each moment was healing a little piece of me that I hadn't known was damaged. It was such a relief that my little boy was starting to trust me to keep him safe, and felt relaxed enough to go back to sleep in my arms.

WISH YOU WELL

Ordinarily, when there isn't a scary virus spreading through the country, the foster carer takes the child to contact sessions with their birth parents, until the judge determines that the child is going to be adopted, then contact reduces and stops completely. Our agency referred to the last meeting as the "wish you well" visit. Others call it the "farewell meeting," or something similar. In our case, Jake's foster carer was unable to take him to the final contact meetings with his birth family due to the pandemic restrictions. They had some contact sessions over Zoom, but the social workers felt it unfair that the birth family hadn't had a chance to say goodbye in person, and asked us to support a face-to-face meeting at a later date. We agreed that it would be wrong not to, but I worried about the effect it would have on our attachment. Our bond was new and fragile. Jake preferred Jon to me. He still cried and pointed at the front door when anyone said "Mummy." I was worried that Jake would be frightened. He wouldn't remember his birth parents. It had been six months since they last saw each other in person. At this stage in the placement, Jake wasn't comfortable with being held by my parents, who we saw several times a week. He still panicked when the supermarket delivery came or when we spoke to anyone on a walk. He clearly didn't feel that he was securely part of our family yet. I didn't want to make that worse.

Jake's social worker told me that she'd pick him up, drive to the contact centre about an hour away and then hand him to a contact centre worker who would take him to his birth parents for an hour, then return him to the social worker. Jake's birth family naturally didn't want to see his social worker, as she was the one who had removed him from their care. I felt panicked, imagining how my precious little boy would feel when handed over to stranger after stranger. He didn't see the social worker regularly enough to feel safe with her. In fact, he cried whenever he saw her on a video call.

I explained my concerns to Jake's social worker. I agreed that Jake's birth parents should have the chance to say goodbye to him, but expressed my concern that the meeting was planned in such a way that their needs were met and emotions protected, at the expense of Jake's. He was going to be terrified! I asked if there was any way we could arrange for me to meet the birth family first, so that they'd know me a bit and then I could take Jake to meet them afterwards, so that he wouldn't be terrified, and they wouldn't be dreading seeing me. I recognised that meeting me would be tough for them, but reasoned that they would probably rather have a happy playdate with Jake feeling relaxed and safe.

Jake's social worker was wonderfully empathetic and seemed to think that might work. She suggested that we delay the whole thing by a couple of weeks, to let his attachment to us grow. She apologised for having told me what the plan was, rather than asking how I felt it could work, and reassured me, "You are now the world expert on Jake. He's been with you for several weeks and you now know all his current likes and dislikes, fears and habits. You know what's best for him. I know we've got a while 'til you can apply for the adoption order, but as far as I'm concerned, you're his parents now, and I respect your views on what is best for him." I welled up with emotion.

A couple of weeks later, I had a call from a different social worker to tell me that the meeting was booked and that we would be sticking to their original proposed plan. When I started to express my concerns again, she told me firmly, "To be honest, Holly, this isn't your choice. He is still a Looked After Child and the Local Authority has responsibility for him, so you have to support this. He's not yours yet. His birth parents shouldn't have to see you. That might be too much for them to handle. And it's not fair on them to make them wait any longer." I didn't want to make them wait longer. I wished they'd had this meeting months ago, when it should have happened. My boy wouldn't have been terrified then. He would have remembered them and had a fun playdate with them. They would have had a happy final memory with him, and could have taken lots of smiley photos and giggly videos. "He won't remember this at all," the social worker tried to reassure me. This went against all of the training we had been sent on that taught us that, even if a child doesn't remember a traumatic event, it can have a lasting effect. "His birth parents will though," I said. "It's not fair on them. They'll have a heart-breaking, sad hour." She agreed that it would probably be pretty horrible and advised me to stay nearby, in case the visit was cut short.

I felt sick at the thought of my little boy not recognising his birth parents. It would be so scary for him, and so upsetting for them to see him afraid of them! *At least he doesn't call me Mama yet*, I thought. That would be awful, if he was screaming to be taken back to "Mama" in front of them. I managed to persuade the social workers to allow me to drive Jake to the contact centre and hand him over there, so that at least he wouldn't be scared for the long car journeys with a social worker driving him to and from the contact appointment. I asked them to send me photos of his birth parents, so that I could familiarise him with their faces. Maybe if he recognised them, after the fear of being taken by the social worker and then the contact centre worker, he might even be relieved and happy. He might even smile to see faces he recognised!

I desperately tried to find ways to make it less scary for him. The social worker assured me that there would be toys galore at the contact centre, so I read Jake a book about a child going to a playgroup, telling him that he was going to go to a place like that to play. I showed him the photo of his birth parents, saying enthusiastically, "They will play with you there! Look, they're fun! They're smiling! They are looking forward to playing with you! And then you'll come back to me and I will bring you home." He beamed and wriggled with excitement. I prayed that he would feel that way on the day! He was now 15 months old and I felt that he understood a lot, but he couldn't say many words yet.

A few days before the meeting, we had a "LAC review," LAC meaning "Looked After Child." It was a video call and included our social worker, Jake's social worker and the Independent Reviewing Officer, who had apparently been involved in Jake's case from before he was born. The Independent Reviewing Officer asked for an update on how Jake was settling in, then went through a list of actions. I had to get Jake weighed by a Health Visitor within the next couple of weeks, to check how he was doing in our care. The Independent Reviewing Officer advised Jake's social worker that, as Jake was in our care now, no more photos were to be given to his birth parents to keep. The social worker was permitted to show him photos on her phone at their next visit, which would be to advise them that he had settled in well and we'd be applying for the adoption order in a few weeks. After that, they would need to book meetings with the adoption agency, to go in and view the photos in their offices, per the original contact agreement.

That logic made sense to me during the LAC review, but after the meeting ended, it dawned on me that this meant that Jake's birth parents would not be allowed any photos of their time with Jake at the "Wish You Well" meeting. Jon and I felt that it would be morally wrong for Jake's birth parents to not be allowed to keep the last photographs taken of them together, so I wrote to the social worker to say that we felt that Jake's birth parents should be given copies of all of the photos taken in the contact centre. We acknowledged that this was against the IRO's recommendation and accepted the associated risks, because it felt like the right thing to do. Ordinarily, that visit would have taken place while he was still in foster care, so his birth family would have been given copies of the photos. It wasn't fair that the coronavirus restrictions had delayed it and now it was happening after they were supposed to stop receiving photos.

When the day came, I did my best to deliver Jake under optimal conditions. I made sure he had eaten a good lunch and had a good nap. I packed a bag with his favourite foods, some milk, his dummy and his favourite toys. Jake's foster carer had given me a list of toys and clothes that were from his birth parents, so I chose an outfit that they had given him, so that they could see him wearing it. It wouldn't fit him for much longer, but I hoped that it would reassure them to see that I was using things they had given us and not erasing any trace of them from our lives. I put two envelopes in the bag, marked with their names. Inside were some cards with paint footprints I had taken of Jake's cute little feet. I just wrote the date on them, thinking that a message would just be something else for them to handle on an already emotional day.

The social worker came out and took him from me in the car seat. The second I handed him over, he started to scream. She ran off, high heels clacking, shouting, "Wait there! I'll be back in a few minutes!" I sat in the car, telling myself that Jake would be alright. A few minutes later, she reappeared and advised me that he'd been handed over to a contact centre worker, and not to worry, because they were very experienced at this sort of thing. I was grateful for her company while Jake was with his birth parents, and she took the time to fill me in on some of the family history that hadn't been in their file. She'd had a brief chat with Jake's birth father, so she gave me an update on him. It was good to hear that he was doing OK. After a while, she went back inside to collect Jake.

A few moments later, I heard her high heels clacking again, and Jake screaming. Howling! I leapt out of the car and saw the social worker running towards me, holding Jake strapped into his car seat. His eyes were swollen and his face redder than I'd ever seen it. I unbuckled his car seat and scooped him up. The noise stopped, but he sobbed silently into my chest as I stroked his back. "The contact worker told me that he was very sad, but very brave," the social worker said, smiling. "Very sad, but very brave..." I repeated, wondering what that meant. *Did he cry the whole time?* She went on to assure me that it had all been done in a "Covid-safe" way. His birth parents had worn medical-grade face masks and visors throughout the visit and they had tried to maintain a 2-metre distance from him while playing. "No!" I gasped. "On their last visit with their baby!" I hadn't realised that would be the protocol. How awful, to not be able to cuddle him. Then again, he might have been too frightened if they had tried to cuddle him. I thought about all the times I'd shown him the photos of their faces in preparation, so that he wouldn't be scared. That had been completely pointless if they were wearing masks and visors! I wondered if he'd been relieved that these masked strangers kept a distance, or if he had just been terrified the whole time. My eyes filled with tears and I hugged him a little tighter. "Well…" she faltered. "There may have been a cuddle and kiss goodbye." I couldn't bring myself to ask how Jake coped with that. It was in the past now anyway.

Jake was very reluctant to go back in his car seat, frantically looking around and pointing, shaking his head and screaming. He was clearly terrified that I'd strap him in and then hand him over to someone else. I reassured him that he was coming home with me and started singing "baa baa black sheep," so that he'd be able to hear my voice even when he couldn't see me. As I drove out of the car park, I saw Jake's birth parents sitting on a hill near the contact centre, smoking and talking. While singing "baa baa black sheep" on repeat, I was fighting tears, thinking about how they'd had to say goodbye to Jake while wearing masks and visors. As I drove past, Jake's birth father turned and we made eye contact. I gave him a nod, feeling that a smile would be cruel, and he nodded back. I don't know if he realised it was me. He couldn't see that I had Jake in the car, because the back windows were tinted, but I hadn't noticed them there on the hill until after I'd buckled him in, so they might have seen us before we got into the car. For a second, I wished I'd hired a car, but they didn't photograph or write down the number plate. I wanted to stop the car and tell them that I'm sorry for their loss. I wanted to tell them not to worry about him, because I'll always do whatever I can to keep Jake safe, healthy and happy. All that would have been wildly inappropriate though, so I drove on and kept singing the whole way home. I had practically lost my voice by the time we got home, but Jake panicked whenever I stopped singing, so I kept on croaking until I got him out of the car seat at home. Jake was visibly relieved to see Jon and Zoe, and he scrambled into Jon's arms. We looked in the lunchbox that I'd packed for him, and could see that his birth parents had offered him everything, but he'd not eaten much, if any, of the food or milk. He devoured it from the comfort of Jon's lap. The letters were gone from the bag, which made me feel a bit better.

Jake cried in his sleep that night. Not enough to wake him up, but enough to tear a little hole in my heart. I stroked his hair and told him, "It's OK, poppet. I'm here. I've got you. You're safe." That seemed to calm him. I felt guilty that I was the one who got to comfort him, knowing that his first Mum was probably also awake, going over it all in her head. The next morning, Jake was more emotional and nervous than usual. He screamed when he saw the car seat, and refused to get in it. Thankfully, his understanding was pretty good for his age, so he eventually calmed down when I kept repeating, "I'm coming with you. You're going to stay with me all day. We're going together." He'd been pushing me away a lot during the days leading up to the visit, but the rejection was less frequent for a week or so after the visit. I tried to imagine what was going on in that little head.

While Zoe was at school, I took Jake to visit my parents and we had a lovely time. At this point, Jake had met my parents a few times and was comfortable being around them, so long as they didn't try to pick him up or hug him. Thankfully, hugs did come a couple of months later, but in the meantime, my parents patiently found ways to play with him without physical contact. He loved rolling balls back and forth, over-watering Mum's plants, and feeding my parents' tortoise. When it was time to go home, Mum picked up Jake's car seat and passed it to me. Jake's eyes widened and he shrieked, shaking his head violently, pushing the car seat away, pointing at Mum. We both immediately realised he thought that Mum touching the car seat meant he might be going somewhere with her. I tried to reassure him, "Grandma's not taking you anywhere, darling. Grandma just passed the car seat to me! I'm taking you home. You're coming with me. We're staying together." It took a bit of convincing, but eventually I managed to get him into the car seat. Mum kept her distance, reassuring him that she wasn't going to take him anywhere, saying "You're going home with Mummy now, Jake. You live with Mummy. Thank you for coming to see me!" I'm so grateful that he was at a developmental stage where he was able to understand that.

A few days later, we had a similar experience at the park. We met one of Zoe's friends there, and Jon carried Jake around the park, taking him on the toys. My friend helped move the buggy at one point, just a few inches, so that I could get to the snack bag more easily, but Jake spotted her touching the buggy handle, and that was it. He refused to get back in the buggy, shaking his head, sobbing and pointing at my friend! For a child who couldn't talk yet, he was extremely good at making his feelings known!

LIFE STORY WORK

We learned about the importance of life story work (talking to a child about their past, to help them to understand and process it) through our training, and some of my adopted friends also shared with me the impact it had had on their lives. The two friends who had known about their biological families from a young age were emotionally well-balanced people. They're two of the kindest people I know. Another friend shared with me that he and his sister found out in their teens, which was very difficult for them and has had a lasting, negative effect on many aspects of their lives. I was determined to do the right thing for my son, so I started doing life story work with him just over a week after he moved in. I could tell he was thinking about the foster family anyway, because he'd been pointing at the door and crying for Karen, so one day, when he was particularly emotional, I thought it might comfort him to see photos of them. Worst case, it might make him cry more, but nothing else I'd tried was helping, so I decided to give it a go.

I'd read that it's best to start off with a reminder of where the child fits now, so I had strategically positioned a photo of our family in front of the photo albums, so that I wouldn't forget this step. I pointed at each of us, and said "That's Daddy, that's Mummy, that's Zoe, and that's you, Jake! We're a family! We live together and we love each other." Then I moved on to the photos we had of Jake's birth parents, and said (using their correct names, rather than these pseudonyms to protect their privacy), "That's

Becky, and that's Carl! Look, they're cuddling you. You grew in Becky's tummy, then you went to live with Karen, and now you live with us and you'll live with us forever, because we're a family!" We spent a long time going through the photos from his time in foster care. He smiled at the photos of his foster family, stroking their faces and babbling. The last few photos in the album were from the introductions, so I pointed out our little family and announced, "And now we're a family! We'll always be a family now."

He seemed reassured by this, so it became a regular thing every few days, whenever Jake seemed to be feeling wobbly. As well as helping him, it was useful for me to be able to fine-tune my words and practise adding little details to my explanation, before Jake was old enough to ask me questions. As Jake got older and learned to talk, he would join in and reel off his abridged life story to me. Sometimes, it felt like he was seeking reassurance that the story hadn't changed. When he asked me questions, I added in more detail, in bitesize chunks, such as, "The social worker looked for the right family to love you and to keep you safe," which eventually evolved into "the judge decided that you should go to live with the foster family, so they could look after you and keep you safe, while the social worker looked for the right family to look after you and keep you safe."

Keeping in touch with the foster family has been instrumental in helping Jake to understand his life story. As Jake was still struggling with the suggestion that I was "Mummy," and he'd recently been through the emotional "Wish you well" meeting, Jake's social worker advised us to delay our first reunion with the foster family by a few weeks, so that he had more time to attach to me before he saw Karen again. I was torn and, as always, overthinking. In some ways, I felt he might be less angry with me if he felt that I wasn't entirely replacing Karen and could see that the foster family were still part of his life and we'd see them sometimes. I was concerned that he might see her and want to go home with her though. I was also worried that he might forget them, which would just be tragic, so I didn't want to leave it too long. The internet was full of conflicting stories and studies. Some articles said that it's best to wait for up to six months, so that the child feels fully embedded in their adoptive family before seeing their foster family again. Newer research seemed to mostly indicate that it's best to maintain regular contact from the start, which can be more upsetting, but has long-term benefits in terms of reducing fears of abandonment and low self-worth. I looked at my giggly little son and wondered if he was going to struggle with those things. Things like this must seem so irrelevant to those not close to the situation, but it felt like a massive, life-altering decision that could affect my son's mental health in the long run.

We delayed by a few weeks, but decided to trust the most recent research and meet up relatively early on, about eight weeks into the placement. By this time, a new baby had been placed with the foster family. Another thing to overthink! Would Jake feel replaced? Would it help to reinforce the life story work that we'd done so far? He did seem to understand what I was saying, but at that point, he couldn't actually speak much, so I was really just making judgments based on his behaviours and the expressions on his curious little face.

Karen suggested that it would be least confusing for Jake if we met somewhere neutral or if they came to us for a short visit, which sounded sensible. We planned to meet for a walk round a lake, but torrential rain scuppered that plan, so they all came to our house. I told Jake that they were coming to see us, emphasising, "and then they will go home, but we will stay here, because we're a family and we live here." He seemed excited, but when I opened the door and he saw them, his eyes widened and he scaled me like a tree, shaking his head at Karen. She laughed, "No? Do you not want to see me?" and he buried his head into my shoulder. "It's OK, Jake," I told him. "You live here now! They've just come to visit! They're looking after another baby now." Jake peeked at Karen, looking unconvinced. Jon came into the room, and Jake flung himself from my arms into Jon's. Sam came through the door carrying the new baby. After they introduced him, I explained, "They're looking after him while the social worker finds the right family to love and look after him, like when they looked after you and then the social worker found us to be your family."

Once Jake was convinced that nobody was going to grab him, he came out of his shell and even hugged some of his foster siblings. He was very wary of Karen in particular, which we hadn't expected. We'd seen that his attachment to her was the strongest of all of the foster family members, so we knew it wasn't that he was least interested in her. It seemed that he was afraid of those feelings. Or maybe he knew that she had the strongest attachment to him, so he felt like she was most likely to want to take him with her. It was all very strange, and quite emotional to watch him trying to figure out what he was feeling.

At one point, Karen said to her new foster child, "Go to Daddy" and pointed at Sam. Jake stopped in his tracks. He looked at Karen, then at Sam, shook his head, then ran to Jon, looking serious and muttering, "No, no, no," over and over. That felt like a significant milestone, and Jake was more accepting of me after that meeting too. He still significantly preferred Jon's company to mine, but he didn't cry and point at the door whenever someone said "Mummy" any more.

THEY KNOW

After Jake had been with us for ten weeks, we were finally able to apply for the adoption order. I filled out a ridiculously long form, three copies of which had to be submitted, along with three copies of various legal documents. It all seemed absurdly inefficient. I was sending the court copies of their own court orders, as well as typing out and triple-checking the seemingly random court order reference numbers, hoping I'd matched them to the right boxes, as there seemed to be slight variations in the terminology used from one section of the form to the next. I suppose some people apply to a different court for the adoption order, so that court won't have copies of the court orders, but it does seem odd that there's no central database for this kind of thing. We just chose the family court closest to Jake's birth family, because we knew that we wouldn't be involved in the hearing, but they would be invited to it.

Another bizarre inefficiency was that the form requested a lot of information that we didn't have access to. We had to ask Jake's social worker to provide contact information for Jake's appointed guardian, whom we'd spoken to in the virtual LAC review, but never met. We also had to include the current addresses and job titles of Jake's birth parents, which Jake's social worker checked and emailed to me. I tried to imagine that phone call, "Hi, I just need you to confirm some details please, so that the family Jake's living with can apply to adopt him." I wouldn't want to be that social worker. They provided their current job titles and addresses, which I thought was good of them. I'm not sure I'd be willing to help someone else to adopt my child, or to talk to the social worker responsible for their removal. Jake's social worker told me that she didn't expect Jake's birth parents to contest the adoption order, because they explained to her that they felt they'd lost him when he was removed from their care a year earlier. They understood that the adoption order was about permanence for him and, although it would also be the point at which he was legally removed from their family, they already knew that they couldn't be a family together. "It's a cruel process really," the social worker commented. "They've already lost him, but now they're invited to go to court to go through it all over again."

A couple of weeks after we had posted the application for the adoption order, we received a letter from the court outlining where and when the final hearing would take place. There were lots of documents and I was surprised to see that one page included a paragraph explaining how to contest the adoption order, then I noticed that that page was addressed to Jake's birth parents. A social worker happened to be visiting that day, so I showed her the letter and she assured me that it was fine, I had just been sent a copy of the letter sent to Jake's birth parents, along with ours, for information purposes. I laughed, "Well, that's a relief! I thought for a horrible minute that we'd been sent their letter, and they'd been sent ours and might have some information they shouldn't!" "No, no," she reassured me, "That wouldn't happen. The court team are very cautious."

Two weeks later, my phone buzzed and Jake's social worker's name flashed up on the screen. An unscheduled call. I felt a tightening in my chest. *I was right. They know where we live.* My mind raced. I wondered if she was calling to reassure us that it would be OK, or to warn us to get out. I looked out of the window, a little part of me expecting to see Jake's birth parents, or a police car coming to escort us to safety before they arrived. As I dragged a feeble "hello" from somewhere, I told myself that running away was probably an overreaction. They wouldn't hurt us, would they?

She got straight to the point. Sure enough, the court had

accidentally sent a letter to Jake's birth parents that should have been sent to us, so they now knew our full names and address. The social worker told me that Jake's birth parents had been the ones to alert social services to the mix-up. They had asked Jake's new social worker (whom we hadn't even met yet) if we lived in this town. She had skirted around the question by saying that she wasn't sure exactly where we lived, then Becky explained that they knew our address, because they had received a letter meant for us. So why ask where we live? Was that a test, to see if the social worker would be honest with them or tell them that she couldn't share that information? They assured the social worker that they had no plans to come to this town. The social worker told me that Jake's birth mother had said, "I'm just glad he's not as far away as I thought. I'm not going to go there. I know you can't just take a baby." *But surely they'll come and have a look*, I thought. I flinched, as a car made a noise outside. I closed the blinds.

I spent a lot of the day on the phone to various social workers. One asked if we still wanted to proceed with the adoption, as we hadn't technically adopted him yet. Of course we did! He was already part of our family, regardless of the paperwork. I panicked that social services might decide not to support the adoption, and assured the social worker that I'd rather move and change our names if we were no longer safe here. The social workers all seemed in agreement that we were probably safe, and that moving Jake to another family would be needlessly traumatic for all of us. Jake's social worker felt that his birth parents would probably not bother to come to our home, as they had actually had the letter for two weeks before they told her about it. She assured me that she had arranged to visit his birth parents the following week, to retrieve the letter. "SO THEY HAVE WARNING THAT YOU'RE COMING, AND TIME TO WRITE DOWN THE ADDRESS?!" I exclaimed, too loudly. She winced. "I didn't want them to feel like I don't trust them," she explained. "It was so honest of them to tell us. They have done the right thing and I feel if I upset them, that could make them more likely to come." I didn't know what to say. I understood her logic, but I also wasn't sure if it was the right move. I became painfully aware of how little I really knew about the personalities of my son's birth parents. I looked back through all the documents we'd received and read everything I could, to try to get a better sense of them. One sentence in a social worker's report of a contact visit made me pause: "Birth mother joked about kidnapping Jake from foster care during contact session." Joked. It was just a joke. My heart pounded a bit harder while I digested that thought. Jon and I spent the evening looking at houses online, in case we had to move, but we couldn't find anything remotely suitable nearby and we didn't want to have to move away from our support network. I messaged Karen and asked what she thought, as she'd met them during contact sessions with Jake. She reassured me that they seemed nice. That helped a little.

I contacted the court, furious that they had caused this terror. I demanded a meeting to hear what they were going to do to ensure that this never happens to anyone else. A phone call was quickly set up, and a couple of senior managers apologised profusely for the human error. The letters had simply been put into the wrong envelopes. They were clearly mortified. One of them sounded like she was on the verge of tears. They kept saying things like "obviously it's nothing compared to how you must be feeling, but we want you to know that the person responsible is devastated." That didn't help. I didn't blame one person and want them to feel terrible. I blamed their process. I asked how they would prevent it from happening again, and was told they'd added more checks to the process. They had also reached out to other courts and asked what measures they had in place to manage the risk of human error. The court managers advised against taking out restraining orders, because they felt that it might just upset Jake's birth family if we did that, and make them more likely to come. The restraining order would also have to include our address, so that would mean that if they had somehow forgotten, or decided not to write down our details before the social worker collected the letter, they would then be given our address again. They assured me that if anything happened, they could arrange a restraining order in a matter of hours.

Jake's social worker called the police and asked for their advice. They opened a case and linked our phone numbers to it. Apparently if we call the police from one of those phone numbers, they'll immediately send someone out, rather than waiting for us to give lots of information. I didn't know enough about Jake's birth family to know whether this was complete overkill or a sensible precaution. The social worker assured me that she felt it was unnecessary, but she wanted to do what she could to help me to feel safe in my own home again. She also offered to pay for a rape alarm for me to carry on walks. I didn't take her up on that, though a few times I wondered if I should have. I think it would have made me more paranoid somehow. Another Jake lived a few streets away and I kept hearing children and his parents calling out to him when we went to the park. Every time, I tensed up in terror and looked around for my son's birth family. They didn't come, and I'd think to myself *it's totally unfair of me to even be afraid of them. They notified the social worker. They told her they won't come. The foster carer said they're nice people.* Too often, I let my mind wander, imagining what I'd do if they did come. Some days, I imagined that they'd just be relieved to see that he's safe, healthy and happy. Other days, I imagined what I'd do if they tried to take him from me. I didn't really believe that they would do that, but I felt like I needed to mentally run through thousands of different scenarios, so that I felt prepared and could to allow myself to relax. Zoe saw me looking at a flyer for a martial arts class and we got talking about how I used to do karate and had dabbled in jiu-jitsu and taekwondo. She asked me to teach her some moves, so I did. It calmed me down a little to remind myself that I can defend myself, not that I really expected to have to do so.

The morning after I heard about the data breach, I woke up covered in painful hives all over my legs, torso and arms. It looked like I'd rolled around in a patch of stinging nettles. For the next few weeks, I woke up with hives. I assumed it was stress. I was prescribed beta blockers, but didn't get on with them. My resting heart rate was already below average and the beta blockers sent it down to 40 bpm, making me feel faint and woozy. I listened to hypnosis tracks to reduce my stress levels and I kept thinking I was getting better, then I'd wake up in the middle of the night, convinced that Jake's birth parents were in the house. The constant hypervigilance was exhausting. Every noise outside made me twitch. Whenever I opened the front door, I expected them to be there. Every morning, when I came down the stairs, I tortured myself, wondering what I would do if one of Jake's birth parents was sitting on the sofa. I knew they wouldn't be really, but these intrusive thoughts persisted for weeks.

When the social worker had advised that I couldn't meet Jake's birth parents before their "Wish You Well" meeting with Jake, she had assured me that we'd book for me to meet them a couple of weeks later, without Jake. Covid made that difficult. It was easier for the social workers to justify holding the "Wish You Well" meeting during the pandemic, because it was part of the adoption process. My meeting with his birth parents was considered more of a "nice to have" that didn't have such immediate benefits for Jake. Now that they had our address, I asked Jake's social worker to speed up and get the meeting booked, so that I could meet his birth parents as soon as possible. I wanted them to feel that there was no need to come here to see what we were like, because they would soon see me in the flesh anyway.

Jake's birth parents hadn't replied to the settling-in letter, so I asked their social worker to ask them if they'd found it helpful, so that she could let me know whether I'd included the sort of stuff they wanted to hear. I wondered if the information in the letters would be enough to keep them going, so they wouldn't have the urge to come here. The social worker got back to me a few days later, having visited Jake's birth parents. "Right," she said, "the thing is, they haven't actually received your letters yet. They didn't sign the contact agreement, so the letterbox team haven't forwarded them on. They say they were never asked to sign it, and I don't know if that's true, because someone else was on Jake's case then, but anyway, I'm going to take it to them to get it signed, and I'll take the letters with me, so they'll get them right away." I groaned, but it struck me that this might be a good thing after all. The agreement I'd signed had been for letters to be exchanged once a year. Jake was growing so fast, I already had lots of material for the next letter, and I'd only sent the settling-in letter a few months ago. I persuaded the social worker to increase the contact to twice a year. I had suggested this to the previous social worker when we were first shown the draft contact agreement, as it felt cruel to update his birth family so infrequently. That social worker had advised against six-monthly letters, because "if they don't reply, that's twice as much rejection for Jake when he's older," but things were different now, so the new social worker agreed that more frequent letters might be sensible, to reassure Jake's birth family that he's OK. Hopefully they wouldn't feel the need to come to our home to check.

RAGE

A couple of months after the data breach, I took the children out to McDonald's for a bit of a treat and to get out of the house so that I wouldn't keep anxiously looking out of the windows. The children each chose a balloon from the "balloon wall," then I sat them down at a booth near one of the ordering machines, so that I was only a couple of metres away from them. Just as I was finishing ordering, a member of staff came over and asked the children what they were talking about. Jake told her that he had changed his mind and he didn't like his balloon any more. He wanted a balloon the same colour as Zoe's. I thought the waitress might go and get him one, but she reached her hand out to him and said "Let's go and get one. Come with me!"

My protective instincts went into overdrive and I saw red. I shouted "HEY! What's going on? Jake, sit back down. Do not go with that lady!" Then I turned to the lady and asked her what on Earth she thought she was doing, and explained sternly that it's not appropriate to take someone else's child anywhere, including to the other side of a (rather large) restaurant, without checking that their responsible adult knows and agrees to that. The lady clearly thought I was being melodramatic. I probably did seem somewhat unhinged. I'm sure my voice and face were murderous, and I was visibly shaking. I felt she had crossed a line. At best, she was teaching my children that it's OK to go with a stranger without telling your parents where you're going. At worst, she was a threat to my child. I was absolutely seething, and it took a lot of focus to return my voice to a normal volume and to resist the instinct to shove her away from my precious children. Zoe and Jake watched wide-eyed, as the lady repeatedly shrugged and said, "I just thought he'd enjoy coming with me to get the balloon" and I explained the many ways in which I found this unacceptable. I over-explained it for the benefit of the children, not caring how patronised this woman felt. I wanted them to understand why her behaviour was unacceptable and I wanted them to know that I will always protect them.

After the woman slunk off, Zoe sheepishly said, "I'm sorry I didn't stop her from trying to take Jake. I thought it was OK, because she's wearing a uniform." I'll try not to digress too far into the pitfalls of safeguarding education, but this is just one of many issues I have with how "stranger danger" is taught in schools. We should be teaching our children about red flags to be wary of, not blanket assumptions like "stranger means danger, but uniform means safe." I reassured Zoe that it wasn't her fault and tried my best to explain that we can't trust everyone who wears a uniform, and reassured her that part of my job as her Mum is to explain to her what's inappropriate, so that she knows this sort of stuff before she's old enough to go out without me.

I look back on this and wonder if it seemed like a total overreaction to the people who saw me telling off the waitress. To me, her behaviour still seems completely preposterous, and I had to take several breaks while writing this, to calm myself as those feelings of rage flooded back. It's likely that the data breach affected how I coped with the situation though. I was already on edge, feeling like Jake's birth family could appear at any moment. For weeks, I tried my best to hide my hypervigilance from the children, but at some point, it turned to rage. That was harder to hide and I found myself being snappy with them. I had no patience and my blood boiled at the slightest inconvenience.

The rashes kept coming back, and I started having random facial swelling. Some mornings, I looked like I'd had Botox on one or both lips. One night, I woke up from a nightmare, covered in a rash. I got up and took some antihistamines and, on my way back to bed, I felt my tongue starting to swell up. I shrieked at Jon, who woke up and leapt out of bed just as I fainted. He sat me up straight and gave me a glass of cool water. I went to hospital and was diagnosed with urticaria and angioedema, triggered by stress. I was prescribed strong antihistamines and told it would settle down, but it got completely out of control. Several times, when my face was swollen, I struggled to breathe and felt like I might die. I kept having to go back to hospital for steroids to get the swelling down. Every time I had an angioedema attack, I felt furious for days after. I was referred to a specialist, who told me that was a chemical response to the spike in histamine levels in my blood and the steroid medication I was having to take. He prescribed some much stronger antihistamines, which eventually calmed things down.

I will have these conditions for life now, but I'm grateful the medication controls it. I considered suing the court for the emotional and physical damage this saga had caused me, but I didn't really feel I had the emotional strength at the time and I suppose I'm just not really the litigious type. I couldn't face it. I decided to focus my energy on trying to find my sanity, so I could be the Mum my children deserved. I felt like something inside of me had been damaged and it wasn't getting better. I couldn't believe this was happening to me. In my high-stress job, I was known for my perseverance. My annual reviews from my bosses had always been littered with words like "determined" and "tenacious." One year, my boss wrote, "I asked some of Holly's internal stakeholders to share their opinions of her behaviours. The word 'relentless' appeared 7 times in their responses." Where was that relentlessness now? I felt that I should be able to get through this!

My parents took me to see a psychiatrist at around 9 years old, to help with anxiety. I hadn't known I was anxious, but my parents tell me it was evident from a nervous cough and fidgeting with my earrings so much that my Mum was constantly helping me to search for lost earring backs that I'd accidentally dropped. The psychiatrist gave me some exercises to help me sleep better, which was fine, but I was deeply offended when he suggested that perhaps my recurring sinusitis was actually due to anxiety. I didn't see a connection and I still feel that it's a separate issue. In hindsight, as an adult, I understand him wanting to explore whether my other chronic health conditions might have been linked to anxiety. I know it can manifest in various ways. At the time, 9-year-old emotionally-ignorant Holly felt that he was saying I was causing the sinusitis myself, by being anxious. That irritated me and I had been insistent ever since that I didn't have any struggles with stress or anxiety. Nothing I couldn't handle, anyway. I would rant at a friend, or go for a walk, then I'd feel better. I listened to hypnosis tracks occasionally to reduce my stress levels and to help me get to sleep.

This was different, though. I was absolutely not coping and there was no denying it. I thought back to when friends had struggled with depression and anxiety and I had encouraged them to get help. I knew that's what they would tell me to do too. Rationally, I could see that something had to change, so I called the doctor. She listened sympathetically and suggested that perhaps the problem was that I have a toddler, because of course toddlers are notoriously triggering. They push boundaries. They feel everything dramatically. She also noted that adopted toddlers can be additionally challenging, due to the trauma they have experienced. I assured her that his behaviours were things I should be able to cope with. I was the one who needed intervention. She sent out the Health Visitor to check that his behaviour was normal, and the Health Visitor diagnosed him as adorable.

At every appointment, sometimes more than once, I was asked if I thought I was going to hurt myself or my children. I answered "no," wondering what would happen if things got worse and I did start to feel like that. Did people really admit to feeling like that? I tried to explain that the reason I needed help was because I was worried that my children would pick up on the simmering rage that I was trying to shield them from, or that I might snap and scream at them and damage them emotionally. I was referred to an online Cognitive Behavioural Therapy course, which I found patronising and unhelpful.

I felt like I was failing my children. I wasn't the happy Mum they deserved. I was grumpy and impatient. Sometimes I was absolutely raging and, though I tried not to show that, they could tell I was angry. Other people were starting to notice it and asked why I was so stressed out. Some offered advice, which ranged from helpful to irritating. I was also angry on Jake's behalf, because his birth parents didn't reply to my letters. The social workers confirmed that they had now signed the letterbox agreement and my letters had been passed on. Replying to my letters was literally the only thing left that they could do for Jake, but they weren't doing it. When it was time to write the next letters, I included lots of questions that I thought Jake would want to hear answers to and I ended each letter with a reminder of the contact information for the post-adoption support team that they should send their replies to. Then it occurred to me that I could make it even easier for them to reply, so I included a stamped, addressed envelope with each letter, addressed to the post-adoption support team.

After I sent the letters off, I emailed one of the social workers in the post-adoption support team and asked if she could go to visit Jake's birth parents and help them to reply. I wasn't really sure if that was in her job description, but I wrote an emotive message about how strongly I felt that they should receive every support possible so that they could reply to Jake. He deserves to know about them and I had limited information. More importantly, he deserves to know that even though they weren't able to parent him, they cared about him. Of course, I'd tell him that, but if there was any chance that he could receive tangible evidence of their love for him, I wanted him to have it.

All of the contact information for Carl was out of date, so the social worker advised that they'd have to keep my letter for him on file until he got back in touch with the agency. She couldn't get hold of Becky or Carl on the phone, so she agreed to include a covering note when she forwarded on my letter to Becky, offering to help her to write a reply to me if she contacted post-adoption support. I felt a little less irate, feeling like I'd done all I could to encourage them to engage in letterbox contact. Sympathy crept back in. Maybe it was just too upsetting for them. I tried to resign myself to the fact that we might not hear from them again and I thought about how I'd explain it to Jake and persuade him that the lack of response wasn't because they don't care.

I went from furious to sad, and cried for two days. I went back to the doctor and was prescribed antidepressants. The intense sadness eased within a few days, but the rage reared its ugly head again and I battled it for several more months. I found a book called "Angry Mother, Assertive Mother," by Cristalle Hayes, and it helped a bit. I joined Facebook groups for angry Mums and followed Instagram experts on maternal rage.

Some strategies helped more than others. I created a "calm down playlist" of songs that helped me to relax. I also found it helpful to visualise smoke coming out of my nostrils like a dragon when I was full of rage. I laughed the first time I read about that method, but it did help a bit. I took the children on more walks and we spent more time on the swings, which I found physically regulating. Fortunately, the Covid pandemic was coming to an end so I could spend more time with friends and family, which was also helpful. My adoption support network grew, as we were able to go to adoption stay-and-play events organised by the local authority and meet more families. I started writing this book, which was in itself therapeutic. Jake's birth parents didn't turn up at our door. A combination of all of these things helped me to start feeling like myself again.

ONE OF US

It felt like Jake loved Jon and Zoe almost straight away, but it took a lot longer for him to allow himself to love me. When social workers were visiting in the early weeks after he moved in, he'd burrow into me. They'd say "This is all very positive! Good sign that he's attaching to you!" I felt like a fraud, because I could tell that he didn't love me yet. He just knew me better than he knew them. It wasn't completely miserable. Once he got used to me being referred to as "Mummy," he wasn't angry with me. He liked me and he was learning that I would keep him safe. He was even starting to trust that I would feed him, but it wasn't love. I can feel it when someone loves me. He would tolerate me when Jon and Zoe weren't around, he'd laugh if I tickled him, and he'd beam at me and say, "Happy!" when I gave him a biscuit, but he didn't light up when he saw me, the way that he did when he saw Jon and Zoe.

I wondered daily whether my son would ever grow to love me, and how I would cope if he never did. It was hard at times, but seeing how much he loved Jon and Zoe was therapeutic. I felt so fortunate that I got to watch those bonds grow. I told myself I could survive knowing that they loved each other even if he didn't love me. The important thing was that he knew that I loved him and that I would keep him safe.

After Jake had been living with us for nine months, I noticed a shift. I had always thought it would be a more gradual change. Maybe it was and it just took us both a while to realise it, but it seemed to me like a switch had been flicked and Jake had decided that it was OK to let himself love me. I felt it. I told Jon that I finally felt that Jake loved me back. He laughed, "Of course he loves you! He's loved you for ages!" I wasn't convinced. The next morning, completely out of the blue, Jake said, "Love you, Mummy!" He had never said "Love you" to anyone! He sounded surprised when he said it. We both were! I spent the rest of the day skipping about, delighted that my son loved me. I was also thrilled to have this confirmation that I was right, because if I could feel that he loved me now, hopefully that meant that he'd been able to feel that I'd loved him for all those months before he felt the same way. A few days later, he asked me, "Mummy, *why* do I love you?" and I happily waffled on about how we're a family, and families love each other.

One reason why I didn't want to sue the court was the knowledge that they were going to remain involved in our lives for a while. We had three more hearings to get through, two of which were legal requirements to formalise the adoption. The first was the Directions Hearing, which we weren't invited to. We were told that this was really more about making sure there were deadlines agreed for all remaining paperwork actions that had to be completed ahead of the Final Hearing. We weren't invited to the Final Hearing either, but that was the one in which Jake became officially a member of our family.

I marked the occasion by baking a rainbow cake, and Jake ate the majority of it over a few days. I enjoy baking, but I am pretty terrible at it, so this was a major effort. I really considered whether it was appropriate to "celebrate" it. Some people feel you shouldn't, that it's a day of loss, linked to the legal separation from birth family. That loss certainly is significant and should be respected. The judge had decided on adoption many months before that day though. This hearing confirmed that we would adopt him, but a previous hearing had already decided that he should be adopted and one long before that had determined that he should be removed from his birth family in the first instance. That loss happened over a year before the Final Hearing so, for us, the day of the Final Hearing wasn't about that loss. It was about Jake's surname changing and him formally becoming a member of our family. Documents finally reflecting our feelings. He'd been part of our family for six months by this point, so it didn't really change anything. We already loved him. We didn't have the option to have a big party anyway, thanks to Covid, but I had to mark the occasion in a small, but meaningful (to us) way, so rainbow cake it was.

The social worker called me while Jake was napping and Jon was working. She confirmed that the court hearing had gone as expected and Jake was now officially a member of our family. As soon as I hung up, I told Zoe that the paperwork was finally complete and her brother was now OFFICIALLY a Marlow. I didn't expect much of a reaction, but Zoe was delighted! She grabbed my hands and danced me round in circles, cheering excitedly. When Jake woke up from his nap, Zoe raced up the stairs and into his room and exclaimed, "Jake, Jake! You're a Marlow now! You're Jake Marlow, like I'm Zoe Marlow!" Her enthusiasm infected him and our little one-year-old ran around with his hands in the air cheering, "I Marlow! I Marlow!"

The court paused all Celebration Hearings for about a year, while the coronavirus levels were alarmingly high throughout the country, so that the court could minimise face-to-face interactions and prioritise the urgent court cases required for child protection. We suspected that we wouldn't have a Celebration Hearing after all, because the backlog was unmanageable, but a year after the Final Hearing, we got a letter asking us if we'd like to be added to the waiting list. I was in two minds about this. On the one hand, I didn't want to make Jake worry that he wasn't actually part of our family yet, but on the other hand, I thought the ceremony might be useful for explaining the process to him. We decided to go for it and in a few months, we made it to the top of the waiting list.

I used the Celebration Hearing as an excuse to order myself a pendant that I'd been admiring for a while, which was the shape of the adoption triad symbol. I didn't usually wear a necklace, so Jake noticed it and asked me about it. I explained that I'd bought it to celebrate that he was part of our family, because I love him so much and I'm so happy that I get to be his Mummy. He was really pleased and still strokes my necklace whenever he notices I'm wearing it. He calls it the "I love Jake" necklace.

We had always imagined that the Celebration Hearing would be a big event, and we'd invite all of our friends and family and of course our son's lovely foster family. Unfortunately, the court wasn't allowing many guests and, as it happened, the foster family had Covid that week. It was still a great day though. We explained to the children that we were going to see the judge who had decided that Jake would be a Marlow and be a part of our family forever. We discussed how that had actually happened over a year ago and this was a bit late really, but we hadn't been there when the judge decided, so the judge was going to show us what it was like on the day that he made that decision. We do a lot of role-play and Zoe loves performing shows for the rest of us, so the children seemed to accept that the judge was going to put on a show for us, to explain things. On the surface, Jake seemed fine, though he asked for extra reassurance a few times over the next week. "I'm Jake Marlow now. I'm Jake Marlow forever, aren't I?" He also asked to see photos of his foster family more than usual during that week, and we talked through his whole life story so far, which seemed to reassure him. I showed him photos of judges on my phone and explained that the judge would probably look like one of those people and wear that sort of uniform.

We got permission for Zoe to miss a day of school so that she could be involved in the Celebration Hearing. She was very excited and asked if she could wear a party dress. Jake's ears pricked up at this and he declared, "I will wear my wedding suit and my wedding shoes!" so he wore an adorable navy suit that he'd worn for my sister's wedding a couple of months before. Dressed in our finest, we reported to the court at 9:45 on a Tuesday morning, where we met our most recent social worker in the waiting room. Jake's social worker had left the agency, so there wasn't anyone from the child protection team there. I was glad they hadn't sent a random person in her place, as we had caught Covid a few weeks earlier, and I was in no rush to widen my exposure to germs any more than I had to. I found it really sad that his social worker missed that celebration though. I often wonder if she thinks about the children she helped. She had what must have been a really emotional job, especially when a child has to be removed from a family. I wished she'd been there to see one of the happier parts of the process and so that I could reassure her that Jake was happy and thriving with us.

The judge talked about how Jake had been officially part of our family for a long time and asked him if he could help her make it "extra, extra, super-official" by banging the gavel for her. He was delighted to oblige!

PRESCHOOL

Nine months into my twelve-month adoption leave, I was dreading the return to work. Zoe's struggle to settle into nursery/preschool five years earlier had just about broken my heart and, although Jake was a year older than Zoe had been at the time, I was still concerned. He still remembered the adoption introductions on some level. Some friends came to stay with us for a week and a few days into their visit, Jake said to me, "I don't want Damien to be my new Daddy." I was dismayed that he thought that was the reason Damien was staying with us, and shocked that a child so young could remember something from nine months ago. I wondered if the trauma had made him hold on to memories in abnormal levels of detail, or if he just had a sort of instinctive nervousness.

Fortunately, my boss phoned to tell me that there were going to be redundancies at work, so they'd be looking for volunteers to be made redundant. It was a no-brainer for me. I'd been considering leaving, to spend more time with my children and to try my hand at writing children's books about adoption, but resigning had been a bit of a daunting leap to take. This was the nudge I needed. My boss was shocked that I volunteered for the redundancy, as I'd always been so driven at work.

Not having to return to work in June made things a lot easier, as I could keep Jake at home with me for longer. In September, we decided to see if he enjoyed going to nursery for a few mornings a week. Frustratingly, Covid restrictions meant that we couldn't go in and have a proper look round any nurseries or preschools. We knew that we liked the nursery Zoe had gone to, but we'd chosen that one because some of her friends were going there and we wanted her to have some familiar faces around. We didn't know anyone who would go to that nursery at the same time as Jake, but one of Zoe's school friends had a little brother Jake's age, called Zac. We'd had a few playdates and Jake and Zac were used to seeing each other and saying hello when we saw each other on the school run most days. They lived near us, so we often walked home from school together and the walk home involved a slight detour to pick Zac up from nursery. The boys got on well, so I decided to look at the nursery that Zac went to, so that Jake would know someone there. Zac's parents loved the nursery, so that was comforting.

I spoke to the manager on the phone about my concerns that he might be nervous and might think it was another transition to a new family, so she suggested I bring him over and we have a look at the garden and peek in through the windows to see the toys. In a way, I think that was actually better than a proper visit, because he could see lots of fun "forbidden fruit" and he was very keen to get in there and try out all the toys! It was also helpful that he'd seen on numerous occasions that Zac's Mum picked him up, so he knew that parents collected their children at the end of the day. I read him books about starting preschool and he seemed excited to go.

We started off with a couple of hour-long sessions to ease him into it and so that I could reassure him that he would be home with me for lunch. Despite that, I packed him a lunchbox full of snacks and made sure he knew that food would be there if he wanted it. I also gave him a snack immediately before we went into the building, to try to prevent him from feeling any hunger while he was there for the first time. The nursery staff joked that there was no way he'd have any time to eat, because he'd be busy exploring the toys, but he ate most of the lunchbox each day.

He was a bit wobbly when I left him for the first time, but nowhere near as distressed as Zoe had been when she had started nursery several years ago. It was definitely helpful that he was older and understood that I was going to come back and collect him. At the end of the first session, he ran to me. I scooped him up into a cuddle, and he said, "I'm safe now." I light-heartedly reassured him that he'd been safe there too, but my heart broke a little at the thought that he hadn't felt safe. On the way home, he happily chatted about all of the toys and how kind the teachers were and told me one of them looked really cuddly and he wanted to cuddle her. He was keen to go back the next day, so he can't have felt that unsafe! Within a few days, he was running in and, over time, he ate less of the lunchbox, because he was happier to eat the food they provided. I still packed a lunchbox every day, so that he'd know it was there and he'd often ask to eat the rest of it as soon as we got home.

A few weeks in, on the way home from nursery, Jake said to me, "I not Sandra's baby." I winced. In the mornings, I'd been handing him over to Sandra, who'd been saying, "Come on, my baby." I'd wondered if we were going to have issues because of that. I reassured him that he wasn't Sandra's baby and would always be my baby, even when he's much taller than me. I thought about asking Sandra to stop using that phrase, but I decided to explain that sometimes people say that when they're just being friendly. It was part of the routine now and he'd only have more questions if she stopped saying it.

One morning, when I was dropping Jake off at nursery, he commented, "You will not fornember to pick me up." It wasn't a question, but he hadn't said it with much conviction. He still needed a little reassurance sometimes. "No, darling. I'll never forget to pick you up, because I'm your Mummy and you're my boy. We're a family. We live together and we love each other." That had become a pre-programmed script in my head. I used it whenever he seemed worried, and it seemed to help. I think it helped that my response to his concerns was consistent.

He didn't go to nursery every morning. Sometimes we spent the day with his cousins or went to a park for some one-on-one bonding time. Once a month, we went to a "stay-and-play" group that the adoption agency put on for pre-school aged adopted children. It was brilliant for getting to know other adoptive families and for normalising adoption in Jake's world. About six months after he started nursery, Jake was assigned a new key worker. This didn't make much difference as he'd been playing with this woman most days anyway, but it meant that she was now the one to write reports on his learning, and she was the one who brought him to the door when I came to pick him up. One lunchtime, when I came to collect him, I said "Jake won't be in tomorrow. We're going to an adoption playgroup." She gasped, and her eyes filled with tears. She choked out, "but why?!" and I realised that she thought I was taking him to a family-finding day, to be adopted out of our family. I explained that he is adopted and we go to these events once a month, to normalise adoption in his world. She pulled herself together and we didn't talk about it in any more detail. I was glad to see that she cared enough about him to be distraught at the thought of me "putting him up for adoption," but saddened that some people think that's what happens.

CONTACT

A few weeks after I sent off the letters with the stamped, addressed envelopes, I got an email from the post-adoption support team, telling me that Jake's birth mother had replied. The email advised that she'd signed it "Mummy" and the social worker had blacked that out with a pen, and written "Becky" next to it. I hadn't expected that. The letterbox agreement stated that she had to sign it with her name, otherwise letters would not be passed on. Perhaps she'd forgotten about that. I was just relieved her letter hadn't been returned to her. By this point, I was desperate to have some evidence to show Jake that his birth parents were keen to have a relationship with him. She had written it herself, without taking up the social worker's offer to help her formulate a response, so that was also hugely encouraging, because I didn't really expect the post-adoption support team to have the resources to do that on a regular basis.

The letter arrived a few days later, and I was buzzing. I told Jake that I'd received a letter to read to him from Becky. He beamed, clearly feeling special. Zoe half-jokingly protested, "Aw, that's not fair, I didn't get a letter!" I had been expecting this and had a reply ready. "Jake has a letter because he can't live with his birth family, so I've been writing to them to make sure they know he's safe, healthy and happy, so that they won't worry about him. You get to live with your birth family, because we keep you safe. If you want to receive letters, you can start writing letters to your grandparents or to your friends, and maybe they'll reply." That seemed to do the trick. We all sat down and I read the letter. It was a beautiful, handwritten letter, full of love for Jake and answers to the questions included in our previous letters. Jake listened intently and was excited to hear about the things they had in common. Becky wrote about her favourite childhood games and her favourite story book as a child. I ordered the book to read to Jake.

I replied to the letter, including another stamped, addressed envelope and got another reply, just as full of love and personal snippets of information. I was starting to feel like I knew her a little. We kept referring to "when we meet" in our letters, because the plan was still for me to meet her at some point. It took a very long time for that meeting to happen, even after the pandemic was over, because the social workers in the post-adoption support team had a backlog of higher priority actions and they lost a few members of staff. I was seriously wondering if it would ever reach the top of the priority list, given the nature of social work in the field of child protection. It was understandable that the agency would have to prioritise the children who needed to be removed, and those who needed to be matched with families, so members of staff were often pulled out of the post-adoption team to support in those areas.

Over two years after Jake moved in with us, someone new joined the post-adoption support team and tried to help clear some outstanding tasks. She left me a voicemail, asking if I thought it might be more appropriate for the meeting to be held in a café with an outdoor play area, so that Jake wouldn't get bored. I listened to the message with increasing alarm and phoned her back straight away. "PLEASE tell me you haven't spoken to Becky about this? This meeting isn't supposed to include Jake! It's meant to be me and her! We've been told by numerous social workers that we can't have direct contact!" The social worker was apologetic and admitted that she had unfortunately already spoken to Becky, who was very excited that "I'd decided" she could see Jake. I was exasperated. I wasn't the one who'd decided that she couldn't! The judge made that assessment, and I'd been told very firmly on multiple occasions by social workers that direct contact with Jake would not be safe for him. The social worker confidently assured me that she'd sort it all out and explain that it was all a misunderstanding. I was worried though that Becky would now feel that I'd taken something away from her. She might think it was my choice and see me as the barrier between her and Jake.

I asked the social worker to tell Becky that I'd bring lots of photos and videos to show her and that I had some crafty stuff Jake had made for her that I couldn't easily post. I also suggested that she bring her mum, sister, or someone else for support. I hoped that that would make it less daunting. The social worker assured me that it wasn't necessary. "We'll have two members of our team there. One will be there to support you and the other will be there to support Becky." I doubted that Becky would really believe that anyone from social services is on her team! The social worker passed the message on and Becky confirmed that she'd bring her Mum.

It would have been easier to just not mention it to Jake, but I've always tried to be as open with him as I can, in a child-appropriate way, so I decided to stick to that approach. We talked through his life story, to sort of lay the foundation for the conversation. Then I told him that I'd persuaded the social workers to let me meet Becky, so that I could tell her all about him. He was momentarily put out that he couldn't come, but thankfully nowhere near as frustrated as I had expected. He seemed to accept that social workers decide things, so he didn't push it. Zoe was actually more annoyed that she couldn't meet Becky. Over the next few weeks, I encouraged Jake to make more artistic creations to give Becky and her Mum. He also helped me to create a list of questions to ask. Predictably, he wanted to know her favourite colour and other such things that matter to young children! I asked him what he wanted me to tell her about him and he decided that she needed to know about his favourite toy of the moment. As our contact agreement states that photos are only to be viewed in the office, I sent a PowerPoint presentation of photos and videos to the social worker, so that she could bring it on her laptop, to avoid any awkward confusion about whether physical photos were a gift to take home.

On the day, I felt quite emotional. I didn't try to change my appearance as I'd once thought I would. I didn't hire a car, as I was no longer worried that she might note down my number plate and try to find us. She'd had our actual home address and not shown up for two years, at least not to my knowledge. I felt that it would have been disrespectful to try to trick her in any way. She'd been really open in her letters, sharing lots of information about her childhood. I felt I should just be myself with her.

At the last minute, Becky's Mum wasn't able to join, but fortunately Becky still made it. The meeting went really well and the conversation flowed easily. We both enjoyed talking about how wonderful Jake is! I talked Becky through the PowerPoint presentation of photos and videos of Jake and we both commented on the physical traits that they shared and his brilliant sense of humour. When I asked how she'd been, she said she had had two good days in the past year; the days my letters arrived, telling her how Jake was doing. That broke me a little bit. We had a laugh, too. She asked me if he is obsessed with dogs, like she is, and I told her that, as a fellow dog person, I was sorry to inform her that she'd created a cat person. She covered her face in mock-horror and we all laughed.

At the end of the meeting, we agreed to meet again on a regular basis. I'm looking forward to our next meeting. I felt drained for a few days afterwards, full of guilt and other complicated emotions, but it was worth it. I hope that this is just the beginning of a relationship that will benefit the wonderful boy we both love so much.

HIS STORY

When Jake was around two years old, we were going through our usual life story work routine, looking first at photos of us as a family, before talking about his birth family and the involvement of social workers and the judge. When I got to the part about him moving to the foster family, he asked, "Were Becky and Carl sad?" "I'm sure they were," I nodded. "They wanted to be your parents. They got to be your parents for a little while, before the judge decided that you needed a different family to keep you safe." We talked in a bit more depth about why the judge decided that, relating it to Delly Duck in the story I'd written to explain adoption to Zoe. "That's sad," he said, "They should have tried harder. If you can't do something, you can just keep trying until you can do it!" My heart ached a bit, hearing his innocent little voice trying to rationalise it in the terms of the world he lives in now, where he just needed to keep trying and he'd learn how to put his shoes on all by himself. I agreed that it is sad, and explained that they did try a bit, but they didn't manage to do enough. I talked about how people are good at different things and that some people haven't been taught how to be good at parenting or aren't able to remember how to do it properly. I also reminded him that I sent Becky and Carl letters sometimes, so that they'd know that he was OK and that they didn't need to worry about him. He thought that was a good idea. I hope that learning about his life story in bitesize chunks is helping him to process it in a more manageable way, though I suppose I won't really know if this was the right approach for him until he's an adult. It seems to be working though, at least for now.

A lot of people associate life story work with the "life story book," which the social workers create and should provide soon after the court order is received. Our book was delayed due to staffing issues and priority calls, but we were fortunate to have a few photos of Jake's birth family. In a way, I think it was helpful that the life story book was delayed, because I had to think outside of the box and use the resources we had. I realise now that I'm doing life story work with Jake all the time, sometimes unintentionally. Even holding hands to cross the road is strengthening the foundation of our life story work because I explain, "I need you to hold my hand, because I'm your Mummy, and parents keep their children safe." When I have to give him medicine or brush his teeth, I remind him that "parents keep their children healthy." This could go wrong, making him think I'm implying that I won't be his Mum any more if he doesn't comply, so I'm cautious not to use these phrases to persuade him to let me do these things. They are an explanation of what's happening, not a tool to control his behaviour. It seems to work for us and I think it's setting the foundation for the more in-depth conversations about why his birth parents weren't able to raise him.

Although the majority of our life story work is focused on helping Jake to understand his past, we also have to make sure we talk about the present and the future. It's essential that Jake believes that we'll be in his future. A brilliant therapeutic social worker once suggested, "Insert yourself into his future. Prove that you'll be there," so when Jake says, "look at that cool car! I'm going to have a car like that when I grow up," I ask "Ooh, where will you take me? Will you drive me to the beach?" I keep clothes in his room that are far too big for him, including some that won't fit him until he's a teenager, so that he has a visual reminder that he'll still be here, in our family, even when he's much bigger than he is now. Sometimes, when he seems to be feeling a bit wobbly, I "accidentally" pull out something that's far too big for him, to instigate a light-hearted chat about how he's going to wear that when he's much older.

Jake has glorious ginger hair and he loves it. He calls it orange and asks everyone he meets if they wish they had orange hair like him. I soon lost count of the number of times I was asked "Where does he get his lovely hair from?" At first, I just said "on his father's side," for the sake of moving the conversation along quickly, but as Jake has grown older, we've talked a bit about how he got his hair colour from his birth father, so I felt that I needed to change my stock answer.

How much you share about your child's story can be a controversial topic. On the one hand, it's their story to tell but, on the other hand, if you're too secretive about it, you could make your child feel that it's something to be ashamed of. My general approach is to be relatively open about the fact that Jake is adopted, but to avoid sharing details about his birth family that I feel are too personal. I share that we've been told his stunning hair colour probably comes from his birth father's side of the family, but I'm not sure, because we adopted him. I don't share much when people respond with questions such as, "Oh, what happened to his parents then?" and "Why did they give him up?" which I've been asked surprisingly often. I have a few well-practised responses to these questions in which I refer to generalities rather than my son's specific family story. For example, I'll say "Oh, people don't really 'give up' their children for adoption nowadays! That's incredibly unusual in the UK. Usually, children are taken into foster care because their birth parents can't look after them and there are lots of reasons for that. Sometimes it's mental illness or addiction. Often, it's because they didn't have great role models themselves, so didn't learn how to parent properly."

This is a response I've crafted in the knowledge that my children will hear me saying it, and it's mostly for their benefit, so that they can use these same phrases. My son knows a lot more about his own story than I'll share here, but I hope that hearing me field these questions is arming him with some phrases he can use to deflect these conversations one day. Sometimes more persistent curious folk ask directly, "but what happened with Jake's parents?" I usually say, "He might tell you about it one day, when he's old enough to decide what parts of his story he wants to share with the world. I'm never really sure how much I should tell people, because it's his story and I don't know how he'll feel about it when he's older."

One of the trickier aspects of having a birth child and an adopted child is finding the balance between respecting my son's ownership of his story and respecting my daughter's right to properly know her own brother. I feel that she has a right to know more than people outside of our family, but I also feel that my son should know some of those things before anyone else. Of course, I won't know which information he is happy for me to share until he's old enough to figure out how he feels about it. Zoe is very inquisitive, so I have to make a lot more judgment calls on this sort of thing than I expected. Sometimes Jake's behaviours have been related to his adoption. When he rejected me for many months after first joining our family, Zoe asked me why he was always so angry with me and I explained that I am his third "Mum" and, although we've kept in contact with the foster family, he probably feels like it's a risk to allow himself to love me, because his other mothers have "left" him. We talked about how they haven't really left him, but to a young child, it may feel like that.

It has also been a delicate balance when writing this book, and I hope that it will help adopters to hear my experiences, and give prospective adopters a sense of what they may be in for. I hope I've judged it right, and that all of my family are happy for these snippets of our lives to be shared, because my wonderful little family is the most important thing in my world.

ABOUT THE AUTHOR

Holly Marlow is a British author and parent to both biological and adopted children. Holly strives for a gentle/therapeutic parenting style and this led her to create stories to help children to understand some of the emotional and practical complexities of adoption. She created her first children's book, "Delly Duck," in response to her daughter's questions about the reasons why a child would be removed from their birth family. Holly is now enjoying life as an author and is grateful for the flexible nature of writing, which allows her to spend more time with her wonderful children.

When she's not writing, or playing with her children, Holly enjoys travelling (especially searching for chameleons, geckos and snakes in the wild parts of Africa) and learning foreign languages. Holly has fibromyalgia and has spent a lot of time trying to raise awareness of the chronic pain condition, giving presentations in schools and universities. Nowadays, Holly also gives a lot of presentations to schools, social workers, and adoptive, foster and kinship families. Holly enjoys baking and gardening, although she is terrible at both.

For more information about Holly, visit hollymarlow.com.

OTHER TITLES BY HOLLY MARLOW

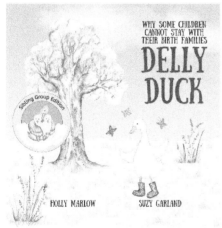

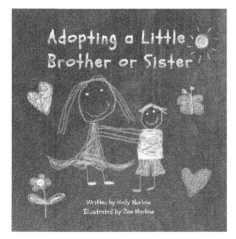

Printed in Great Britain
by Amazon